D1567903

MANAGING SALES LEADS

MANAGING SALES LEADS

HOW TO TURN EVERY PROSPECT INTO A CUSTOMER

Bob Donath
Carolyn K. Dixon

Richard A. Crocker
James W. Obermayer

Printed on recyclable paper

NTC Business Books
a division of *NTC Publishing Group* • Lincolnwood, Illinois USA

Library of Congress Cataloging-in-Publication Data

Managing sales leads: how to turn every prospect into a customer / Bob Donath . . . [et.al.].
     p.   cm.
    "American Marketing Association."
    ISBN 0-8442-3599-7
    1. Sales management.   2. Customer relations.   3. Communication in marketing.
  I. Donath, Bob. II. American Marketing Association.
  HF5438.4.A45   1994
  658.8'1—dc20   94–16180
                                                             CIP

Published in conjunction with the American Marketing Association, 250 South Wacker Drive, Chicago, Illinois 60606.

Contents

Part 3

Managing Leads   253

Preface

Welcome to a book about finding and nurturing new customers, the life blood and future of every business.

Intelligently managing sales leads to make your selling efforts more efficient should be a top priority in every company's marketing plan. Despite the importance of the subject, however, we've been surprised that so little has been written about the art and science of handling sales leads.

We wrote this book to fill that information gap and create the first all-inclusive source on sales lead management. Along the way, we draw on many sources in addition to our own experiences. A few deserve special mention here:

Cahners Advertising Research Reports—widely known as *CARR Reports*—published by Cahners Publishing Co., provide extensive marketing communications research findings to industry.

Penton Publishing Co. and its *New Equipment Digest* published an excellent overview of lead-management topics in 1991, as well as extensive inquirer survey research.

Thomas Publishing Co., publisher of *Industrial Equipment News* and the voluminous *Thomas Register* directory, conducted a number of insightful buyer surveys and focus groups in the 1990s.

The Trade Show Bureau, promotional arm of the exhibition industry, sponsors and publishes a wide array of excellent research about its medium's contribution to sales lead development.

Beyond those sources, numerous publications, trade associations, consultants, and academic researchers have made important contributions to lead-management knowledge. Among them, we especially want to thank Rick Kean, executive director of the Business Marketing Association, for his support, particularly when he held his previous post as the American Marketing Association's director of publications.

Finally, of course, there are the many staff members of Inquiry Handling Service, Inc. who kept us on track and assisted us throughout the writing of this book. They include Steve Noble, vice president of telemarketing services, whose thoughts and guidance proved invaluable, and Cindy Kagy, who designed graphics to illustrate our data and cheerfully assisted us with many of the details that make a critical, if otherwise unsung, difference in reader value.

—The Authors

Introduction

Confronting a National Marketing Tragedy

A short time ago, while speaking to a group of about 200 marketing communications managers, market specialists and marketing managers, we asked them, "How many of you generate leads for your companies' sales forces and distributors?" Nearly everyone raised a hand. Many nodded knowingly, sure that they knew what would come next.

"How many of you know whether salespeople follow up your leads?" we then asked. Significantly fewer hands reached for the ceiling. Some wiggled tentatively in mid-raise. Then we popped the crucial question: "How many leads actually become orders?"

Just a couple of people claimed to know such numbers. But their hands did not stay aloft for long, in fear the speaker might ask their owners to declare that confidence publicly.

Audience reactions like that are no surprise. We see them repeatedly wherever marketing people gather. True, those attending seminars to learn lead handling aren't experts on the subject. But, at least they understand what they need to know. For many in marketing, sales lead *mis*management continues to be a frustration they would like to avoid if they had the time and resources to do so.

What could be a simpler concept in marketing? A company tells the world about its wares, inviting interested prospects to ask for more information. When prospects indicate their interest, the company dispatches a salesperson or dealer to make the sale ahead of the competition. Our experience and independent research repeatedly finds that for the average product's marketing campaign, *nearly half* of those prospects eventually make the purchase from one vendor or another.

So, it's astounding that, for whatever reasons, most companies do not follow this straightforward path to sales success. Even when companies do gather the right kinds of prospect inquiries—by no means a foregone conclusion—many ignore the information. Or they blithely dump the inquiries on their sales forces and distributors, who dismiss them as a waste of time. How can sensible people be so cavalier about genuine prospects, people who've taken the time to say they are ready to buy?

The problem, of course, is that some inquiries are worth pursuing and some are not. Some will buy now, some later, and some never. Good intentions run aground over the difficulty of figuring out which inquiries are which, and what to do with the promising ones. To one degree or another, most companies underestimate the power of their sales leads. We hardly overstate the case in calling this a national marketing tragedy of massive proportion. The billions of dollars in wasted marketing communications makes waste in government programs paltry by comparison.

Failure to cash in on sales leads in turn creates a backlash, and yet another crisis. Awash in inquiries their marketing departments do not understand and their salespeople despise, companies chop marketing communications budgets to fatten profits, figuring as nobody uses them, they don't need more leads. Trouble is, this is like stopping your watch in order to save time. It doesn't work.

Without the support of the advertising, mail, telemarketing, and trade shows that produce inquiries from the new buyers constantly entering the marketplace, salespeople run helter-skelter for any business they can scrape up. Sales and marketing managers switch to red alert, committing what we call "corporate triage" to save some products in the line at any cost. They panic and cut prices, hoping to clear the warehouse and make year-end volume goals. But that only erodes profits further, leaving less money for next year's promotion—the advertising, direct mail, telemarketing, and trade show appearances the company needs to survive. The downward cycle continues and accelerates, dooming products to extinction or ignominious sale.

Sometimes, however, corporate triage is required medicine, for even the best of managements can be hit by unanticipated competition, economic changes, and other sudden threats. Fighting to survive a calamity, a company must concentrate only on its strongest products or services. In times of crisis, marketing and sales needs the quick-results tools of lead management: to focus only on business that can be closed quickly; to use telemarketing and quick direct mail drops that generate leads rapidly; and to pull leads from the prospect database. Without those tools, attempts to survive a sudden sales free fall become a rout rather than a strategy.

While such shabby realities hardly bode well for the economy overall, they are good news for those who *do* know how to capture the full potential of sales lead management. Companies can as much as *double* their sales with effective lead management. These companies understand how to use potent tools to outsell their competitors and find the most loyal and profitable customers. They know that successful business is built on relationships, and they consider inquiries and leads the front end of long-term relationship building. This book's mission is teaching how and why behind the lead-management tools marketing and marketing communications managers should use to confront and exploit the national marketing tragedy that hobbles so many others.

Follow-Up: The Key to Effective Sales Lead Management

Winners know the central tenet of sales lead management: sales leads must be followed up by salespeople and distributors. Follow-up requires some kind of reply to the prospect. For most consumer durable goods or services, sales literature with an invitation to visit the dealer is the most effective and efficient way to fulfill information requests. Industrial and business products or services generally require effective follow-up through a personal contact—generally a phone call or visit—from a company's central office, its field sales staff, or its distributor personnel. The large potential profit of the sale and long-term value of a new customer justifies the special effort.

But, corporate track records are weak. Despite billions spent to promote and solicit an annual harvest of 300 million inquiries from buyers, in our experience only about a tenth of all business and industrial leads receive personal follow-up.[1] Business magazine giant Cahners Publishing Co., surveying its own readers, finds that only about 15 percent of business and industrial advertising inquiries receive a salesperson's personal attention on the phone or with a sales call.[2] Either follow-up rate is dismal, considering that nearly half of all business and industrial inquirers will eventually buy!

Consumer products muddle along with worse inquiry follow-up ratios. That's not surprising, because so much consumer-oriented advertising is "pull-through," designed to spur retail sales.

Follow-up is weak even among those lead-oriented companies advertising in business and industrial product tabloids, publications specifically designed to generate prospect inquiries. A remarkably low 20.7 percent of their inquiries receive sales force follow-up, according to 22 years of reader surveys by *New Equipment Digest,* one of the nation's leading pan-industry tabloids.[3] As a result, the $5 to $1,000 companies spend to generate each sales lead largely goes to waste.

Even though their field follow-up might be terrible, most business-to-business marketers nonetheless claim they have some sort of lead-handling program in place. Just 28 percent acknowledge that they do not.[4] But follow-up being the step essential for producing a payoff from leads, it is obvious that most companies have an excellent opportunity to perform better.

When Programs Fail and Succeed

Lead-management logic often succumbs to the daily pressure of business and the inevitability of human error. We authors—who collectively have more than a century of lead-management experience—have seen countless "little things" ruin sales-lead programs. Perhaps it's the harried mailroom employee charged with processing advertising inquiries "when there's time," or the clerk, annoyed at the interruption by something that's "not my job," perfunctorily handling a phone inquiry from a possible customer.

Salespeople, predisposed to believe that they actually know every bona fide buyer in their territories, ignore new names on the inquiry list. Or we can blame the advertising manager who mails inquiries off to field sales, then forgets about them, fueling the fears of the marketing vice president prejudiced against ideas that "We tried once, and they didn't work." Poor training, weak morale, inadequate staffing and inattentive planning combine to create a rogues gallery of errors more easily overlooked than corrected.

Fundamental organization problems create more serious stumbling blocks. One of sales lead management's biggest benefits is linking the marketing and sales functions so they work together to reach corporate goals. Often, however, marketing and sales departments pull in different directions, as we'll discuss in Chapter 1. When they fail to work closely together, a well-run, complete lead system is impossible.

Profitability Through Growth

Ironically, improving lead management will provide more of an immediate and durable boost to sales at many companies than will the grandiose strategic initiatives senior managers somberly hand down to the corporate rank-and-file with great fanfare. And, unlike staff downsizing which has preoccupied so many firms in recent years, lead management emphasizes profitability through growth, not retrenchment. In our experience, sales increases ranging to 100 percent or more are not uncommon when marketers fine-tune their lead-management programs. That sales lead management can double your sales is not merely a theoretical or exaggerated promise.

Achieving such gains with lead management requires that a firm have sound marketing and sales strategies in the first place. Lead management is not a panacea. It cannot by itself overcome the futility of chasing the wrong markets with the wrong products through the wrong channels at the wrong time.

Yet competent sales lead management, with the analysis that's part of the process, will yield essential information for understanding—and, if necessary, changing—corporate strategic direction and the tactics supporting grand plans. It addresses critical questions such as: Can a product have a chance in newly discovered markets? Are distributors providing sufficient sales support? Which salespeople are coasting, and which are working too hard for the company's good? If you don't mine your leads for that kind of information, your marketing program is flying blind, no matter what its sophistication elsewhere.

We recall, for example, a corporate planner from a Fortune 100-size company, griping about inquiries and leads at a recent senior executive-level conference. Asked if sales lead conversion data validated his strategic models, he dismissed the impudent question. "Leads? Just try and get anyone to follow them up!" he sputtered. He knew his expensive programs didn't work as well as they should because front-line troops weren't following relatively inexpensive lead-handling basics.

Is Lead Management for You?

To get you thinking about your current lead-management practices, evaluate the competitive strength of what you are now doing, or not doing, according to the Lead Management Checklist on page xviii. It lists just a few of the features that characterize a professionally competitive inquiry handling program. If you check more than three items with a "no," it is high time to rethink your lead-handling system and decide whether it supports your sales force properly. You have started this book none too soon!

Although a powerful tool, formal sales lead management isn't for everyone, however. If we define the process as that of using promotional tools to find prospects whom we then telephone or visit, lead management is ideal for firms with per-order profits large enough to justify the selling expense. Capital equipment, corporate services, manufacturing raw materials and components, and bulk supplies are among the categories that come to mind in the industrial arena. On the consumer side, durable goods and high-ticket services provide the margins justifying formal lead-management programs. Selling small, relatively inexpensive, frequently purchased, low-margin items through retail to business and consumer buyers alike usually does not require a full-bore lead-management capability. The buyer orders from a catalog, or visits the retail outlet and buys.

Database marketing, still in its infant stages compared to its potential, erases those distinctions, however. All database marketing involves handling leads. The consumer joining a supermarket discount club or asking a food product maker for a recipe becomes a database record. No longer a faceless member of a mass audience described by statistical averages, the consumer develops an identity to a marketer tracking his or her product preferences, purchase patterns, media habits and other characteristics. The consumer, the "lead," might not receive a personal phone call from the manufacturer, but will receive direct mail, a company magazine, or other tailored promotional attention. That, too, is sales lead management in its strictest sense.

In this book, however, we'll concentrate on the prototypical lead-handling scenario, emphasizing how the process makes sales and distributor sales forces more efficient. That inevitably tilts our discussion toward business-to-business marketing examples.

Who Needs to Read This Book?

This book is for those people actually generating inquiries and managing the lead program, and their bosses who control a business unit's marketing activities.

We are writing for the hands-on, front-line managers whose day-to-day effort should include keeping the company's sales-lead lifeblood circulating. Titles at that level include marketing communications or advertising directors or managers, exhibit program managers, telemarketing directors, marketing services managers, sales support managers, database managers, and the like.

The well-run lead-management system rewards its key players professionally with more efficient sales operations, more enthusiastic dealers and distributors, more powerful marketing communications, more efficient trade show exhibiting, better sales forecasting, and more successful new market development. Personally, managers gain valuable skills that enhance their careers.

We are also writing for their superiors, the senior- and mid-level management executives who need to know the strategy of designing a lead-management program, who to hire to run it, and what the system is supposed to produce in terms of sales, profit and information. Titles such as marketing vice president or director, group product directors, marketing and sales directors and managers, and sales managers to whom marketing departments report are typical.

Corporate top managements will recognize and applaud the contributions marketing makes to profitability, because lead management allows managers to measure their contributions with precision rather than guesswork, proving how much bang they deliver for the buck.

Finally, but hardly as an afterthought, we recommend this book to sales managers. Being in charge of the most critical personnel management link in the lead-management chain, sales managers can make or break a program. In reading this book, they will fully understand what *should* be happening in a lead program. If the program is deficient, they should demand that the marketing department fix it.

Lead Management Checklist

Review your inquiry handling program against the following checklist to determine whether or not it is competitive:

	Yes	No
Processing		
1. Do you process inquiries so literature is sent within 72 hours?	☐	☐
Within 48 hours?	☐	☐
2. Do you send sales leads to the sales force weekly or more frequently?	☐	☐
3. Do you have a "Fax-on-Demand" service for instant response to those who need information *now?*	☐	☐
4. Are you capable of sending sales leads electronically via diskette or E-Mail?	☐	☐
Qualification		
5. Is your 800-number professionally staffed to capture vital prospect profile information (i.e., need, desire, budget, time frame)?	☐	☐
6. Do you telephone senders of inquiries of unknown value before giving them to salespeople?	☐	☐
7. Do you collect profile information on every prospect, add it to the sales lead database, and give it to salespeople?	☐	☐
Reports		
8. Does sales management receive monthly reports on the leads generated in territories, districts/regions, and nationally?	☐	☐
9. Does marketing management receive monthly promotional effectiveness reports showing lead sources and products of interest?	☐	☐
10. Does senior sales management receive sales lead follow-up reports?	☐	☐
11. Can you prove the value of leads with a report showing the sales produced by your promotional efforts (advertising, trade shows, publicity, direct mail, etc.)?	☐	☐
Database		
12. Can your database be used for future mailings and offers?	☐	☐
13. Will the prospect profile and lead disposition information be used to evaluate marketing mix elements (promotions, salespeople, etc.)?	☐	☐
14. Is the system a genuine "closed loop" that includes lead performance experience to influence subsequent marketing decisions?	☐	☐

If you answer "no" to more than three questions, it's time to rethink your sales lead handling system.

Part **1**

Sales Leads for Marketing and Sales Planning

Chapter 1

Sales Leads for Tough Markets

"**I**t's a jungle out there, where only the savviest operators survive," George likes to tell his troops. As division sales vice president, George is proud of his devoted effort and the reputation he has earned as a "real hands-on guy." He enjoys his regular Friday after-lunch ritual, a relaxed time to phone friends to arrange weekend plans as he sifts the pile of sales lead forms that accumulate during the week.

Passing by in the hall, Janice, the company's new marketing communications director, stops to watch George at work through his open office door. What she sees alarms her.

With a wastebasket positioned strategically alongside his desk, George plucks forms from the stack before him. He squints at each thoughtfully for a few seconds. He lays some respectfully on another much smaller pile that he will send to his road warriors in the field. But, he flicks most of the forms disdainfully into the trash. George is screening advertising inquiries, raw leads from trade publication reader service cards indiscriminately passed on to the sales department.

"Those leads cost us 28 bucks apiece!" Janice protests, striding into George's office like cavalry to the rescue. She works hard to run an advertising campaign to excite the marketplace and motivate likely buyers to ask for more information. Brochure requests have skyrocketed. Inquiry counts have soared. It's a numbers game to Janice, and she boasts about her marketing communications program's sizzling scoreboard.

But Janice worries that salespeople, and boss George in particular, treat the extra volume as an imposition, possibly even a threat. Not that anyone has said anything, Janice realizes. It's just that tone of voice she hears from salespeople on those rare occasions she travels to the field.

"How can you tell so quickly who's a good lead and who's not? Who's going to buy and who's not?" Janice demands. She wants to add, but doesn't, that the sales department is breaking the rules. Each inquiry should be followed up with a salesperson's phone call, she believes, maybe even a visit. That is the sales department's job. Summarily trashing leads without checking them out defeats her program at the start, Janice seethes.

She worries because she doesn't really know what happens to all those names and addresses her marketing communications department shovels to George's office across the hall. Spending so little time making calls on prospects with salespeople, Janice never sees how most of the inquiries she forwards actually frustrate salespeople, waste their time, and justify their muttering that "the leads are no good."

George tries to protect his people with his home-grown lead-qualification system. "It's easy to tell which are which, with my experience," George calmly answers Janice, a parent educating a child. "Sit here and let me show you how it's done."

George slides a lead from the stack and with a flourish offers it for their mutual inspection. "See, this has no phone number; he's obviously not a serious buyer." George flips the lead card into the wastebasket triumphantly.

"Here's another one 600 miles away from our nearest office—so we can't follow it up right away. We'll call on them when one of our people get up there next month," George promises without conviction.

"This one's for a $200 meter, and we sell $200,000 complete power systems." George holds the lead with two fingers at arms's length as if it were vilely soiled. "Let this guy call back later if he just wants the meter," he proclaims.

"And what about this heavy hitter?" George chuckles. "A hair salon? They must have some powerful blow dryers! What are we going to sell to Tess's Tresses? We got one from a biology lab last week, and we've never sold to those outfits," George scoffs.

On it goes, George's decision rules, enraging Janice. The marketing communications director frets over the fate of the advertising inquiry database she wants to create, so she can earn recognition upstairs for the inquiry count's rapid growth. Janice also knows she will not win points arguing with the senior sales executive, so she remains silent.

Meanwhile, George sneers at a lead from someone who has inquired three times before. George remembers those "freeloaders. They've never bought anything from us yet, so I'm not going to waste any more time with them. If they really want to buy something, they'll call and order it."

Then another from George's rogues gallery of inquirers: "This lead says 'general' on it. We never follow those up. If they don't know what they want, they waste our time."

He turns to Janice and smiles victoriously. George knows his markets.

Closed-Loop Marketing

If George and Janice remind you of real-life characters in your company, you are hardly alone. Companies across the nation, in virtually every manufacturing and service business, let tremendous amounts of additional business slip through their fingers. George and Janice caricature the crisis in sales lead management today, the national tragedies of misguided communications and misled selling that cause so many companies to underperform.

George is right about "the jungle out there," but he is seriously deficient in survival techniques. Nor does Janice have her act together. To their company's detriment, each pursues different objectives. Each uses sales leads, which should link their efforts, as a political football instead. "Salespeople never follow up," Janice complains. But to George, it's clearly a case of "Most of this stuff is junk."

Old-fashioned attitudes die hard.

Despite her apparent mass communication skills, Janice does not stay in close touch with the sales department, or with prospects one-on-one. Market research printouts clutter her office, but she has only the dimmest understanding of what is happening in the field sales operations she's supposed to support. She does not design marketing communications to give salespeople and the company what they need most: the quantity and quality of leads appropriate to the sales quotas George must meet. She does not help salespeople maximize their selling time.

George meanwhile suffers the myopia of a subjective, even eccentric approach to separating inquiry wheat from chaff. His prejudices bubble forth on Friday afternoons, for George hardly gives leads Monday-morning attention. Much less does he give inquiries the objective, systematic examination that would allow him to spot more potential business.

Nor does he protest convincingly when his salespeople grouse about "big brother watching" whenever someone from across the hall asks what happened to the inquiries. He's on the side of his troops, and they know it. He allows them to nurture their own little conceits: that they already know everyone who is anyone in their territories; that they don't need telemarketers or bothersome paperwork meddling in their markets.

Confused Organizations

Combatants in today's business-to-business and consumer markets cannot afford the problems the Georges and Janices of marketing create. The way things are supposed to work, the "marketing" department and the marketing communications function reporting to it identify markets and develop strategies and tactics for selling to them. "Sales" does the actual selling, negotiating and closing the orders. That is the classic model of the well-integrated marketing operation, and the strategy behind the well-tuned sales lead-management system.

But, it's a confusing model because the selling *function* is actually part of the overall marketing *function* charged with the task of finding and keeping customers. Treating "marketing" as some process over-there-across-the-hall from "sales," as home-office turf warriors are wont to do, drives a wedge between the finding and keeping. What should be a seamless partnership throughout the marketing process succumbs to rivalries like George's and Janice's.

As a result, one of the chief lead-management problems companies encounter is deciding who should be screening inquiries: which require priority sales force or distributor attention, which should be ignored altogether, and which fall between those extremes? Should it be "marketing" ensconced in the home office? Or "sales" out in the field with all those ears presumably closer to the ground? How a company answers that question will make the difference between so-so lead management and true double-your-sales success.

Most companies' sales lead management will perform best when they follow the simple rule: *marketing identifies; sales closes.* Generating inquiries with advertising, direct mail, trade shows, and other media is only half the marketing department's job. It must also determine which inquiries are bona-fide leads, sparing salespeople and distributors the drudgery of sifting a glut of time-consuming unqualified leads. The job in the field is to pursue the prospects who are ready to buy. The more marketing can insulate the field from unqualified leads, the more it contributes to overall marketing efficiency.

A Lead by Any Other Name . . .

Leads and inquiries are not the same. Although we frequently will use the terms synonymously in this book for style reasons when it does not affect the points we make, there is a strict difference between them. And although the two terms are interchanged promiscuously in daily business conversation, here are the strict definitions.

Marketing communications, trade shows and other sources produce *inquiries,* requests from people for more information. Some, but hardly all, of those inquirers are likely to buy within some finite time period, usually a year or less. Those are the *leads* worth pursuing. Research shows that, on average, within a year nearly half of all inquirers will eventually buy, from one company or a competitor, the type of product or service they inquired about.

Raw leads are the same as inquiries: requests for information, regardless of the inquirers' likelihood of buying.

Qualified inquiries, the same as *leads* or *qualified leads,* are inquiries which appear to be from likely buyers. The inquiry may on its face meet a company's screening criteria, or the inquirer might have asked specifically for a sales call. Someone might have contacted the inquirer, and determined that he is a genuine prospect.

Converted leads or *closed leads* are those leads which led to an actual sale.

These are the sales lead-management steps that link marketing and sales in a smooth process known as "closed-loop marketing:"

- *Inquiry generation:* motivating prospective buyers to identify themselves and their specific interests via an inquiry.
- *Inquiry tracking:* creating and updating a database of inquiries by source (800-number calls, business-reply cards, publication reader service cards, etc.) and by medium (trade publication ads, direct mail campaigns, trade shows, press releases, etc.).
- *Inquiry qualification:* determining who among the inquirers are most likely to buy.
- *Inquiry fulfillment:* providing the information promised to the inquirer, thus furthering the selling process in a timely fashion.
- *Sales lead follow-up:* informing the sales force and distributors about quality leads, motivating them to contact those leads.
- *Sales lead tracking:* collecting sales reports and conducting field surveys to determine the disposition of leads, and updating the database of inquirers who might someday be prospects.
- *Sales lead analysis:* examining the inquiry and sales lead databases by source, disposition, timing, purchasing patterns, and other criteria in a systematic way to aid decision making.

A complete sales lead-management program is a self-correcting closed loop of information. Analysis allows you to improve the quality and/or quantity of the inquiries you generate and qualify as your program continues. Refinements surface from the answers to questions such as: Which media produce the most qualified leads, the most leads converting to sales, and the biggest returns on your promotional investment? Which products in the line require more leads and therefore more promotional support? Which sales territories are not covering potential business adequately? Are prospects receiving your literature fast enough to aid their buying decisions? Who are the individuals specifying products and brands in large customer organizations? How much should the company spend on advertising?

Barriers to Success

Conceptually, lead management is not a complicated process, but it is a time-consuming one. Perhaps that's a major reason why many companies do not treat their inquiries and leads with the respect they deserve.

To put the problem in perspective, U.S. industry sold nearly $7.2 *trillion* in goods and services to other businesses in 1992, accounting for six out of every 10 dollars of all domestic sales volume.[1] Industry spent nearly $70 billion a year during the early 1990s to advertise, publicize, exhibit and otherwise promote those sales to business,[2] generating what we estimate to be roughly *300 billion inquiries annually.* In consumer product and service markets, advertising and sales promotion spending alone runs well into tens of billions of dollars, $44.2 billion in 1992,[3] for example. While most of that supported sales at retail or through the mail, a significant portion—many billions of dollars still—produces leads that, when followed-up, eventually become sales.

Still, a variety of reasons and excuses behind poor sales lead management cause the $5 to $1,000 companies spend to generate each business-to-business inquiry largely go to waste. We call them the Six Barriers to Sales Success.

The Six Barriers to Sales Success

Barrier #1: Senior management does not care. Paid to lead the organization in the big-picture issues of market strategy, quality, and customer satisfaction, senior managers are tempted to dismiss operational fundamentals and assume all is well. They are not aware of the tactical need for complete lead follow-up, rapid inquiry fulfillment, accurate qualification practices, or actual measurement of communications and sales performance.

Barrier #2: Salespeople remain uninformed. Unless they understand the potential value of qualified leads, salespeople—an independent-minded breed—think they do not need the help. Sales managers who fail to insist on follow-up imply that leads are at best an option just for slow days. Marketing departments that fail to qualify leads in advance contribute to the problem, giving leads a poor reputation.

Barrier #3: Poor coordination hobbles marketing and sales. Marketing and marketing communications people frequently have little idea of the quotas salespeople must meet, the timing of their sales contests, their need for seasonal boosts in lead volume, the products needing extra lead support, and the geographical balance needed to apportion leads sensibly among sales territories. Meanwhile, the sales force does not understand why lead follow-up reports are essential if marketing is to fine-tune its advertising, mail, and other promotion tools.

Barrier #4: The company mismanages its prospect lists. Inquiries become orphans in a netherworld between marketing and sales. As a result, the company sends the wrong information to inquirers, sends it late, and does not tailor it to inquirers' specific interests. Marketing collects limited and uninformative data and updates them infrequently. Marketing rarely compares separate databases— one for orders and one for inquiries, for example—and even more rarely merges them into a marketing information system.

Barrier #5: Management does not hold salespeople accountable. Sales management does not insist on follow-up and new prospect status reporting, even though it fusses over detailed expense and call reporting.

Barrier #6: Management does not hold marketing people accountable. Chief marketing officers do not hold subordinates accountable for lead-handling performance. They do not insist on program return-on-investment reports, for example, evidence that inquiry generation ties in with company sales goals, or analyses of inquiry source productivity.

Leads and Corporate Strategy

All six barriers are the product of poor communications, inattention, lack of knowledge, human frailties, and the sublime dysfunctionalities that lurk within all organizations. None is the result of weak strategies, poorly designed products, sloppy manufacturing, competitive pressures, government regulation, or inadequate capital—the classic management issues that preoccupy most companies.

But, lead management is a critical tactic in pursuing many of today's most important customer-oriented marketing strategies. Let's examine some of this decade's major marketing management trends to see the important role lead handling plays within each. Properly generating, tracking, and following up leads might not put a company ahead of savvy competitors, but *not* using lead-management techniques will leave a company way behind. Reengineering their lead-handling practices should be a top priority for such firms.

From Transactions to Relationships

Part of the confusion between the terms "marketing" and "selling" stems from old-fashioned thinking about the function of marketing within a company. Its goal has been the transaction: closing the order, making the sale. In other words, marketing has traditionally been treated as a part of the selling function.

Modern thinking in this information age turns the relationship around to examine it from its proper perspective. The true objective of marketing, say today's marketing Solons, is building customer relationships, particularly with customers who will remain loyal to a supplier. The longer they stay, the more profitable they become. Frederick Reichheld, a leading exponent of customer loyalty strategies, argues that sustained long-term profitability is impossible without nurturing long-term customer commitment.[4]

Naturally, many factors determine who will become a business or consumer customer, and who will stay with a supplier for how long. One of the most important of those factors is the nature of the customer. How much will he or she, or members of a buying committee, value the unique qualities a supplier offers? How easily can other vendors woo the customer away? How quickly will the customer's needs change?

When pursuing new customers, say Adrian Slywotsky and Benson Shapiro, two proponents of what they call the "marketing mindset," seek prospects who are most likely to switch from other suppliers, those that could be your most profitable customers, and those that are growth-oriented and thus might help you build more long-term market share.[5]

- "Switchables," according to their thinking, are competitors' unhappy customers, vulnerable to your pitch. Acquiring them can cost a fifth to a tenth of the amount required to switch a competitor's loyal customers.

- "High-profit" prospects aren't always easy to identify, even after they become your customers. Some customers are easier and less expensive to service than others that require heavy selling and support. But, the factors differentiating high- from low-cost customers often don't conform to neat divisions of SIC or class-of-trade. You might need detailed activity-cost accounting to determine which are which.

- "Share-building" customers might cost a lot to acquire at first. But they deliver better returns in the long-run. They could be destined for market dominance, bringing their suppliers along with them. They might serve key customers in their own markets. They might be opinion leaders, conferring status on their suppliers. They might dominate key distribution channels.[6]

It is important to know how loyal a prospect might be if converted to a customer. Sales lead qualification and analysis will reveal clues about a potential buyer. Are the decision makers unhappy with current suppliers or casually looking around with no real thought of switching? Is the prospect the kind of company or individual demanding expensive services that eat into your profit?

Is the prospect a dominant supplier to its customers in a growing market? Consider examining how well your technology and capabilities fit the business customer's applications and service needs. Will the business customer buy from you again as it builds experience using your product or service? Can your consumer product brand keep pace with a customer's changing lifestyle needs? Is the prospect a one-time buyer? Or a price buyer with little allegiance?

Information gathered throughout the selling process, from inquiry generation, through the first sales call, to sales-performance analysis will help answer those critical questions and pinpoint the characteristics of your best and worst customers. You will also learn which media produce the most qualified leads from desirable prospects, and which territories have a greater saturation of them.

For similar reasons, lead management also abets the formation of closer supplier–customer ties. They range from "outsourcing" what used to be produced internally, to full-blown vertical strategic alliances. Such arrangements have become extremely popular in theory and, although tough to manage and sustain,[7] more popular in practice as well. In 1993, 44 percent of purchasing executives polled in one survey said their firms "outsource"—buying rather than making components—more than they used to; 47 percent expect to outsource even more by the year 2000.[8] Not all customers will want the same degree of cooperation with a seller, however. For those that are the wrong kinds of customers to cozy up to, transaction-based, arm's-length dealings continue to be the best way to sell to them. Information about prospects drives the process, with sales lead management providing some of the critical data. A company should fine-tune its Power Profiling™ of prospects—how it qualifies them in advance of a sales call. (Power Profiling is described in Chapter 2.)

From Mass to Database Marketing

Attention to the characteristics of individual customers—second nature to most business and industrial marketers—is the core of database marketing. Lead management is the up-front, first stage in marketing database construction.

Voguish now, the database marketing concept has been around for quite a while, well before it became a buzzword in the 1980s. As an approach to customers, database marketing has its roots in traditional account-by-account selling strategies for high-priced, high-margin products and services, particularly in business and industrial fields. Each customer and prospect in the salesperson's call book is a database record, each an individual known by the company to one extent or another. Marketing success is measured account by account.

In contrast, mass marketers sell to groups of customers, identified no more finely than, say, all U.S. women 18 to 36. Television and mass-audience publications have been the unquestioned media of choice for "pull-through" promotion designed to propel the prospect to the retail store. It wasn't important if a specific person bought; winning a large enough share of the mass-market segment's purchases was what counted.

Now, however, fiercer brand competition is forcing most consumer product manufacturers to segment markets hoping to dominate the preferences of discrete market niches. Technology adds to the pressure, enabling that ultimate expression of database marketing, the customer segment of one. Supermarket checkout scanners collect information about individual consumers' buying habits. Merging it with other data such as media exposure and lifestyle and demographic profiles, packaged goods marketers can infer why Mrs. Jones on Elm Street bought what she did. When Mrs. Jones inquires about a product, marketers log the requests to their customer databases.

Packaged goods marketers have been slow to implement database techniques, trapped as they are in maintaining competitive presence through promotional price concessions to the trade and consumers alike. Consumer marketers spent 70 percent of their marketing budgets on promotions, and just 30 percent on advertising, database marketing researcher Donnelly Marketing reported at the start of the 1990s. Ten years earlier, promotion grabbed just 57 percent of the pie and advertising cornered 43 percent.[9] Price concessions such as couponing, deal pricing, and manufacturer rebates turned far too many consumers into price-sensitive buyers with little loyalty and long-term profitability for vendors.

Other types of promotions such as booklets and complementary product self-liquidating premium offers elicit an information-oriented customer response. That is a more solid foundation for long-run marketer strategy. Those devices can pinpoint customers who respond to value-added appeals. The technologies and techniques to do so are available now. The trick is balancing the cost of servicing customers individually vs. the long-term value of the average customer.

Interactive Media Explosion

The rapid growth of telemarketing to businesses and consumers in the 1980s, aided by advancing telephone technology, foreshadows the interactive media future. Even companies selling high-priced items once thought to be impossible to sell over the phone learned that outbound telemarketing to the right prospect lists can yield a promising crop of leads.

The trouble is, outbound telemarketing's own intrusiveness, its strength in getting through to the prospect, might be its undoing. Consumer advocates push for restrictions, insisting that households be able to easily remove themselves from telemarketers' databases. Some argue that marketers should pay consumers for allowing their names to be part of saleable databases. Outbound telemarketing has been less controversial on the business-to-business side, largely because people on the job are paid to use their phones for business purposes.

But while outbound telemarketing has built substantial ill will, inbound telemarketing has proved to be wildly popular with both business and consumer buyers. Toll-free inquiry numbers are a major part of the appeal. So is the fact that the prospect retains full control over the decision whether to communicate. In the future, cable TV and two-way multimedia communication will put much more information exchange at customer fingertips, under their command.

All this is likely to leave marketers awash in inquiries, their computers bulging with customer data. Consumer product marketers will look for more direct sales—such as infomercials and home-shopping networks now provide—and more inquiries as a first step in motivating individual customers to visit local dealers. Business-to-business marketers will have many more leads to sort before sending them to the field for sales follow-up. Sales lead management properly applied will accomplish the mission. Without it, companies will choke on the inquiries they generate—or risk producing too few inquiries to provide a required base of qualified leads.

Marketing and Sales Automation

In the last half of the twentieth century, computer applications expanded, function by function, to dominate business information management. Marketing and selling proved to be the fields most resistant to automation, largely because of the so-called "soft" productivity benefits computers provide. How does a marketer measure the productivity boost caused by, say, faster communication between field sales, the home office, and customers? The analysis defies traditional productivity measurement, particularly if the computer system enables managers to make better decisions than they otherwise would. Putting a dollar value on that is risky, because you do not know what decision would have been made without computerized decision-support and how good it might have been.

Sophisticated marketing information systems and extensive computer-aided sales tools now conquer the automation frontier. But not easily. Building systems, training staff, and learning how to cope with an information glut are challenges that confront all firms, regardless of size. Companies can turn to sales lead management for their starting point, building a system to surmount the challenges. The lead program becomes their initial template for organizing knowledge of the marketplace around them. And, unlike many computer uses in marketing, productivity gains are obvious and easy to measure when companies install computerized lead-tracking systems. As a result, clumsy, paper-based lead systems are giving way in whole or in part to automated solutions.

As of 1990, 63 percent of its advertisers used computers in their lead systems, reports product tabloid *New Equipment Digest,* compared to 33 percent six years earlier.[10]

Information technologies have revolutionized every phase of sales lead management. At its fastest, a lead system can cut weeks off the inquiry–fulfillment–qualification–follow-up cycle. Prospects can fax an inquiry to a supplier and receive an instant response. The marketer in turn notifies the sales force, while comparing the inquiry against a database of hottest prospects. There's little excuse for taking a month or more—as many firms do—to answer a prospect who wants to know more about you.

The so-called "information superhighways" predicted for the twenty-first century promise greater change to come. Desktop videoconferencing, video-on-demand, global database searches, and other innovations will join today's fax, phone, and electronic mail as basic standards of supplier-buyer communication. Exploiting those technologies will not be luxuries; they will become competitive necessities.

Customization required. Database marketing will enable the best marketers to customize their products to individual customer tastes. Worldwide, manufacturers hope to adopt more efficient "lean manufacturing" and "agile manufacturing" techniques, all designed to meet the individual business or consumer customer's requirements better, faster, and cheaper than the competition can. The marketing information system databases that will drive those programs will be built around marketing information systems: market research results and data gathered from inquirers, qualified prospects, and customers. Without sales lead management, critical information will be missing.

Leads and Total Quality Marketing

Quality has become the religion of business, with the "total quality" movement proving to be an extremely popular management concept. It puts the marketing function and customer satisfaction squarely at the heart of competitive strategies. Sales lead management, controlling what usually is the first contact a prospect has with a firm, plays a critical role in shaping a vendor's quality image.

Once thought to be solely a concern on the factory floor, the quality movement now stands for the customer's total involvement with and perception of a supplier's product—the way it's sold and serviced as well as its physical attributes. Service must stand similar tests in terms of customers' comfort levels and meeting customer expectations. In crowded marketplaces where competing brands share indistinguishable physical features, it's up to marketing to create the perceived benefits that make the sale.

The quality movement has lasted long enough to be more than a passing management fad. Consumers and industrial buyers have learned to demand superior goods and services for which they will pay a premium. In searching for better value, buyers look for clues to a supplier's integrity, responsiveness, and expertise in every contact they have with a company. Sloppy lead handling helps to create an inferior image.

When the wrong fulfillment literature arrives, arrives late, or does not arrive at all, prospects have a reason to think the vendor is not attentive to customer needs. When salespeople fail to follow-up, when telephone service operators do not have the right information for callers, the company appears disorganized. Poor-quality literature connotes a sloppy or penny-pinching outfit. Making it hard to get information suggests to an inquirer that "the company doesn't want my business."

Pursuing quality in the lead-management process also contributes to quality elsewhere in the operation. Regularly tracking inquiry and selling activity keeps essential marketing databases current. It helps sales management lead the field force. It measures marketing communications quality. It promotes good relationships with distribution channels because distributors and dealers consider qualified leads an important part of their supplier relationships. In the many industries where channel members own most of the information about end-user customers, eliciting their active support is a matter of manufacturer survival.

Faster fulfillment. Although the nation suffers today from inadequate sales lead management as we pointed out earlier, the situation used to be worse on a critical quality-image dimension: inquiry fulfillment. Twenty years ago, a broad-based industry study by the Advertising Research Foundation discovered that nearly half of all requested information arrived "too late" for inquirers to use "in time to be really helpful for current projects." By "current," the researchers explained, they meant purchases planned for the three-month period following the inquiry. Considering that a third of the sample also said it purchased the product within three months, slow response probably created a substantial number of lost sales.[11]

Apparently, industry has cleaned up its fulfillment performance somewhat. Cahners Publishing Co., using a different sample base nearly 15 years after the Advertising Research Foundation study, reported that 74 percent of requests to advertisers in its publications said fulfillment literature "almost always arrives quickly."[12] In yet a later Cahners survey, 82 percent said the information came "in time to be helpful with current projects." On average, inquirers received the material they sought in 3.4 weeks (two-thirds of them receiving the information in two to four weeks), Cahners says.[13] Among industrial magazine readers surveyed by product tabloid *Industrial Equipment News,* 56 percent said they generally received information within one to two weeks of sending in a reader service card; 85 percent received information within four weeks.[14]

Better fulfillment. Twenty years ago, 18 percent of an Advertising Research Foundation survey respondents said they received *none* of the information they requested with their inquiry. About 59 percent of respondents to that pioneering survey said they threw away one or more pieces of information they received, judging it worthless. They also complained about the lack of price information, or direction on where to get more help and details. Unclear literature, the wrong material, and information they couldn't file easily also spoiled the quality of many companies' first contacts with inquiring prospects.[15]

Nowadays, however, surveys report much happier outcomes. Among industrial publication readers polled by *Industrial Equipment News,* 92 percent said they are at least "somewhat" satisfied by the information they receive.[16] At Cahners, the nation's largest publisher of specialized business magazines, 95 percent of inquirers polled said "almost all" information they have received "has clear and easy-to-understand" text.[17]

Competitive pressures. Problems aren't limited to the reader service card inquiries that predominate in those surveys. We've often seen inbound telephone inquiry handling bungled by behavior that turns off the hottest inquirers, those who've picked up the phone to take action. A lack of professional response, or no response as inbound calls go uncovered, creates a negative first impression with potential customers. Among the biggest sinners: companies that mistakenly think inbound calls can be handled by any untrained staffer who just happens to be unoccupied at the moment.

Disappointed or not, inquirers generally do not wait for information from just one vendor. They also ask competitors about 60 percent of the time, according to our surveys. Will the competitor's response be better than yours? What will an engineering prospect think about the technical depth of a company whose product sheets don't provide full specifications? Will the management prospect feel like sharing, much less recommending, a vendor to other members of the buying committee when the vendor's literature is garish and cheap looking? What does the prospect think when the salesperson she asked to see doesn't call?

Leads and Genuine Buyers

Those who ignore the importance of sales lead management and the value of closed-loop marketing also ignore other truths of the marketplaces in which they struggle. They assume, for example, that "everyone knows us"—a classic conceit used to kill marketing communications budgets or otherwise discourage ventures beyond the comfort of the current customer base. People who say it usually realize too late that they will have to replace most of those customers down the line. The equally myopic corollary is, "We know all the buyers," a mistaken notion nurtured by the vanity of salespeople who only *think* they know all the players in their territories. Sometimes, those who dismiss the importance of inquiry management state their excuse bluntly, with something like, "We don't need leads."

Those attitudes tend to afflict business-to-business marketers more than their consumer-oriented brethren who deal with mass audiences. Only a small fraction of business and industrial marketers do not need leads. Some have such small and unchanging markets for their highly specialized products or services that they can know all the key people with buying clout. Perhaps some are monopolies. But for the rest of us, succeeding in competitive marketplaces means constantly finding new customers.

Sales lead-management techniques find buyers—individuals with purchasing authority—who otherwise remain invisible to salespeople. Of those buyers, nearly half will make or recommend a purchase within a year of their inquiry! Ignoring lead management simply throws away a tremendous amount of sales and profit opportunity.

Finding Hidden Buyers

Despite their best efforts calling on business customers, salespeople usually do not get to see everyone who influences a buying decision. Usually they get to see fewer than half. Calling on mom-and-pop operations is an exception, but companies with several specialists on staff naturally divide management responsibilities. One manager becomes the purchasing agent, the prime contact for salespeople, who writes the purchase orders. The others remain invisible to all but the most tenacious and talented sales representatives.

In larger organizations, engineers, plant managers, and other executives running various functions and staff operations typically do not consider it part of their jobs to see salespeople. Even if a salesperson works hard at "linking," using contacts to make additional contacts with other executives in the prospect firm, he or she usually does not succeed in getting to pitch to many of them, much less all the people who have a say in corporate purchases. They are the "hidden buying influences," whom marketers must reach with their supplier story.

But while they will not see salespeople, those hidden buyers actively study their industries and the products and services that might help them. They read; they attend trade shows; they request product information.

New Equipment Digest, a leading new-product tabloid covering many industries, reports that about 82 percent of advertising inquirers—people with obvious product interests—had not seen a salesperson from the advertisers' companies.[18] That startling statistic is based on 20 years of surveys among 125,000 inquirers. Earlier surveys across several industries report similar results, and not only for advertising inquirers. Trade shows also reach purchasing influences whom salespeople do not get to see.

Skeptics still ask if those hidden buyers really matter. Isn't the key individual the one who fills out and signs the purchase order?

In some fields for some purchases, that might be the case. Exactly who has how much clout in a buying situation depends on many factors. Broad averages, however, suggest that hidden buyers really do matter. They are the bulk of advertising inquirers, for example. And about 95 percent of inquirers claim they have authority to one extent or another that influences purchasing decisions, according to a broad industry survey.[19]

Rapid Turnover

Not only are key prospects hidden. They also change frequently, adding to the value of up-to-the-minute sales lead information. In the computer industry, for instance, personnel turnover has averaged 38 percent a year.[20] Corporate downsizing and more frequent job-hopping in all but the sleepiest fields means salespeople no longer can rely on "good ol' Joe" remaining steadfastly at his buying post. As a Penton Publishing Co. report felicitously puts it, "Buyers are in a passing parade, not a grandstand."[21]

Patterns of buyer authority change, making it more difficult to track who in an organization will have influence as companies rearrange their organization charts. When firms decimate layers of middle managers, salespeople's carefully nurtured contact lists obsolesce overnight, particularly when the new faces of younger staffers assume more responsibility. The median age of U.S. managers, executives and administrators declined from 41.8 years to 39.6 from 1978 to 1988. Over the same period the median age of engineers slipped from 41 to 38.4 years.[22]

A multi-industry study of industrial buyer motivation sponsored by Penton Publishing Co. reported that seven of every 10 companies it interviewed claimed to be doing more work with fewer people. And, 81 percent of interviewees said decision making is "trickling down" in their companies. Flushed with the confidence of youth, 55 percent of the same sample also thought buyers are "often smarter" than sellers, even though they acknowledge that they rely on vendor salespeople for information more than ever before. They are eager to grab the reins, but they want the active support of problem-solving vendors with a sense of "co-destiny." As one senior executive explained the shift in responsibilities, "We've moved the decision making down to people who really know what the problems are and how to fix them. The people who do the work know more about what they're doing than I do."[23]

Recent research by *Industrial Equipment News* found similar attitudes. More than 80 percent of the industrial magazine readers surveyed "agreed strongly," the publication said, that their jobs have become more complicated with greater involvement in more phases of manufacturing.[24] Stereotypes about who buys what no longer apply.

Another source of power-buyer turnover is the changing role of women. In business-to-business selling, women increasingly play a role in purchasing, even in the grittiest industries. Penton's study found women in half the decision-making posts at a personal care products company and the same ratio at a computer company in California. There are exceptions—Penton did not find women making parts-purchase decisions at auto makers[25]—but the long-term trends are clear. On the consumer side, the traditional influence patterns for household purchases change accordingly: more women select the family car; more men do the family shopping, for example.

We will examine the implications of turnover and hidden buying influences in Chapters 2 and 3. But all evidence supports what sales managers have always known: salespeople tend to call on individuals they know and like, typically at current accounts. One wag has called it "Labrador retriever marketing: salespeople go where they get petted." Add to that the physical reality that salespeople cannot be in enough places at once, and you can see that achieving complete coverage of buying organizations requires the lead generation, tracking, and analysis steps of the closed-loop marketing system.

The Rule of 45

Not all inquirers buy the products or services for which they request information. Non-buyers might have decided to delay a purchase or buy a different product or service. Perhaps they wanted to maintain a file of currently available products to have on hand for quick reference. (As we'll later see, those literature collectors also are important prospects.)

But, within a year, on average, about 45 percent of inquirers buy, from the advertiser or from a competitor. We call it the "Rule of 45." It is the broad average of a wide range of business-to-business marketing programs in many industries.

Our research finds that six months after expressing their interest, 26 percent of inquirers from all sources actually purchased the type of product promoted, 56 percent said they still planned to buy, and 33 percent reported they still had a budget authorization for the purchase.[26] (See Exhibit 1-1.) Those are remarkable statistics that have remained fairly stable over a decade of continuing Did-You-Buy? studies.

Individual lead programs often find the proportion of year-later buyers and hot prospects varying around the 45 percent average, depending upon product and market conditions. Yet we've found that the ratio is unlikely to vary more than 10 percentage points either way. Economic conditions might affect the ratio even more. Recessions force companies to delay purchases, particularly for products of a year-or-longer purchase-decision cycles. For example, one company selling a $5,000 computer peripheral surveyed its inquirers 12 months later, which happened to coincide with a recession. It found 31 percent had bought the type of product advertised. But 32 percent said they still planned to make a purchase in the category. Had most of those buying intentions panned out, as was likely, about 45 percent of inquirers would have purchased within 18 months.

The Rule of 45 is stable enough to make it, in our judgment, a worthy guideline companies can use for planning their *return on promotional investment* (ROPI) if they don't have records of their own specific experience. We will review the evidence behind the rule and how to use it for planning in Chapter 5.

Exhibit 1-1
Lead Conversion Ratios

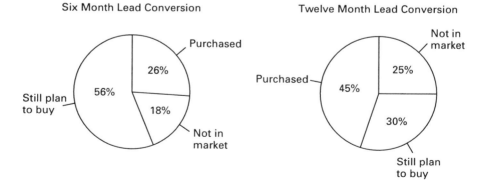

Six Month Lead Conversion

Twelve Month Lead Conversion

Source: Did-You-Buy? Study Database, Inquiry Handling Service, Inc.

Follow-Up Is Essential

The Rule of 45 has a catch, however. To fully exploit the market opportunity it represents, salespeople and distributors must follow up *all* qualified inquiries. If they just follow up some, they do not have a chance to sell to the other potential buyers they missed. As we've seen, however, most companies pursue only a small fraction of their inquiries. They will never have a crack at most of the future buyers who inquire!

To put yourself in the inquirer's shoes, think of being snubbed in a store or restaurant. You wait for service, but no one approaches, leaving you complaining, "They don't care about my business here!" Why would you then allow your own salespeople to treat your potential customers in the same shoddy manner? All successful businesspeople agree: you must approach the people who ask for information. You call them, show up in person, or leave at least three messages. You don't leave inquirers figuratively standing at the counter for weeks before you grace them with your presence.

As we noted in the Introduction, however, our research of advertising, mail, trade show, publicity, and post-card deck inquiries finds only 10 percent receive sales follow-up either in person or by phone. Cahners Publishing reports that although 94 percent of advertising inquirers said they received a reply of some sort, just 11 percent received a telephone call and four percent received a salesperson's visit.[27] (See Exhibit 1-2.) Even the inquiry-oriented advertisers in the giant product tabloid *New Equipment Digest* respond to prospects poorly: just 21 percent follow up inquiries with a phone call or visit.[28]

Exhibit 1-2
How Companies Contact Inquirers

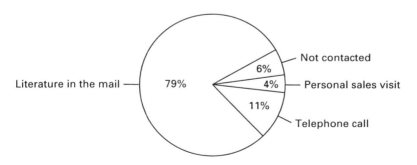

Source: *Cahners Advertising Research Report No. 210.5C* (Newton, Ma.: Cahners Publishing Co., 1993).

Inquiries must be followed up with an interactive, person-to-person contact by a sales rep or a telephone salesperson, working for the manufacturer, a distributor, or a dealer. Sending literature and awaiting prospects' "bounceback" replies through the mail used to be the recognized standard for the fulfillment–qualification–sales contact cycle. But no longer. Today's prospects expect quick response to their needs. They know how easy modern telecommunications allow it to be—for you and your competitors.

Also, bounceback cards only skim the cream of the prospect pool. Plenty of inquirers who do not return the bounceback are worthy leads as well. Experience shows that only a small portion of those who buy will bother to "self-qualify" by returning the card, especially if the fulfillment package provides enough of the information they seek. On average, we find that only *five percent* of inquirers self-qualify, just a portion of the 40-plus percent qualification rate the average company attains through all means of qualification.

Aggressive qualification and follow-up inquiries make a big difference in the likelihood of closing a sale. Judging from Did-You-Buy? studies we have conducted, which ask inquirers how things turned out, inquiry follow-up almost always boosts your market share. For example, a computer peripheral manufacturer advertised a $5,000 unit. Its distributors' salespeople followed up some inquiries but ignored others. Its share-of-sales among buyers followed up was more than 80 percent, and *twice* the share achieved in the other group. Without follow-up, competitors got much more of the available business. (See Exhibit 1-3.)

Exhibit 1-3
The Value of Inquiry Follow-Up

Source: Did You Buy? Survey Database, Inquiry Handling Service, Inc.

In another research project, eight high-tech product advertisers surveying inquirers six months after their requests collectively achieved more than twice as large a market share among accounts they followed up, compared to those their sales operations did not follow up. (See Exhibit 14-20 in Chapter 14.)

Vulnerable Process

Follow-up is the Achilles Heel of most lead-management systems. It constitutes the information–feedback stage that completes the closed-loop marketing cycle, yet it depends on the enthusiastic cooperation of salespeople whose top priorities are not information-gathering, but closed sales. Even with sufficient training, motivation, sweet-talking, and desk-pounding, it is unrealistic to expect complete lead follow-up from most sales forces. Day-to-day pressures will stand in the way of 100-percent follow-up; salespeople frequently will not be able to get to all the leads. Attitude will also stand in the way. Salespeople believe they are paid to be experts in their territories, knowing when anyone is buying. They are reluctant to acknowledge the help leads from the home office give them.

"The inquiry program probably has greater impact than the sales reps give it credit for, but that's not atypical among salespeople," says Allen Owen, marketing communications manager of Hewlett-Packard Analytical Products Group. His business unit's direct sales force claims 90 percent of their advertising, direct mail and trade show inquiries are from people they already know, he explained.[29]

When follow-up lags, however, management largely has itself to blame. Failure to present a program properly to sales builds an antipathy for leads. Then, when the marketing department does not provide screened, high-quality leads to the field, it creates outright hostility. Asking salespeople, particularly those on commission, to take the time to chase inquirers of unknown potential and qualify them usually is a poor idea. Yet so many companies expect that because they confuse raw inquiries with qualified leads, and fail to recognize how efficiently they can screen inquiries centrally.

Reports Must Follow

Distrusting the quality of leads spills over into salespeople not reporting whatever follow-up calls they do make. Whether they shun paperwork, fear acknowledging that the lead program found some new prospects, or distrust the specter of Big Brother watching them, salespeople often fail to return information about inquirers whom they did contact. The information is critical for fine-tuning the closed-loop marketing system.

You can, however, get by with a less than complete follow-up. Given sales reps' reluctance to report and the realities of day-to-day business, it's wise to choose a more practical reporting target for your company's sales force than 100 percent. Sales organizations following up and returning field information on two-thirds of their qualified inquiries are doing exceptionally well compared to their corporate peers. Perhaps your company can beat that ratio, or maybe you will need to build toward it step by step. Remember, too, that *any* follow-up reporting is better than facing the black hole into which many companies' leads disappear when sent to the field.

Uncovering new buying influences and improving market response are just some of the sales and profit benefits provided by lead management. More effective, more efficient marketing communications, improved sales productivity, happier and more committed dealers and sales representatives, plus improved forecasting and return-on-investment analysis round out the list of advantages important to all levels of the organization.

As you read through this book and study successful lead-management techniques, keep in mind the threats and opportunities facing your brand, your business unit, your division, and your corporation. It's been said that the ability to learn faster than one's competitors might be the only sustainable competitive advantage in an information-intensive marketplace. That is the ultimate benefit of a comprehensive lead-management system.

Chapter 2

Lead Management Supercharges Sales and Marketing

Armchair home office sales quarterbacks gratuitously joke that all sales reps really want are purchase orders they need only carry to the customer for signature. A well-managed sales lead program actually gives salespeople the next best thing: information to make more productive sales calls.

Lead management points your salespeople squarely toward companies and consumers that are likely to buy what they're selling, saving reps the drudgery of fruitless prospecting. Lead management gives salespeople the information to make calls at the most propitious times: when a prospect recognizes a need to purchase, has the money, and seeks a supplier. In business-to-business selling, lead management identifies who in the prospect organization salespeople should see, including powerful product specifiers far removed in the organization from purchasing agents. On the consumer side, lead management offers salespeople a prioritized list of prospects standing out from the masses.

The average salesperson spends just 30 percent of his or her working hours each week in face-to-face selling, and 21 percent in telephone selling.[1] The rest is swallowed by service calls on current customers, traveling, waiting around, and paperwork. (See Exhibit 2-1.) All that non-selling time costs money, considering how much potential new business it keeps salespeople from chasing. According to one widely quoted story, a major manufacturer studying the problem determined that a 10 percent improvement in selling time will generate more than five percent additional sales volume.[2]

Exhibit 2-1
How Do Salespeople Spend Their Time?

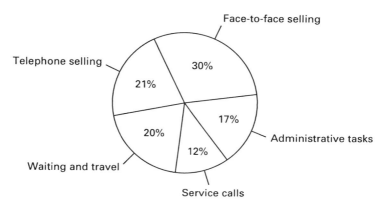

Source: Dartnell Corporation, *26th Survey of Sales Force Compensation.*

Lead Management Will Cut Your Selling Costs

Non-selling time makes a huge contribution to the expense of selling. One of the most notorious statistics in sales management is the cost of the typical personal sales call.

The most-quoted estimate has been $292, as of 1992, according to Cahners Publishing Company's biennial survey of its magazines' advertisers and prospects, primarily a business-to-business sample. That price tag—which includes all direct selling costs such as compensation, benefits, travel, entertainment, promotional materials, and product samples—is 13 percent larger than in 1989, 22 percent more than the average cost of a call in 1984, and more than double the $128 tab Cahners estimated in its 1980 survey.[3]

Sales & Marketing Management magazine, using different sources, finds less aggressive cost escalation in the 1990s. It pegged the median consumer product sales-call cost at $210.87 in 1992—little changed from its $210.34 estimate for 1990—based on its subscriber information and a variety of industry cost data. The median industrial product sales call cost $227.27 in 1992—*down* nine percent from the 1990 level despite a modest long-term uptrend, the magazine reported. The median service sales call tipped the scale at $213.64, down a mere four percent. Those estimates, medians rather than averages, include compensation, travel, entertainment, training, meeting, recruiting, support materials and administrative costs.[4] (See Exhibit 2-2.)

Exhibit 2-2
Costs per Sales Call

Median Cost per Sales Call by Industry

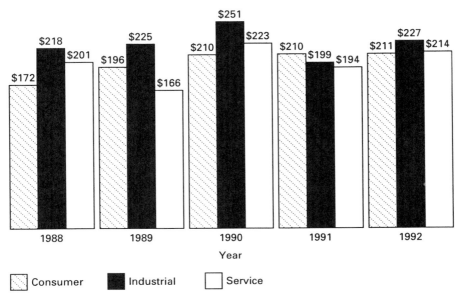

Source: 1993 Sales Manager's Budget Planner, *Sales & Marketing Management,*
(June 28, 1993): p. 75

Average Cost of a Personal Sales Call

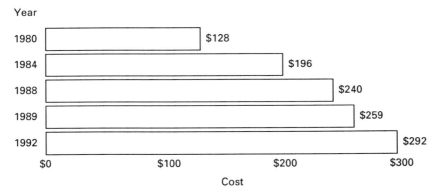

Source: *Cahners Advertising Research Report No. 542. 1H*
(Newton, MA: Cahners Publishing Co., 1990)

Cahners reports some interindustry differences based on the publication audiences it has surveyed. In 1992, for instance, electronics and computer manufacturing sales calls led the list at $322 each. Service industry calls were least expensive, Cahners said, estimating them to be $235 each on average. Understandably, costs-per-call vary by the type of product sold: from $306 for capital goods to $243 for consumer goods, by Cahners' estimate. Also, the average cost-per-call varies by region, ranging from a high of $330 in the south to $262 in the midwest.[5]

Representative cost-per-call data are, of course, very rough estimates. "Ask a dozen sales managers what the cost of a sales call is these days, and you're likely to get 12 different answers, ranging anywhere from $100 to $1,000," *Sales & Marketing Management* says, citing variations among selling organizations and cost accounting differences among industries.[6]

Cut Wasted Calls

The point for marketing and sales executives to remember is that personal sales calls are hardly cheap, especially by the frugal standards of the 1990s. And of course, it takes several calls to make a sale; 3.7 on average, says Cahners.[7] Information systems that eliminate unnecessary, unproductive visits should be welcome at any sales organization—particularly in markets where getting the order requires prolonged selling activity and several calls to close.

"Cold-call prospecting"—visiting a company without first determining its level of interest in your wares—is rarely among a salesperson's favorite activities. Oddly enough, however, it lives on in sales road-warrior mythology: The knight errant swaggers into a new town, opens vast new markets, and wins the adulation of colleagues, bosses, and spouses. Too bad that some companies still think selling is that easy, that gassing up the buggy, packing the sample case, and sallying forth with Willy Loman's "shoe shine and a smile" will win the day. Salespeople do not know whether the next appointment—if they have an appointment—is a call on someone with buying influence, with an interest in and application for their product or service, and with money ready to spend.

Sales leads, sent to the field with qualification information attached, answer those questions *before* the initial call on a prospect. Salespeople are better prepared to size up the account quickly and move the prospect toward closing faster. Spending $100, or even more, to generate and qualify a lead that allows a salesperson to close an account with one less $300 call is an attractive trade-off.

Optimize Timing

Additional features of the lead-management system ensure that salespeople concentrate on prospects whose buying interest is peaking. Sales automation expert Richard Brock argues that in the "natural sales cycle," telemarketing and timely mailings keep a supplier in close touch with prospects, monitoring whether they stay qualified, and spotting the moment when the personal attention of a salesperson will be most productive.[8]

The trade show industry provides some startling evidence of lead-qualification efficiency. Compared to 3.7 personal calls to close the average business-to-business sale, exhibitors make the sale with just 0.8 calls—less than one—on the average buyer who had visited the booth. A trade show contact is itself a personal sales call of sorts, so 54 percent of all sales linked to a show lead do not require any salesperson follow-up, says the Trade Show Bureau, that industry's marketing organization.[9]

Lead Management Will Help You Reach Hidden Buyers

Sometimes it seems that you really get to know a customer only when things go wrong. Then it isn't just the person who signed the purchase order who's complaining. A chorus of individuals you never knew existed claim intimate roles in the buying process and, they imply, the supplier-switching decision as well. That's how to find hidden buying influences the hard way.

The easy way is using marketing communications to sniff them out and get your company's story in their hands. It's a well-documented benefit from using advertising, publicity, direct mail, telemarketing, trade shows, and other marketing communications media. Then, you use sales lead management to propel those initial contacts toward the eventual sale.

In business and industrial marketing, studies repeatedly find that salespeople do not reach everyone with buying clout. Penton Publishing's *New Equipment Digest* polled many industries' advertising inquirers for 22 years, learning that 82 percent of advertising inquirers had not seen salespeople from the advertisers who sparked their interest.[10] The phenomenon hasn't changed much over time. An early 1980s study by *New Equipment Digest* found a comparable hidden-buyer ratio, as did extensive mid-1970s research by Cahners Publishing Co.[11] Whatever the ratio of hidden buyers among inquirers, nearly all inquirers—95 percent says Cahners,[12]—claim some role in purchasing decisions at their companies.

Trade show statistics show a similar pattern: 83 percent of show attendees visiting the average company's exhibit had not seen a salesperson from that company during the prior 12 months.[13] Yet, more than 80 percent of them influence purchase decisions, according to projectable research among dozens of shows surveyed annually by Exhibit Surveys, Inc.[14]

On the consumer side, statistics comparable to business-to-business selling are not available, nor would they be that meaningful. Mass marketing requires heavy emphasis on marketing communications to promote new products, build brand preferences, and encourage prospects to contact dealers.

Stay On Top of Team Buying

Hidden buying influences stay hidden because the salesperson working a territory can't find them, can't get in to see them, or doesn't try because he or she concentrates on people already known. As it is, the average sale closes after calling on more than two people—2.3 by Cahners' estimate.[15]

Turnover makes it harder to find hidden buyers, particularly in fast-moving fields such as electronics where turnover and job-hopping by professionals is commonplace. The problem promises to get worse, as purchasing becomes more complex, involving more decision makers. Nearly nine of every 10 Fortune 1000-company purchasing executives expect cross-functional buying teams will dominate purchasing decisions by the turn of the century, compared to 60 percent using teams in 1992.[16] Consistent lead management is the only way for most marketers to keep up with who's who.

Sales Lead Management Will Boost Your Selling Effectiveness

Once you've delivered your sales message to the purchase influences who matter and identified who among them is interested in your product and service, your sales lead-management system will boost your selling effectiveness in a variety of ways.

Manage with "Power Reports"

Although lead-management systems should not threaten salespeople by looking over their shoulders, lead tracking provides valuable selling-performance information. It gives sales leaders a real-time measure of individual territory sales potential. For example, qualified lead volume compared to sales and closing activity per territory produces powerful decision-making data.

Several things can throw lead activity and sales volume out of balance so that a territory generating, say, 20 percent of your inquiries provides just 10 percent of your closing activity. Local economic conditions, competitive activity, a changing prospect base, and other factors beyond a salesperson's control may be the culprits. But the leads-to-sales ratio does alert sales management to potential territory problems that bear investigation.

If sales leads are not getting the attention they deserve, often that is the first indication that salespeople are losing interest in your company or your products. They could be looking for a new job, particularly when they stop calling in or asking for leads. Or they could be selling someone else's products on the side, or even selling someone else's products with your leads!

Therefore, we call monthly and quarterly lead and sales tracking summaries the "Power Reports" of sales management. They provide market-potential ratings, sales performance tracking, territory forecasting and quota-setting data, and other insightful knowledge. Information is power in business today, but unfortunately, Power Reports are the most underused and least understood part of corporate lead-management systems.

Improve Lead Follow-Up

Formal sales lead-management programs, properly developed with the sales force's needs in mind, boost enthusiasm for follow-up and lead status reporting. Salespeople are more likely to follow up leads when they know the leads have been screened and that follow-up reports will improve the lead-management program even more. Comparing detailed reports of companies with and without formal lead-management programs, our research has found that the average follow-up rate *quadruples*—from 10 to 39 percent—with a structured system.

Despite their legendary grumbling and ambivalence toward home-office leads, salespeople do learn to love them. We will explore how to accomplish that in Chapter 12. At least, managers enthusiastic about the sales potential of inquiries also believe their field people share the feeling. Seven out of 10 *New Equipment Digest* advertisers—companies that advertise in that product tabloid specifically to generate inquiries—told the publication that their salespeople appreciate specialized business publication advertising inquiries. Those sales reps must, because 56 percent of the advertisers also claimed that their salespeople follow up inquiries promptly.[17]

Build Powerful Databases

Inquiry and lead tracking information should become the core of direct marketing and sales prospecting databases. Lists based on actual responses to your communications and sales efforts are far more productive than compiled lists or response lists generated by others, as we will explore in Chapter 8.

The best response lists for a company are, of course, its own. The single most important one is the customer list, followed in priority by its prospect list of bona fide potential buyers on whom salespeople are calling. A well-designed system goes beyond that, however, and keeps track of all those who've shown an interest in the company's product or service. It is segmented so it doesn't confuse hot prospects with, say, inquirers who should receive mail and periodic telemarketing calls, but are not yet ready for personal sales visits.

Sales lead management updates databases as new information on the prospect arises: qualification data, sales follow-up reports, bounceback replies, and purchases. The system also cross-checks lists in order to spot duplicated inquiries, advertising inquirers from customer companies, or leads to the same multi-location company pursued by different reps in different territories, for instance.

Fulfill Sales Literature Fast

The lead-management system makes sure that sales literature gets out the door and into inquirers' hands quickly. Strive to ship fulfillment material within 48 hours of receiving the inquiry. There's a discipline to fulfillment and getting the right mix of materials to the right inquirer. Far too often, however, companies treat it as a task to "get around to when someone has the time." Competition no longer allows such a casual attitude, nor do modern technologies, which can fulfill inquiries instantly.

Pre-sell Before the Call

Sales lead management provides a one-two punch paving the way for sales calls. The very act of generating the lead helps to make sales calls more productive. Marketing communications help to build a company's reputation, pre-selling prospects who then inquire seeking more information. Lead fulfillment adds the second punch, advancing the closing process with a prospect before the salesperson even shows up.

Conversely, failing to maintain adequate awareness imperils a company's future. A lesson learned the hard way by Tredegar Molded Products of Richmond, Va., epitomizes the problem. Long enjoying a quality reputation for serving major manufacturers with custom plastic injection molded products, the firm watched sales slide as it concentrated marketing effort solely on its big accounts. "New, small customers weren't calling in like before," according to Bernie McDonald, marketing manager. Research found that "deemphasizing smaller customers caused us to lose an overall market presence." Stepping up marketing communications, along with reconfiguring dealer programs and sales coverage, overcame the problem.[18]

Pricing and quality research repeatedly shows that vendors with superior market reputations have more power to maintain their prices during negotiations, and enjoy greater market share and profit than equivalent firms with weak images. We will look more closely at the evidence in Part 2 of this book.

In addition, a good reputation opens doors. Salespeople who represent "name" brands find it easier to get appointments with key purchase decision makers. Communications educate buyers who would otherwise be unimpressed and uninterested in a vendor's name. In one large business-to-business survey, nearly three out of every four inquirers to ads did not know that the advertiser made the advertised product.[19] Try setting up appointments when the prospect answers your greeting, "You represent *who?*"

Link Sales and Marketing Forecasts

Inquiries put sales and marketing on the same forecasting track. In "top-down, bottom-up" forecasting, marketing management reconciles differences between its econometric sales forecasts and the field's territory-by-territory and account-by-account predictions. Inquiries provide an objective index of market changes, the value of which is acknowledged by both marketing and sales.

Set Detailed Quotas

Rather than set annual performance targets by arbitrary percentages across the board, management can adjust territory quotas in line with changing lead activity, and refine them to achieve specific goals. Setting quotas and incentive awards by individual products, classes of trade, or applications protects a company from motivating the wrong selling activities.

Design Sensible Territories

One of the authors created sales territories for a former employer, a medical equipment manufacturer, by determining the number of physicians each representative needed to contact in order to make quota in his or her area. Physician counts by specialty are available by zip code.

Building territories that way rather than by state or county lines, north of this freeway, west of that freeway, etc., gave each salesperson a fair shot at making quotas based on potential business (physician count), known market share (closing ratios), and the number of leads needed from the doctors in the assigned area. Knowing what the replacement market is for a product, plus expected new installations, gave management an idea of how many eventual sales it could anticipate from aggressive lead-generation campaigns.

Profile Buying Patterns Precisely

Inquiry tracking profiles a marketplace, indicating the patterns of purchasing influence and the key players at companies in each territory. One large high-technology manufacturer, for example, keeps a database of inquiries arranged by account. Salespeople who tap it can better prepare for calls, knowing who specifies, buys, and approves purchases in which areas.

Spot New Opportunities at Current Accounts

Inquiries reveal personnel changes and shifting responsibilities among buying influences at customer companies already known to a rep. Two-thirds of manufacturer and distributor sales reps receive inquiries from current customers, according to an independent survey.[20]

Spotting new sales possibilities at a current account lets a salesperson approach decision makers early, before competition, when it's easiest to nudge purchase specifications in the vendor's direction. It also adds to an image of speed and customer orientation.

Sidestep Purchasing Agents

Inquiries from those hidden buying influences give salespeople justification for outflanking purchasing agents (PAs) and any other gatekeepers trying to shield the rest of the organization. Particularly in the case of major one-time purchases requiring significant engineering input and technological risk, buyers with clout who determine needs, set specifications, and grant final approval generally aren't found in purchasing departments, where salespeople are told to call.

Typically, purchasing executive expertise isn't technical, but resides in knowing the reliability and quality of suppliers. Purchasing managers recommend vendors among those who can deliver to specification. And they negotiate the price and terms of delivery. Their involvement becomes proportionally greater the more routine the purchase. But, that does not stop them from insisting on regulating vendor access to the firm, and griping bitterly about sales reps who go around them. Sidestepping around the PA is the single biggest complaint purchasing people have about sales reps.[21]

Having authority over a company's purchase orders, purchasing agents with their noses out of joint over "back-door selling" become a substantial occupational hazard for sales, particularly when they play a role in picking a vendor for a given set of specifications. A classic study by *Purchasing* magazine found that slightly more than half the requisitions PAs receive from their companies do not specify a manufacturer.[22] The PA is expected to pick a vendor from an approved-supplier list.

As a result, hot leads become a mixed blessing. The sales rep can't burn bridges and anger PAs, yet he or she must move quickly to contact, say, the engineer drawing specs for a new product. Six out of ten times, our research shows, the inquirer has also asked the competition for information. Fortunately for reps, the more complicated the buying decision, the more likely hidden buying influences will cast a wide net for information and rely heavily on vendor-supplied data.

Jump-Start Sales Calls

Information gathered by the lead-management system gives the salesperson a leg up on the first objective of the first call on a new prospect: identifying the prospect's need. Trade show leads should be particularly productive on that score because they're based on in-booth interviews with prospects. But astute telemarketers qualifying inquiries can draw out useful information for the field, as can well designed business reply cards.

The best lead-management systems will provide what we call Power Profiling™ capability: procedures that capture inquirer qualification information (need, desire, buying authority, time frame for purchase, etc.), get those data to the field, and integrate them into the marketing database. Power Profiling integrates reports from all "portals of entry"—telequalifiers, trade show booth personnel, information the inquirer provided on coupons, postcards, bounceback mailings, etc.—and data from other company databases, as needed. For instance, merging the inquiry and customer databases will reveal whether a customer has asked for more information—and might have asked other vendors as well.

Small tidbits of knowledge can be surprisingly useful. One electronics marketer remembers the prospect who revealed, during an inbound phone inquiry, that his boss insisted on "buying American" whenever possible. "That let our rep in the field know his initial presentation could deliver subtle strategic digs at foreign competitors, and have them land on sympathetic ears," he told us.

Prioritize Calling Patterns

A list of qualified leads with associated Power Profiling data yields information that allows salespeople to categorize and prioritize prospects according to their selling strategies. Deciding whether a potential $500,000 sale that will occur in nine months is better to pursue than a $350,000 sale planned for six months is part of the selling job, but reps cannot choose without knowing which account is which.

Get New Recruits Up and Running

The sales lead system also gives new salespeople a boost in setting up appointments. A new rep's success making productive calls on well-qualified leads right at the start builds enthusiasm at a crucial point in training.

Feed More Information to National Account Teams

Inquiries are a special help to major account and national account selling teams, alerting them to new buying influences and projects in their customers' complex organizations. National account marketing coordinates sales teams servicing major customers, often those with multiple locations, divisions, and product lines. The account's right hand might not know what the left is up to, but the vendor rep who knows has potentially useful information.

Keep Salespeople Informed

Lead management keeps reps in the marketing information loop. Salespeople not only want to know who is ready to buy in their territories, they want to be kept up to date about company advertising, direct marketing, and literature activities. Is the company planning new customer incentives? Adding new dealers? Appearing at a new trade show? What will affect "their" turf and "their" customers. Salespeople feel embarrassed, demoralized, and insulted when they first learn about new marketing programs from customers and prospects. Procedures to track leads should include telling the field what is generating those leads.

Sales Lead Management Will Power Up the Pipeline

The key marketing and sales advantages gained from sales lead management also work in the pipeline, the dealer and distributor channels serving manufacturers and service companies. Lead management properly handled is just as important for maintaining distributor support as are training, merchandising, and financing. Leads build rapport and support from dealers. And maintaining a dealer-locator service allows the manufacturer to steer prospects to its best dealers.

Yet, getting channel members to follow up and report on inquiries usually is a trickier proposition than dealing with one's own sales force. Channel members have learned to wield power, particularly since database marketing makes it abundantly clear in many markets that distributors and dealers control valuable information. They often know the ultimate customer and the competition better than their suppliers do. In many markets, they jealously guard their control over customer data, ever fearful of the manufacturer who tries to "go direct" and poach on territories distributors claim as theirs alone. Many refuse to tell suppliers who is buying the suppliers' own products.

Distributors and dealers, middlemen, resellers and retailers, wholesalers, jobbers, and reps have an ambiguous identity with manufacturers, for whom they are both customer and marketing partner. Sometimes adversaries, sometimes pals, distributors share the ambivalence that manufacturer salespeople have toward leads. At its worst, they demand to receive leads, then gripe that they are no good. Then dealers won't tell the factory which leads *did* pan out.

Build Dealer Support

Many dealers and distributors know, however, that leads represent found money for them. Those selling well-advertised products are likely to be the most enthusiastic. After polling industrial distributors, *New Equipment Digest* said 88 percent claimed their salespeople "appreciate" manufacturers' advertising-generated leads. And 85 percent said they look for aggressive advertisers when scouting new lines to handle. Still, a whopping 78 percent of the same sample of distributors agreed that only about a quarter of manufacturers bother to screen inquiries. Less than half their suppliers even send leads regularly, the distributors complained.[23] Their answers to such surveys might be biased slightly, however. Why would a distributor claim satisfaction if complaining might improve a negotiating position with suppliers?

Then again, manufacturers and service providers are not above suspicion. Some want to lavish their best leads only on their direct sales force. Others fear that dealers will use good leads to sell competitive products. Cutting off the supply of quality leads isn't the answer, of course; better all-around relationship building is.

The smart manufacturer recognizes, too, that lead management can police channel strategies. Carefully apportioning the lead flow mitigates channel conflicts between dealers and the supplier's direct sales force. That assures distributors that suppliers aren't unfairly skimming the cream of new business.

The even smarter manufacturer also collects qualification information from telephone inquirers seeking the names of local dealers. Then the manufacturer gets a better idea of who might be buying from distributors. Also, smart manufacturers add returned warranty-card information to their databases. This way, distributors aren't the only ones with lists of their customers.

Sales Lead Management Will Add Communications Muscle

Comprehensive sales lead-management systems offer substantial benefits to marketing communications in cost reduction and improved planning, budgeting, media placement, message creation, and management reporting. Planning and budgeting are, in fact, the areas of most dramatic benefit.

Companies with satisfactory lead management also tend to be satisfied with their marketing communications (marcom) programs,[24] in large part because leads allow them to measure marcom performance and spend money much more efficiently. That's no small benefit in the 1990s, as advertising budgets suffer cost-accounting attacks more than ever before in both consumer and business-to-business marketing.

Enhance Professionalism

Unfortunately, many marketers do not know what effects their communications have on revenue and profit. Media advertising, publicity, and, to some extent, trade shows, are the biggest problems. Their effects are not as closely linked to sales as are those of mail order and telemarketing. Business and industrial marcom managers, in particular, often protest that direct causal relationships between advertising and sales are very difficult to measure because sales results depend so heavily on field and distributor selling.

That response frustrates marketers and their bosses who demand cash-flow accountability throughout the organization. As a result, companies have sent old-line thinking packing, cut their marcom staffs, and demanded more professionalism and productivity from those who remain. "Technical (editorial, graphics, marketing) or managerial skills will not be enough for the top positions in communications," warns a 1993 report by consultant McKinsey & Co. and the Business Marketing Association. Marcom managers will also need strong budgeting and research skills, and "the ability to conceptualize powerful, new ways of getting the message to key external and internal constituencies."[25]

Plan with Precision

While not the all-inclusive answer to the problems facing communicators, tracking inquiries from source through their eventual disposition provides the Power Report data that fine-tune marcom decisions. Rather than rely on surrogate measures of performance, such as awareness and attitude changes, or coincidental trends ("new business is up and so is the advertising"), sales lead management allows you to trace a specific sale to a specific advertisement, press release, trade show, etc. Later, we will show how to calculate your return on promotional investment (ROPI) and use it as both a diagnostic and planning tool to give management the accountability information it demands.

Synchronize Communications and Selling

An important benefit is the way lead management puts the entire marketing process in synch. Salespeople get the right number of leads at the right times, and don't go begging when they need leads the most. We call it planning to your "promotional window." If, for example, your company's leads tend to close six months after the initial inquiry, plan communications six months ahead of the closing activity needed to support new product introductions, sales contests, customer buying cycles, quota periods, and the year-end scramble to close pending business. We've seen sales increase 10 to 15 percent at some companies when they adjusted lead flows to the times they're most needed.

Avoid "Corporate Triage"

Promotional window information and communication Power Reporting also prove to management that leads must be generated at various points throughout the year. That should go a long way toward ending the budget give-back charade so common at many companies.

The chaos goes like this. Management starts to worry about cash flow and the bottom line, particularly when investors demand quarterly earnings gains. So starting about mid-year, management looks around for expenses easy to cut, invariably fingering the ad budget. They nibble at it as the year progresses, drying up the lead flow sales needs to keep order books perking.

Nor does the company dig into the rich lode of sales leads in which it has already invested. Sales doesn't ask marketing, "How many identified prospects do we have in the database?" Instead, sales management panics and demands more cold-calling, and throws sales incentives around haphazardly in a vain attempt to catch up. Marketing management panics, and sacrifices effort on some of the product line in order to throw more support behind the rest. It's another poor implementation of the "corporate triage" survival strategy we mentioned earlier. With profit down, management budgets less for communications, accelerating the downward spiral in leads, sales, and profit.

Without the evidence derived from a sales lead information system and promotional window analysis, marketing communications goes to management empty-handed, arguing that advertising and other programs should continue in a regular pattern. Advertising schedules linked to lead flows and eventual sales speak a language everyone can understand: revenue.

Hone Tactical Strengths

Beyond planning, budgeting, and forecasting the effects of the marcom program, the lead system provides invaluable tactical performance feedback. A system worth the effort will report the number and average cost of inquiries, by source and specific vehicle, by product and by promotion program (specific ad, trade show, mailer, etc.). That allows marketing communications management to choose the most productive media, avoid waste circulation, concentrate on the right messages, and promote products and services in the most productive media.

When a system really hits its stride with strong field follow-up and reporting along with Did-You-Buy? inquirer surveys, management can assess each communications element in terms of cost-per-qualified lead, and even cost-per-closed lead. That cuts through the sales promotion clamor of competing media by evaluating each on the same basis: the qualified leads each produces.

"Integrated marketing communications" became an advertising buzzword in the 1980s, when the rapid expansion of direct mail, telemarketing, and database marketing convinced marketers to use multiple paths to reach target markets. The key question became how to balance the effects of each communications tool. Companies with sales lead management in place already have a leg up on integration with their valid and objective media-measurement standard.

Measure Advertising Properly

Any advertisement's or brochure's ability to inform, persuade, and generate a response is a function of what it says and how it says it, and whether prospective buyers stop to read it. So, many advertising managers reason, they can base creative decisions on ad readership scores.

However, qualified lead flow, not readership, should be the primary measure of advertising success when ads support a sales force. That begs the next question: Do high-readership ads produce more inquiries? That's usually a subject for lively debate in business-to-business advertising circles. No one to our knowledge has been able to answer conclusively. Multivariate analysis on product tabloid ads has found a weak but positive relationship between lead volume and readership scores.[26]

Our advice is to sidestep the debate and cut to the chase. If attracting attention to your ad is your goal, judge your program by readership scores. But if attracting attention to your product is your mission and you seek prospective customers, judge your program in terms of qualified inquiry yield. You'll need a lead tracking procedure to do it.

Measure Media Objectively

If possible, avoid judging media options only by the raw inquiries they produce. Those are numbers the media can manipulate easily. For example, by the late 1980s, a number of specialized business publications started hyping their inquiry production by adding so-called "bonus leads" to advertisers' lists of reader service card inquiries. The additional names might be people checking a special box to receive material from *all* advertisers in the category appearing in the issue. Or, worse yet, they could be the identities of rival advertiser's inquirers, as some industry sources privately allege happens at a few publications. To savvy advertisers, however, those are "bogus inquiries" of dubious value, to be screened out of their inquiry flows.

Some will argue, with some justification, that media evaluation must include softer measures, such as a publication's relationship with readers, or fit with readers' psychological and lifestyle profiles. We agree, to the extent that information helps the marketing communications planner make decisions. If such intangible data were comparable across media, marketing communications managers could use them for planning. But they are not. Qualified lead yield continues to be the most accessible and objective media measurement for marketing communications that support a sales force.

Save Money on Collateral

Lead management also cuts sales-literature expenses by trimming waste distribution. Printing a literature package, complete with letter, business reply card, brochure, articles, where-to-buy information and perhaps other elements can cost from a few dollars to $15 or more apiece. Handling adds to the bill. Qualification allows you to determine who should receive the expensive mailings, who should not, and who should receive specialized information.

The engineer interested in a specific product, for instance, or asking for help with a particular application might not need your entire catalog. A single sheet sent by fax might do. Some companies claim as much as 30 percent literature savings thanks to inquiry qualification before fulfillment.

At trade shows, a lead system allows you to limit literature distribution intelligently. Handing out expensive brochures to everyone who visits your booth is a colossal waste. Those casual passers-by will probably toss them out before reading them. Instead, concentrate on collecting qualification information from booth visitors. Then mail the literature the next day so qualified prospects have it in their offices or homes where it will do the most good.

Measure Wear-Out

One of the evergreen sports in consumer advertising is pondering whether an ad has run its course and become too familiar to excite the audience any longer. Often, however, wear-out is more a matter of the advertiser tiring of an ad and mistakenly thinking the marketplace is, too. Wear-out is even less of a problem among business-to-business advertisers, largely because so many of them run minimal ad schedules. But it is a legitimate cause for concern for frequent advertisers. Management armed with a lead system can monitor wear-out by watching inquiry volume changes over time.

Sales Lead Management Can Enrich Marketing Plans

Well-engineered sales lead-management systems also provide substantial strategic input to brand, product, and marketing management. Fluctuating inquiry volume might reveal new markets and applications for products and services, or point to more effective segmentation schemes and sales forecasts. Lead qualification and Did-You-Buy? survey information supplement field intelligence reports. Leads provide the standard for measuring strategic choices throughout the marketing program. Should you mail brochures frequently or lavish literature packages infrequently? Are you best served by an off-site technical seminar at the industry's big annual show, or an in-booth demonstration? Which offer will pull best, a free-trial period or a premium? Testing logical alternatives and building a base of corporate experience is the best way to approach those questions.

Find New Markets

Smart companies scout new markets and applications for new products or services efficiently through marketing communications and inquiry analysis. Field reports, discussions with customers, engineering hunches and assorted executive what-ifs produce lots of suggestions, many of which can be tested economically through advertising and publicity.

Rather than test an idea with an expensive series of sales calls, focus groups, surveys, and trade show appearances, run a limited series of ads in the prospective market's specialized media. Send press releases to those media and see if your proposition interests the editors. Even better, publications might assign a reader service card number to your release or article, ensuring that interested readers have an easy way to ask for more information.

Although the test is a toe in the water and not a full-blown communications program, it might not be enough to send out releases alone. It takes months for publicity on a novel idea to diffuse throughout the new market, be studied, and then accepted—even by editors who might not immediately see the value in an innovation. Accelerate the process by running a few advertisements. Then count the inquiry response and qualify it. That will suggest whether further investment in the new market, new product, or new product application could pay off.

Discover Better Segmentation Strategies

As markets for products and services mature and become more competitive, companies must choose market segments for concentration. A segmentation strategy for a product or brand specifies the market niches it intends to dominate and details how the brand will meet the unique needs of those segments better than competitors. The better your segmentation plan, the more you will be able to keep rivals at bay in your prime niches.

Lead generation, qualification, and Power Report analyses can profile customers and prospects by geography, customer type and size, application, and virtually any other factor that might influence a product's or service's appeal. The data will reveal which market segments show greatest interest. Does geography best differentiate the best prospects? Is it the type of application? Does customer size make a difference? Will changing the creative or media strategy in a segment boost response? Can you afford to drop an unprofitable product from the line without jeopardizing your market share in a key segment? You design the questions and use your lead system to find answers.

Gather Competitive Intelligence

Lead-management data provides valuable input to competitive intelligence databases. Rather than rely solely on information filtered back from the sales force, use inquiry qualification and Did-You-Buy? survey data to get an unvarnished view of prospects, market trends, and competitive activities. Shop the competition by replying to their ads to see how fast and how well they fulfill their inquiries, or how successful they are screening you out of the lead flow.

How well do they follow-up inactive leads with phone and mail contact? Who are their distributors?

Delight Top Management

Lead management offers many benefits to sales, marketing, and marketing communications, making corporate top management the ultimate beneficiary. By painting an early picture of future sales volume, lead systems answer corporate management's main question—What will sales and profits be?—faster than actual bookings can. While examining order volume alone does not reveal precisely which marketing elements might be lagging, lead systems monitor every stage of the customer-contact cycle. Corporate management gets hard data, not feelings and impressions, about how well communications, marketing, and sales work together, and where weak links in the chain might be lurking.

In addition, well-managed, comprehensive lead management breeds team-work that is often missing in large and even small organizations. Lead management regulates the interdependencies among marketing, selling, and marcom, holding everyone accountable to unambiguous, measurable standards. A top management insisting upon the application of those standards not only knows what's going on, but, more importantly, is confident that subordinates know what they are doing.

Chapter 3

Who Inquires and Why?

Incredibly, some companies seem to treat inquirers as annoying freeloaders, to be ignored unless they beg to have a salesperson call on them. A vocal minority of executives who don't know better mutter darkly about "literature collectors," "tire kickers," and other presumed low-lifes bent on sucking up brochures and wasting sales force time. Some inquirers fit that description, of course, which is why a firm must make every effort to qualify them. Not everyone who raises their hand to make an inquiry is screaming, "Sell me!" But almost all are taking the first step toward being sold and saying, to one degree or another, "Tell me more!"

People like to buy. They are happy to find satisfactory solutions to their problems and ways to fulfill their wants and needs. Perhaps they have a rational, easily discerned desire: the productivity improvement a company will get from a new computer system, or the larger capacity a homeowner needs in a refrigerator. As is often the case, however, emotion plays a role, maybe a dominant one, in the decision to buy and the choice of brand. The home refrigerator buyer and business computer purchaser likely will gravitate toward brands they feel they can trust, for instance. They're not just buying a "product" or a "service;" they're seeking future performance, reassurance, and the satisfaction that they've arranged a good deal for themselves.

How Buyers Buy

Buyers work their way through a succession of steps in the buying process, each of which requires appropriate action from the seller. The process begins with the buyer's reason to act. At that initial stage of the sale when the prospect becomes aware of a problem or opportunity and first enters the market, initial contact with manufacturers and service providers usually occurs through communications media. The seller uses relatively low-cost, far-reach vehicles such as advertising, direct marketing, trade shows, publicity, catalogs and directories to build awareness for his or her claim to have the best solution for the money.

First Contact

Prospects Seek Information

Sometimes, such as in advanced technology markets, prospective buyers aren't aware of new solutions to their problems. That adds an extra educational burden to the communications and sales objectives of the vendor. The engineer, for instance, wants more process reliability but remains unaware that a new technology could provide it. Or a consumer won't know of a new, environmentally safer lawn fungicide. The marketer must sell the technology as well as the brand.

Nor do prospects always know who offers the solution. Business publication giant Cahners Publishing reports that among 6,000 inquirers to 12 of its business publications, just 28 percent had been aware prior to seeing an ad that the advertiser made the product or provided the service advertised. The rest did not know of the advertiser's involvement in the product category.[1] Penton Publishing's *New Equipment Digest,* a major industrial product news tabloid, reports similar market unawareness. In 22 years of conducting Did-You-Buy? studies, an average of 61 percent of inquirers didn't know the vendor provided the product of interest until they saw the ad.[2]

Once aware of vendors' proposed solutions, the prospective buyer seeks more information, turning to specialized publications, libraries, colleagues, and other sources to learn more. The prospect inquires of advertisers, visits trade shows, pores over catalogs and directories, and is especially attentive to mail and telemarketing offers helpful to the search.

The prospect (still really a "suspect," with buying intentions unknown at this stage) certainly is not ready to buy yet, and may not even be committed to making a purchase at all. Yet it is a critical time in the buying process for the supplier who must educate and build preference for his or her brand. The inquiry generation and fulfillment program becomes a key competitive tool.

Having gathered background information, the potential buyer starts to narrow his or her specifications. Must the dishwasher have a fine china cycle? What clock speed must the integrated circuit provide? How much risk should a mutual fund offer? Should the office-cleaning service have bonded workers? Must the law firm have a litigation division? Should the caterer have his own full-time staff? At this stage, the critical marketing role often requires helping buyers set those specifications in ways that will tilt decisions toward the vendor—getting "speced-in" in selling parlance—or at least exclude marginal competitors.

Be There at Decision Time

Communications and sales must work side-by-side at the specification stage. Once known, and with his or her name entered in the vendor's database, the prospect (a "suspect" who's been qualified) should receive follow-up communication via direct mail, telemarketing, newsletters, trade show contacts, and the like. The more probable the prospect will buy, the more communications contact he or she should receive.

As the buying decision nears, it becomes time for salespeople (for products and services so supported) to make personal contact to learn the buyer's real desires, tailor the vendor's product or service solution to those specific needs, and maintain communication through follow-up calls. Sales reps must be sure to reach as many of the people involved in the specification and approval process as possible, setting the stage for closing when the buyer is ready to commit.

At the commitment stage, the buyer or buying committee is ready to make a decision. Sometimes an individual may not even recognize that psychologically he or she is ready. Objections raised at the commitment stage usually are designed to elicit reassurances and additional evidence (such as a minor concession from the seller) that the pending decision will be the correct one. The astute salesperson turns those objections into opportunities to restate the value of the offer, and uses those occasions to attempt to close. Salespeople must handle the close and ask for the order. Unless the communications medium can handle the actual close itself—as in direct response and trade show marketing—it's a job for direct or distributor personal selling in the field. Still, marketing communications continues to play a strong supporting role by contributing to product-feature awareness, interest, and brand preference throughout the closing process.

Keep Them Sold

The selling process isn't over once the buyer signs the purchase order, however. Because keeping current customers is more profitable than acquiring new ones, it is critical to maintain and strengthen relationships beyond just the first purchase. Customers may require specific after-sales services provided by reps or a separate field service force. The better the vendor performs them and exceeds the buyer's initial expectations, the stronger the relationship. Communications act in the absence of personal contact, continuing to reassure buyers of the wisdom of their choice, and fending off competition trying to convince them to switch with their next purchase.

Also, communications combat a phenomenon called post-decision dissonance: the decision makers' nagging fear that they've made the wrong choice, especially in risky, expensive, high-stakes situations. Seeking relief, the customer craves information justifying the selection. Marketers have learned, for example, that after buying, automobile purchasers pay close attention to ads for the brand they chose and avoid messages from rival car makers. In a business-to-business setting, decision makers want colleagues and bosses to see proof that they made the right choices.

Who Inquires?

Inquiries can come from anyone, consumers with money to spend and business buyers looking for solutions. But, the inquiry flow will also include students, competitors, and compulsive mail recipients. Even prison inmates have been known to circle numbers on reader service cards, hoping to receive something they can barter away.

While hardly as serious a problem as die-hard critics of sales leads portray, the weird, offbeat and obviously freakish inquiries constitute a tiny fraction of what comes in the door. The real value in sales lead-management qualification procedures is identifying the best prospects requiring immediate follow-up attention, and prioritizing the rest. The effort is worth it, particularly for personal selling-oriented business and industrial marketers. The great majority of the 300 million or so business inquiries generated annually are sincere attempts by serious buyers to collect useful information.

The available statistics tell us that inquiries come from any size buying unit. The individual consumer household is the typical unit in durables marketing. In the business-to-business marketplace (one and one-half times the size of U.S. consumer markets), four out of 10 advertising reader service card inquiries (42 percent) originate from mid-size companies with 100 to 1,000 employees, according to Cahners. About a fifth come from firms with more than 1,000 employees; companies with fewer than 100 staffers generate 37 percent.[3] That pattern seems to be stable; more than a decade ago, the Advertising Research Foundation found that 25 percent of inquirers worked in companies with more than 1,000 employees.[4]

Buyer Profiles in Flux

Figuring out who to pursue first is getting tougher in the 1990s as buyer behavior and demographics change radically in many markets. Consumer purchasing has become more conservative compared to the flamboyant consumption of the 1980s. On the business side, the once clear distinction between home and office inquiries no longer applies. The so-called "soho" market (small office/home office) of telecommuting employees and home-based businesses is a fast-growing part of the serious business landscape. Even if they do not work at home, increasing numbers of corporate employees receive business mail at home, either for convenience in reading or because glutted corporate mail rooms insist upon it. The time-honored rule of thumb that a home address indicates a poor-quality lead is woefully out of date today.

Those working in the traditional corporate office meanwhile face unprecedented pressure as corporate downsizing forces them into new and unfamiliar areas of responsibility. That puts salespeople and the systems backing them into new roles. Researcher Howard Gordon, author of Penton Publishing's "Know the Buyer Better" report, tells an instructive tale about the educational challenge facing today's marketers.

> A very competent manufacturing engineer was given the responsibility for acquiring a new piece of machinery for the production process in her personal care products plant. When she met with the sales rep from a supplier company, the rep asked her what her objectives were for the new machine.
> While she could provide a general concept for the machine, she wasn't sure about the needed specs. The rep replied that he couldn't help her until she knew the specific objectives. She needed assistance with identifying the objectives but she didn't get any help from the rep.
> She subsequently purchased machinery from a company whose rep did indeed help her develop specific objectives. And the rep from the first company simply lost a sale—largely because he wouldn't educate.[5]

Increasing foreign and domestic competition, mergers, and intense pressure for profit and market share require manufacturers to bring new products to market faster and more frequently than ever before. Even "low-tech" industries are compelled to innovate more than ever. And consumers have become particularly choosy about value for their money.

Multiple Buying Influences

In consumer markets, manufacturers and service vendors research buying units, typically households, to determine the relative decision-making clout of spouses and, in some product categories, children as well.

In business markets, typically several individuals influence buying decisions, particularly in large organizations. Each might play a dissimilar role in the process and bring different objectives to the decision, making the marketing and selling job much more complex. Marketing literature offers a variety of descriptive models that generally focus on the steps in the buying process and on who determines a need, sets specifications, recommends suppliers, approves purchases, and places the order. Together, the executives handling those functions are known as the "buying committee," whether or not they meet formally as a distinct committee.

Sales lead qualification and follow-up are designed to determine who wields what kind of clout in an organization. Sometimes, hard evidence dispels mistaken assumptions. For example, a 1,700-interview survey by International Data Group among computer buyers found four distinct groups influence purchases:

- End users, who the study says exert just 13 percent of the buying authority, are concerned primarily with ease-of-learning, ease-of-use, and working smarter on their desktops.
- Department managers, with 18 percent of purchase decision clout, worry about departmental team productivity.
- Senior managers, focused on corporate strategy, competitive pressures, and returns on investment, also wield 18 percent of the influence in a decision.
- Corporate staff computer professionals, often mistakenly considered to be the only purchase decision makers who count, have 51 percent of the clout. That's a formidable, but hardly uncontested say in what a company will buy.[6]

Who has how much decision-making power varies, of course, by company, industry, and the purchase itself. Street-wise sales experts typically seek the prime player or two who, they believe, have unmatched authority to approve the organization's buying decision. Thus that purchase influence towers over lesser buying committee members.

As sales consultant Jim Holden portrayed such concentrated power in what he calls the "Power Base" of buying:

> Everyone on a buying committee, influential or not, has a personal agenda they wish to fulfill through the committee. Some actually relish the role of "figurehead," wishing they can avoid responsibility for decisions.
>
> At the other extreme are the committee members pursuing ambitions within the organization. Invariably they try to influence the charter of buying committees, influence who will participate and influence the outcome in terms of their own personal agendas.[7]

Successful salespeople spot the differences among the groups and concentrate effort on the committee members who count. It's an essential sales training lesson: "linking" throughout the organization, using contacts and persistence to reach all relevant buying influences. Persistence in following up leads from those individuals puts a salesperson ahead of those competitors who are content to live with the dismally low lead follow-up rates characteristic of industry today.

Purchase influence patterns are flexible, however, depending on the situation. One carefully controlled experiment, for instance, simulated industrial purchasing with the participation of actual corporate buying committees. It found that the riskier and more expensive the decision, the more all members of the buying committee exert collective influence to share the decision, and possibly the blame. For routine, low-risk choices such as repurchases, committees appear to be willing to let one or a few members make the selection.[8]

A Decision Scenario

At the start of the purchasing process, an executive somewhere in the bowels of the corporation—one of those notorious hidden influences—will determine a need and ask a technical person such as an engineer to draw up specifications for the application. That's usually a critical point for vendors who need to be sure that the specs written will include their product or service or, if they're fortunate, tilt the decision in their favor. Then the decision must be approved up the line, typically by a more senior executive in control of the purse strings, who also needs to be convinced of the wisdom of the purchase and choice of supplier.

Communications reaching everyone involved throughout the process are extremely valuable sales tools at this key juncture. As Exhibit 3-1 points out, 58 percent of respondents to a Cahners survey said they meet with suppliers. But that is *after* making their inquiry. They only want to see salespeople when they are convinced they need to see them to collect more useful information. Whether they see salespeople or not, however, buying influences inquire just as frequently, research has found.[9] In other words, making personal sales visits cannot substitute for vigorous lead generation and fulfillment.

Inquirers Have Authority

Purchase specifiers, approvers, recommenders, and the like almost always have some sort of decision in mind. Exhibit 3-1 indicates the buying roles claimed by a sample of 5,000 inquirers to 10 publications polled by Cahners Publishing Co.

In a similar vein, *Industrial Equipment News* found that 89 percent of controlled-circulation subscribers to product tabloid *Industrial Equipment News*

Exhibit 3-1
Inquirer Buying Responsibilities

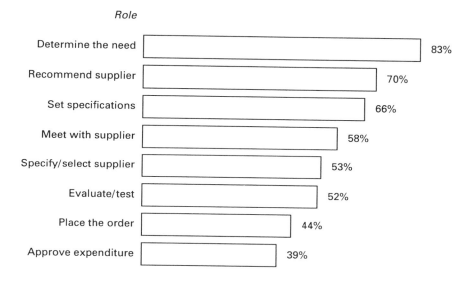

95% of Inquirers Have Some Form of Buying Responsibility

Role

Role	Percentage
Determine the need	83%
Recommend supplier	70%
Set specifications	66%
Meet with supplier	58%
Specify/select supplier	53%
Evaluate/test	52%
Place the order	44%
Approve expenditure	39%

Source: *Cahners Advertising Research Report No. 210.9A* (Newton, Ma.: Cahners Publishing Co., 1993).

say they're involved in the process of making the product or service their companies vend. And 93 percent of them request information from that publication's advertisers.[10]

Similarly, trade show attendees generally have a specific type of buying decision in mind. Trade Show Bureau data report the primary purchasing roles illustrated in Exhibit 3-2.

Note the heavy involvement inquirers have at early stages of the purchasing cycle, when it's most critical that vendors get on the short list of considered vendors. In contrast, relatively few, though still nearly half, of Cahners' respondents (Exhibit 3-1) claim involvement in the later stages of approving expenditures and placing the order. The pattern is consistent with other studies. Inquirers tend to be upstream purchase influences gathering information in the early phases of decision making. Product tabloid inquiry data, for example, find that 4 out of 10 inquiries come from professional and technical experts, half originate with management people, and fewer than a tenth come from purchasing executives,[11] the executives presiding over the final buying steps.

Exhibit 3-2
Trade Show Visitor Buying Responsibilities

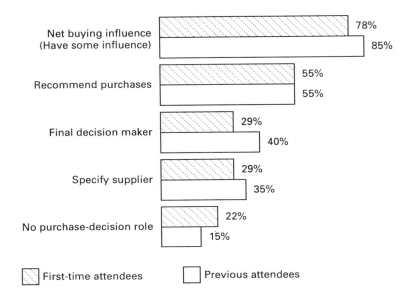

First-time attendees   Previous attendees

Source: *Understanding and Influencing Your Audience: Report AC23* (Denver: The Trade Show Bureau, 1991).

By the time buying decisions get to those downstream influencers, firms probably have already picked a short list of suppliers, and certainly have settled on specifications. We've generally found that purchasing agents are not as a rule responsive to advertising that solicits leads by offering technical information. Besides, they've already collected plenty from the salespeople who call on them.

Inquirers Look Around and Move Fast

Those approved-vendor short lists probably will get shorter. Some 69 percent of Fortune 1000 corporation purchasing executives said they expect to use fewer sources of supply by the year 2000.[12] Also, business buyers tend to consider fewer suppliers for contract services—which require a relationship be built— than when buying equipment and machinery, according to Penton Publishing's "How Business and Government Buy" research studies. On average, Penton says, buying influences of any type spend less than a month investigating potential suppliers.[13] Would-be vendors have to move fast once they receive an inquiry.

Still, at the inquiry stage, prospects do not want to overlook possible solutions. As we noted earlier, our own research finds that about 60 percent of inquirers overall ask more than one vendor for information. One survey found that different kinds of buying influences consider different numbers of vendors:

- Purchasing managers/agents, 5.4;
- Engineers, 3.7;
- Managers/administrators, 3.5;
- All decision-makers on average, 4.4.[14]

Why They Inquire

In technical fields, specifiers frequently turn to current product literature before completing their purchase specifications. Even if they have already made up their minds about suppliers, they might want more data on hand, just in case they need to justify a decision to others in the authority chain. A vendor's salespeople and supporting literature must be there to stay in the game.

Support materials—literature often called "collateral"—are crucial to the sale. Among Cahners publications readers, for example, 96 percent like to examine printed vendor information before making a purchase decision. Nearly two-thirds, 63 percent, said they limit their lists of potential suppliers to those from whom they've received collateral or catalogs. And 94 percent said they prefer to specify and purchase advertised products.[15]

That penchant for printed material extends to more than just specification sheets. Buyers need reassurance after committing to a decision, as we noted earlier. A large part of it derives from the brand image, in part shaped by the quality of a vendor's marketing communications. Brand reputation is no small matter, even to industrial buyers. Independent personal interview research conducted for Cahners Publishing found four of every five buyers interviewed saying that brand reputation is as important as technical specifications in their product choices.[16]

According to a poll of reader service card users, three-quarters of them inquired in order to build reference files with fulfillment literature. (See Exhibit 3-3.) Nearly 7 out of every 10 have an immediate information need in mind. Just a sixth say they inquire in order to update files routinely.

What happens to fulfillment literature after it's received? Another survey of 6,000 business publication reader service card inquirers found nearly 30 percent purchased the advertised product or a competitive brand, while the rest either filed the information once they received it or passed it along to colleagues. (See

Exhibit 3-4.) But whether they filed the literature or not, 80.5 percent said the information was used for "immediate needs," which apparently include studying future purchase specifications in advance.[17] Evidently, those files don't sit around and get dusty.

Exhibit 3-3
Why Reader Service Card Users Inquire

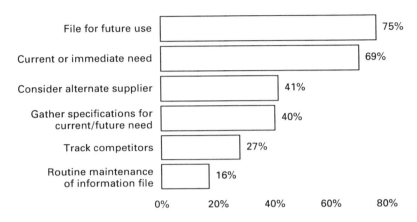

Source: *Cahners Advertising Research Report No. 210.2A* (Newton, Ma.: Cahners Publishing Co., 1989).

Exhibit 3-4
What Reader Service Card Inquirers Do with Information Received

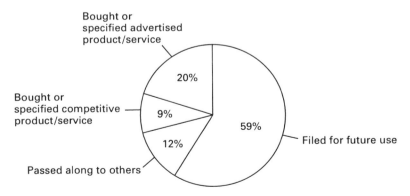

Source: *Cahners Advertising Research Report No. 210.0A* (Newton, Ma.: Cahners Publishing Co., 1993).

Building Knowledge Databases

A favorite complaint with the leads-are-no-good crowd is that "literature collectors" aren't serious prospects with buying on their minds. Those sales lead skeptics seem to think the only good inquiry is the name of someone anxiously hovering over the mailbox, ready to pounce on a fulfillment package and place an immediate order. The worst of the breed, they insist, are capricious "heavy circlers" of reader service card numbers. The industry's slang for reader service cards, "bingo cards," fuels the misperception. We are not, however, talking about the occasional mischievous inquirer who uses reader service cards like a game board, but of those prospects making many more requests than the three-to-five numbers circled on the average reader service card returned to publishers.

There is, however, no objective standard about how many requests are "too many." Some advertisers ignore heavily circled reader service card leads in order to avoid a glut of "bingo-card junkies." Others disregard all reader service card inquiries, concentrating only on phone, fax, coupon, postcard, or business reply card leads, which generally do have greater value. Reader service card inquirers aren't serious enough to approach the manufacturer directly, the reasoning goes.

We do not agree. Bingo card inquiries have value to the companies who know how to qualify them. To ignore them is to ignore potential business. Yet, in the face of skeptics' complaints, many publications won't pass names from heavily marked reader service cards on to advertisers. A few publishers will send the names along, indicating how many other items the inquirer circled. Most publications, however, do nothing and transmit names uncritically. There's room to debate how much a publisher should intervene in the process and prequalify leads for advertisers. We favor disclosing the number of items circled, and letting the advertiser decide.

Jewels, not "junkies". There's evidence that ignoring the alleged "bingo-card junkie" is shortsighted. Heavy circlers can be very good buying influences. Because they were curious about the breed, adman Roger Brucker of Odiorne Industrial Advertising and his client, Gardner Publishing's *Modern Machine Shop,* surveyed those who had circled 10 or more items on the magazine's reader service card. Their unique study found the heavy card-users involved in 35 percent more projects that might require a purchase, compared to the average reader service card user. Heavy circlers said they planned to spend 40 percent more, on average $340,000 each.[18]

Heavy circlers told the researchers that they stock up on literature because advertisers do not send information fast enough; they couldn't risk waiting if they really needed something. But a phone inquiry, they feared, would subject them to qualification questioning and requests for sales appointments for which they didn't feel ready.

Although Brucker's mid-1980s survey predates today's widespread use of the fax machine and fax-back services, which could have soothed some inquirers' apprehensions, patience seems to be warranted on the vendor's side. Heavy circlers are preparing for projects down the road. "Although our Did-You-Buy? studies show strong activity," one advertiser reasoned, "the problem is that lots of design engineers are catalog collectors. Sometimes it's a year or more between the design engineering and the time they buy," says the promotions manager at an electronics manufacturer.

Call it the "buyer's right to remain silent," quipped sales automation expert Richard Brock, head of his Brock Controls Systems. He cites an implicit understanding between inquirers and vendors that starts with a prospective buyer's right to avoid the vendor while he or she mulls options. And then, when ready to talk with a salesperson, the prospect invokes the "Buyer's Bill of Rights," thinking, "You must educate me, and I, you, concerning my needs, before you have the right to ask for my business."[19]

Where Buying Influences Seek Information

When consumers search for information about services and durable goods, they usually have a sizable expenditure riding on their decision. When business buyers need purchasing information, often it's their jobs on the line. Buyers are serious. And they usually are thorough. Consumers typically check with friends, associates, published sources, and opinion leaders—knowledgeable individuals within their social group—for advice. Business buyers, specifiers, approvers, etc. generally have more structured information sources at hand.

The Advertising Research Foundation conducted the most complete research quantifying the relative popularity of information sources ("When you wish information . . . how do you go about getting it?") in the 1970s. Although dated and eclipsed to some extent by today's emerging technologies, the study illustrates the breadth of resources available to the typical business-to-business purchasing influence. Exhibit 3-5 shows the relative popularity of different sources for current and future purchases.

Note that for current purchases, and those contemplated for the future (more than three months distant, according to the study), business publication readers ranked personal files as the single most important source for them. Their files act as up-to-date versions of the second-most popular information source, catalogs. As we've seen, more recent research also attests to the importance of reference files. Were the Advertising Research Foundation survey repeated, however, we would expect relatively greater use of phone and fax inquiries, with correspondingly less reliance on physical mail and reader service cards.

Exhibit 3-5

Where Buyers Turn for Information

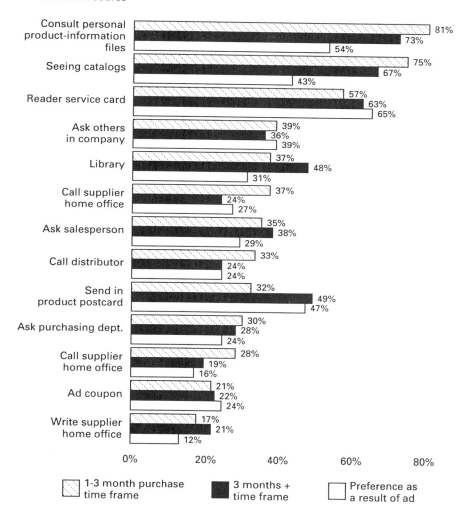

Sources of Information and Their Influence Upon Purchases

Information source

Data report those respondents saying they "always or usually" of "frequently" use the listed source when seeking product information for current (within three months) and future (beyond three months) needs. The third column indicates product information source preferences "as a result of seeing ads in business and technical magazines."

Source: *Inquiry Cards: Their Potential and How to Exploit It* (Princeton, N.J.: Center for Marketing Communications, 1976), p. 34.

Not everyone has the information they need when they need it, however. More recent surveys by Cahners Publishing find 41 percent of business publication readers saying they were unable to easily get their hands on suppliers' catalogs and brochures when they needed them.[20]

Apparently, no one source for information has automatic, top-of-mind status with business buying influences. Focus groups run by Thomas Publishing's *Industrial Equipment News* report that industrial buyers routinely cite a list of sources they check, ranging from print media through trade shows, seminars, salespeople and distributors, and vendors' other customers. "None of these are used exclusively," the magazine concludes.[21]

How Inquirers Ask for Information

When purchasing influences decide to ask manufacturers and service providers for information, inquiry-generation media typically inspire the request. Advertising, direct mail, telemarketing, and publicity are the major inquiry-generation media in both consumer and business markets. Trade shows are a powerful lead source in business, but play a minor role in most consumer markets.

Those media also provide one or more response methods inquirers can use to contact a vendor. For example, publication advertising can generate requests via reader service cards, phone and fax calls to the vendor (inbound telemarketing), in-ad reply coupons, and bound-in business reply cards. Direct mail inspires phone, fax, and reply card inquiries as well as actual orders. Outbound telemarketing—calls made at the vendor's initiative—solicits an immediate oral reply. Visitors to the vendor's trade show booth can ask that a salesperson visit, they can mail a literature bounceback card later, or they can purchase right on the show floor.

The generation medium itself, the kind of material offered, and the inquirer's degree of interest and urgency determine how someone will request more information. Your specific product and service type, media availabilities and costs, and other specific factors will determine which media and response methods work best for your situation.

Benchmark Averages

Broad industry averages nonetheless will suggest roughly how different media and response mechanisms might work for you. Such benchmarks are especially useful if you do not yet have a sales lead-management analysis system up and running to track your own inquiries and leads. The data can help you provide a more balanced lead flow for your sales force and distributors, and set marketing communications budgets accordingly. Naturally, adjust your expectations to the specifics of your program. You cannot, for instance, expect your reader service card inquiries to match the norm if you run few ads in publications providing them.

Here, we will discuss four business-to-business inquiry-activity databases that profile lead sources from different perspectives.

1. An actual count of inquiries over five years and hundreds of companies by Inquiry Handling Service, Inc. (IHS).

2. Data from a random-sample survey of readers of Cahners Publishing Co. publications.

3. A random-sample survey of Cahners' advertisers in several business-to-business markets.

4. Inquiry activity in a single medium, Penton Publishing Co.'s *New Equipment Digest,* representative of a lead-generation mainstay for many business and industrial vendors: the product tabloid publication.

In most cases, data are not comparable among the four profiles, but collectively they give a rough feel for inquirer behavior. Choose the benchmark average that best fits your circumstances. In Chapter 5, we will examine specific ways you can use averages, and your own lead-tracking data for planning and budgeting.

The IHS Inquiry Performance Survey. This database of approximately 5.7 million inquiries made over five years (1989-93) to about 200 vendors with active lead-management programs, profiles a largely high-tech marketplace. Those vendors thrive on sales leads as competitive weapons in fast-changing markets. Few, if any, can afford to treat inquiries lackadaisically.

The most important conclusion to draw from the data shown in Exhibit 3-6 is the year-to-year consistency in inquiry performance among generation and response methods. The averages do not fluctuate widely year to year.

Business publication advertising reader service cards and ad coupons produce the most responses from business and industrial buying influences, according to the Inquiry Performance Survey. Publicity and trade shows rank second and third respectively. Direct mail and postcard decks trail, as one would expect from an expensive, targeted medium (direct mail), and a medium that does not flourish in every market (postcard decks).

As for response mechanisms, toll-free and toll calls provide roughly comparable volume. Phone inquiries are considered a separate source because of their high cost compared to reader service leads and their superior closing ratios.

Exhibit 3-6
Leads Generated by Source Type

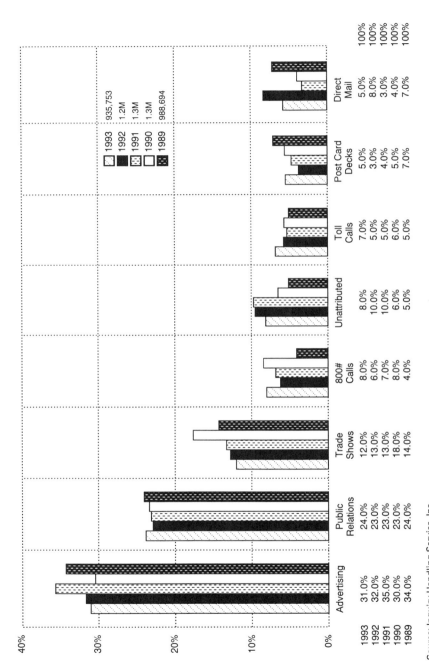

	1993	935,753
	1992	1.2M
	1991	1.3M
	1990	1.3M
	1989	988,694

	Advertising	Public Relations	Trade Shows	800# Calls	Unattributed	Toll Calls	Post Card Decks	Direct Mail
1993	31.0%	24.0%	12.0%	8.0%	8.0%	7.0%	5.0%	5.0%	100%
1992	32.0%	23.0%	13.0%	6.0%	10.0%	5.0%	3.0%	8.0%	100%
1991	35.0%	23.0%	13.0%	7.0%	10.0%	5.0%	4.0%	3.0%	100%
1990	30.0%	23.0%	18.0%	8.0%	6.0%	6.0%	5.0%	4.0%	100%
1989	34.0%	24.0%	14.0%	4.0%	5.0%	5.0%	7.0%	7.0%	100%

Source: Inquiry Handling Service, Inc.

Such calls normally are generated by advertising, publicity, card decks, direct marketing, catalogs and directories.

Cahners' reader survey. Cahners Publishing, a leading producer of article-oriented specialized business magazines and newspapers, asked a sample of 6,000 inquirers how they obtain information about products they see advertised. They use reader service cards far more often than other methods, including the telephone, as shown in Exhibit 3-7.

Cahners' advertiser survey. Cahners Publishing also asked a 4,000-strong sample of its active and prospective advertisers to report the proportions of their lead volume ("the sales leads you give to your representatives") by source and, separately, by response vehicle. The sample spanned the food service, electronics and computers, building and construction, design, printing, and general manufacturing markets. The results, shown in Exhibit 3-8, show the dominant role of advertising as a lead generator, not surprising given the sampling frame. Trade shows also prove to be strong inquiry sources.

Reader service card, telephone, and 800-number responses comprise more than half the leads received. The strong reader service card performance is consistent with the popularity of advertising among respondents.

Exhibit 3-7
How Readers Request Information about Advertised Products

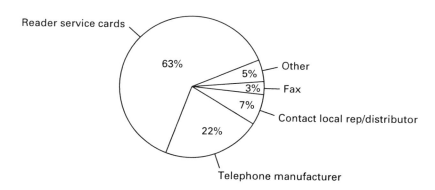

Source: *Cahners Advertising Research Report No. 240.1A* (Newton, Ma.: Cahners Publishing Co., 1993).

Exhibit 3-8
How Leads Are Generated and Received

How Leads Are Generated

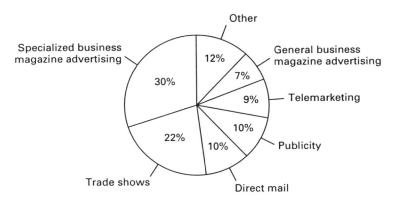

Source: *Cahners Advertising Research Report No. 560.3*
(Newton, MA., Cahners Publishing Co., 1990)

How Leads Are Received

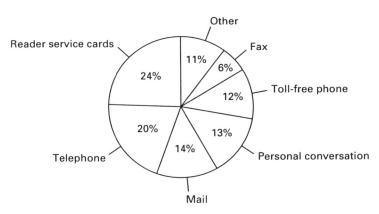

Source: *Cahners Advertising Research Report No. 560.3*
(Newton, MA., Cahners Publishing Co., 1992)

New Equipment Digest **advertiser survey.** One of the leading pan-industrial product tabloid publications, *New Equipment Digest* specializes in business and industrial lead generation. Like others of its genre, it devotes its pages almost exclusively to product advertisements and editorial product announcements— all with reader service numbers and reply cards that collect some qualification information from inquirers. Exhibit 3-9 indicates the proportion of *New Equipment Digest* advertisers receiving inquiries from other sources. The results imply, for example, that product tabloid advertisers may be underutilizing direct mail, which we believe to be essential in a well-balanced business-to-business communications program.

Exhibit 3-9 also shows the relative popularity of advertising response vehicles, with reader service cards the overwhelming favorite. About 71 percent of their advertisers think the reader service card is their best lead generator, for inquirer convenience and advertiser handling ease, the publication says.[22]

800-Number Power

The year-to-year Inquiry Performance Survey data in Exhibit 3-6 show inbound telemarketing—receiving inquiries on 800-number phone lines—growing faster than any other source. Ubiquitous among even small businesses, 800-numbers have become a standard business communication device. Calls to 800-numbers totaled nearly 13 billion in 1993, compared to 11 billion the year earlier, according to AT&T Corp. More than a half-million companies offered 800-lines by the end of 1993.[23] Consumer catalog sales and electronic communications drove that growth, along with greater corporate emphasis on database marketing to business and consumer customers alike.

Inquiry-oriented publishers such as giant product tabloid *Industrial Equipment News,* which has researched the subject extensively, anticipate that as technology proliferates and competition accelerates the demand for information, the best prospects increasingly will turn to phone and fax. We expect the average quality of reader service card inquiries will suffer. The hottest leads will not wait several weeks for information to reach them. Staying on top of technology and possible solutions is their high priority. Experts such as engineers are paid to know the answers. Among readers of *Industrial Equipment News,* for example, 97 percent agreed with the statement, "Getting information is a necessary part of the job."[24]

Exhibit 3-9
Product Tabloid Advertiser Inquiries

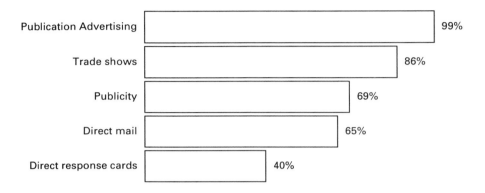

Inquiry Sources Among Product Tabloid Advertisers

Publication Advertising	99%
Trade shows	86%
Publicity	69%
Direct mail	65%
Direct response cards	40%

How Product Tabloid Advertisers Receive Inquiries

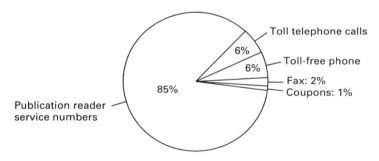

Source: *Profiting from Industrial Advertising Sales Leads* (Cleveland: Penton Publishing, 1991).

Snail Mail Shortcomings

Conventional mail-dependent lead management, perfected in a more casual era than prevails today, runs at a snail's pace in an electronic age. It requires as much as several weeks to get information to prospects: several days for the reader service card to reach a publisher who waits a week or two to batch-process inquiries and get lists in the mail to advertisers; then at best the advertiser takes 48-hours to fulfill the inquiry, get material into the mail, and notify the sales force. Traditionally—as recently as the mid-1980s—four weeks from inquiry to receipt of information was pretty good. For many inquirers the delay was much worse.

Nowadays, industry has cleaned up its act somewhat, cutting average reader service card inquiry fulfillment to 3.4 weeks, as noted in Chapter 1. And eight out of 10 inquirers say they have "almost always" received material in time to be "helpful with current projects." But, does "helpful" mean it came in time to influence purchasing specifications? The point at which a vendor could be "speced-in" or "speced-out" of a product design easily could predate the purchase approval stage by six or more months. Once a supplier is speced out, it is out. Salespeople trying to "sub a spec"—getting specifications changed so the vendor is back in the game—face very slim chances of success. They have to try to wedge their way in on the basis of price, which does no favors for the vendor's bottom line, and usually does not overcome more critical design and quality considerations.

Even when they have literature on hand, buying influences want to ensure they have the latest data. "The part that has intrigued us, is that readers say they don't trust the data books anymore. The fact is, specs change quickly," said David Allen, publisher of *Computer Design* magazine, as he launched a fax-back service for readers and advertisers. "An engineer or engineering manager who has taken responsibility for design of a system does not want to use a spec that may or may not have been updated. What they do is go to the manufacturer, semiconductor people particularly, and ask them to fax their current data sheet. There's a time and date stamp on the fax. They're protected. They don't say it that way, but that's what seems to be on their minds."[25]

Certainly, the fax machine, now commonplace in even the smallest of businesses, allows inquirers instant, interactive gratification via fax-back, also known as "interactive fax." Call a toll-free number on a fax line and a data sheet complete with graphics instantly comes back to your fax machine. Many publications such as *Computer Design* increasingly offer to handle the fax-back job for advertisers. "With the way the Postal Service has become, fulfillment of inquiries, even if everyone is working very hard, is probably three weeks," Allen observed.

Publishers are also learning to save time by sending reader service names to advertisers electronically via e-mail, shortening the transfer and rekeying time by as much as a week. That in turn encourages progressive advertisers to use the phone and fax to fulfill inquiries and qualify leads, a growing trend.

Immediate vs. Future Needs

Time haunts every stage of the inquiry-management process. Certainly inquirers themselves feel the stress. As shown in Exhibit 3-10, phone and fax are the

Exhibit 3-10
Advertising Inquiry Methods Used

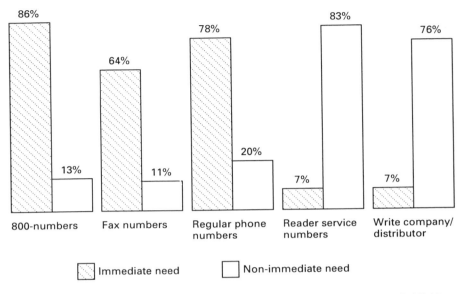

Source: *Cahners Advertising Research Report No. 550.2* (Newton, Ma.: Cahners Publishing Co., 1990).

overwhelming choice for advertising inquirers seeking information immediately, according to a Cahners survey of 4,000 business publication readers.

Looking at the same behavior from a different angle, a 1990 survey of Thomas Publishing's *Industrial Equipment News* subscribers found that 69 percent of inquirers using the product tabloid's reader service card had "no immediate need" for the information. Meanwhile, 63 percent of those who called an advertiser said they "needed the information fast." The phone users, by the way, were more heavily involved in purchasing decisions and were three times more likely to buy the product—26 percent vs. nine percent of the sample—than reader service card users.[26] Nine out of 10 *Industrial Equipment News* reader service card users nonetheless seem to be "very" or "somewhat" satisfied with reader service card fulfillment, the publication said.

Industrial Equipment News also conducted focus groups research to diagnose a slump in its reader service card usage. Tabloids such as *Industrial Equipment News* and its archrival, *New Equipment Digest,* go to extraordinary lengths to make reader service card programs especially useful to advertisers and inquirers alike. *Industrial Equipment News* readers said they use reader service cards for long-term needs, file building, and multiple information requests. The inquiry card process, they complained with a familiar refrain, is too slow and often the information sent is not what they requested. Those same reader groups also cited the problems of calling companies: connecting with telesales operators who cannot answer technical questions, then bouncing around in voice mail jail and playing telephone tag to reach the people who can. The phone scramble gets worse with multiple information requests to several advertisers, they added.[27] *Industrial Equipment News* has attempted to ease the calling problem by listing phone and fax numbers, and contact names for each advertiser in an issue. The tabloid also publishes a "fax inquiry form" within its pages, making it easier for readers to fax requests directly to advertisers.

Seasonality

Are they really old wives tales, those hoary advertising stories about response heading south in July, August, and December when everyone presumably is vacationing or holiday partying just like admen? It's not so, according to the evidence. Seasonality doesn't affect business inquiry flows, at least across industries in general.

Counting the quarter-by-quarter flow of more than 8.8 million inquiries its publications received in a year, Cahners Publishing found the first quarter produced the greatest proportion, 26.8 percent. The fourth quarter produced the least, 24 percent. But no quarter varied far from the expected 25 percent average.[28]

Month-to-month inquiry flow, according to the IHS Inquiry Performance Survey, suggests slightly larger seasonal swings than Cahners reported. Exhibit 3-11 shows 1993 inquiry volume, with fourth quarter claiming the largest portion, 27.4 percent.

Some large month-to-month differences exist for individual media. But are we to conclude that the jump in postcard inquiries from May to June reveals some immutable truth about postcard deck reading habits? Neither month's volume varies significantly from the medium's overall share of annual lead flow. Other anomalies, such as the slump in trade show leads from October to November, certainly are a function of the show activities of the vendors in the database.

Of course, the seasonality of your lead flow depends on the specific needs of your prospects, and should also depend on how well your lead-generation program dovetails with the selling cycles of your sales force and distributors. Naturally, each company's own experience is its best guide for forecasting performance. For example, the Solid State Division of the then-RCA Corp. analyzed nine years of monthly advertising inquiry volume. It found that in its

Exhibit 3-11
Inquiries by Month by Source

1993 Inquiry Performance Survey
935,753 Inquiries from 200 Participating Companies

	JAN	FEB	MAR	APR	MAY	JUNE	JULY	AUG	SEPT	OCT	NOV	DEC
Ads	29.8%	28.7%	24.8%	30.0%	29.8%	35.7%	32.9%	34.2%	28.3%	27.9%	31.5%	35.8%
PR	23.9%	18.9%	20.9%	22.6%	24.5%	25.1%	23.3%	20.6%	23.0%	27.0%	28.8%	26.5%
Trade Shows	13.7%	20.3%	20.4%	13.2%	11.5%	6.7%	8.6%	11.8%	11.8%	13.7%	4.9%	6.3%
800 # Calls	7.0%	8.5%	8.8%	7.7%	8.3%	8.5%	8.5%	7.2%	7.4%	7.5%	8.8%	7.3%
Unattributed	9.4%	6.9%	8.7%	9.8%	9.4%	7.9%	8.6%	8.2%	8.5%	6.9%	11.3%	10.7%
Phones	6.7%	6.8%	6.7%	6.0%	6.9%	6.4%	6.2%	6.9%	7.2%	6.3%	7.3%	5.2%
Postcard Decks	4.5%	4.7%	6.3%	4.3%	3.7%	6.1%	5.3%	5.9%	6.9%	5.0%	3.5%	3.1%
Direct Mail	5.1%	5.1%	3.5%	6.5%	5.9%	3.6%	6.7%	5.1%	6.9%	5.7%	4.0%	5.1%
Total Responses	7.2%	8.0%	7.3%	7.3%	8.3%	8.6%	9.1%	8.4%	8.3%	10.9%	7.9%	8.6%
Quarterly Percentages	1st Qtr 22.5%			2nd Qtr 24.2%			3rd Qtr 25.8%			4th Qtr 27.4%		

Source: Inquiry Handling Service, Inc.

particular high-tech electronics experience, there was a 77 percent chance that any month's reader service card inquiry flow would not vary significantly from the average month's volume. As far as his program planning was concerned, said advertising and sales promotion manager Dale Ludlum, "Betting on that assumption with 77 percent assurance is better odds than you'll ever get in Las Vegas."[29]

Look for opportunities in the inquiry patterns of your target markets. Do not simply assume, for instance, that seasonal differences might not exist. Sometimes patterns are easily discernable and predictable, suggesting opportunities to snatch a competitive advantage. Your industry's trade show schedule, for instance, will indicate light-activity months that might be appropriate for your own technical seminar road show. Other patterns will remain hidden, however, unless you collect and analyze inquiry and qualified-lead data—processes we'll cover in this book.

Armed with a sales lead-management database, you will spot periods when your lead flow should be stronger. Also examine other data sources. For example, publishers' reader service inquiry reports often reveal overall lead activity in your product category. Look for months where competitive promotion activity ebbs, so you can boost your "share of voice." Then, prospects are more likely to see your message.

It may be that in your field, there really are times your market *is* on vacation or holiday partying. Just be sure that your marketing program isn't on the beach or lounging around the punch bowl.

Chapter 4

Launching and Upgrading the Lead-Management Program

Examine just about any organization, and you'll find that somewhere in its ranks lurk procedures and policies—the ways you do things—that should work better. Sometimes they simply don't make sense. In well-managed firms one must look hard to find the problems, but, at the other extreme, entire companies just rumble along, apparently with fate as their only protection from disaster.

Unfortunately, sales lead management at most companies falls into this trap. A minority of organizations not only know how to manage a complete program, they actually do it right, earning significant competitive advantage. Other companies do not have a clue about what to do with those leads that arrive in the mail, beyond dumping them on a hapless sales force.

Among companies in the vast middle majority, however, marketing and sales managers have at least a basic understanding of what sales lead management could provide to them, but they do not follow through. They either put lead management aside in the "get around to it" file or they dismiss it out of hand with "It's too expensive," "It's not right for us" or that favorite show-stopper, "We tried it before and it didn't work."

When they do try lead management, managers often commit a commonplace blunder. They assign the job to junior assistants, mistaking it for a strictly clerical task rather than an important first step in relationships with future customers. First impressions count, and bad first impressions can last a lifetime.

This chapter will concentrate on certain key steps that ensure your sales lead management program gets off to a good start and meets and exceeds the expectations of even the skeptics within your organization.

Set Objectives

Incomplete objectives are generally a result of misinformation about sales lead-management procedures. Much of what is written on the subject emphasizes its most immediate and obvious benefits, but fails to stress the importance of a *complete* program—one that includes the back-end data analysis and closed-loop marketing readjustments that continuously improve sales productivity.

Industry commentators usually stress how rapid inquiry fulfillment beats the competition, satisfies prospects, and gets hot names to the sales force. That's certainly important and, arguably, it's the single most important benefit of a lead-management system. It's also the domain of literature fulfillment services whose advertising and technical publicity shape what appears in trade publications. The impressions stick. For example, a revealing survey by *Business Marketing* magazine and Chicago ad agency Starmark, Inc. asked business-to-business marketers which elements they considered "part of a successful inquiry program." Fast turnaround received the most votes—80 percent of the sample. But only 23 percent cited inquiry-based information as an adjunct to telemarketing and research. Just 18 percent of the sample considered performance reporting an element of inquiry program success.[1]

A company can do so much more with lead management than rapid fulfillment alone. It's really a matter of marketing information management: building and using the databases that create and sustain profitable customer relationships. That's the strategic picture. On a day-to-day basis, think of lead management as continuous sales support, performing tasks such as finding prospects and nudging them closer to a closing situation more efficiently than field salespeople can on their own.

Any of the lead-management benefits cited in Chapter 2 can be a lead-management objective. It depends on your marketing strategies. Are you emphasizing new market development? New product launches? Building new distribution relationships? Rebuilding neglected sales territories? Realigning territories? Pumping new leads into the field to compensate for languishing sales? Providing more information to prospects and hidden buying influences than you can communicate in an ad? Gathering market information faster for real-time planning? Justifying budgets?

Choose Appropriate Goals

Whatever your marketing and sales objectives, lead management is likely to play an important role in achieving them. When you've chosen and pursued objectives consonant with senior management's goals, you are well positioned to win corporate support.

Account-driven goals. If, for example, your company or business unit strategy is account-driven, focusing on a relatively small number of customers and prospects the company already knows, salespeople concentrate on maintaining ties within account organizations. The selling objective is keeping current customers happy, getting more of their business, and getting competitors' customers to switch vendors. Mass market lead generators such as advertising are relatively less important. The comparatively smaller numbers of inquiries received at the home office require little formal qualification; they are much more likely to originate from prospects salespeople already know.

The communications goal serving account-driven strategies is staying in touch with the relatively stable prospect and customer base via regular mailings, newsletters, and updates of sales support literature. Trade show appearances are opportunities to maintain known buying contacts. Middlemen such as distributors, dealers and value-added resellers are less likely to be active users of manufacturer-generated leads. Presumably, they know their territories.

Market-driven goals. On the other hand, market-driven strategies aimed at large or rapidly changing customer and prospect bases require much more emphasis on attracting inquiries from previously unknown companies and buying influences, and from those hidden buyers salespeople cannot reach. Advertising is an efficient way to troll those waters. Trade show booths must attract people who you don't know and who don't know your company.

In following a market-driven strategy, direct mail and outbound telemarketing actively test new lists seeking more unknown prospects. Inquiry qualification is a must for sifting through blizzards of names. Salespeople must limit their calls to the hotter prospects who are close to a purchase. Concurrently, tracking market changes through inquiries, sales follow-up reports and Did-You-Buy? studies becomes more important for marketing planning. Middlemen are major inquiry users.

Market maturity. The choice of lead management goals must also address the maturity of a market. For instance, new technologies and those in a fast-growth phase rely on "tech-driven" strategies: emphasizing superior performance while trying to overcome buyers' fear of the unknown. Communications must arouse desire and curiosity to generate the inquiries that flush the risk-prone "early adopters" from the larger mass of buyers, and solicit invitations for sales calls and demonstrations.

At the other end of the product or service life cycle, the mature offering, managed to maximize cash flow and return on assets, seeks a steady stream of low-cost inquiries for low-cost follow-up. Buyers, familiar with the technology and the field of parity-product competitors, buy on the price and terms of the offer, which must be stressed in lead acquisition. Formal telemarketing is an efficient and effective follow-up tool.

Competitive pressure. The appropriate lead-management system also must address competitive performance. Strive to make the speed and quality of competitors' best inquiry response the *minimum* standard for your developing system. Provide fulfillment by fax, for example, and emphasize receiving phone and fax inquiries directly from inquirers. Tirelessly preach to the sales force the importance of "getting there first," and recognize the salespeople who do.

Profit margins. Finally, how much clerical and data processing overhead can the lead program afford to carry, given product profit margins and the unit sales growth better lead management will produce? Available profit often determines how much a company is able to spend on communications and sales lead management.

For example, with a $100 product with a 35 percent gross margin and a 5 percent pretax profit of $5, you will be hard pressed to spend: $1.50 on literature per inquiry, 75 cents to $1.50 on postage, $1.40 to $2.00 on handling, and $3 to $15 to qualify the prospect. A $500 product with a 5 percent pretax margin can find a few dollars to manage the inquiry. A product costing several thousand dollars is very well equipped to manage an inquiry properly. And a product in the $10,000 to $1,000,000-plus range is suffering criminal neglect if its inquiries do not receive lavish attention!

Study the Lead System Anatomy

Think of sales lead management as an information-sorting process. Exhibit 4-1 illustrates the data flow of the complete closed-loop marketing system, with the Power Profiling™ database at its heart. Let's walk through it.

Inquiries and Lists

An integrated marketing communications program generates inquiries from a variety of media, approaching the marketplace from different angles simultaneously to build reach and frequency to varying degrees among different target audiences. Periodical advertising will attract the attention of some prospects, while direct mail reaches others. Business buying influencers attend trade shows to see new products. The exposure also reinforces messages they might have seen in their reading or their mail. As we will see, lead management provides the key unlocking the complexities of media integration.

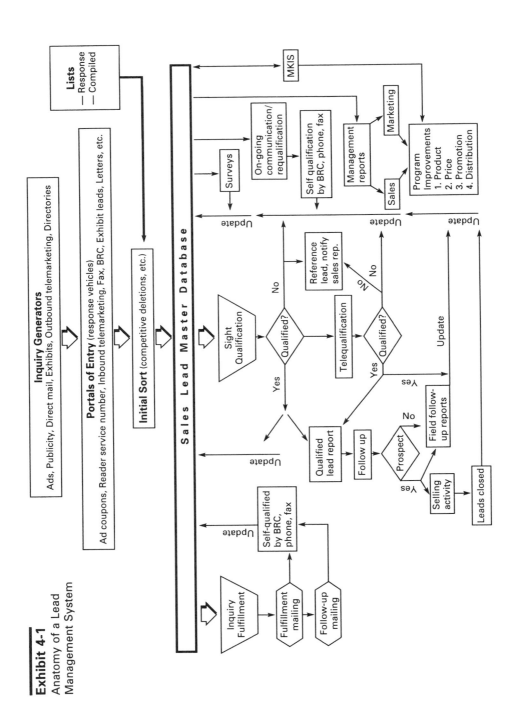

Exhibit 4-1
Anatomy of a Lead Management System

Each medium provides inquiries through one or another "portals of entry"—the ways in which your company receives them. Advertising inquiries appear as reader service card replies, phone and fax queries, coupons, bind-in reply cards, and letters. Trade show inquiries should derive primarily from the people manning your booth. Mail generally produces reply card or phone and fax inquiries, etc. Inquiries produce an active database, composed of individuals who have expressed an interest, however casual or intense, in your company, its products, or its services.

Lists taken from directories or compiled by direct marketing firms provide another input to the lead-management system. We call them lists, rather than leads, as many in business mistakenly call them, because they are passive and non-specific to your company. That is, response and compiled lists do not represent people who've shown an interest in you specifically. The individuals on response lists once acted on an offer somewhere, perhaps for a product or service related to yours. Those on compiled lists are names culled and combined from a variety of passive sources such as other lists, directories, or government records. If you hand them uncritically to salespeople and call them leads, you are mixing qualified prospects with names of relatively unknown quality and accuracy.

Initial sort. Each raw inquiry undergoes an initial sort to isolate duplicates (a hot prospect might hedge her bet by inquiring more than once) and identify inquiries from competitors, students, pranksters, or other obviously unqualified individuals.

Competitors are worth sorting out of your lead flow. Why make it easy for them to receive your sales literature and fulfillment offer? As for students, you might have good reasons to send them some sort of fulfillment information, to build goodwill with future customers. Then there are the reply cards filled with profane or otherwise mindless scribblings, testimonies to the fragility of human reason.

Sales Lead Master Database

At the center of lead management is its core database, repository of *all* the information you gather about an inquirer throughout the process.

After you sort raw inquiries, ideally you check each against the existing database to determine if the inquirer sought information before, is already a live prospect, or already a customer. Matching old and new records isn't always possible (more than a two-thirds hit rate is considered good), but it is worth the effort to let a computer attempt a match at the same time you key an inquiry into your system. Record-matching algorithms and tools such as artificial intelligence and fuzzy logic promise greatly improved hit rates in years to come.

Each new inquirer becomes a new database record, a dossier of everything you learn about an inquirer during the steps of inquiry acquisition, fulfillment, qualification, and follow-up.

The original inquiry, for example, is likely to provide only sparse information about an inquirer's interest, need, application, timing, budget, etc. Telequalifiers will learn more, if necessary, and lead follow-up reports from the field should add much more data to the individual record. Each step contributes to a deeper understanding of the market and to more efficient, effective marketing programs. Detailed knowledge of its customers can be a company's most important source of competitive advantage, particularly firms selling technically undifferentiated products and services.

Once logged into the database, inquiries move in two directions simultaneously: to fulfillment and to qualification.

Qualification

Does a particular inquiry come from someone with enough need, desire, money, authority, and other characteristics to suggest he or she is likely to buy? Qualification answers that question, making it a key step in lead information management. Qualification is also the first step in building an efficient lead-value assessment model: techniques and rules of thumb for sorting inquiries without collecting more information.

Yet, qualification is the Achilles heel in many a company's inquiry handling escapades. The typical company's blunder is fobbing the job off on field salespeople. Except in unusual circumstances, make initial qualification a marketing department function, not a task for sales. Eventually, the sales department determines if a lead is worth pursuing with selling effort. But sales should be making those decisions only for inquiries with obvious potential, lest your expensive sales force spend too much time qualifying unknown "suspects" and not enough time attempting to close known prospects.

Even worse in the long run, dumping raw, unqualified inquiries on the sales force erodes their confidence in all leads, good and bad. Salespeople sometimes dismiss the very concept of leads developed by others in "their" territories, so treating inquiries cavalierly contributes to the dismal lead follow-up rates we cited earlier.

Reference notification. We recommend that once you've either sight-qualified or telequalified inquiries as described below, you send even the unqualified ones to your direct sales force, and maybe to your distributors. Such a *reference* *notification* clearly states that these names are not deemed qualified, and need not be followed up except at the salesperson's discretion. Print and send each of the reference notification names on a lead form, to encourage reporting back just in case the sales rep does follow it up. But make it plain that you *do not expect follow-up on reference notification names;* they have much less priority than qualified inquirers.

The reference notification is part courtesy to salespeople whose support is critical to the lead-management process, and part good territory management. Seeing who inquires gives salespeople more information about their territories. Just make sure that salespeople know the difference between the reference notification list and the qualified lead list.

Of course, be sensible and sensitive to the needs of salespeople. Do not expect them to tie up their time in clerical duties, shuffling a large number of reference notifications and qualification reports, unless their own systems are well automated.

Depending upon your selling strategies and relationships with your dealers, distributors, manufacturers' reps, etc., you might want to send all relevant raw inquiries to them as well. If they are truly marketing partners, the inquiries list will help to strengthen the sharing implicit in such partnerships. But if your dealers are more "customer" than "partner" and you trade with them at arm's length, a reference notification list might cause more harm to your interests than good. That's particularly true if you are managing potential channel conflicts, such as friction between a direct sales force and distributors. Do not throw gasoline on that contentious issue by sending the same inquiries to both distributors and direct sales!

Sight qualification. The first step in separating inquiry wheat from chaff, *sight qualification* refers to lead-status decisions based on the information provided with the original inquiry, without collecting more data from the inquirer. Experience and pre-existing knowledge of the market provide the decision context.

Most often, sight qualification relies on a staffer who knows a product's best markets and can spot which inquiries have potential. Company names, certain industries, particular applications, company size, etc. can all be potent clues. Sight qualification also includes using the various types of statistical or expert system models gaining increased popularity as management science tools.

Of course, many raw inquiries come in the door with little ancillary information beyond inquirer name, title, company, address, and phone number. Unlike trade show and inbound telephone inquiries that allow you to gather all needed qualification information on the spot, other portals of entry usually leave several key qualification questions unanswered—reader service cards or in-ad reply coupons, for example.

Savvy marketers cope with that problem at the start by encouraging information-rich inquiries. They achieve 55 to 65 percent sight qualification ratios by emphasizing 800-number inquiries, and by using coupons and reply cards that ask for more than just a name and address in their publication advertising and direct mail. They also train trade show booth personnel to use comprehensive lead forms.

Timid marketers, however, waste money in the mistaken belief that it is somehow impolite to pose qualification questions or ask if the inquirer would like a salesperson to call. Usually, the ones who gasp and agonize the most have never been in the field themselves, and have never had the chance to learn just how vital such information is to the selling process.

Telequalification. This is where telequalification comes in: picking up the phone to ask the inquirer for more information. Inquiries with a "maybe" status, that look neither like probable winners nor likely losers to sight qualifiers, should be telequalified before you expend more expensive sales force effort on them.

Those savvy marketers know that by collecting qualification information as early as possible, they can cut the number of inquiries requiring telequalification to 30 to 40 percent. The timid marketer could get stuck telequalifying as many as 90 percent of inquiries in order to do a conscientious qualification job. But even with a high volume of inquiries, telequalification pays off compared with the egregious waste of selling time and money when salespeople qualify raw leads.

Sight-qualified and telequalified leads go to the field where the company sales force, distributors, etc. *must* follow them up. Telequalified leads obviously have value; the telemarketing department has contacted the inquirer, who wants to proceed in the selling process. Many sight-qualified leads will be really hot prospects, such as those who circle the "have salesperson call" number on a reader service card.

Note that the field should also receive telequalifier reports on inquiries that do not telequalify positively. The information might be interesting and useful to the salesperson in the territory. She might see potential in such a lead because of detailed knowledge of local conditions.

Updating the database. Regardless of an inquiry's status, it stays in the sales lead master database. If it fails either sight or telequalification, do not discard the database record, but update it accordingly. If the inquiry passes and makes its way to the field, that's noted too and, hopefully, more information about the inquirer will soon return from the field. That is why Exhibit 4-1 shows all data flowing back to the sales lead master database, the Rome of all inquiry-handling roads.

Even if they do not qualify initially or in the field, inquiries might have value in the future. Some are worth adding to promotional mailing lists in hopes they will respond with a qualified lead later. Other inquiry records will provide additional market, competitor, or prospect information for the corporate marketing information system (MKIS), of which the sales lead master database is a part. And data about poor-quality inquiries as well as the good ones say a lot about the media generating them.

Fulfillment

Along with reference notification and qualification, inquiries that pass the initial sort must be fulfilled. You promised them something, and you should deliver, even to inquiries that do not pass qualification muster.

As we've noted, 48 hours between receiving an inquiry and getting fulfillment material out the door is a competitive turnaround time. Bouncebacks—fulfillment package reply cards returned by inquirers—indicate a self-qualified lead; the prospect has asked for more information.

Avoid locking prospects into the "literature loop" of bounceback-and-fulfillment cycles that have literature and reply cards passing back and forth in the mail without advancing the sale. A self-qualified lead is an open invitation to a salesperson from an interested prospect.

Bounceback replies used to be the gold standard of lead qualification—but that was three decades ago. Today, with ubiquitous phone, fax, and electronic mail providing instant communications between prospects and vendors, we find just 5 percent of fulfillment literature recipients return a business reply card on average. Many qualified prospects will not respond at all, by mail or phone or fax. The literature answered their questions, and they're ready for a salesperson to call! It is yet another reason why sales follow-up is so critical in gaining full value from your investment in generating inquiries.

Fulfillment includes follow-up mailings to inquirers who did not respond to your fulfillment package. Remind prospects about the information they received; ask if they need more or want to see a salesperson. Ask if they received the information originally sent, if they've already bought, their time frame, etc. You'll generate more qualified leads, possibly as many as you generated through bouncebacks in the initial mailing. And you'll keep your name in front of prospects, whether or not they respond. We recommend following up at 30 days and again at 70 days after your initial fulfillment mailing.

Field Follow-Up

As Exhibit 4-1 shows, qualified leads go to the field, to distributors, or to direct sales as required by your sales and distribution strategies. Make it clear that the leads represent new business, extra commissions, contest points, etc. for the rep or distributor. Include whatever background information you have about each prospect; telequalifiers can collect considerable amounts.

Your sales force and distributors should follow-up and report the status of each lead, with additional information about each, back to the master database. If the lead warrants their continuing selling activity, "leads closed" reports on leads converted to sales should also be recorded in the database.

Achieving follow-up is, however, one of the great challenges of sales force management. Without sufficient encouragement and motivation, the average salesperson will not follow up qualified leads comprehensively, but will cherry-pick the obviously good and convenient ones. Research by Dartnell Corp. has found that 80 percent of all sales are made after the fifth contact with a prospect firm, yet 48 percent of all salespeople give up after the first contact!

Not that the others are persevering all that well, 25 percent more give up after the second contact, 12 percent more throw in the towel after the third contact, and 5 percent give up after the fourth contact, Dartnell reports. In other words, just 10 percent of salespeople stick with the prospect for at least the five contacts required to make the sale![2]

Follow-up, and reporting the outcome of a follow-up contact, are two separate issues. Even good salespeople, hot to pursue a promising lead, can drag their feet reporting back to the master database. In a later chapter we'll look at ways of increasing reporting rates. As a practical matter, however, receiving follow-up reports on two-thirds of the leads sent to the field is a very good reporting average.

Surveys

To compensate for the weak follow-up and reporting that can plague a sales lead-management system, and to gather information objectively without sales force intervention, wise marketers maintain a regular schedule of Did-You-Buy? surveys of qualified inquirers who did and did not buy.

Such surveys fill an information gap that develops in most companies' lead-management systems, the "black hole" marketing managers decry when they complain, "I send leads to the field, and I never hear about them again." Some inquiries resurface as booked orders, but what of the rest? Did anyone contact them? Did anyone buy? Are they still considering purchase? Did they buy from competitors? Polling inquirers by phone or mail provides enough information for closed-loop marketing decision making. Surveys also flag weak spots in your fulfillment and follow-up, and collect more information for master database record updates.

By telephoning inquirers at precise times following fulfillment of an inquiry—say 6 months and 12 months later—you can profile the market's buying and purchase intention patterns. You generally cannot, by the way, achieve the same precise timing in a mail survey unless you go to extraordinary lengths requiring a professional researcher's involvement in the project. Your own telemarketers can handle the relatively simple questionnaires required for a Did-You-Buy? study.

Ongoing Communications

Experienced salespeople know that some of their best prospects are companies and individuals on whom they called but who didn't buy, or those who bought from competitors but can be switched to another brand easily. And, even unqualified prospects might become hot prospects sometime later.

All should be "kept warm" by ongoing communications. Send them new product announcements, your customer/prospect newsletter, trade show invitations, and include them in your direct mail campaigns. Often, seeming nonprospects will change their policies, strategies, or personnel, putting them back into play for your salespeople. A bad experience with a vendor can return them to the market. Because you've already established a relationship of sorts with them, they are predisposed to buy from you when they are ready to switch suppliers.

Make sure each communications device gives them a chance to respond—via business reply card, a toll-free phone number, or a fax number—and provide requalification information to update your database.

Gil Cargill, noted sales trainer and nationally recognized speaker, says that customers must be contacted, "touched" as he puts it, "6.7 times before they buy." Touches can include the original literature package, telemarketing qualification calls, follow-up mailings, and the sales rep calling on the prospect. Leave all of those contacts to just the salesperson, aside from the initial literature package, and you'll probably delay the sale, or throw it over to the more energetic "high-touch" competitor.

MKIS and Management Reports

A marketing information system (MKIS) is a broad, enterprise-wide network of databases, and client/server decision-support tools that organizes marketing data for decision makers. Desktop computing enables managers to combine internal and external data sources for product, price, and distribution planning. The sales lead master database is a critical internal source for MKIS.

Forecasting, financial reporting, and budgeting marketing communications should rely heavily on inquiry statistics. Vague notions that "the ads are working," or indirect evidence such as market awareness and preference-rating changes over time, don't meet MKIS input standards. Trying to link marketing communications activity with sales volume down the road comes too late to meet the decision-making demands of MKIS users. Your lead-management system will be the one quantitative source of communications performance data meeting MKIS requirements.

For example, any competitive analysis should deduce why some buy from others instead of from you. Ongoing Did-You-Buy? survey results combined with the prospect records in the sales lead master database reveal a valuable clue—how your customers differ from competitors'—unavailable elsewhere except through expensive research studies. Are your communication and selling plans sensitive to those competitive strengths and weaknesses?

Closer to home, the sales lead master database provides real-time guidance to marketing, marketing communications, and sales management, as we will explain in detail in Chapter 14. Inquiry activity foretells what will, or should, be happening in the field tomorrow, and which media should be used to generate the leads needed for the day after tomorrow.

Audit Your Current Position

In designing your lead-management program, assess how well you've been handling inquiries. Whether you use an outside service or do the job in-house, are you satisfying customers, company management, your sales force and your marketing department with your performance? Turn an inquisitive eye on what you're doing now, solicit the opinions of colleagues throughout the company and those of customers, too. Consultants and lead-management services can help, particularly because they know what programs work and they can assess your current position objectively. You might decide to have your inquiries handled out-of-house, yet the consultation can suggest great ideas for improving your own system. Also, compare your performance to the standards recommended in this book.

You might not need outside help to determine if things are out of kilter. Try responding, disguised of course, to one of your own ads, mail pieces, directory listings, etc. Call your own 800-number for product information, for instance. Does a bored voice answer? Or does a cheery voice announce the company name clearly and ask that simple but critical question, "How can I help you?"

Playing prospect can be a real eye-opener, as one sales manager learned when she called her own corporate headquarters posing as an inquirer. "I had to interview that woman on the other end of the line to be sure I was at the right place to get whatever information I was supposed to be calling for. The ad never said exactly what they could send to me," she complained.

"I asked if they sold the advertised component with the right size and specs to fit my application. And if so, at what price? From which distributors?

"The reply? 'I can't help you with that,' said a weary voice at the other end. 'The person who can isn't around.' Had I gotten a receptionist? Someone's secretary?" the sales manager wondered. "Whoever picked up, it wasn't who it should have been, at least I hope not!"

The audit should continue by examining what happens to inquiries forwarded by publishers or collected at trade shows. Are those names simply tossed back out to the field where they're routinely ignored as some sort of bad joke from the factory? Do inquirers merely receive a brochure stuffed in an envelope? Maybe a bounceback card that only offers to send them more brochures? Do the inquiries that ask specifically for a sales call get lost in the shuffle?

Checking current data integration is an important part of your audit. Can database users compare order, customer, and inquiry information to track marketing performance? Do you suffer a systems gap within the marketing department, with separate databases handling lead generation and fulfillment, sales follow-up, proposals and quotations, etc.?

Obtain feedback from customers and prospects. A Did-You-Buy? study, augmented by questions covering the speed and quality of your inquiry fulfillment and sales follow-up, will be revealing.

Custom-Tailor Your Approach

Planning the lead-management system best for your company's unique needs, we recommend that you complete a Sales Lead Management Matrix form and an Inquiry Handling Objectives form, as described below. Both are useful not only in guiding your thinking, but also for communicating your priorities to management and others in the organization who will be affected by lead management.

List your problems and solutions. The Sales Lead Management Matrix shown in Exhibit 4-2 is a simple four-column field for writing down the goals, problems, strategies, and tactics supporting each distinct product or service group. The exercise takes the audit stage of planning from a description of what is occurring now to a prescription for what should be happening.

Exhibit 4-2
Sales Lead Management Matrix

Goals ⊗	Problems ?	Strategy ⇨	Tactics ℞

For example, the widget line may be enjoying a growing market share, and the lead-program goal is, say, 15 percent more qualified leads for the sales force over the next fiscal year. The problem is that your current inquiry-handling system is swamped already, with no additional telequalifying capacity. Your problem-solving strategy could be increasing qualification capacity, or altering lead generation to improve the quality of raw inquiries.

Tactics for the first strategy will include more staff for telequalifying leads, adding advanced telemarketing equipment to build efficiency, or hiring an outside telemarketing firm. You could pursue the second strategy, gathering inquiries of greater quality, by shifting communications emphasis to media (e.g. trade shows) and messages (free "buying guide" 800-number offers) yielding proportionately more inquiries that can be sight qualified positively.

At another level of planning, use the matrix to address the product's overall strategy, saving the tactics column for the role lead management should play in support. For example, suppose the widget line must continue to build share against traditional competitors and defend the market against a substitute product technology making headway based on lower price. The strategy marketing has chosen is a value-added approach, offering free trials and installation services that low-price substitute technologies cannot match. Tactics include heavy promotion of the new value-added positioning to produce a heavier inquiry flow, with more telequalification to identify genuine prospects for the free-trial offer.

Rate your performance by objective. The Inquiry Handling Objectives form in Exhibit 4-3 continues the analysis by focusing on specific lead-management

---

Exhibit 4-3
Inquiry Handling Objectives

Objective	1	2	3	4	5	6	7	8	9	10	Status
Quick Lead Turn-Around											Slow Lead Turn-Around
Database											None
Computer System											Manual System
Pre-Screening											None
Qualification of Leads											"Shot-Gun" Selling
Response Mechanism											None
Tailored Literature Packages											Generic Package
Follow-Up by Sales											None
Measurement & Analysis											None
Surveys											None
Did You Buy? Surveys											None
Personalized Response											Preprinted Response
Inbound Telemarketing											None
Outbound Telemarketing											None
Flexibility											Rigid System
Supported by Sales											Not Supported
Accurate Lead Records											Inaccurate Lead Records
Ad Hoc Reporting											Rigid Reporting
Integrated with Marketing											Not Integrated
Prospecting New Business											No Prospecting
State-of-the-Art System											Antiquated
Established Training											None
Monitor All Costs											Costs Unknown
Exploit Present Customers											None
Updating Procedures											None
Determine ROI											ROI Unknown

Current Status = _____   Future Goals = _____

These objectives can be set for each element of your program (telemarketing, etc.). The grid can graphically show where you are and where you realistically want to be. You may want to set up your own criteria.

goals. Deciding how much emphasis to devote to specific lead-program features is rarely an "either–or" choice. We recommend a 1–to–10 rating scale for profiling the relative importance of each task. To use the form, indicate both your current status and where you need to be to accomplish program goals. For example:

- Did-You-Buy? surveys have greater or lesser importance depending upon the quality of field follow-up and the degree to which known customers and prospects comprise the market.

- Providing ad hoc reporting from the database will be more important to marketers and product directors frequently checking the status of fast-moving markets and new products. (Database marketing requires ad hoc reporting.)

- Flexibility is important when the lead program must accommodate peaks and valleys in the inquiry flow, new products and services in the system, new markets and new data-reporting demands from management.

- The ability to determine one program's return on investment (ROI) will have a greater priority where performance accounting is required practice, as is frequently the case in publicly owned corporations.

Set measurable objectives. An important consideration at this stage is setting objectives properly. The plan should start taking a more specific shape than a simple promise to "increase the number of qualified inquiries" or "boost sales follow-up reporting." To be accountable, your program needs objectives stated in measurable, time-dimensioned terms, such as "increase monthly volume of telequalified leads by 20 percent by the end of the year."

Otherwise, how can performance be judged? Without objective evidence that you attained an agreed-upon standard, how do you know you achieved it? "Increasing sales force satisfaction" is laudable, and "boosting lead volume" is a noble sentiment, but one could say such imprecise goals were met merely by notching performance up a point or two.

Preplan Every Step

The next stage in planning the lead-management system is to preplan *every* step of the process, rehearsing it in your head and on paper so that nothing is left to chance once the program is up and running. Use the steps in this chapter as a guide.

Then, consistent with setting objectives, add timelines to your program. Design a descriptive flow chart for every step. It need not be fancy, just a device for indicating how long it will take to accomplish each task. Stringing sequential steps together, can your plan meet its timing goals?

Police time dimensions carefully once they're in the plan, or delays will ripple throughout the entire system, killing its effectiveness. When more than one task is to be performed at a time, the timeline becomes a *critical path schedule,* indicating which jobs must be completed on time for the entire project to remain on schedule. Suppose, for example, that it takes three months to prepare new promotion materials in advance of the big annual trade show, and that your agency requires two and a half months to get the advertising insert ready for a publication's show issue. Adding the publication's "month-before" closing date for materials moves the critical path for show promotion artwork and design to three and a half months.

Or suppose marketing needs two working days from receipt of an inquiry to get a fulfillment package in the mail and the inquiry ready to send to the field. At the same time, the inquiry sits in a queue for three days before a telequalifier gets to it. The critical path for the individual lead getting to the field with qualification information attached is three days. If that's too long a time, decouple the fulfillment and qualification steps, sending the lead to the field immediately in a "reference notification to field report," with qualification information tagging up later.

Write a Manual

Preplanning every step implies a specific, standard procedure be written for every step. Many a well-planned system fails or seriously falters when personnel turnovers bring in new people who apply their own ways of doing things. Or, people take shortcuts because they have nothing to guide them.

For example, fulfillment will require editing the inquiry to determine which combination of literature pieces to send the inquirer, entering the inquiry in the database, and printing the lead form, mailing label, and cover letter. The inquiry goes to the literature storage area where someone collects the required items, checking them off a list as they are picked from inventory. Literature and the cover letter go in an envelope to which the gummed label on the lead form is attached. The envelope goes to the mail room where it's mailed that day. The lead form is forwarded to the sales department for distribution to individual sales representatives.

Written out in a comprehensive operations manual, the plan leaves nothing to chance or misinterpretation. Distribute it in loose leaf binders to accommodate changes. Include a style manual designating when and how to use literature. New personnel, part-timers, and backup people should be able to turn to the manual and take over any step in the process immediately.

To be successful, you must impart a sense of urgency to the process. Lead-management staffers have to understand they are dealing with a perishable commodity. Even though the majority of leads will not close for months, who wants to arrive later than competitors with literature or a salesperson's phone call?

And although no written procedure can anticipate everything that can go wrong, strive to add contingencies to the plan. What happens when required literature is out of stock? What if the 800-number goes down? And, most important, who makes decisions if something happens that isn't in the contingency plan?

Plan Your Organizational Support

Problems not likely to be revealed in writing, except in confidential memos, concern organizational resistance to the program. Each function of the company has its own agenda, and tends to evaluate problems and opportunities from its own short-term perspective. To get them to anticipate the long-term benefits of sales lead management, you, the planner, must bring everyone aboard carefully lest resistance scuttle an otherwise sensible design.

Salespeople seek more orders, while brand managers jockey to meet broader objectives for their individual products. Marketing management wants sales to report field results for analysis, but sales reps will resist "number crunchers" looking over their shoulders. Sales managers like the idea of controls assessing rep performance, lead qualification, customer coverage, selling cost efficiency, etc.—as long as they have it on their terms. It's not uncommon for sales management to take over the downstream portions of the lead-management program to be sure it stays in control.

Meanwhile, senior company management wants bottom line profit and market share gains, expecting to see all that productivity documented with hard data. And the communications staff wants to prove how many raw inquiries it can generate per dollar, without being overly concerned about what happens to them downstream.

The lead-management planner is stuck in the middle of what could become factional warfare if the lead program is poorly designed and presented. Getting everyone behind the plan means fashioning compromise, giving each faction something to meet its objectives. In a word, people have to see what sales lead management does for them.

Win senior management commitment. Selling the sales force on lead handling is a subject worthy of a chapter on its own. We discuss it in Chapter 12. But, salespeople are not the only ones with tender sensitivities. Senior marketing managers may have an agenda inimical, or at least indifferent, to the objectives of your nascent program. They might be skeptical because of prejudices inherited from years climbing up the sales ranks ("we already know all our customers and prospects"), or up through engineering ("only literature collectors inquire"). Corporate kahunas long in tooth are sure they've tried everything before sometime, and they vaguely recall it didn't work and that's why they don't do it now. Or they're convinced their product/market/strategic position is so unique that "none of that stuff applies to us."

On the other hand, enlightened managers yearn for the innovations that build marketing conquests. Not that they jump at every new notion in the suggestion box, but they do respond well to a good idea from someone who has done their homework. Just remember, however, that such a leader will keep asking you for evidence of performance, out of genuine interest in how it all turns out. That's when the diagnostics your lead program provides become valuable tools for your own personal promotion.

Strive to get management commitments and approvals stated in writing. We all laugh at the clichéd "cover your tail" mentality of incessant bureaucratic memo swapping. But the extra time spent making sure understandings are clear is nothing compared to the frustration of dealing with miscommunication and forgetfulness later. We recall one company chieftain, for instance, who stipulated that his lead program's top priority was achieving a 20 percent closing rate on inquiries. But, when later shown progress toward that goal, he insisted that new market penetration was his main concern for the lead program! Or imagine the confusion caused by a marketing honcho asking for a spiffy image-oriented ad campaign, then later complaining it wasn't producing enough inquiries.

Build a task force. Top management can kill a proposed lead-management system outright, but others can kill it slowly—with repeated stabs in the back. Preplanning therefore requires keeping everybody in touch, to establish and perpetuate everyone's sense of ownership in the program. Start your internal selling process by forming a task force to review your plans and suggest adjustments. Present your ideas not as something others approve with thumbs up or down, but as a concept you will all shape together. And include the foot soldiers as well as the bosses in the planning. The "grunts" are, after all, the ones on whom lead program details most depend.

The Inquiry Handling Objectives form in Exhibit 4-3 is particularly helpful at this stage. By filling it out for themselves, everyone gets a chance to think hard about present strengths and shortcomings, and to indicate their choices for improvement priorities.

Next, plan in advance how you'll keep all players informed once your system is up and running. Don't wait for them to ask you how's it going. And, don't leave it to chance that they will recognize how your program contributes to their goals. Articles in your company house organ calmly noting progress probably work best for routine information sharing, unless there's an extraordinarily good or bad event at hand. Without a house organ, start your own "Lead Lover's Newsletter" for periodic distribution to program constituents.

Organize Personnel Responsibilities

Having sold the program to management and colleagues, make sure you've got enough of the right people in place to run it. The list starts with a "sales lead czar," so to speak: the person who knows the system, takes responsibility for it, and considers it his or her highest priority. The program's planner is likely to be its biggest champion and hence the best choice. It must be clear to the entire organization who runs the lead program. And whether full- or part-time, the "czar" must have enough time for periodic review and system planning beyond the day-to-day duties of keeping it running.

Avoid the "clerical extra" fallacy. One of the biggest causes of lead program disappointment is the mistaken notion that it can be a thoroughly clerical function, an extra tagged on to the duties of employees with other things to do. The smallest of companies receiving just a dozen or so inquiries a week may be able to get by with passing attention to the task. But any larger program, especially one that hopes to track and analyze lead information, requires someone making lead management his or her top priority. The "let Suzy do it" thinking that puts the fate of inquiries in the hands of receptionists, secretaries, or other preoccupied clerical personnel may look cheaper, except for the high opportunity cost of botched lead handling, lost potential sales, inadequate data analysis, and the frazzled nerves of salespeople and distributors.

"Suzy" and her male equivalents aren't dummies. They know the jobs they're paid to do, be it answering the phone properly, managing the boss' schedule and letters, keeping office services humming, etc. Inquiry handling as an add-on to their "real" duties invites them to save the lead program for Friday afternoons or, inevitably, let the accumulated batch of inquiries slide untouched to the following week.

The lead czar has to have sufficient presence in the organization to report directly to senior management if need be, and sufficient rank to work with the various departments contributing to lead success. The stereotypical "Suzy" isn't in a position to cajole sales or communications managers, demand faster action from the mail room or stay on top of the computer department's handling of the database.

Depending on its size, the inquiry program likely will need other staffers assisting the czar. If they are not full-time workers for the lead program, they at least must have inquiry-handling duties explicitly part of their job descriptions and salary reviews. For instance, answering inbound phone inquiries should be the top priority of the person assigned to the job. Otherwise those "interruptions" become an annoyance to someone under pressure to complete other tasks.

Motivate and support. How inbound telephone service representatives handle calls, for instance, reveals their satisfaction, or resentment, on the job. Callers will sense the attitude and, as with all first impressions, will judge a company by what they hear. Will prospective buyers hear a bright, on-the-ball voice eager to help? Or a bored couldn't-care-less indifference connoting an unresponsive company that's best avoided?

Within reason, make sure telephone service reps and other personnel dealing directly with prospects and customers are contented, motivated individuals. In contrast to outdated, traditional practices that put front-line staffers on the bottom of the employee totem pole, modern service-management strategies stress the critical role those people play in shaping the company's public face. According to what's emerging as a 21st century approach to customer service, front-line people deserve investments in technological aids, training, performance-based compensation, and management attention commensurate with their true value creating and keeping customers.

How to keep lead-management personnel motivated isn't a mystery. A management style that encourages ownership of the job, recognizes superior performance, sets realistic goals, and treats employees with respect is the key to strong performance in any organization.

Compensation and team-building incentives are also part of the formula, of course. Because lead management plays such a critical role in presenting the company to its markets, pay the staff well. Existing sales department and corporate personnel policies will dictate the right mix, or at least pay as high as the company will approve.

Finally, in preparing for the day the system is up and running, don't assume that the lead-handling staff will operate without supervision. When things settle into a comfortable routine, it's tempting for the lead czar to turn to other problems, presuming all is well. But Murphy's Law *will* intervene. Stay in touch with what's happening with the people to whom you've entrusted your system's success. Do not let employees who tend to turn over rapidly shape your system to their desires by default. Staying in touch would have saved a lot of embarrassment at a company where the program manager insisted his operation provided 24-hour fulfillment turnaround. However, his mail room staff brightly acknowledged to a visitor that they try for 24 hours, but at that point they were two weeks behind!

Design Adequate Facilities

Motivation and job satisfaction depend heavily on the physical environment established for the lead-management program staff. Also, the quality of literature and the accuracy of fulfillment depend on storage facilities that protect inventory and facilitate accurate paper management.

The model office arrangement for staff isn't particularly different than arrangements one would make for office workers in general. Clean, well-lit workstations with low wall dividers to impart a sense of privacy, each with power outlets for office equipment and supplemental lighting. Give the staff its own distinctive area where people can work together easily. Place the group within or adjacent to the marketing communications department, the staff with the most immediate stake in proper inquiry handling.

Do not ignore the back room. Insist on having adequate space for every aspect of the program. Make sure the office manager is part of your planning task force, so he or she will realize the importance of the process that shapes the company's public face.

Literature and premium storage and fulfillment areas require particular attention. We've seen otherwise well-laid plans go awry over little details, such as someone finding out that forklift trucks delivering pallets of product literature can't fit through the door to the literature storage area. Or that the designated area has the wrong humidity and temperature for adequate storage.

Plan a system of well-marked storage racks that make it easy for literature pickers to find the fulfillment literature and forms they need. Mark the positions indicating when a stack of literature is small enough to require reordering. We recommend placing a reorder card in the last box of literature as the trigger to reorder. Or, figure your average monthly literature flow (accounting for special promotions, etc.) and the time required for literature reordering. Add two weeks to the time estimate and estimate the stock you'll be dispensing before the new material arrives. Usually, that translates to about three months' normal supply as your reorder point.

And be sure a specific individual has responsibility for checking literature inventory frequently. It's hardly rare, for example, that salespeople will raid a stack of literature, depleting it faster than expected, unbeknownst to the inquiry department. Try and accommodate such requests, making sure they always have the lead-program manager's knowledge and approval.

Fulfillment package assembly will require its own large table area near the literature storage racks, as well as cubbyholes for whatever forms and tags package assembly must use.

And by all means carefully plan where you'll put computers, terminals, and other sensitive electronic gear. Certainly not alongside the forklift route in the warehouse!

Maintaining security will always be important, but it becomes critical when warehousing expensive premiums. Establish inventory controls and check up frequently, matching physical inventory to fulfillment mailing records and special tally sheets filled out by stock pickers, which they know will be double-checked against other records.

Budget Your Program

The key point to remember, and to promote to management in selling your budget upstairs, is that lead management is not an *expense*. It's an *investment* in greater sales efficiency. In fact, if the lead program is operating properly, it is funded by "found money." That is, it will produce more incremental cash flow than it absorbs.

Fixed vs. Variable Cost

It might be helpful to promote sales lead management to your accounting colleagues as a *fixed* cost of doing business, rather than a *variable* cost. The difference is critical to accountants and financial managers. We have seen on many occasions that describing what you are doing in their language can win you more support.

Fixed costs are those a company incurs no matter how many product units it produces and sells in an accounting period: overheads such as plant and equipment charges, office rent, heat, and light, for example. *Variable cost* totals change with volume in an accounting period. For instance, the cost of raw materials and shipping. Of course, many types of costs lie in a gray area of partial variability.

The problem for marketing and communications arises by the way most companies traditionally budgeted selling and marketing expenses. Accountants charged expenses to the products sold in the same period. And when it was time to budget for the coming year, they took the easy way out and forecast marketing costs based on anticipated sales volume. Conceptually, that means that actual sales will determine actual selling and marketing costs, which therefore must be variable costs. Certainly, that's backwards thinking; the real world doesn't operate that way. Marketing activity produces sales, not the other way around!

Unfortunately, cost accounting-oriented managers who think of marketing solely in variable-cost terms reason that if sales decline, marketing costs should fall as well, to keep cost percentages in line and protect profit.

Advertising, the easiest marketing cost to cut, gets trimmed first. That cuts the flow of leads to the field, further eroding sales volume, triggering the "corporate triage" crises as we noted in Chapter 1. As a result, treating lead management as a variable cost risks triggering a vicious downward spiral in revenue.

Instead, think of lead expenses as fixed. They are a steady cost of staying in business, the source of tomorrow's ongoing sales activity every bit as important, and fixed, as the accounting department itself. The typical business marketer selling direct or through distributors cannot stay in business for long without sales leads. Many consumer durables makers cannot either.

Cost accountants have been improving their ability to link individual expenses with discrete marketing activities, and treat some marketing costs as capital investments in future business. A few pioneers in the "momentum accounting" school persuasively argue that marketing investments should be evaluated by their influence on sales growth rates rather than absolute unit volume.[3] But you do not need to fuss with such detail to make the case for steady investment in your lead program.

Relevant Cost Categories

At the budgeting stage, concentrate on the costs directly relevant to inquiry handling. The broad expense categories cited on the worksheet in Exhibit 4-4 do not include the cost of generating leads, typically media charges, nor the cost of following them up which generally become sales or marketing department expenses. Those categories provide the bulk of overall expense in the lead generation–fulfillment–qualification–follow-up cycle.

It is not unusual, even among business-to-business marketers, to spend 10 times or more on media than on lead handling. (We discuss media budgeting in the chapters devoted to inquiry generation.) As for the additional follow-up costs carried by the sales department, enlist its aid in estimating how more and better leads will cut selling costs per order. Those are sales statistics, however, and not part of the inquiry-handling budget even though they can help you sell your program "upstairs."

Budget inquiry-handling procedures first, because essential functions such as fulfillment and qualification must be in place regardless of the amount you spend on media. In the same vein, don't sacrifice lead handling speed and accuracy for the sake of running a few more ads. Those will produce more inquiries that your debilitated system cannot handle professionally.

Estimate Activity in Advance

An up and running system provides data proving that it works. But at the start, absent any formal data specific to your company's experience, estimate lead flows and thence operating expenses using the broad all-industry averages we've cited earlier in this book.

Use the return on promotional investment (ROPI) model presented in Chapter 5 to show others the relationship between promotion, inquiry volume, and revenue. Then estimate the cost of receiving, processing, and analyzing the forecast inquiry flow. Absent more specific evidence, use the all-industry Rule of 45, introduced in Chapter 1, to estimate the lead closing rate.

You are working with a dynamic organism, however, not static ratios. Be attentive to changes in the sales function that are likely to occur when salespeople know they've got a new lead-management system contributing to them. Improved follow-up on their part will increase their lead-closing ratios. And knowing management is keeping better score on performance might prompt more effective lead generation from the communications department.

What you don't want to try is fobbing a low-ball budget on management, one designed to make your plans nearly too good to be true. They'll probably turn out that way, making you look foolish, diminishing management's confidence that the system has been well conceived from the start, and possibly costing you your job.

Facing uncertainty predicting lead flow, lead-closing ratios, and other performance metrics, try to put likelihoods on different budget levels. At this early stage of the process, provide a range in which costs probably will fall: a "best estimate" flanked by "high side" and "low side" approximations. Not only will that add reality to your budget, it will reduce the chance of surprise. Unforeseen deviations from the plan, either good or bad, drive corporate accountants up the wall.

Finally, strive for cost-accounting fairness. It's likely that corporate accountants will consider lead-management costs part of general sales expenses to be allocated among the products it serves. Fairness argues that product groups be charged on the basis of inquiries processed, rather than in the old-fashioned, inaccurate method of lumping all overhead together then allotting it all according to department staff size. You don't need any line managers with their noses out of joint thinking they're paying for more than they're getting.

Operating Cost Categories

Exhibit 4-4 shows the Inquiry Handling Operating Cost Analysis form (in-house), a useful guide to budgeting operating costs. It isn't a budget presentation form, but a planning document listing the major operating expense categories under the lead program's control. Each category will have its own worksheets enumerating subcategory expenses.

Note that it includes *only* operating costs directly attributable to the lead program per se. Fulfillment literature and mailing costs are not included, for example. Those are advertising costs, not part of the lead-management budget. They can vary widely by program and, presumably, a company will incur them anyway when it mails fulfillment packages without the benefit of a formal lead-management system.

For each cost category, we give "typical" expenses for a moderately sized system, handling about 12,000 inquiries annually on a $62,400 operating budget and run by a part-time lead czar. Consider the following percentages to be a rough planning guide to apply to your own program budget, recognizing that your own circumstances might require sharply different spending proportions. Alter the line items in Exhibit 4-4 to suit your own program design.

Exhibit 4-4
Annual Inquiry Handling Cost Analysis—In-House

LABOR

1. Employee salaries (@ $11.50/hr, Counting, Data Entry, Stuff, Telemarketing) .... $ 24,000
2. Employee benefits (Full- and part-time 35% of gross salary) .... $ 8,400
3. Supervision costs (20% of $12/hr + Benefits) .... $ 6,600
   (Prorate the costs of supervisors who assume responsibility
   for lead processing, plus add 30-35% for fringe benefits)
4. Anticipated extra labor for computer & peak time/shows/etc. .... $ 9,600
   (Four heavy months with four shows/year (@ 1/3 full-time employee)
5. Receiving literature, delivery to post office (@ $50.00/mo)............ $ 600

EQUIPMENT

6. Cost of special equipment and maintenance (i.e., postage meter, scales, typewriters, etc.) .... $ 1,200
7. Cost of computer (i.e., pc, software, printer, supplies, etc.) .... ** $ 5,400
8. Cost of literature storage areas (square footage, lights, heat, etc.;
   500 sq. ft @ $.50/sq ft) .... $ 3,600
9. Cost of work areas (tables, chairs, etc.) .... $ 1,200

FORMS/SUPPLIES

10. Cost of lead forms .... $ 1,200
11. Supplies other than literature, i.e., tape, paper clips, etc. .... $ 600

TOTAL: $62,400

$62,400 ÷ 12,000 inquiries/yr = $5.20 per inquiry

Note: $ amounts have been used in certain calculations and may vary between geographical areas, i.e., per hour and per square foot rates.

**Non-recurring

- *Salaries and benefits* for full- and part-time staffers and supervisors comes right off the payroll budget, pro rated by the amount of time each individual will devote to lead-management tasks. Roughly estimate they will run around 60 percent of the total.

- *Anticipated extra labor* is no small consideration for most companies which need to exert special effort preparing for trade shows, handling the extra phone volume of a major special promotion, etc. On average, we've seen these costs comprise 15 percent of lead handling costs, but the ratio varies widely between firms.

- *Special equipment and maintenance,* those charges for equipment not already charged as overhead to your system, typically comprise 2 to 5 percent of operating expense.

- *Computer costs* are a sizable cost category, whether they are corporate system allocated charges, or the annual amortization of your own dedicated system. Roughly 8 to 15 percent of inquiry-handling costs mark the ballpark; software and staff training are the big wild-card expenses in this category.

- *Literature storage/work areas* are a direct allocated charge against your budget; estimate seven to nine percent of the total.

- *Cost of lead forms* is a modest annual charge when large order runs are spread across several years. The two to five percent range will apply unless you change your forms more often.

- *Miscellaneous* supplies and other charges are not likely to run much more than two percent of the total in a typical system.

Having completed the detailed budgeting exercise, divide the cost by the total number of inquiries you expect to handle. This will determine the average cost per inquiry of your program. In the Exhibit 4-4 example, the average is $5.20.

Cost Fluctuations

Some lead program costs will fluctuate more or less in step with inquiry volume changes—lead forms and supplies, for instance. Others vary only indirectly with inquiry activity, such as the extra labor required to handle a major promotion or trade show project. Activity-based costs allocated to your department, such as time-based computer department charges, also fall in such variable cost categories.

Fixed costs of your program do not change with inquiry volume. They remain the same, at least in the short term. Department staff, and storage and work area charges, for instance, remain the same whether a particular lead generation project produces a blizzard of inquiries or a trickle.

Part of the program planning task may include budgeting capital expenditures, such as computers, networks, phone systems and other equipment outlays required by the new department. In larger companies, the additional capital equipment may take the form of corporate system upgrades: new lines added to the PBX, additional computer capacity, and the like. Deciding how much of these one-time start up expenditures to amortize yearly is a matter for company finance policy, accounting standards, and tax law.

The Make or Buy Decision

It is always wise to compare expenditures for in-house inquiry management with the prices outside services charge. Because those services typically offer all or parts of the complete inquiry management process—with expert consulting thrown in—you can combine what you can do most efficiently inside with *à la carte* services purchased elsewhere.

The Inquiry Handling Operating Cost Analysis form facilitates a direct cost comparison between in-house and outsourced services. Solicit bids concerning fixed charges such as monthly fees, volume-based charges, and add-ons such as telequalification charges. Find out how quickly they fulfill inquiries, get leads to the field, and update databases. Do they have the right equipment to service your account now, and when you grow? Can your company afford to assign employees to lead management, making it their top priority? Are you big enough to be an important client to a service of a given size?

Other factors might bear consideration in your decision. Often, small companies with modest lead-management needs, and large firms able to enjoy economies of scale, find in-house lead management the most efficient option. In between those extremes, however, the picture varies. Companies with sophisticated needs might find the decision tipping toward outside services that already have equipment and trained personnel on hand.

Keep These Tips in Mind

Upcoming chapters will discuss lead generation, fulfillment, qualification, and analysis in detail. Here are a few key considerations to keep in mind as you ramp up your system.

Lead Generation

Be sure you plan the communications program and the lead-handling system with the same inquiry volume in mind. An unanticipated flood of leads straining the qualification process, for example, is likely to cause difficulties downstream for the sales department. On the other hand, inquiry handling overcapacity wastes money at the start.

Your lead-generation strategy must balance somewhere between the "loose leads" and "tight leads" extremes. The loose leads approach seeks as many inquiries as possible, relying heavily on in-house qualification to guide sales follow-up. It's appropriate for building large databases and mailing lists—such as when entering a new market—when wide reach has a higher priority than qualification efficiency. Advertising, publicity, and mailings to broad-coverage lists, achieve high reach for the dollar, but produce many leads of relatively low average quality.

The tight leads strategy attempts to generate fewer inquiries, but of a higher average quality. Making very specific literature offers and concentrating promotion in niche mailing lists, vertical trade shows, and outbound telemarketing are appropriate strategies for a tight leads approach.

Receiving Inquiries

Your company's sales lead-management manual should specify the exact steps to be taken for inquiries arriving through every portal of entry. Each new method of receiving inquiries complicates the process for clerical personnel who, if frustrated, will put the inquiries aside for handling "later."

We remember one publisher's special circulation promotion that generated hundreds of what circulation department mail room people called "funny cards." Not having received instructions, they filed the cards for later distribution, once they'd investigated where the cards should go. Not surprisingly, the cards sat around for a month or more before someone became curious. Throwing inquiries into a file drawer or, as the industry cliché goes, stuffing returned business reply cards into shoe boxes, isn't uncommon.

As soon as inquiries arrive at the door, in whatever form, they must be handled immediately. Strive to make it a continuous process, rather than a batch process of once-a-week or slower frequency. Inquiries must be dated, screened, logged into the inquiry database, and coded for appropriate handling before they are sent on to the field, to qualification, and to fulfillment. Initial sorting and sight-qualification standards must be clear, accompanied by written instructions just about anyone can follow.

Fulfilling Inquiries

Speed is essential. Technology and competitive pressure might make the current 48-hour turnaround standard too slow in fast-paced markets. But to hit even that standard consistently, your manual should instruct how to address envelopes, and specify the order in which brochures are placed in folders. Plan it before inquiries start arriving at the door, and that literature is ready and waiting. Also decide in advance exactly how you'll handle bounceback requests for more literature and send information about those requests to the field. Fulfillment is labor intensive, and everyone involved must be scripted well.

Promoting Field Follow-Up

You will improve follow-up by adding drama to the field notification package. Big type splashed across the front of the envelope declaring "Hot Leads Inside" may sound hokey, but it attracts attention the minute it hits the salesperson's in-box. Try to show reps copies of the inquiries. Seeing the actual prospect's handwriting on a card asking for a sales call makes the inquiry a more urgent priority.

Then again, why use mail and envelopes? Fax notification of such hot leads makes much more sense. Even better, communicate leads via a computerized sales automation system, allowing reps to load lead data directly into their laptop computer databases.

Unless you make follow-up reporting effortless, however, you'll never get close to your goal. Salespeople are renowned for hating paperwork. And if they have scores of detailed forms to fill out for each batch of leads they receive, their aversion almost seems justified.

Use notification devices, or sales lead notices, that make it easy for salespeople to report back to you. Simple check-the-box questionnaires on the lead notice, preprinted with the lead name, take only seconds to fill out and generally will provide all the follow-up status information the home office needs. Sales automation speeds the process even more.

Remember a golden rule about working with the sales force: because you're asking for information that you need to meet *your* goals, if the data gathering is to be hard on anyone, make it hard on the lead-management staff, not field staff. Ultimately, of course, your success makes their sales job easier. But salespeople often do not think that far ahead when they're sweating to make this quarter's quota.

Stay Flexible and Venturesome

Marketing information systems at their best are designed to organize details from diverse sources. Certainly the market's first response to a company's offers provides an early warning of purchase activity to come. Therefore, the sales lead-management system should not be allowed to sit in a corner to merely count leads.

Planning, revising, adjusting, monitoring—it's a never-ending process in managing inquiries and leads. A system that's too rigid, too deeply engraved in stone, begins to lose its lustre as markets and the company itself change around it. Ironically, the better the planning, the better the system can accommodate unplanned adventures, the kind of healthy experimentation that discovers new ways to achieve competitive advantage.

Be venturesome with ideas at every stage of program planning and implementation. Try to pick winning ideas, testing and trying new things, sometimes failing but always learning. Otherwise the competition will prevail.

Part **2**

Qualified Leads
from All Media

Chapter 5

Planning Leads to Reach Selling Goals

No doubt most of us are familiar with, and tired of hearing, the chestnut attributed to retailing magnate John Wanamaker, or various other marketing luminaries: "I know that half my advertising is wasted. I just don't know which half."

Actually, whoever said it was nearly right. As noted in Chapter 1, our research shows that an average of 45 percent of all inquiries generated by business marketers lead to a sale within 12 months by the company receiving the inquiry, or by a competitor. Appendix A, Lead Planning Math, provides more detail about those statistics.

We're not suggesting you engrave all these ratios in your media plan. Despite the preponderance of data, and the research vigor behind them, they are broad industry averages around which the experiences of individual industries and firms within them will vary. What each company must determine for itself is its own closing ratios over different time periods for each of its products. In our experience, a company's observed relationships will be stable and are likely to continue in the future, barring fundamental marketplace or marketing program changes. Most likely, a company's own leads-to-sales ratios will vary from the norm by 10 percentage points or so.

Rather than get hung up on the numbers, however, keep in mind what Gen. Dwight D. Eisenhower said as he led allied forces to victory in World War II: "Plans are nothing. Planning is everything." In other words, examining and understanding how you generate leads, how they are used in the field, and what happens to them is more critical to success than calculating specific ratios. Lead management is not an exact science. Your lack of control over markets and distribution channels makes forecasting a game of chance, not certitude.

But if you use the techniques we discuss in this chapter you will be using the same forecasting and planning approaches that key managers running your company employ to predict corporate growth and earnings. Your planning will make marketing and marcom invaluable to the sales department and product managers. Once you show that leads and your communications plan deserve credit for sales growth and selling efficiency, your programs will be more secure and less vulnerable to budget cuts. Planning, not numbers per se, links sales and marketing to a shared vision and combines their strengths in achieving shared goals.

Choose Your Lead Sources

Enticing prospective purchasers and buying influences to raise their hands and signal their interest in your product or service generally falls within the scope of marketing communications: print and electronic advertising, direct mail and telemarketing, plus public relations and publicity. Then there is exhibition selling, which combines the characteristics of a marketing communications medium and direct selling to prospective buyers. For many firms, particularly business and industrial marketers, trade shows are the most productive tool for beginning the selling process because they generate very high quality leads.

As we saw in Chapter 3 and Exhibits 3-6 through 3-9, each medium contributes to the overall mix of inquiries companies generate annually. Some, such as telemarketing, direct mail, and electronic media with an 800-number produce an immediate response. Use them to produce a quick shot of extra leads when needed. Others, notably publicity and public relations, build a steady month-to-month inquiry flow and a long-term market presence and awareness of your company. Electronic and print advertising can be long- or short-term in its effect, depending on how you design it.

Keep a Balanced Viewpoint

Choosing among lead sources, begin with a big-picture that considers the suitability of all media as response-generating tools. This ensures that you'll have a coordinated program, appropriate to your overall marketing strategy, that balances the strengths of individual media.

Sometimes, however, planners bias a program by overemphasizing some tools and shortchanging others that could have made a more useful contribution. An advertising expert, for instance, might put more faith than warranted in mass media. A sales manager might overspend on trade shows, while the corporate communications director might rely too heavily on product publicity and corporate image building.

A balanced media mix is essential because your target audience members have their own media biases. Some business buyers like to collect product information from trade shows, others from industry publications, still others from catalogs and directories. On the consumer side, some people read widely while others spend more time watching television.

With powerful media and their trade associations touting their respective wares, it is easy to lose a balanced perspective. Trade shows, for instance, tout strengths such as the statistic that appeared in the April 1991 edition of *Ideas*, the house organ of the International Exhibitors Association: Of nearly 21,000 advertising and trade show leads, telequalification judged nearly 40 percent of show inquiries qualified compared to less than 30 percent of advertising inquiries. Does that mean that trade shows leads are "better"? Show leads should be of higher quality than advertising inquiries, but the cost per raw inquiry is likely to be higher, too.

Meanwhile on the advertising side, research by the American Business Press, Inc., the major trade association for specialized business publications, claims that across several business and industrial markets surveyed, 76 percent of buyers consider vertical publications to be "useful" sources of product and service information. Buyers ranked publications highest among all media. Trade shows rated second at 68 percent. Does that mean publications are a "better" media choice? Not at all, because perceived usefulness of an entire medium doesn't necessarily mean it's a more efficient inquiry source.[1]

Beware, too, specious comparisons among media. One of our favorites is the way some business publishers make straight-faced comparisons of their "cost per call" to that of field salespeople: just a few cents per reader vs. the $200-plus spent on a sales call. Obviously, the possibility of exposing a reader to an ad doesn't have quite the same selling impact as a visit.

Each medium contributes unique strengths to your overall lead-generation program. Just as an army combines the respective strengths of air cover, ground assault, artillery, and armor to achieve an objective. Used individually, however, such tools are usually less than fully effective.

Consumer packaged-goods advertisers traditionally have been prone to put most of their promotion eggs in one media basket: television. But growing recognition during the 1980s for *integrated marketing* popularized the notion of balance and messages coordinated across media advertising, direct marketing, sales promotion, and public relations. Integrated marketing proponents also struck a responsive chord among business-to-business marketers, some of whom need to overcome a one-trick-pony approach to communications and sales coordination. Lead management coordinates integrated marketing by evaluating all lead sources according to the same standards, adding precision rather than rough guesses to the process.

Business-to-business marketers balance a variety of marketing communications tools, as Cahners Publishing reports in Exhibit 5-1. The data, representing a cross-section of industries, show significant stability year to year.

Exhibit 5-1

How Business Marketers Spend Their Budgets

Allocated for:	1991 %	1989 %	1988 %	1987 %
Specialized Business Magazine Advertising	23	23	22	21
Trade Shows	18	18	16	16
Promotion/Market Support	9	10	12	12
Dealer/Distributor Materials	11	9	9	9
Telemarketing/Telecommunications	7	6	9	9
Direct Mail	12	12	9	8
General Magazine Advertising	5	6	7	8
Publicity/Public Relations	5	7	7	7
Market Research	4	4	5	5
Directories	5	5	3	4
Other	1	2	1	1

Source: *Cahners Advertising Research Report No. 510.1B* (Newton, Ma.: Cahners Publishing Co., 1992).

We do not recommend following those allocations slavishly. For one thing, Exhibit 5-1 represents the experience of companies that advertise, biasing the data toward that medium. Running with the herd is often the recipe for mediocrity, yet, a manager should have sound reasons for any allocation plan, particularly if it differs greatly from industry norms. One sound basis for deviation can be the opportunism of exploiting competitive weakness—advertising where the competition ain't.

The importance of balance is no mystery to marketers who track their leads. They already have measurement programs in place that hold all media up to the same standard of sales lead productivity, looking for the sources that provide the most quality leads, unduplicated by other media, for the dollar. Unduplicated qualified-lead yield might not be the only criterion important to a specific communications program, but it's the single best measurement for comparisons that relate directly to a company's revenue and profit objectives.

When Cahners polled several thousand business advertisers about their satisfaction with different methods for attracting new customers (not how they allocated their budgets), responses averaged out to broad support for all approaches, as shown in Exhibit 5-2.

Advertising, trade shows, and other media provide other benefits in addition to inquiries, of course. They build awareness, recognition, and reputation. Those factors help salespeople make calls and penetrate buying organizations. Also, extensive performance records from about 3,000 business units in the renowned Profit Impact of Market Strategies (PIMS) database suggest that higher-than-

Exhibit 5-2
Methods for Attracting New Customers

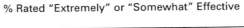

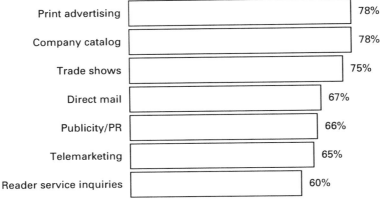

% Rated "Extremely" or "Somewhat" Effective

Print advertising	78%
Company catalog	78%
Trade shows	75%
Direct mail	67%
Publicity/PR	66%
Telemarketing	65%
Reader service inquiries	60%

Source: *Cahners Advertising Research Report No. 560.2A* (Newton, Ma.: Cahners Publishing Co., 1989).

average advertising spenders also have superior reputations for quality, which allows them to maintain higher prices.[2]

Yet those relationships generally appear clearly only in detailed statistical analyses. For most companies, a relatively modest amount of lead-system monitoring will ensure that they are getting value from the money they spend to generate inquiries.

Set Your Objectives

The first step in choosing inquiry-generation media is specifying what your program is to accomplish, over what period of time, and how that accomplishment will be measured. In some markets with few stable buyers, your selling program, and thus your lead program, plays a much different role than in, say, a field with many prospects turning over rapidly. How you employ marketing communications to support that selling effort—by establishing contact, creating awareness, exciting interest, building preference, and provoking response—differs accordingly. Each of those steps can be measured through survey and laboratory research. Response is concrete; you can count it when inquiries roll through the door.

Each lead-generating medium has generic strengths and weaknesses for building your inquiry yield. Although cost-per-qualified lead is the *single* best number for rating specific media, it isn't perfect. Different messages and the quality of creative treatments will affect inquiry yield, among other factors beyond the medium's direct control. So experimentation and thoughtful analysis of lead data must accompany cost-per-qualified lead comparisons.

The future of communications media promises an even greater role for sales lead management in business and consumer markets. Broad socioeconomic trends decades in the making are thrusting specialized business and consumer media to the forefront, as every marketer tries to get closer to individual customers. Media no longer are merely places to advertise. Think of them as keys to customer access.

Specialized publications. Magazines and newspapers appealing to focused interests tend to be efficient lead sources, especially in business and industrial markets. For example, a broad survey of industrial salespeople, manufacturers' representatives, and distributors found 86 percent claiming they had received sales leads from specialized publication advertising.[3] In consumer markets, so-called "enthusiast magazines" or "buff books" also provide sales lead feedback.

Specialized publications have a relatively narrow—or *vertical,* to use the publishing industry phrase—editorial and advertising focus, emphasizing news and features about an industry or hobby and the products and services it uses.

Most provide some sort of inquiry mechanism for products and services advertised or featured in editorial columns. Some publications make lead generation their main objective, new product news tabloids being the outstanding example. They provide low-cost inquiries relative to other media.

For products with vertical appeal, specialized publication circulation offers relatively inexpensive target audience reach with little waste compared to other advertising media. In many business and industrial markets, for instance, marketers also consider specialized publication circulation databases to be the most accurate lists of prospects available, often used as a de facto census of a particular market.

And because they contain editorial fare to entice readers to their pages, publications are less likely to be ignored than direct mail pieces. Do not assume, however, that subscribership equals readership; people might receive a magazine yet not read it. Give close scrutiny to free publications distributed to readers who did not even ask to receive them.

Direct mail. A surgical medium, direct mail reaches well-defined audiences, depending on the quality of the list. Database sorting by, say, consumer demographics and business *firmographics* (industrial classification, customer size, location, previous purchases, applications, etc.) allows the advertiser to reach target market niches without waste and without spillover to other segments. Modern technology allows substantial personalization for each recipient.

Consumer marketers have long called direct mail the easiest medium to measure because, unlike brand image advertising, it solicits specific, measurable responses. The advertiser knows how many pieces went out, and how many reply cards or orders return. Of course, business marketers can apply the same standard to virtually all media they use by tracking inquiries.

Successful direct mailers make a fetish of testing different lists, offers, and promotion packages. Typically, they credit list selection (response lists, compiled lists, warranty-card lists, and lists of inquirers and customers) with 50 to 60 percent of the response, and the value of the offer with another 25 to 30 percent. The glamour and expense of the package that goes in the envelope surprisingly receives just 25 percent or less of the credit for generating replies.

A mailing can produce a faster response than a publication advertisement, arriving at a recipient's desk in a more or less predictable number of days after it is "dropped" into the mail system. It does not wait for publication subscribers to get around to reading a specific page in a magazine they might pick up many times during a month. The ability to give the sales force extra leads when really needed can be critical to building sales department support for a lead-management program. Generally, you can expect to receive about 90 percent of your total response within five weeks of your mail drop.

Use direct mail for emergency lead generation. For example, if a salesperson has only 20 leads on the 25th of the month and needs an average of 30 leads a month, mailing to within 50 miles of the area in which she will be traveling can put extra leads into her hands within ten days.

Those virtues come at a price, however. Mail packages can easily cost several dollars per piece, an expenditure that may be necessary to get noticed amid the clutter of "junk mail" inundating businesses and households. Unlike a publication welcomed into the home or office, mail is frequently treated apathetically, and occasionally with antagonism. Secretaries and assistants screen it for busy bosses, and some corporate mail rooms refuse to deliver third-class mail to intended recipients.

Beyond the response numbers, mail will supplement other media in your balanced lead-generation plan. It can improve the efficiency of other media. Trade show booth visit invitations, for example, can be mailed to prospects. Mail also paves the way for sales calls, and can cut the cost of calls needed to close a sale by as much as 25 percent, we've found.

One low-cost lead generation option has proved to be a potent way to tap business publication circulation lists: postcard decks. When designed properly to collect qualification information, they effectively supplement other media aiming at a vertical market. Then again, they are low cost because one advertiser's single postcard shares the ride with dozens, or maybe a hundred or more, other advertisers' cards.

Pay attention to the lists to which postcard deck publishers mail. Response and circulation lists are very likely to be much more current and accurate than compiled lists.

Telemarketing. An intrusive and often controversial tool, particularly in consumer markets, outbound telemarketing is a highly productive medium for many consumer and business products and services. Telemarketing combines the database targetability of mail with the ability to make a sales pitch person-to-person.

Many people define telemarketing loosely, applying the term to just about any phone call a business makes to a customer or prospect. A more professional definition, in keeping with its status as a measurable sales tool, specifies that telemarketing is a discipline requiring trained representatives delivering a prescribed message, keeping call records, and measuring contact and sales performance against objectives.

Cold-call telemarketing cost-per-lead can vary widely depending upon the number of call-backs required to reach members of the target audience. For instance, even after many calls, a telemarketer still has slim chances of reaching large corporation chief executives well-insulated by staff. Telemarketing to existing customers with whom you have a relationship costs significantly less.

Outbound telequalification is essential to the well-managed lead program, as discussed in Chapter 4. The phone is also the preferred medium for conducting Did-You-Buy? studies.

Inbound telemarketing—when inquirers call you or your inquiry management service—has become the competitive standard for receiving leads generated by other media in most business and industrial markets. On the consumer side, more than two-thirds of manufacturers maintain toll-free inquiry phone numbers[4] for product information and, when appropriate, dealer-locator assistance. Their willingness to offer such service is more than a matter of goodwill; inquirers become the foundations for consumer database marketing strategies.

Facsimile transmission and, increasingly, electronic mail are fast-growing variants of telemarketing in business and industrial markets. Many publications invite readers to inquire by fax, either to the publication or to advertisers directly. Expanding numbers of them provide fax-back services which instantly return information to a telefax number.

Trade shows. Expositions bring prospects to your salespeople. Shows should generate inquiries of higher quality than other media: leads requiring fewer subsequent sales calls to close. Trade shows permit live demonstrations of equipment and services that salespeople may not be able to illustrate easily on their calls.

But, exhibiting is an expensive medium requiring strict professionalism and training about what to do during a show and after it. Unfortunately, many firms haven't gotten the message. In our experience, 70 percent of trade show inquiries do not receive proper follow-up! That's an astounding statistic, considering the overall value of inquiries qualified on the spot at the show booth. Savvy companies and their sales forces capitalize on the superiority of trade show leads, and follow them up more energetically than leads from other sources, providing yet another reason why show inquiries outperform others.

Trade shows are not an efficient medium for shouting product news to a wide, diversified audience with proportionally few prospects for your product or service. Advertising and other media are likely to be better options, particularly when a marketing budget only allows an underfunded, small exhibit.

When the show appearance is warranted—and the importance of being seen at a specific industry's principal trade show is considerable in many industries—it benefits from the support of other media that help attract qualified prospects to an exhibitor's booth. Pre-show and during-show promotion via advertising, direct mail, telemarketing, publicity, and the like build the right kind of booth traffic.

Avoid relying on gimmicks to increase traffic indiscriminately. Gimmicks will boost the booth yield lead, but with a sharply higher proportion of poor leads while cutting the time your booth personnel have to chat with genuinely hot prospects. Eschew lame lead-building efforts, such as inviting anyone and everyone to drop their business card in a fishbowl for a drawing.

Even if shows produce the most expensive leads in your mix, as is likely, they provide a face-to-face contact at a price well below the cost of a field sales call. Shows also provide other benefits that don't necessarily show up in lead statistics: the value of entertaining customers, prospects, and distributors at a show, and the efficiencies of holding a sales meeting in conjunction with a show.

Exhibition and conference attendance may be a problem for otherwise promising purchase influences, however. Travel expenses climb and time to spend away from the office becomes scarcer in today's leaner-and-meaner, cost-cutting corporate environments.

Directories. When available in an industry or product category, vendor directories edited for buyers can be very efficient lead generators. More so than any other medium, and perhaps more than your own catalogs and literature kept on file, buyers turn to directories when they've got a specific purchase in mind. Buyers tend to keep directories around, passing outdated editions along to subordinates.

An ad supplementing information already contained in the directory's standard vendor listings can draw more attention to your offering, and allow buyers to learn more about you before inquiring. That could cut the number of unqualified "literature collector" inquiries one might otherwise receive from a simple listing.

Like the trade shows important to an industry, key directories become venues where it is important to be seen. But not every directory gets proper distribution or attracts sufficient use. It is easy to publish directories of dubious value, so it's not surprising that some entrepreneurs do. Compared to newspapers and magazines, relatively little audience research attests to readership and use. That makes inquiry tracking particularly useful for assessing a directory's value specifically to you.

As a medium, directories run the gamut from detailed, product-specific listings to the general class of trade listings characteristic of the best known directory, the Yellow Pages. A small number, sure to grow, of directories are computerized, available on-line through the Internet, Electronic Data Interchange, or on CD-ROM. New forms of security will allow companies to inquire, buy, and even pay for purchases over otherwise public computer systems.

General publications. Covering either business or consumer subjects, general publications are less efficient sources of inquiries suitable for salesperson follow-up. Their ability to zero in on bona fide prospects with little waste circulation is limited to products and services with broad appeal. Cost-per-inquiry tends to be too high for specialized products, particularly when clutter forces you to run large ads frequently to be noticed.

Then again, providing a non-product-oriented editorial environment—such as a newsweekly or management publication offers—can be congenial to broad appeal business services (hotels, for instance) and products (office equipment), especially when the advertising stresses corporate image themes about the advertiser. An office equipment maker promoting specific models with specific technologies in vertical publications, for example, could supplement that campaign with a quality story that is not model-specific in, say, a business newspaper. Such advertising aims more at building awareness and market positioning than generating inquiries, however.

Those well-established patterns are changing as marketers demand greater accountability and response from their choices in print and electronic media. New publications serving narrow market segments increasingly blur the distinction between the traditional "buff book" and general-audience media. New printing and binding technologies permit publications custom-tailored to the individual recipient. Free-standing newspaper inserts revolutionized newspaper advertising during the 1980s, particularly as suburban newspapers acted on their unique access to local audiences.

Electronic and interactive media. The most discussed and egregiously hyped media formats in years, whatever eventually does make money for advertisers on the vaunted "information superhighway" is bound to depend heavily on lead-management skills in both consumer and business marketing.

On the business side, except for occasional campaigns on local or regional television, TV commercials traditionally have not been a congenial format for generating inquiries. Broadcast TV wasted too much expensive reach on non-prospects. Office equipment advertisers and others selling to a broad swath of businesses learned, however, that news and sports programs could deliver image messages to sizable professional/managerial audiences. And some used the medium to reach critical buying influences such as secretaries and clerical workers. A few would place a phone number at the end of their spots, inviting a response.

Radio, less costly and more likely to reach commuters and office workers, has been more popular with business advertisers. Some markets even have business-oriented news and talk radio—formats that include paid infomercial-style programming options for business-to-business advertisers.

In consumer markets, however, mass-market advertising powered broadcast media to the top of the promotion firmament. The dominant strategy: create brand preference to pull product sales through retail channels. Meanwhile, toll-free phone number technology has matured a whole class of direct-response television advertisers much more respectable than the late-night household utensil hucksters of the 1950s and '60s.

But now all that is changing at unforeseen speeds. Socioeconomic forces in a post-industrial age have been killing mass markets, replacing them with increasingly customized products and promotions tailored to ever fussier business and consumer customers. Technology accelerated the change, as cable TV and other new media segmented once-monolithic markets. Recognizing the need to tailor their appeals to narrow niches, marketers now turn to relationship marketing and the critical role of collecting and enhancing information about individual customers and buying influences.

As of this writing, lots of talk and a few pioneering experiments indicate that no one—advertiser or media purveyor—has yet figured out how to make money on the information superhighway and the convergence of computer, telephone, and video technologies. From infomercials—program-length product pitches—to the Internet linking computers worldwide, so many options confuse advertisers hoping to someday harness new communication technologies.

Wherever it's all headed and whatever the winning media, lead management undoubtedly will be critical to success. Marketers will be awash in inquiries as never before. Competitive pressure will demand that those leads be qualified, fulfilled, and followed up swiftly, with information updated to support relation-ship marketing. The value of the new media will extend far beyond lead-generation alone, to the very fabric of ongoing customer-vendor affiliations.

Promotion and response databases galore. The significant development un-derlying the rise of new media is the growth of marketing information systems, most notably those handling customer and prospect records. No longer can companies consider their account lists to be some sort of amalgam of order-entry records and salespeople's territory lists. Consumer sales promotion and scanner data spew information marketers are just beginning to exploit. Publicity, event marketing, and other forms of public relations increasingly must provide inquir-ies and customer information to satisfy marketers no longer content with mere "feel good" market reactions.

Tight Leads vs. Loose Leads?
We've said cost-per-unduplicated qualified inquiry is the single most important statistic for assessing the relative value of media in your program. But it is not the only consideration. Your choice of media will also depend on whether you pursue a *loose leads* or *tight leads* strategy, which are not directly comparable on a cost-per-lead basis.

The loose leads method seeks as many inquiries as possible, relying heavily on inquiry qualification to sort them out before sending the qualified leads to the field for follow-up. Markets with many buying influences and high turnover, new products, and forays into new markets will benefit from casting a wide net in the search for likely prospects. Calculating your actual cost-per-qualified lead includes the expense of sifting all those raw inquiries.

In the tight leads approach, you attempt to generate fewer leads of higher average quality. Relatively stable markets, limited additional selling capacity, and high cost-per-sales call argue for emphasizing cream-of-the-crop inquiries. Those you receive will require less telequalification expense added to the media cost-per-lead.

Your choice of strategy, tight or loose, should be a conscious selection because it will affect your lead quality vs. quantity balance. Your message and offer, your media selection and timing, and response format within media are the tactics you can use to serve your strategic choice.

Different promotional choices. Seeking loose leads argues for media with wide reach and high frequency. You might want to send many tepid inquiries to the field to stimulate prospecting activity (although, as we've stressed, too many unproductive leads will anger salespeople and distributors, making them apathetic). Even if you want to send only the red hot leads to the field, you might want many inquiries in order to build a database. Consumer packaged-goods marketers can benefit from that approach. High-volume loose-lead programs also favor business marketers spreading leads across extensive (100 or more) domestic dealer networks. Sending inquiries regularly to dealers maintains the manufacturer's visibility.

Loose-lead media choices will favor less specialized publications, high frequency in postcard decks, traffic-building enticements at horizontal trade shows and directories, industry newspapers, compiled mail lists, and maybe even broadcast advertising.

Tight leads strategies will favor media such as specialized publication advertising and technical publicity, the interactivity of vertical trade shows, and narrowly defined response lists for mail and telemarketing.

Messages and offers will vary, too, depending on how narrowly you position your product and service and what you offer: an on-site demonstration for tight leads, or an information booklet with obvious value for loose leads. Be attentive to the message and offer; too often advertisers mistakenly blame the medium alone for poor lead yield.

Response formats. Your promotional response mechanism also affects the response. Generally, the more information you ask from an inquirer and the faster you receive it, the fewer leads will require extra pre-field qualification. You'll have enough information to sight-qualify more inquiries. Also, give a prospect a chance to self-qualify and indicate, for instance, whether you should "just send literature" or "have a salesperson call."

Publication response devices that favor tight lead generation include toll-free phone numbers, in-ad coupons, tipped-in reply cards, and publisher's reader service cards that collect demographic data, information about purchase plans and timing, and ask the prospect to specify the action expected from the advertiser. The more effort a prospect expends to inquire, the more qualified the response. If the prospect elects to send you a letter, the product interest behind that exertion hardly seems casual.

The tighter the lead strategy, the more information you'll want to collect from direct mail bounceback cards, and through telemarketing scripts. At trade shows, you'll eschew card-in-the-jar and other nondiscriminating response mechanisms and opt for qualification cards filled out by booth personnel during or immediately after each visitor contact.

In contrast, simple reader service card number circling doesn't collect much inquirer information. But making the response easy favors a loose-lead strategy. So do postcard decks; devoting most of their space to making an offer, the cards offer little opportunity for detailed inquirer information beyond the basics.

You can use other tactics to manipulate the quality vs. quantity balance of your communications. Make it tougher to respond by, for instance, requiring a stamped, self-addressed envelope, or a modest price or handling fee for sending material to the inquirer. Ask for letterhead responses only, or for business cards only. Provide detailed coupon and reply card questionnaires, and ask inquirers to pay reply card postage. Make it clear that whatever fulfillment you offer, a salesperson must deliver it personally. Don't provide a toll-free inquiry number or, more dramatic yet, offer information to consumers only on an extra-toll 900-number.

Prudent balance. Generally, avoid the extremes of loose-lead and tight-lead policies. Don't overspend on qualification and waste money with too wide a loose-leads fishing expedition. Pre-qualifying response by discouraging the casual inquiry is cheaper than telequalifying it once it's in your door.

Yet it makes little sense to artificially cut response as some advertisers do by refusing to run a reader service number or an 800-number in their ads, or by ignoring reader service card inquiries. Making it harder to respond will reduce the ratio of tire kickers among inquirers, but it will also trim the absolute number of genuine prospects registering their interest. Rather than go through extra steps to ask you for information, they'll turn to your competitors. Therefore, even if you seek only a highly specialized audience, make your offer more specific and application oriented, but still make it easy for the interested to respond. A sound lead qualification procedure will winnow out the chaff.

A tight-leads strategy should not become an excuse to shortcut the qualification job that *must* be done before inquiries will be welcomed by field sales. Whether or not inquiries coming in the door are of uniformly high quality, those that leave must be qualified and ready for the field.

Competitive Intelligence

A final word about your media selection procedures: don't forget the virtues of checking around, finding out what the competition is up to and why. There's a reason the competition does what it does, maybe a valid one. Remember, though, that if you follow the competition's media plan, you have to outspend them and provide a superior creative message to beat them. But if the competition has left open an opportunity you can exploit by running a different type of media plan, you can outflank them.

Advertising agencies are professionals at media selection. Any program worth buying from them will include a competitive media analysis. Other suppliers also have an inkling of what's working on the street. Talk to printers and space reps about who is promoting where and why. Within limits, they can discuss the market in general terms without violating their professional ethics.

Frequently, competitors themselves will tell you, either through speeches and interviews they give, or even by answering your "casual curiosity" directly.

The Response-Generating Offer

Beyond your choice of media, you will need to select the type of offer to make in your advertisement, press release, broadcast commercial, direct mail piece, trade show presentation, etc. to generate the prospect response most useful to your communication goals. Remember that the reader, the viewer, the booth visitor, the direct mail recipient also has objectives. Keep in mind this fundamental communications axiom that's too often forgotten by marketers hot to make a sales pitch: *prospects don't care about you or your company; they only care about themselves.*

Communications designed with that thought in mind cannot wander far from having audience appeal. All behavior is motivated, and anyone making that split-second decision to read an ad, open a direct mail piece, view a commercial, or stop to visit a trade show booth constantly asks, "What's in it for me?" The single biggest reason communications fail to reach an audience effectively is the message's failure to answer that fundamental question clearly right at the start.

Regardless of the medium you use to deliver your offer, make sure you do offer *something* of informational or intrinsic value. And build a sense of urgency, inviting a response to "Call now!" or "Write today!" perhaps offering an incentive to do so.

Merchandise the offer to make it compelling and attractive. A large photo of the "planning kit," for instance, a picture of a happy engineer using it, or a photo of a friendly telesales agent answering a consumer's phone inquiry are devices that convey value in a reader's mind. Even financial service advertising giants like Citibank and American Express, and airlines such as Delta, show friendly phone operators in their commercials to imply how easy it is to buy from them. Print your telephone number large, separate it from the copy block, and print it in color if possible, making the number hard to miss.

Product literature is the perennial favorite offer supporting consumer durables and business-to-business products and services. *New Equipment Digest,* a leading industrial product tabloid, cites it as the most common offer in its pages, made by 62 percent of its advertisers.[5] The literature can be as simple as a single sheet of technical specifications, or as elaborate as a multimedia CD-ROM catalog of the entire product line.

Invest your literature with extra value by giving it a "product selection guide," "planning kit," "application notes," or similar label that connotes usefulness. Technical publicity reprints are an excellent giveaway to technical buying influences. Managers, however, are likely to be more interested in productivity and financial results (e.g. "Cut waste production 35 percent!") than how they are achieved.

Ask inquirers to choose from among two or more offers. It invites thought and involvement in your selling proposition. And, if one of the options you offer indicates a salesperson will call to arrange a demonstration or deliver a sample, the multiple choice becomes a method of inquirer self-qualification, indicating the respondent's level of interest and need. *Dual bingo numbers,* which we'll discuss in the following chapter, use the multiple choice approach to substantial advantage.

The Power of "Free"

Free periodicals and the offer to put someone on your mailing list are excellent ways to build a database of prospects with distant as well as immediate needs. Promise a technical newsletter or house organ with some general reader value. Or simply offer a sample issue with a bounceback offer for a full year's subscription, etc. The technique works beautifully, even at trade shows.

Free samples are growing in popularity, boosting response by breaking through competitive clutter. *New Equipment Digest* says, for example, that more than 17 percent of its advertisers have offered a sample.[6] Sometimes the sample is the only way a prospect can evaluate your product. Your sample may not be of the product, but of its output. For instance, send an attractive blow-molded plastic part rather than a small bag of resin pellets.

Your offer need not be tangible. Offer demonstrations, free trial periods, free estimates or free consultations, all of which have the benefit to you of requiring a sales call. Or invite the prospect to visit your plant for a demonstration. Make sure the trip is not perceived as a junket, however. You're asking prospects to surrender some of their valuable time.

Be aware of the free sample's possible drawback: its allure to non-prospects. It does you little good to fulfill and qualify inquiries from people who only want a sample and not your product or service. Oddly enough, even the most trivial trinkets can attract responses from the most unqualified of inquirers.

Premiums, call them a "free gift" in your offer, are not product samples or sample output. They are advertising specialties designed to pump up response for a loose-leads strategy. Field studies find that promotional products can boost goodwill toward a company by as much as 80 percent, compared to the absence of a prospect gift.[7] Better yet, use premiums related to your business proposition—the roofing manufacturer giving umbrellas to qualified booth visitors, for example. Best of all are premiums with value primarily to qualified prospects, such as slide rules for process control calculations, to underscore your expertise and understanding of their unique needs.

Contest and sweepstakes offers are proven consumer attention-getters, and work well with business buying influences. Ensure that they are not perceived as unprofessional, or excessively lavish come-ons to hide an otherwise weak proposition or bribe an employee to act outside his or her company's best interests.

Avoid Non-Starters

Make it clear in your communication what inquirers will receive. You can use salesmanship to promote your offer in its best light, as noted above, but don't lie about what you'll send. There's no sense tarnishing your company image at the start.

And avoid the bland, mousy offer. Closing your message with an insipid, "For more information . . ." invitation hardly implies helpfulness on your part, and it certainly doesn't inspire interest.

Also refrain from promising literature not designed for informative fulfillment. Starkly technical product sheets with no promotional flavor, sales call leave-behinds not designed for "first impression" distribution, copies of ads or technical articles mailed without a cover letter, or, need it be said, items in bad taste (be careful in foreign cultures) belong on the forbidden list. People will take offense over the most innocent of lapses.

Impact in the Details

Certainly, your offer must be crafted to support your need for loose or tight leads. As a general rule, the greater the intrinsic value of whatever you are offering, the looser the leads. But the greater the information value, the tighter the leads. And the more the offer furthers the selling process, the tighter the leads.

The greater the commitment asked of the prospect by the offer, the more the quality vs. quantity balance tips toward quality. For example, offering general application information will draw inquiries, but offering descriptive literature about your product will cut response somewhat because it asks the target audience to acknowledge a specific interest in you. And asking prospects to respond only if they want a salesperson to call will cut gross response dramatically, because it involves an even greater degree of commitment on the inquirer's part.

Information intensity alone will affect response. Product or service details in an advertisement or mail piece add to the prequalification you can expect from the communication. In other words, more detail tends to cut the number of people who will retain a casual interest in your product or service. The more information they have, the more they can decide whether you have something for them. Prices have particular power to filter response, so don't mention price unless it provides a clear competitive advantage consistent with your product or service's competitive positioning.

Those who stick with a detailed message and register an inquiry are much more likely to buy and can be sight-qualified more accurately, as *New Equipment Digest* points out in a tale from its experience. A machinery vendor promoted two very similar products with ads of virtually identical format and response mechanisms in the same issue of the publication. One ad "put product capability in the headline and mentioned that it was affordable. It briefly covered features and benefits and offered more information by request." The second advertisement "offered extensive product detail and described the benefits," also mentioning the price, *New Equipment Digest* said.

The first ad outpulled the second by 400 percent in terms of total inquiries. But response to the second ad was just about entirely qualified.

Even so, the advertiser judged the first ad the winner, because the advertiser had a lead-qualification mechanism in place. When it came time to talk price with prospects, salespeople handled it and overcame objections on the spot.[8]

Offer Efficiency vs. Penetration

A final consideration may be worth keeping in mind when choosing a tight-leads vs. loose-leads strategy and engineering the quality vs. quantity balance of your lead generation program. Your company's ultimate goal is not necessarily achieving the most efficient sales, that is the lowest possible cost-per-sale or cost-per-qualified lead. Most likely your objective is net profit in a given period of time.

It is shortsighted, therefore, to make a lead-program decision solely on the basis of the lowest cost-per-qualified lead. In the real world, some qualified leads are more valuable than others, a condition the ROPI formula takes into account by its lead value weighting mechanism discussed in the next section of this chapter.

If expensive leads produce larger sales, and therefore more net profit per sale even when all selling costs are taken into account, by all means go for the expensive leads. If you track your leads fully through the sale, you will see how economical those seemingly expensive inquiries really are.

There are some who argue that cost-per-lead matters little in the big picture, as long as a company is able to make as many profitable sales (gross margin less all marketing and selling costs) as it can. That's true in theory, and occasionally in practice as well, when a market is small enough so a company can put its sales pitch in front of every possible buyer and buying influence and still make a marginal profit on every sale.

But as a practical matter, in most fields, and particularly in consumer product and service categories, companies don't have enough cash or personnel to reach everyone. The size of their overall profit requires reaching the best prospects first, getting to the ones who can be closed most efficiently before the competition does. That's when the cost-per-qualified lead, tempered by lead timing and relative quality, become important in lead-generation planning.

Planning for Selling Goals

Marketing communications is no longer a matter of simply "getting the ads out." Downsizing, cost-cutting, and redefined job responsibilities across corporate America have put marcom in the hot seat. As a 1993 survey of Business Marketing Association members found, companies are demanding a more strategic outlook from their communications staffs, "the ability to conceptualize powerful, new ways of getting the message to key external and internal constituencies." Budgeting, the study continued, is a critical skill needed to meet that challenge. "Respondents are looking for measurement systems that can justify expenditures based on results."[9]

In other words, the bottom line for marketing communications is supporting the sales effort that generates profitable revenue now and sets the stage for more sales in the future. When direct and distributor selling are the prime sales methods, leads are the tool to accomplish that.

The next question is calculating how many leads a company will need, and how much and where it will spend to get them. (In Chapter 14, we'll show how to analyze the leads you do receive.)

We recommend a three-stage process for lead-generation planning:

1. Determine how much account turnover you will have to replace in a year. To achieve your sales target, how many new customers must your company acquire? Research says that 25 percent of business-to-business sales each year go to new customers.[10]

2. Calculate the number of qualified leads you'll need to find new prospects. Use your current lead-closing ratios, and the number of inquiries from advertising, mail, trade shows, etc. required to provide that qualified lead volume. If you don't yet have enough data to estimate your own firm's ratios, or you've radically changed your product mix, selling operations, or market environment, use the Rule of 45. Based on overall marketplace averages, the Rule of 45 is a rough estimate to use while you collect information specific to your firm. Actual sales conversions may vary as much as 10 percent around that average.

3. Schedule communications to produce lead volume tailored to your "promotional windows" to support a new product introduction, a sales contest, customer buying cycles, a fiscal year end, quota periods, etc. We've seen sales increase 10 to 15 percent at some companies when they adjusted lead flows to the times they're most needed.

Calculate New Business Needed

Inquiry handling and lead management provide many benefits, but the most important one is the ability to spot new sales opportunities not already known to your organization. Circumstances may require that some companies set different objectives for their systems. Perhaps the key mission for their lead management is producing information that keeps existing customers happy, builds repeat business, and prevents brand switching. Or maybe dealer relations are the highest priority a lead system will serve, at least in the short term. Even so, planning lead generation to meet those goals requires a numerical estimate. Calculating it is easy; estimating components of the calculation may not be.

Appendix A includes the New Business Calculation Worksheet, a straight-forward process of forecasting sales and customer attrition. Subtract from your target sales level the dollar or unit sales you expect from current customers, add the sales you'll have to make up to compensate for departing customers, and you have the unit or dollar volume you will need from new customers—to be found through sales leads.

Calculate with ROPI

Having an estimate of the sales volume needed to meet an annual target, you can determine how many inquiries you'll need to provide enough qualified leads that close, and how much you will need to spend to generate those inquiries. An impossibly complex and imprecise task? Hardly. Yet, like every type of business decision, it relies on making some judgment calls that, one hopes, are backed by reliable performance data.

At the core of the planning process is what we call the return on promotional investment formula. It quantifies the relationship between leads and sales. Appendix A illustrates the math involved. The ROPI formula states that a certain proportion of leads produces closed orders, a share of which is yours. Solve the equation for the number of inquiries you need to produce a target sales level. Your database indicates your cost-per-inquiry, allowing you to specify how much you need to spend to generate the leads you require.

Obviously, having an inquiry master database, well stocked with several years of past marketing and sales performance information, makes using ROPI easier than relying on broad industry statistics. Your own selling experience best indicates the proportion of raw inquiries that will qualify, as does your industry's unique lead conversion rate: the percentage of inquiries that close in a given time period, such as a year.

You can apply those statistics directly to lead planning *if your sales department follows up nearly every lead and reports the status of each back to you.* That's not the case for most companies, however. So when your field follow-up and reporting ratios are weak, we recommend that you instead use Did-You-Buy? survey results in you ROPI calculations. Those surveys (see Chapters 11 and 14) ask inquirers directly whether they bought the product about which they inquired.

Did-You-Buy? surveys do not require sales force follow-up, but they provide a statistical estimate, not a complete census, of inquirer activity. Often, Did-You-Buy? studies do not accurately report or even ask which brand the inquirer purchased, although they should collect that information. Without it, assume that your share of sales among survey respondents equals your overall market share.

Apply judgment. There is one caveat we must stress again. The ROPI formula can produce accurate projections *only* if your salespeople and distributors follow up every qualified lead. When they pursue only the best leads and disregard the rest—which seems to be the case at most companies—the ignored leads cannot fulfill their potential. So, suppose your salespeople only follow up half your leads, should you factor that into ROPI and double your lead-generation target? Perhaps, if doubling the number of leads sent to the field boosts follow-up activity accordingly. Usually, however, follow-up will not increase proportionately, although the extra lead volume might prompt salespeople to pay more attention to your leads. That's a very expensive, budget-busting way to buy respect. Your cost-per-lead would skyrocket, particularly if your extra spending scrapes the barrel and comes up with only marginal leads.

The ROPI formula works best when the company has great control over its channels, such as employee sales reps on salary. They provide the most accurate ROPI results because a company can insist on performance standards. For companies using distributors, dealers and other channels, the accuracy and value of ROPI calculation diminish the more the manufacturer's control diminishes.

The ROPI formula also is most appropriate when budgeted lead-generation programs identify nearly all new prospects. The formula needs to be adjusted if the company regularly learns about new prospects through referrals or salespeoples' unbudgeted prospecting activity. When salespeople can rely on heavy referral activity, they quickly reach a comfort level. Failure to follow up new leads is a normal result.

And, ROPI assumes that the sales supported by leads provide enough profit margin to justify the cost of the lead program. Spending $50 or more to acquire, fulfill, and qualify an inquiry makes sense for a sale providing much larger returns, but not for orders of $50 net profit or less.

The ROPI calculations are deceptively simple, and can lead to trouble if used uncritically. For example, an unadorned ROPI formula will always produce a better return even if the input exceeds what's realistic. One reason is that a simple ROPI model assumes a linear relationship between leads and sales. A company doubling its inquiry flow probably shouldn't assume, however, that sales will double, too. Not unless it has a substantial untapped market opportunity, and salespeople follow up just about all the additional qualified leads. Considering that the great majority of business marketers spend very little on advertising, many are far from reaching the point where extra spending will flatten their lead yield appreciably.

Nor is the cost per lead of an advertising program likely to stay the same as the advertiser increases the budget significantly. Without untapped market opportunity, additional spending is likely to produce fewer qualified leads per extra dollar of lead generation. The designation "qualified" is also a matter of judgment. Change your qualification criteria significantly and you will have to readjust your cost-per-qualified lead benchmarks.

Also, too many leads can overtax your sales force. For example, at 15 to 20 leads a month, a salesperson becomes very busy. At 25 to 30 leads, the follow-up undoubtedly begins to slip on call-backs and other hard-to-reach inquirers. At 35 to 50 leads a month, salespeople begin to cherry-pick and follow up only with the hottest, need-to-buy-now prospects. They will ignore most future buyers, including the 56 percent of inquirers whose decisions are more than six months away.

More is not necessarily better from a cost-control viewpoint. Respecting selling constraints is a part of program planning that's often abused. The miscalculations usually come in small doses and build up over time. But sometimes, bold moves of the "more is better" variety can wreak havoc. One sales manager, for instance, bragged that he had increased his average inquiry volume per month from 1,200 to 2,000. He simply spent more on advertising; his acquisition cost-per-lead did not change. In the field, however, the average monthly inquiry count ballooned from 30 to 50 per month per territory, with hot territories receiving 100 or more. Follow-up ratios dropped precipitously, and the cost-per-closed lead soared, indicating wasted advertising expenditures.

Nevertheless, a sales lead-based ROPI analysis provides the best and easiest communications planning estimates available to a company that relies on leads to identify potential customers, particularly business-to-business marketers. It's easy, that is, *if* you've got a comprehensive lead system in place. And, because you should have a lead system in place anyway, you'll be ready to measure your program strategically.

Plan Lead Timing

The budget generally should be spent evenly throughout the year to ensure a steady, manageable stream of inquiries. Put your best month-to-month inquiry flow estimate on a spreadsheet. Your initial lead generation schedule, built from your media and exhibiting plans, will create some peaks and valleys in the flow. Smooth them by adding an ad insertion here, or a direct mailing there. Then, add spending peaks with some fraction of the budget held aside to add oomph to special promotions and end-of-quota period sales pushes. Often, 10 percent of the budget is sufficient.

Planning a constant lead flow also illustrates how cutting the ad schedule precipitously—creating advertising blackouts—will disrupt the even flow and your selling efforts. Because leads produce predictable closing ratios over defined periods of time, blackouts will create measurable and predictable slumps in closed sales and orders.

Lead-generating marketing communications provide inquiries that, for most companies, will produce sales extending for many months, including those more than a year after an insertion appears, a letter mailed, or a commercial aired. Therefore, a promotional blackout won't cause sales to decline precipitously at first. Sales and profits will more or less brown out if a steady flow of new leads is not provided for the sales force. The effect is something like sailing a large ocean liner. Cutting the engines from full speed to stop won't cause the liner to stop immediately. It will slow down over 5 or 10 miles, gradually losing speed. And, like the ocean liner, getting back up to full selling speed is going to take time and investment.

Try What-If? Scenarios

Loading your ROPI calculations into a computer spreadsheet or similar software makes it easy to test the effects of different options you might pursue. Use it to ask questions such as:

- How much lead conversion ratio deterioration can you stand before you've exceeded your promotion budget?
- How will the lead flow change if you alter your marketing mix?
- How much will profit increase if follow-up improves?

- What is the effect of smaller dollar sales per order as you bring new and perhaps marginal customers into the equation?
- What happens when follow-up ratios slip badly?
- How much can your achieved market share differ from your forecast, and how much should you adjust promotional spending to compensate?

Information management is a hallmark of marketing sophistication, and computerizing your calculations with appropriate software is a step in the right direction. It allows you to prepare management reports more quickly and professionally.

Inquiry Handling Service offers an efficient program, Sales Projector, which runs on Microsoft Windows and automates ROPI calculations. Exhibit 5-3 shows the Sales Projector screen. The program is available from IHS.

Exhibit 5-3
IHS Sales Projector Screen

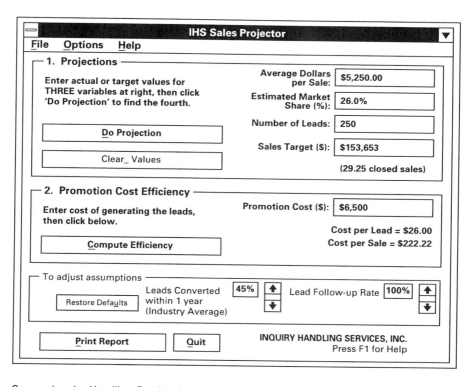

Source: Inquiry Handling Service, Inc.

Return on Investment

When a company knows what it will cost to generate the leads it needs to reach a sales target, it can easily calculate its *sales return on promotion*. A $100,000 campaign producing inquiries leading to $3 million sales over 12 months has a percentage return of 3,000 percent—30 times the lead-generation cost, for instance. Each dollar in advertising reaped $30 in additional sales.

What's typically known as *return on investment* (ROI) is a different figure, comparing the net profit from extra sales to all the incremental costs of making those sales. Return on investment is widely used to measure and compare the efficiency of different investments designed to generate profit.

Note that ROPI is a different measurement, focused as it is on the cost of leads. While that's of immediate importance to budgeting, marketers should also keep track of their sales return on promotion, to track whether their marketing communications are becoming more or less efficient over time. Appendix A contains a sample sales return on promotion worksheet with representative numbers, crediting advertising with two years of subsequent sales.

Estimating over a 2 year period is actually a conservative way to calculate return. Direct mail marketers, who always kept records of individual customer purchases, have taught the rest of the consumer and business marketing world to calculate the *lifetime value* of their customers, or at least account for the profit they produce over a three-, five-, or ten-year period. When companies do that, they realize just how profitable an existing customer can be. Evidently, the old saw that it's five times more expensive to acquire a customer than keep one is certainly the truth for most of us. Having seen the profitability in long-term customers, marketers have embraced loyalty and customer retention as key management metrics. Some studies have shown that a mere 5 percent increase in customer retention can boost profit in high-turnover fields an astounding 75 percent or more![11]

Rate Media for Lead Quality

Each medium produces a unique mix of qualified and unqualified inquiries. A lead from a trade show—the person who visits a company's booth, chats with a sales rep and shows continuing interest—is more likely to become a customer than the person circling a reader service card number. The difference between advertising and show inquiries is likely to be smaller if the advertising inquiry arrived by phone or via a filled-in reply coupon. The ad inquiry may even be equivalent or better than the show lead if the inquirer has checked a box, or circled a special reader service number to invite a sales rep to call. Whatever the differences, the marketer must estimate the quality of inquiries each medium will provide when using ROPI to budget and plan a complete communications program.

You should grade inquiries according to qualification criteria appropriate to the selling plan. Give sources credit for providing the best inquiries, and downgrade the scores of those generating large volumes of lesser-quality responses. Appendix A shows a worksheet approach to the task.

Beyond ROPI

Analysts willing to invest extra effort in more comprehensive planning tools can choose from a number of statistical and modeling techniques. Knowing the strengths and limitations of each is part of the problem. The other is having enough good data.

Perhaps the most popular of more advanced methods is *regression analysis,* which calculates an equation that best describes how different variables interact *simultaneously.* One of the so-called *multivariate* techniques, regression analysis provides a more realistic view of the relative strength of each variable as it affects the test variable.

A simplified example might look like this:

Leads = A × Insertions + B × Size of show booth + C × Reputation

A, B, and C are coefficients of factors which the analysis identifies as important. One factor affecting lead yield in this case is the vendor firm's reputation relative to competitors. Another is the number of ad insertions. A third is the size of the company's big annual show booth. Individual variables don't operate in isolation, and multivariate analysis accounts for that.

Exploit Promotional Windows

Planning the lead flow to meet sales goals also means capitalizing on special opportunities. We call it the Promotional Window Concept, the recognition that some periods of the year are especially critical for communications and lead generation.

It may take as little as 10 percent more than the monthly average promotion dollar to provide enough extra leads to support a quota period or sales contest, to uncover extra business that can be closed before year-end, or to cash in on an expected surge of buying in a market segment. Regardless of the specific reasons, supplementing a continuous promotion program with "bumps" ensures that special sales activity will occur.

Promotional window timing depends on three factors:

- The closing time needed to complete a sale determines how far in advance the firm must bump up inquiry volume.
- The customer buying cycle may depend on specific events: tax periods, government regulatory deadlines, a major trade show, the buying cycles of your customers' customers.
- Quota and incentive periods, business cycles, and financial reporting calendars will influence promotional window timing.

For instance, if the average sale takes five months to close, salespeople will appreciate extra lead volume five months ahead of the end of their quota periods, even if doing so accelerates some of their business that would otherwise close in the sixth month. And senior management, knowing promotional reserves can be called up to save what's expected to be a sagging financial period several months down the road, won't cut communications budgets at the slightest provocation.

Make sure you are ready when it's time to mobilize those reserves. Have a plan to ramp up extra outbound telemarketing and inquiry telequalification support for an emergency. Keep mailers in stock, ready for a quick drop. Turn to publishers' bonus inquiries if you must, mining them for hidden gold. Sometimes, the sales emergency occurs only in some territories, so have a plan for redirecting the lead flow to where it's really needed.

Chapter 6

Harness the Lead Power of Advertising and Publicity

Advertising and publicity are by far the workhorses of inquiry generation for most marketers. Advertising produces more than 30 percent of business-to-business inquiries; publicity is second with about 24 percent.[1] In consumer markets, enthusiast publication advertising draws inquiries from well-defined audiences. Even consumer packaged-goods advertising is slowly turning toward lead generation, as more brands attempt to capture the names of their best customers.

And, in all markets, publicity about new products and services, about using products, and about the companies behind the products fuels the editorial fare of thousands of publications, audio and video programs, and other news media. The advertising/publicity one-two punch continues to be the most economical way for most companies to promote new products to the world.

Although mass communications have suffered a great deal of marketing criticism in recent years, the main complaints center on the difficulties of measuring their value. Even though this most ubiquitous tool of modern capitalism is more than a century old, debate over how and why commercial mass communication works or doesn't continues to preoccupy the marketing services industries. The problem is that communicating persuasively mixes art and behavioral science, and is ever ready to surprise by succeeding when "the rules" have been broken, and failing when the experts pronounced things to be just right.

Sales lead management helps to solve those problems, making advertising and publicity as accountable as any other marketing tool for their contribution to the selling process. Keeping that in mind, let's examine what the rules, and the common sense of experience, tell us about mass communication lead-generation sources.

Make Your Advertising Work Harder

Paid-space advertising spending in 1993 totaled more than $138 billion in the United States, according to ad agency McCann-Erickson.[2] About $3.2 billion of that volume appeared in specialized business publications. Yet the medium has lost ground to competition in the early 1990s. Companies, especially consumer packaged-goods firms, spent an average of 70 percent of their advertising and sales promotion budgets on promotions (inducements paid directly to customers and dealers), leaving 30 percent for advertising. A decade earlier, advertising received 43 percent of the pie.[3] Companies are learning, however, that excessive promotion hurts many brands' short-term profit while providing no long-term benefit.[4]

Rather than try to buy consumer loyalty with prizes, contests, coupons, and discounts, advertising attempts to wrap brands in quality images that add to the value customers think they are receiving. And, advertising can carry that message deeper into buying organizations than salespeople can, to the "hidden buying influences" we discussed Chapter 2. A number of major business-to-business research studies[5] and dozens of investigations in consumer markets credit advertising with the ability to improve market share, perceived quality, and brand preference, producing more sales and larger profits.

Good advertising also produces lots of qualified inquiries. Research suggests that advertising weight correlates more closely with inquiry generation than with eventual business-to-business sales.[6] That makes sense, because advertising inquiry volume depends entirely on advertising, while many factors in addition to advertising influence sales.

Set Budgets to Objectives

Fortunately for the marketers who stress inquiries as the prime goal of their advertising, ad campaign analysis and budgeting are relatively simple because they rely on the direct relationships among advertising performance, inquiry cost, and lead productivity. The return-on-promotional-investment (ROPI) formula from Chapter 5 calculates how many qualified leads you need to achieve a specific sales goal. Other methods are not so straightforward, but are used widely nonetheless.

The *percentage-of-sales* budgeting approach still has a major grip on advertising because it's easy and simple to manage, even though it's conceptually backwards. Comparing promotion costs to sales realized does measure efficiency. But setting the next period's ad budget according to the sales forecast implies that sales cause the ad spending rather than the other way around. The method fails to address a critical budgeting question: How will changes in ad spending affect revenue?

Budgeting to task is the preferred approach. Sensibly, it requires that promotion plans accomplish specific *communications goals.* Inquiry flow is the goal most easily measured and tracked through the eventual sale. Changes in marketplace awareness, brand preference, and customer perceptions can also be measured and tracked through research, although it's tougher to link those effects to eventual sales. That's why it is usually not enough to simply set your communication objective as "increased sales." Advertisers without lead programs must rely on indirect measures of advertising selling power such as awareness, etc. But even marketers with lead-management systems should measure more communications effects than lead flow alone, particularly when weak field follow-up provides an incomplete picture of qualified leads converted to sales.

Another approach, not widely used, attempts to determine how much advertising (or, more properly, the whole communications program) contributes to the selling process. By breaking the sales function into its component steps and determining how much communications adds to what salespeople accomplish, you can determine the dollar value of the advertising program as an upper limit to the advertising budget, its proponents say.

For example, one general machinery manufacturer turned to the *steps to the sale* model developed by McGraw-Hill Publications Co., reckoned how much each step contributed to an overall sale, and estimated the extent to which marketing communications participated in each step. It multiplied the factors and summed them to calculate a weighted estimate of the marketing communications revenue contribution, as shown in Exhibit 6-1. Complicated yes, intellectually elegant, perhaps. But the contribution-to-selling method suffers from the same inflexibility as the percentage-of-sales approach. It treats the sales forecast as preordained, regardless of the advertising support it receives.

Despite such attempts to budget comprehensively, many advertisers fail to set objectives properly, and that means they wind up setting budgets improperly—usually with a percentage-of-sales ratio. Evidently, advertisers seldom express their objectives in measurable, time-dimensioned terms. For example, a study of advertisers who submitted publication advertising entries to the Gold Key Awards competition of the Business Marketing Association examined how each wrote the statement of objectives that had to accompany each entry. Although nearly all, 94 percent, cited a communications task as their goal, just 68 percent specified the target audience, and *none* indicated either the time period or the amount of change desired.[7]

Conceptual models, targeted levels of "soft" advertising goals such as awareness or preference, and competitively superior spending levels are all important considerations. But the single most important budgeting input for a company with salespeople and distributors who need leads is the number of leads

Exhibit 6-1
Weighted Marketing Communications Contribution

Task	Contribution to Sale %	×	Marcom % to Task	=	Marcom Weight %
Making Contact	10		30		3
Arousing Interest	15		33.3		5
Creating Preference	25		10		2.5
Making Specific Proposals	15		0		0
Closing	10		0		0
Keeping Customer Sold	25		10		2.5
Total marcom revenue contribution = 13%					

Source: Cyril Freeman, "How to Evaluate Advertising's Contribution" *Harvard Business Review* (July–August 1962) as quoted in Charles H. Patti, Steven W. Hartley and Susan L. Kennedy, *Business to Business Advertising: A Marketing Management Approach* (Lincolnwood, Ill.: NTC Business Books, 1991) pp. 106–113.

they actually do need to meet sales targets. Complicated, no. Intellectually elegant, certainly. The ROPI formula is the best approach for budgeting lead-generating communications.

Your Advertising Media Choices

The range of advertising formats touted over the years testifies to the ingenuity of communications entrepreneurs. New in-store and other out-of-home media ranging from shopping cart cards to TV monitors to shelf-talkers that really talk get publicity, often fleeting, whenever an innovative "medium of the decade" starts promoting itself to advertisers. New technologies such as interactive television, multimedia CD-ROM, and on-line information services all insist that now, finally, their time has come. On-line services, for example, are expected to have nearly 20 million users by 1998.[8]

But for most marketers generating inquiries, the mainstream advertising media continue to be periodicals edited for specialized audiences and directories. Those have the highest concentrations of audience members focused on a product or service category: prospective customers likely to want more information from vendors.

Optional Media

Other media certainly should be part of a balanced program, particularly to build awareness and supplement the lead-generating power of special-interest publications. Also, the premier mass medium, television, is undergoing radical change as special-interest cable TV channels, infomercials, and interactive programming attempt to assert themselves beyond the experimentation phase. Many expect those will supplant print for special-interest marketing communications, at least to consumers. As computer, telephone, and video technologies merge, marketers will be flooded with inquiries they must manage to stay competitive. Getting started now by handling well the leads received from today's media is the best way to prepare for that future.

Outdoor. Consumer and business services advertisers have been flocking to billboard advertising, a $1.48 billion ad medium in 1992. The service category grew by a third in that year, according to the Outdoor Advertising Association of America.[9] Traditionally a local medium, outdoor is increasingly regional and national, as large outdoor operators acquire local outdoor advertising "plants." The medium features low-cost impressions and the ability to link a brand name to an 800-number for inquiries—if the passerby has time to write it down.

Outdoor is an attractive supplement to mainstream business-to-business communication campaigns, particularly for reaching business travelers. Outdoor displays near trade show venues can boost an exhibitor's booth traffic. Outdoor's geographic orientation makes it a useful tool for local service providers. The medium cannot deliver a complex message, however. A billboard has only a few seconds to make its point.

Broadcast. Television and radio advertising, strong awareness- and reach-building media, increasingly offer response telephone numbers for direct selling and information offers. The response tools of the late-night vegetable slicer pitchman, if not his midway barker's enthusiasm, have been updated and repackaged for mainstream advertisers selling direct and building user databases.

Business product and service advertisers find TV and radio news and sports formats deliver better-than-average business and professional audiences. Corporate image advertising supplementing detailed print messages appears in public-affairs programming. And regional business services and dealers find local broadcast congenial to their needs. But broadcast requires short, punchy messages and at least two repetitions of an inquiry phone number to generate a lead. Those who use the medium find that toll-free phone number mnemonics—such as American Express' 1-800-THE-CARD, or Teleway Inc.'s heavily promoted 1-800-FLOWERS—are invaluable.

Broadcast provides a quick shot of inquiries. Commercial "spots" can run immediately if time is available. The nature of the medium inspires inquirers to call soon after the spot runs.

Television is expensive, however, particularly in terms of the cost-per-lead it incurs for the geographically dispersed, special-interest audiences sought by most business and industrial products and services. Radio is much more economical, permitting a commercial to run many times.

Radio, primarily a local medium, focuses tightly on special formats and audiences (e.g. news, talk, rock, classical, even all-business news). Commuting "drive time" is the most expensive, but it's considered the best for reaching businesspeople. Some 53 percent of adults also listen to radio at work, according to the Radio Advertising Bureau.[10] But if it's playing in the background, are listeners focused enough to comprehend commercials?

Emerging media. Call it the "information superhighway" or "junk mail at light speeds," the interactive electronic future promises hundreds of electronic communications options available to home and office through cable television and telephone lines. The future is taking a while, however. There's more hype than happening in all today's press coverage fuss, vaporware product announcements, and merger deals that don't go through. Cautious investors remember the early attempts at interactivity such as videotex and teletext, breathlessly promoted in the 1980s before they disappeared with just a whimper. Now, however, the momentum seems unstoppable, even if the communications industry cannot figure out exactly what's ahead. One public opinion poll found that "Most people may not know exactly what the term 'multimedia' means, but by 54 percent to 21 percent, their initial reaction to the idea is positive."[11]

Fast-growing and now moving an estimated $1 billion in goods, infomercials will someday soon have their own cable TV channels, their advocates claim. Those slick 10-, 20-, or 30-second product pitches designed for direct selling, represent the newest special-interest medium receiving close scrutiny from leading national advertisers. Infomercials offer plenty of time to solicit an order or an inquiry, and narrowly focused cable TV channels undoubtedly will include special-interest business-oriented programming. Engineers will turn to the technical lectures cum new product pitches, for instance. Business marketers will advertise within infomercials produced by others, or produce their own (at time charges running from $50 to $500,000 an hour[12]). So far, two-thirds of consumers seeing infomercials for the first time have a better opinion of them, research says; 92 percent of those who buy from an infomercial say they are satisfied, according to a National Infomarketing Association survey of 3,500 infomercial shoppers.[13]

Whatever its final shape, electronic communication technology will alter marketing communications in two major ways. As we said, two-way communications will require companies to provide response options no matter what their product or service. That will flood marketers with leads for which prospects will expect instantaneous fulfillment. Interactivity will also put the audience in full control of message delivery.

The viewer's ability to jump forward, backward, and sideways hypertext style, through a commercial or program-length infomercial, eliminates the sequential presentation control of today's television commercial. That puts electronic advertising on the same footing with print. Today's CD-ROM-based promotions, well-menued and branched, with games and other devices designed to lure audience interest to the sales pitch, illustrate what will come over the wire to homes and offices. When the wires are up, that is. Providing the high-bandwidth lines and computer servers to make it all happen nationwide will cost about $100 billion.[14]

The fax medium? Certainly, what was once called facsimile transmission, now the ubiquitous fax, is a communication tool that emerged and flowered to the great advantage of sales lead management. But we prefer to think of fax as a response and fulfillment tool rather than as a lead-generating medium per se.

Unsolicited fax messages are illegal in many cases and annoying to recipients in most. Even businesspeople who do not mind receiving cold-call telemarketing bristle when unsolicited sales pitches tie up the relatively few fax machines they have on hand. We do not recommend fax for lead generation as we would cold-call telemarketing. But as a response option for prospects and a fulfillment tool for you, fax provides an immediacy for text and graphics that other methods cannot match.

Periodical Diversity

Think of any activity, business, lifestyle, hobby, or job description. Chances are there are one or more periodical publications serving it. When a defined market niche is attractive enough and the cost of advertising through the publication is efficient enough, you get an advertising medium.

Among business publications, the main lead generators, some are *vertical.* They serve several different job functions within an industry by writing for management and technical executives alike. Other publications, called *horizontals,* typically serve a particular job function or technical specialty across many industries. Publications for plant maintenance managers, sales executives, information officers, engineers, chief executives, etc., fall into the horizontal category. In consumer markets, specialized publications serve audiences with common interests, such as a hobby or sport.

Audiences and interests. Another way of classifying publications is the difference between *special audience* and *special interest,* phrases coined by veteran media commentator Jim Mann in the 1970s. Special-interest publications are designed to attract readers with a shared interest. But special-audience publications are those designed to accumulate a certain type of reader attractive to advertisers.

The difference is not academic. The special-interest publication serves the audience (e.g. skiers or electronic engineers) and hopes to find advertisers to support it. The editors' mission is clear: write to readers' shared information needs.

The special-audience publication, however, is designed to serve advertisers and hopes to find enough readers fitting advertisers' target audience profiles (e.g. 18–35-year-old professional/managerial women). In pulling together an audience of people with common demographic characteristics, the special-audience magazine can look highly efficient on an advertiser's media plan. But its target audience probably has diverse information needs. It might be tough or impossible for the editorial package to span enough of those needs often enough to build strong reader loyalty.

The differences in loyalty show up in circulation renewal rates. The dissimilarity in reader appeal also shows up in the quality of leads each type of publication generates. Shared special interests provide an audience that will consider a well-edited publication an essential source of information. Under those circumstances, readers look to advertisements as well as editorial fare for the knowledge they crave, and that helps to produce qualified inquiries.

General vs. specialized business publications. As an old saw in the magazine business puts it, the three categories of information that attract readers are sex, news, and service. Business advertisers generally expect sales leads only from the last two.

Business news publications can be either general in their orientation, such as *Business Week, Fortune, Forbes* and *The Wall Street Journal,* or specialized, catering to one industry, such as *Multichannel News* or *Adweek.* The same distinctions apply to service-oriented business publications that are more "how-to" than news oriented. But, lacking a tight focus on any one field, broadly circulated business news or service publications might not enjoy as much reader devotion as specialized periodicals. According to a Simmons Market Research Bureau study, 81 percent of specialized business publication readers are "regular" (three of the last four issues) readers of such a publication, compared to 63 percent of general business publication readers who read one of those periodicals regularly.[15]

For the lead-minded advertiser, how-to publications generally offer the most attractive environments because they devote editorial coverage to buying and using products and services. Some publishers even attach reader service numbers to editorial features to facilitate inquiries. A problem-solving resource for readers, feature articles and entire service publication copies tend to be read, passed along, and saved for later reference. And, well-written advertising actually becomes part of the magazines' editorial appeal. Seven out of 10 readers told a Cahners Publishing survey that advertising is a regular part of what they read in specialized business publications. (See Exhibit 6-2.)

Making formal distinctions between horizontal/vertical and news/service publishing formats can get messy. Publications can exhibit all those qualities to different degrees. What counts to the advertiser is the efficiency with which its message is exposed to readers, in the context best supporting the objectives of the advertising insertion. That is, if market awareness and preference are key goals of an ad campaign, relatively broad circulation and readership is called for rather than exposure to narrow audiences.

Broader audiences also favor generating more inquiries, but of lower average quality—the loose-leads strategy. *As a general rule of thumb, the more specialized the audience of a publication, the higher the average quality of the inquiries it generates, even though the total number of inquiries is likely to be smaller.* That assumes, of course, that your advertising message is sufficiently well-crafted and tailored to that audience for a tight-leads strategy to work.

Exhibit 6-2
Is Advertising As Popular As Editorial?

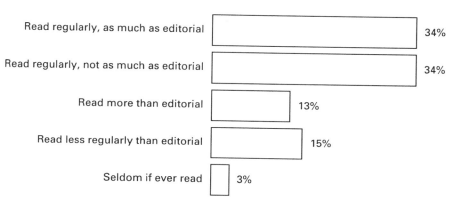

Read regularly, as much as editorial	34%
Read regularly, not as much as editorial	34%
Read more than editorial	13%
Read less regularly than editorial	15%
Seldom if ever read	3%

Source: *Cahners Advertising Research Report No. 412.4* (Newton, Ma.: Cahners Publishing Co., 1990).

Product tabloids. Product tabloid publications, highly efficient inquiry producers, rely on neither sex nor service. They carry product announcement advertising that readers peruse like a general catalog. Their editorial fare generally relies on manufacturers' new product announcement press releases. Literature distribution publications, which list available technical and product information and provide a means for ordering it are a subset of the tabloid category.

Product tabloids (which may or may not physically take tabloid newspaper form, although most do) are designed specifically to generate inquiries. Publishers of some of the biggest, such as *New Equipment Digest* and *Industrial Equipment News,* go to extra lengths to boost inquiry yields and help advertisers prequalify them. Product tabloids shoulder the majority of the press release burden that other books shun. Without them, business and industrial new product introductions would suffer.

Some in the advertising business denigrate tabloids—unfairly, we think. Their editorial fare of reprinted press releases won't win journalism awards. And their page upon page of fractional-page ads does not thrill designers. But product tabloids do not pretend to be something they are not. We've seen many advertisers buy much more expensive space in publications claiming high reader-value journalism, only to receive poorer inquiry yields.

Readers frequently peruse product tabloids with buying on their minds. They seek solutions, and are curious about what's new. Unlike service magazines about which they are choosy, engineers peruse whichever tabloids cross their desks, according to focus groups conducted by *Industrial Equipment News.* Even though they consider tabloids "all advertising," engineers like to scan them to see if something catches their eye, the publication states.[16] In a follow-up field study, *Industrial Equipment News* reports, a third of surveyed engineers said their most recent inquiry was to an ad in a standard-size magazine; 26 percent said they responded to a product tabloid ad.[17]

By offering only advertising and product releases, the tabloids don't tell readers much about the solutions so offered, however. That tends to breed a large number of casual inquiries, best suited to a loose-lead strategy as discussed in Chapter 5, requiring an effective inquiry qualification system.

Directories
Designed to be used usually for year-long periods, editions of industrial and business directories have a long useful life that grows when subscribers hand their old editions to subordinates. Whether published on paper, CD-ROM, diskette, or on-line, directories appear in two generic types: one for sellers, the other for buyers.

Many industrial directories cater to marketers and contain lists of companies, addresses, and phone numbers organized geographically, by industry, etc. Usually they are compiled, based on combining information from other sources—directories, public records, newspaper lists, etc.—rather than being lists of active buyers. Such directories are an inexpensive source of names many companies use for mail, telemarketing, and direct selling campaigns. But those undifferentiated lists aren't really "leads," although some mistakenly apply that term to directory names. Generally they yield the lowest qualification rates of all prospect lists.

Product and service directories designed for buyers offer an advertising opportunity similar to product tabloids: readers have products on their minds as they turn the pages seeking useful information. Readers consult directories with an immediate buying need in mind more than 80 percent of the time.[18] A well-used directory can be a good place to tell your product or service story with a display ad supplementing a regular listing.

In consumer markets, the Yellow Pages is the best-known directory. Yellow Pages advertising is expected to approach the $10 billion mark in 1994. A strong business-to-business lead provider, Yellow Page listings for business and consumers generated 17.6 billion phone inquiries in 1990, according to U.S. Yellow Pages, Inc. Nearly 88 percent of those calls ended with a sale or probable purchase.

Industrial directories range from national all-industry titles such as *The Thomas Register of American Manufacturers* and *U.S. Industrial Directory,* to regional and industry-specific directories, to special annual issues and buyers' guides published by many vertical business periodicals.

Catalog compendia. Some publishers also produce so-called "pre-file catalogs," which are similar to directories because they carry the product catalogs of several manufacturers in a field. Thomas Publishing Co., for example, publishes *The Thomas Register Catalog File,* nicknamed "Thomcat," an 8-volume portion of the 26-volume *Thomas Register of American Manufacturers.* Because pre-file catalogs contain more extensive product information than directory listings of who makes what, they can be an important source of information for buyers just beginning their search. Some feel they've collected enough information, so rather than ask for more product literature, they ask manufacturers for a sales call or a quotation.

Electronic distribution. Additionally, electronic directories, still more experimental than an established medium at the start of the 1990s, will become increasingly important as the decade unfolds, particularly to technology marketers. Directories easily distributed on computer diskette, CD-ROM, or, more instantaneously, via on-line services, promise to displace many a bulky set of printed documents with electronic data retrieval aids. As electronic sales calls, they can interact with buyers, helping them pick the right components for applications and configure orders, for example, before zapping the order on-line direct to the manufacturer.

Digital Equipment Corp. (DEC) has had glowing words for its Electronic Connection, on-line service for customers and resellers. It provides interactive shopping, product news and information, order tracking and quotations. It even carries information and ordering wherewithal for non-DEC products that complement the DEC line. Sales through the service have grown 40 to 60 percent a year, Digital executives said, calling the system "phenomenal."[19]

Your Advertising Media Tactics

Media costs—space and time charge—probably will be the largest part of your advertising lead program. Roughly figure charges will break out this way:

- 60 to 70 percent for space;
- 10 to 20 percent for ad production;
- 5 percent for fulfillment literature;
- 1.5 to 2 percent for fulfillment postage;
- 1.5 to 2 percent fulfillment clerical and handling costs.

Choosing media involves not only broad choices among media types, but analyses and decisions about reach, frequency, readership, and timing—plus attention to editorial and advertising environments. Here, we'll look closest at publications, the source of most mass-communication leads.

Circulation Metrics

Too few advertisers begin and end their media selection process by eyeballing publication gross circulations, then calculating the cost-per-thousand circulation. That's where to start, but there's more to the story if you want to optimize your inquiry flow. Of course, once you've had experience advertising in a publication, you'll know its cost-per-qualified lead. Even then, however, you should be attentive to other media qualities that also affect your long-term marketing health.

Research finds that advertisers typically value editorial strength and circulation vitality more or less equally when choosing publications for advertising.

In the specialized business press, for instance, a survey asking advertisers which criteria are most important found 71 percent citing circulation quality, 69 percent pointing to coverage of buyers and specifiers, and 62 percent citing editorial quality.[20] Inquiry production received just a 42 percent rating in the survey, but it's not known to what extent members of the sample, recipients of *Cahners Advertising Research Reports,* track leads and maximize inquiry generation. Circulation is the lifeblood of a publication's existence. Reputable publishers spend a great deal to keep circulation lists current to cope with turnover in the fields they cover. (Cahners, for instance, finds that 30 percent of its specialized business publications' circulation changes annually.[21]) Publishers in highly competitive media markets can be quite creative, even misleading, in promoting their reach. Read the fine print carefully.

Audits. The fine print starts with circulation audit statements which, oddly enough, usually do not receive the in-depth attention they deserve from advertisers and ad agency media departments. The two leading publication audit services are the Audit Bureau of Circulations (ABC) and the Business Publications Audit of Circulation (BPA), the latter being particularly important for controlled-circulation business publications. Between the two leading services, just about all important business publications receive audit scrutiny. Audited publications issue reports every six months. Always use the latest one in your analysis.

Some publications provide "verified" circulation reports which are backed by a publisher's sworn statement. But it is actual audits, similar to financial audits, that represent the acceptable standard of circulation reporting. Auditors' reports, publicly distributed as publisher's statements, reveal much about a publication's ability to attract readers. The requalification rates listed on BPA Publisher's statements, for instance, indicate the recency of circulation updates and the proportion of readers specifically asking to receive the publication. Circulation breakdowns by a variety of business and job function criteria specific to an industry indicate who receives the publication, and the circumstances under which they receive it (personal request, bulk subscription, discount subscription, etc.) Advertisers might report more information from their own reader surveys, but circulation audits are an independent watchdog's actual counts.

In broadcasting and cable TV, rating services survey audiences to determine station and program audiences. Controversies flare periodically over the accuracy of ratings, whether collected by diaries or machines attached to TV sets, but the numbers collected daily in major cities and several times a year nationally are generally accepted, at least as benchmarks for price negotiations.

Audiences. Demographically, does a publication do a better job than others in reaching your target prospects? Common demographic criteria for consumer media selection are: age and gender; income (usually household); region; product/service purchase/ownership. In business-to-business markets, the relevant demographics include the reader's job title and function, the nature of his or her business—often expressed as a Standard Industrial Classification (SIC) code—and the business "firmographics": the location and size of the business and the products/services sold, etc.

In some advertising situations, lifestyle and behavior characteristics may be more important than demographics, particularly in consumer markets where the special-interest vs. special-audience distinction can be quite important. Do readers prefer physically active or sedentary activities? Do they tend to buy at discount or premium outlets?

On the business side, where purchases generally must have a rational benefit for a company, the behavior factors in a publication's audience most important to advertisers are reader role and clout in buying decisions. Are they specifiers or final approvers? Do they initiate purchase activity or complete it by issuing the purchase orders? Publishers generally provide insight on those questions. But also study the editorial fare. The type of person editors write for is the type who will read the publication.

Use audit and research data to adjust your circulation cost comparisons to include only the type of readers who interest you. Do not, however, immediately discount a publication because it has a large proportion of circulation that does not interest you. It's possible that you could economically reach a highly desirable market segment that's just a portion of a periodical's total circulation by renting a portion of the publication's circulation list, or by purchasing *demographic edition* space distributed to part of the publication's audience.

Pass-along audiences. Does a publisher's circulation claim include pass-along readership (secondary circulation), which typically is a very crude estimate? Are pass-along readers as interested in a publication or its advertisers as a primary reader, the one who purchases the issue?

Pass-along isn't something to ignore. Cahners Publishing found, for instance, that one-third of nearly 9 million reader service inquiries, received by its specialized management and technical publications, came from non-subscribers. The pattern had been the same a decade earlier, the publisher says. And a survey asking readers about pass-along behavior reported that the average specialized business magazine reaches three primary and secondary readers.[22]

Cumulative reach. In addition to the individual circulations of publications selected for your advertising, you'll want to know their *cumulative reach*. In business markets served by several publications, many target audience members receive and read more than one publication. You should estimate how much overlap, or duplication, exists among publications in your media plan, and therefore how much net, or cumulative reach you are actually buying. For instance, publication A might have 100,000 primary circulation, while publication B has 80,000. But because 60,000 of publication B's subscribership also receive A, the cumulative reach of an ad appearing in both publications is 100,000, plus the 20,000 unduplicated subscribers of publication B.

Circulation duplication doesn't necessarily translate to readership duplication. Few readers actually see every issue of a publication they receive. Fewer still see every page in an issue they do read. The available specialized business publication industry statistics, from a Cahners Publishing survey, say that 95 percent of readers know they receive the publications they get, 92 percent read at least one out of four issues, and 72 percent read at least three of every four issues.[23]

Circulation duplication probably will not pose real problems for a lead program. A prospect inquiring from publication A is likely to not inquire again from publication B. That's particularly so if it's an "effort lead" requiring the prospect to make a phone call, complete a coupon or reply card, or take some other action requiring more exertion than circling a reader service card number. We have seldom seen more than 5 percent inquiry duplication in a given month from magazines and reply cards. Duplication might occur later, however, if the inquirer who did not receive fulfillment literature or a sales call inquires again.

Major consumer and general business magazine primary and pass-along duplication information is available from syndicated research services. And a few business-to-business advertisers and specialized business publications have mounted expensive, and therefore infrequent, studies of the cumulative primary and pass-along coverage they and their competitors provide. Generally, however, advertisers in specialized business titles or in smaller consumer publications not covered by the syndicated services have to rely on their own market surveys, or the primary circulation research publishers conduct, to estimate roughly how much duplication will occur in a given media plan.

One relatively inexpensive way is to build a magazine plan based on your own market survey of reading preferences. The logic is that people have their favorite publications, so you build your schedule around them. Here's how. For the publications you are considering, ask members of your target audience which they receive. Also ask them to indicate "the one publication you would choose if you could receive only one." Encourage them to choose only one. The publication receiving the most "only one" votes from the relevant target audience becomes the core buy.

Then remove the responses of those who voted for the core buy from the database. Examine the remaining responses and count the percentage receiving each publication other than the core buy. If, for example, publication A is the core buy, look for the publications with the largest market penetration among those who did not make publication A their top pick. Add those publications to the schedule in descending order of penetration, allocating your budget among them in proportion to their contribution to net reach.[24]

That approach might not provide the most efficient media selection on the basis of circulation cost-per-thousand, but it will help you wade through the duplication problem and balance your exposure to a market. Remember, also, that the method does not account for niche publications you should have on your list in order to deliver your message to hard-to-reach audiences.

Finally, the method is just a starting point for the lead-oriented advertiser for whom lead efficiency, not circulation efficiency alone, is the prime promotion goal. Armed with cost-per-lead data from your past experience with candidate publications, you will adjust the media plan to reduce the cost of reaching your lead target, or to increase the lead count within your budget limits, while keeping duplication under control.

Paid vs. controlled. Exercise judgment when publishers tout the respective merits of paid vs. controlled circulation. Both types have their strengths and weaknesses, often overblown when publishers debate.

Paid circulation is generally less an indication of reader loyalty with business publications than with consumer periodicals. Companies frequently pick up the paid-subscription tab for employees anyway. But someone did plunk down some cash, evidence of some degree of commitment.

Controlled circulation, often dismissed as "free" circulation in consumer marketing, is designed to help a publication reach as many qualified readers in a defined target market as possible. While paid-circulation publications must distribute to anyone who pays the subscription price, controlled circulation is supposed to include only those people of value to advertisers. That's a critical issue in special-interest publishing. The subscribership of a controlled-circulation publication and its controlled-circ rivals defines the size of a market, especially in business and industrial fields. Those circulation lists probably are the best, and quite possibly the only, rosters of buying influences in an industry.

Be wary, however, of the genuinely "free" publication sent to anyone on a given list—such as a directory—whether or not that reader wants it. The best controlled circulation is so-called *direct request,* in which a subscriber must sign a request form (and often provide extensive business and buying information) before getting on the list. Controlled circulation audits scrupulously monitor and report controlled circulation requests, and how recently those names were requalified by a new signature.

Also, determine how many paid subscribers paid full price. Publishers in business and consumer fields alike generally charge lower prices to first-year and multi-year subscribers, but be on the lookout for large portions of circulation sold at giveaway prices. Often, it's a tip-off that a publication has had trouble holding its readers, and has to buy new ones on the cheap in order to maintain its circulation guarantees to advertisers.

Finally, business publications often have both paid and controlled circulation, not charging target readers but expecting all others (that is, those of less interest to its advertisers) to pay. Treat the all-other category as a bonus; what counts are the number of *your* kind of prospects reading the publication.

Readership

Temper circulation claims by examining readership. How many readers actually peer inside a given issue, how often, and for how long? Competitive publications jockeying to put their answers to those questions in the best light spark some of the publishing industry's favorite dust-ups.

Overall, specialized business publication averages from a number of readership surveys by Cahners Publishing report that:

- About nine out of 10 manufacturing industry purchasing influences read specialized business magazines.

- Eighty-five percent of specialized business publication readers have staff supervision responsibility.

- Almost nine out of 10 subscribers read at least one of every four issues of monthlies or semimonthlies, with 65 percent on average looking into a specific issue two or more times.

- On average they read the magazines 1 hour and 27 minutes a week. (That statistic, published in 1993, compares with 2 hours, 22 minutes average reading time in 1979.)

- About 56 percent of readers read specialized business publications only at work.

- Eighty-five percent of specialized business publication readers say they take some action with an issue: saving it, clipping, it, passing it along or placing it in the company library.[25]

- Nearly half (48 percent) of all magazine recipients in 1991 said they read at least some of the ads, up from 40 percent in the late 1980s.[26]

- Seasonality doesn't appear to affect the readership of either advertising or editorial fare.[27]

Issue readership is not the same as the advertising readership scores many publishers routinely collect for their individual advertisers. (We discuss ad readership later, in the message development section.) Make sure that when publishers throw numbers from a study at you, you get to see all the numbers. Ask to see a copy of the questionnaire used in a survey; Advertising Research Foundation ethical guidelines insist on it.

Affinity. For decades, media researchers have tried to develop summary measures of a publication's overall relationship with readers and thus its value as an advertising environment. Early in the 1990s, Cahners Publishing Co. applied the notion to specialized business publication readers, developing an *Affinity Index*. Detailed research measures a publication's overall usefulness and ability to engage its readers. The stronger the affinity, the more readers are likely to read, believe, and remember ads in the publication, purchase advertised products, and inquire for more information, Cahners maintains.[28]

Frequency

How often should you advertise? The frequency question is a matter of evergreen debate in advertising. Experts agree that advertising recall decays over time and that readers need to be exposed again to be able to remember the message. The more you advertise, the better the recall. But just how many exposures are required to break through competitive clutter and pass the threshold level for a message to stick in the mind?

The question is especially critical for advertising designed to build awareness and favorable attitudes for an advertiser, product, or brand. Advertising designed to generate leads should appear with whatever frequency provides the right number of inquiries at the right time for the sales force and your promotional windows (as discussed in Chapter 5). Don't assume that one ad will generate all the potential inquiries out there; prospects move in and out of the market constantly. Repeating an ad designed to generate leads is likely to keep paying off, up to a point.

With the right offer and the right message aimed at the right audience, your total inquiry volume will peak out proportional to your market sales estimates. For example, if you expect 15,000 new customers will buy this year, your qualified leads over the year should be around twice that amount, assuming that around half of all inquirers actually buy. Trying to generate more leads than that is a waste of money.

Advertisers frequently fret about *wear-out,* when an ad or commercial loses its appeal to readers and viewers. Often, however, advertisers flatter themselves thinking the audience is paying that much attention to their messages in the first place. Seeing it every day, the advertiser grows tired of an ad far faster than the public. As the old ad agency joke goes, the client, bellowing about wear-out, wants a new campaign even before the old one starts running!

Wear-out can be a serious problem for consumer packaged-goods advertising relying on novelty and wide exposure to attract attention. Most business-to-business advertisers, however, run far too few ads a year to worry about it. Even when they do mount hefty schedules, solid, reader-oriented, and information-rich messages appeal to new buyers in the market each time they run.

For example, the Ludlow Corp. repeated the same ad in the same industry publication for 41 consecutive quarters. While quarter-to-quarter inquiry yield varied, it remained high throughout the 10-year period, and was highest the 21st, 29th, and 36th times the ad ran. The 41st appearance produced more inquiries than any of the first 19 times the ad ran. A division of Johns-Manville Corp. achieved a similar effect, running an ad 13 times; 5 of the insertions produced more inquiries than the previous insertion.[29] Surcom Associates, a specialty electronic components distributor on the West Coast, selling primarily to the aftermarket rather than original equipment manufacturers, had rotated a pool of three ads in every monthly issue of a magazine, finding no reduction in lead volume over a nearly four-year period.[30]

Clutter

Does it matter when your ad runs in a thick publication laden with page after page of other advertising? Eye-tracking research, which literally maps how reader focus bounces around a page, finds that as more ads compete in a publication, the harder it is for them to attract reader attention. Yet the same type of research credits business and industrial advertising with holding its own well against clutter, compared to consumer print ads.[31]

Publishers point to readership research to support their contention that clutter should not be a concern. Examining advertising readership scores for 379 issues of its publications, Cahners Publishing found little difference between average-ad scores in magazines of different sizes, ranging from fewer than 200 to more than 500 pages.[32] Considering that the folio (total page count) of most publications depends on their advertising space, the number of ads doesn't seem to affect average ad readership scores.

Another Cahners study of 124 of its publications found a slight but statistically insignificant increase in inquiries per advertisement, the more ads there are in an issue.[33] Again, the clutter doesn't seem to matter. One could reason that the fattest issues get that way because they attract more reader attention, giving each ad a better chance to produce leads.

Print is an interactive medium. Unlike the linear presentations of broadcast advertising, the audience controls what it sees, for how long, and in what order.

That certainly suggests that the solution to clutter problems in print rests largely with the advertiser's obligation to create engaging, reader-oriented messages in the first place. Then, the lead-based media analysis will indicate whether the ad can produce up to par in a cluttered environment.

Advertising Placement

The common wisdom from consumer advertising dictates that readers will ignore ad pages unless they trip over them when reading. Advertisers with partial page units should have editorial matter on the same page, the reasoning goes, and full-page advertisements should appear on the right, facing editorial fare, so that eyes attracted to an article will drift toward the ad.

Advertisers often demand such placement. But common wisdom probably doesn't matter as much in specialized business publications, where the ads themselves have news and service value. Research finds that left- or right-hand page placement makes little difference in reader recognition scores for specialized business publication advertising.[34]

There is even some evidence that running an ad alongside high-impact editorial features could cut the attention it receives. Eye-tracking studies have found that, on occasion, strong editorial material will attract readers to a page, then divert attention from an ad on or adjacent to the page. Two ads in proximity seem to have the same competing effect.[35]

Advertisers also routinely ask that ads appear in the first half or first third of a publication. The more polite ones ask for it, "if possible," while others demand it on insertion orders as a divine right. The idea is that readers start perusing an issue at the front. Actually, only 60 percent are so orderly, says Cahners. According to its research with thousands of readers, 8 percent start from the back, and all the rest use the table of contents to choose how they move through the issue.[36] And, when Cahners examined the readership scores for nearly 74,000 business and industrial ads, it found that placement in the front or back half of a publication didn't affect median reader "noted" scores (readers who recall seeing an ad).[37]

Eye-tracking research contends, however, that position does matter, favoring the second quarter of a publication's pages. The reason, wrote eye-tracking expert Joan Treistman, is that too many advertisers jockeying for up-front position create clutter in the first quarter of the folio, depressing the average ad's ability to win reader involvement. Also, the high-impact editorial fare generally concentrates in a publication's opening pages, competing with advertising for attention. By the time the reader gets to the second quarter of the folio, the editorial and clutter competition eases a bit, allowing ads to generate more involvement.[38]

Position and memorability. Does location within an issue affect inquiry volume? Absent research tracking a direct relationship, the answer lies in whether the readership scores of individual advertisements correlate with their relative inquiry yield. The little research that exists on the subject finds a small but significant positive relationship between ad recall and response. In other words, the ads that are better remembered tend to produce more leads, all other things being equal.

Drawing on cross-tabulations from its readership score database, Cahners found that better scoring ads produced more inquiries on average.[39]

A limited, although technically precise regression analysis, of the readership score-to-lead connection in product tabloids found that about 27 percent of variation in inquiry response could be explained by variations in readership scores. Not surprisingly, the advertisements that rated highest in lead yield and readership simultaneously tended to be large four-color units promoting multiple products in a product category highly salient to readers, with reader service card numbers for each product.[40]

Readership studies have their own inaccuracies and biases, so we are extremely cautious in accepting them as surrogates for lead analysis. For example, does the reader who recalls seeing an ad remember where she saw it? Also, ads from well-known advertisers which advertise a lot tend to be better remembered. That budget-based research bias initially clouded ad page positioning research by Starch INRA Hooper, one of the nation's oldest advertising research firms. It first found that advertisers appearing in the first third of magazine achieved higher noted scores than those in the back. But the advertisers most often appearing in the front were the big accounts apparently receiving favored treatment from publishers. When researchers controlled that effect by limiting their analysis to similar advertisers, the readership advantage of up-front position disappeared.[41] (The advantage of the inside-front cover [or *second cover*] position did hold up, however).[42]

Eye-tracking research, a more probative tool, claims that recognition scores can produce substantially large errors: 30 percent of respondents incorrectly say they saw an ad in an issue. Also, as much as half the time, people will look at an ad but not remember it.[43]

Then again, the ad that's looked at and remembered isn't necessarily a good ad from a marketing viewpoint. People will remember the tasteless ad, the ones with egregiously ugly artwork, the sexist ad, and the ads with "borrowed-interest"—themes irrelevant to any reasons for buying. Cahners found that 47 percent of the top-10 ads in nearly 400 readership studies had borrowed-interest headlines.[44]

In other words, even weak ads offering little to prompt a genuine qualified inquiry can get decent readership scores. Your best approach to ensure your ads work hard for you is to examine their message quality according to principles of ad communication, and to keep tracking qualified-lead performance.

Publisher Support

When evaluating media choices, remember that publisher involvement can extend beyond selling the space, running the ad, and returning the names of reader service card inquires.

Research services. One valuable research tool many provide are publisher's Did-You-Buy? studies. An advertiser should conduct its own research, but publisher studies, usually provided at no charge, have value despite the limited information they provide. They will indicate a valuable number for ROPI planning: the proportion of inquirers in a category who actually bought the advertised product or service. For example, *New Equipment Digest* regularly tracks salesperson follow-up rates as reported by inquirers, the percentages buying the advertiser's or competitors' products, the percentages who never saw a salesperson from the advertiser, those with a specific application in mind, and the proportion of inquirers who didn't know the advertiser made the product in question.

Publishers usually provide some sort of ad readership research, but the motivation behind those studies isn't altruism alone. Publication readership studies are chameleon data. Sometimes the publisher uses readership study results as sales promotion; sometimes the numbers offer valuable ad diagnostics. When analyzed carefully, keeping in mind their shortcomings, readership reports add to your market feedback.

Additional help. Beyond research, intense competition among publications prompts most to offer a range of value-added services to their customers. Assistance with direct mail, trade show, point-of-purchase, and distribution channel promotion has become standard at many publications.

Be a careful media buyer, however, avoiding ploys such as the "bonus leads" offer that portrays other advertisers' recycled ad and publicity leads, or the names of subscribers with specific interests, as leads for you. One publishing gimmick offers readers the option of checking a box to receive information from all advertisers in a category. Those bonuses are bogus too; such names must be clearly separated from bona fide inquiries. Chances are bonus leads have relatively little value, but, on occasion, some advertisers find them productive and worth pursuing. To determine what's right for you, use your lead-management system to test any bonus leads that come your way.

Your Advertising Creative Tactics

Advertising relies on several steps to present information to prospects. As enunciated decades ago in a scholarly classic, those steps to a sale are: awareness, liking, preference, conviction, and purchase.[45]

In terms of lead-generating advertising, the last step, purchase, should be thought of as "action," as in taking the action to respond. We also like to add a sixth step, reinforcement.

As we interpret those steps, the advertiser should:

1. *Build awareness.* Getting attention, arousing a "this might be interesting and useful" curiosity, requires a word and graphic package that catches the eye and presents evidence why the advertised product or service is the solution to the reader's needs.

2. *Win rapport.* At this stage of "liking," the prospect has determined that the product or service warrants consideration.

3. *Create preference.* The advertisement's objective at this stage is to illustrate and dramatize the superiority of the sponsor's offering compared to competitors.

4. *Generate conviction.* Persuade the reader to accept the message.

5. *Promote action.* The reader takes an overt step toward purchase. If not purchase itself, the prospect inquires, recommends the product or service to colleagues, or saves the information for later use.

6. *Sustain reinforcement.* Advertising must continue to keep the customer sold by maintaining awareness of the product or service and the conviction favoring its selection.

Rules of Engagement

The communication process has inspired advertising experts to pronounce all sorts of advertising "rules" over the years, some better than others, but all striving to suggest how messages should be constructed to accomplish the steps to a sale. We have our favorite rules, the 12 Copy Clinic Canons enumerated on pages 154–158. They address tactical rather than strategic decisions. Strategy, *what* you say to your audience, is determined by your marketing plan and advertising goals. The tactics concern *how* you say it. Use the Canons to guide your own advertising and evaluate what you've already created.

The Copy Clinic Canons

1. ***Arrest attention.*** An advertisement's first obligation is to get noticed, particularly by that portion of a publication's audience comprising the likeliest prospects for the sponsor's product or service.

   If an advertisement fails this test, not succeeding in overcoming the clutter created by competing messages, it has failed its mission and will produce few inquiries. Business readers, busily searching for useful and interesting information, will not pause for the dull and lifeless.

   The headline and the main illustration must complement each other, arousing excitement and curiosity consonant with the intended overall tone of the message.

   Either the headline or illustration should be the dominant visual element drawing attention to the page. Together they must create a single focused message for the eye and the mind.

   Avoid advertising design that does not provide a dominant focal point for the eye and a single dominant concept for the mind. Eyes left to wander undirected around the page will wander off the page. And without a single clear statement about what the ad is about, the busy reader will look elsewhere for useful information.

2. ***Promise a benefit.*** Having attracted attention, the advertisement's next obligation is to address reader needs clearly and engagingly. Being human, prospects respond best to their self-interest, their desire to perform their jobs better, win recognition, and achieve career success. They must be told, right at the start, the answer to their universal question: "What's in it for me?" Give them the right answer, and they will inquire for more information.

   Good salespeople, who know how buyers think, can be the best headline writers. Listen carefully to what they say on a sales call; you'll get winning headline ideas you'd never pick up from the engineering department.

   The benefit promise may or may not be explicit, but it must not be ambiguous.

   If explicit, the benefit statement should promise specific levels of performance. Stating "cut overhead cost up to 15 percent" is more effective than claiming "cut overhead cost."

If implicit, the promise must be supported immediately by specifics in the subheadline and body copy.

In contrast, the advertisement that does not promise a benefit to the reader delivers no benefit to the advertiser.

Remember, however, that the more specific the facts contained in the benefit statement, the more likely it is the ad will generate a response from those with a genuine interest and need, thus satisfying a tight-leads strategy.

3. *Excite the heart and head.* Communication that creates the most believability and conviction operates on two levels: logic and emotion.

Reasoned argument and credible statements of fact are essential evidence for readers deciding to purchase or at least take further action toward buying the advertised product or service.

Yet true commitment to the decision rests in the heart as well, with the assurance that one is making the right choice.

The most powerful advertising satisfies readers at both levels, ensuring a favorable reaction to the message, inoculating the prospect against competitors' claims, and prompting an eager inquiry.

4. *Speak their "language".* Target prospects as a group share common tools, ideas, symbols, and goals of their craft or profession. Successful business-to-business advertising uses those concepts to enhance communication.

For example, charts and graphs speak strongly to engineers, who live in worlds of technical detail and process integrity.

Advertising to managers should stress end results and staff productivity.

Salesmen often respond to the promise of personal recognition as well as financial success.

Advertising should avoid jargon, however. It risks confusing the message and limiting its potential audience.

5. *Use the magic word "you".* The effective ad leaves no misunderstanding. It speaks directly to readers' needs and interests.

Formal expression using the third person usually fails to build the bond of shared purpose between reader and advertiser accomplished by liberal references to "you," "we," and "us."

6. ***Speak friend-to-friend.*** The best advertising copy reads the way a friend would tell a friend about a good thing.

   Short sentences, a familiar tone and writing as one speaks are more persuasive than solemn phraseology, which may seem pompous.

   Sound copy uses expressive verbs in the active voice.

   Advertising should avoid clichés. Those signs of poor writing trivialize the message, and imply to readers that an inquiry would only bring them more of the same.

7. ***Back claims with evidence.*** Proof that what the ad says is true is essential in business-to-business advertising. Without it, claims appear to be mere puffery, not to be taken seriously nor to be pursued via an inquiry.

   Persuasive copy uses one or a number of devices to present proof, or its semblance, that audience members will accept as evidence that a solution to their problem is at hand:

   • Product descriptions and specifications;
   • Performance statistics;
   • Customer testimonials;
   • User case histories or consumer "slice of life" stories;
   • Scientific research findings;
   • Credible spokesperson (expert or celebrity).

8. ***Make the ad readable.*** Sometimes even the best-written advertisements founder because of design and typography that obscure the written word rather than make it easy to read.

   Whether the product of overzealous art direction or plain sloppiness, hard-to-read headlines and body copy, tiny illustrations and confusing layouts motivate readers to turn the page in search of accessible information elsewhere.

   Sound presentation avoids reversed type, tiny body type, all caps type, running type over complex artwork and dark backgrounds, running type around other design elements, and text columns set the full width of the page. Those and other distractions make it tough for readers to stay with the presentation and determine if they want to know more.

   Writing short paragraphs, adding subheads within body text, using a typeface with serifs, employing white space to guide the eye and eliminate clutter—all add to the reader's visual pleasure, comprehension, and conviction.

Layouts must provide logical, clear paths for the reader's eye and not interfere with communication. The most common layout—dominant illustration, headline, body copy, and advertiser logo at lower right—is common because it never obscures the message.

9. ***Tell them to act, and make it easy.*** Having told readers *why* to choose the advertised product or service, the effective message tells them *how* to take the next step. The ad asks for the order. Or, it invites readers to inquire by offering more information, a sales call, a free sample, etc.

   The ad should provide a potent response mechanism: reply coupons large enough to be usable, phone numbers printed in large type, and other devices that facilitate reader action. They should gather more information from the interested reader than just a name and address.

10. ***Kill extraneous elements.*** Once the advertisement is written and designed, writers and art directors should go back over it, pruning all elements, save those required to explain and support the selling proposition and the requested action.

    Messy irrelevancies, unnecessary colors, tangential copy and other visual and verbal asides only confuse the reader.

11. ***Exorcise the corporate ego.*** The greatest sin in advertising is writing to please the advertiser rather than the target prospect. Unfortunately, it's also one of the most frequent mistakes made in business-to-business advertising.

    Readers don't care about the advertiser's company, its depth of self-esteem and its claims to "dedication," "commitment," "quality," and other vaguely defined virtues. They only care about what the advertiser can do for them. That is what motivates them to respond.

    Good advertising always speaks to the reader's need. For example, corporate longevity is only important as an indicator of current and future competence. Market share becomes an interesting statistic when the ad explains why the advertiser has it.

    One of the most convincing approaches uses customer testimonials so that the credible words of others say what the company cannot believably claim for itself.

12. ***Build the right company image.*** All advertising, good and bad, affects readers' perception of a company. Messy ads connote a sloppy attitude throughout a company. Boastful messages imply the company puts customers second. Dull ads suggest an indifferent organization.

But friendly, clear, persuasive communication indicates a customer-oriented company and contributes to the consistent nurturing of a favorable corporate image. Make an exciting offer to connote a company that understands and values its customers.

Size Matters

The larger the ad, the greater the chance that readers will notice it. But does that pay off in commensurately more readership, comprehension, and inquiries? For many inquiry-minded advertisers, the ninth of a page fractional ads common in product tabloids are all that's needed. But other advertisers will require larger ads in order to tell a story, build competitive preference, explain a technology, or contribute to an image—steps that pave the way for better-qualified inquiries.

In the spirit of "all other things being equal," bet on the larger ad for more readership and more response. For instance, Starch Tested Copy research finds the average full-page ad has 61 percent more readership than the average half-pager.[46] Larger ads also generally cost less per square-inch of space than smaller units. And, among nearly 86,000 business and industrial ads in Cahners Publishing's readership study database, encompassing 48 specialized business publications, the median noted score for two-page spreads was 55 percent, compared with 40 percent for single pages and 24 percent for fractional ads.[47]

In terms of inquiry averages, Exhibit 6-3 compares the average inquiry volume of different size ads, as reported by:

- Cahners, for 8.8 million inquiries generated by about 86,000 ads, and
- Penton Publishing's *New Equipment Digest* product tabloid, for its 1989 advertising volume.

We indexed the data against the volume from a single page, for clarity.

The data from *New Equipment Digest* concentrate on combinations of ninth-page units, that being the dominant advertising format in its pages. Cahners' data is more reflective of standard-size magazine ad performance. Given the different origins of the data, we recommend against comparing Cahners' data to *New Equipment Digest*'s numbers in Exhibit 9-5; make comparisons among the different ad sizes only.

Exhibit 6-3
Inquiry Generation by Ad Size

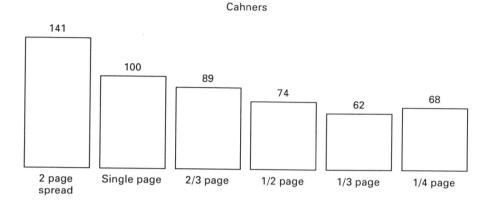

Performance Indexed Against Single Page Inquiry Yield

Cahners

Source: *Cahners Advertising Research Report No. 250.1A* (Newton, MA: Cahners Publishing Co., 1988)

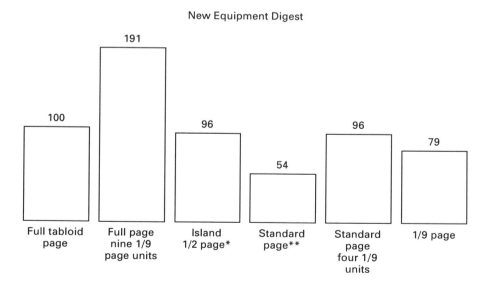

New Equipment Digest

* Island half-page is half the space of a tabloid page.
** Standard 7 × 10 inch page is also known as a junior page.

Source: *Profiting from Industrial Advertising Sales Leads* (Cleveland: Penton Publishing Co., 1991), p. 25.

Small-unit efficiencies. Fractional-page advertising can be a powerful inquiry-generation budget stretcher. Keep the message short to reduce clutter. Emphasize the reason the reader should respond. Fractional advertising generally provides a lower cost-per-lead than full-page advertising, but also lower average quality. By spreading your spending out by running, say, three fractional ads on different pages of an issue rather than one full-page, you are likely to increase your overall campaign exposure.

Then again, there's proven value in running several fractional ads together on the same page. *New Equipment Digest* notes that multiple ninth-page units ganged into larger ads, each with its own reader service number, produce more leads than a single ad occupying the same amount of space.

An advertisement for Zero Corporation in Exhibit 6-4 illustrates the approach. Zero sells cabinets, cases, and enclosures for delicate equipment. Prices among its 37 different product lines range from inexpensive to several thousands of dollars. Zero learned that nine different ninth-page units promoting different product lines—each with its own reader service number—promoted all the company's lines more efficiently than one big ad with a single all-inclusive photo. With the traditional approach, customers ordering one product never knew about Zero's other offerings. But ganging the fractionals changed that awareness and boosted the average number of product lines sold per order from three to five. Although Zero executives initially questioned the aesthetics of the ad, they couldn't quibble with the response.

Running several fractional units on a page in rows, columns, or diagonals boosts response synergistically. An individual ad appearing within a three-ad grouping will generate at least 20 percent more inquiries than the same ad appearing alone, *New Equipment Digest* states.[48]

By the way, some advertisers fear too many reader service number options will only add to the number of junk "bingo circler" leads they receive. That might happen if your multi-unit ad is poorly planned and doesn't clearly explain what you're offering. A well-planned ad, however, designed to make specific and different offers to readers, will improve inquiry pre-qualification and reduce casual "fishing-expedition" requests. The more specific the offer tied to a given reader service number and the less ambiguous the advertisement, the more qualified the average inquiry will be.

For example, *New Equipment Digest* cites a multiple-unit ad with six reader service numbers, each referring to a different product. The ad ran three times, with fewer than half a percent of inquirers circling all six numbers. Eighty-eight percent sought information for just one or two items, and 76 percent asked for information on just one product.[49] Even when high lead duplication occurs, it might still be wise to run the ganged ad if it produces superior unduplicated response. Rely on a sound sales lead-management system to catch those duplications.

Exhibit 6-4
Zero's Page of Ganged Fractionals

Size and inquiry cost. Publishers charge more for larger ad space. Does lead volume growth justify the price? All other things being equal, apparently not. The smaller unit is more efficient. The average cost per reader service inquiry increases with larger units, Cahners reports. Its database finds larger ads producing more inquiries, but the cost-per-lead grows as well, from $32 for quarter-page ads to nearly $68 per inquiry for full pages.[50]

A greater inquiry yield and space to deliver more information might argue for using the larger ad anyway. Don't be a slave to cost-per-lead statistics; they are important but they do not reflect how your campaign may be serving other objectives that matter.

Finally, remember that the lead-cost averages cited here are based on reader service card replies and do not include inquiries mailed or phoned directly to an advertiser, which a publisher never gets to see. Conceivably, the better the ad the more direct responses it will gather, generating correspondingly fewer reader service inquiries and raising the apparent cost-per-lead.

Colorful Effects

On the basis of readership scores, four-color ads produce 39 percent greater readership than black-and-white, Cahners reports, while two-color ads provide only a marginal improvement.[51] According to eye-tracking research, color ads average 13 percent more reader involvement.[52]

Those are just the averages, however. The smart advertiser uses color strategically, to operate at the high end of the curve, so to speak. Color effectively differentiates a key point from a colorless background. Even two-color can have impact if it appears within an otherwise black-and-white environment.

For years, a major chemical and industrial products company ran red headlines in black-and-white business publication ads. It reasoned that fact-oriented headlines are more important than illustrations or photos in industrial advertising, and therefore should draw the eye first. Graphically dominant ads best serve the emotion appeals of consumer products, the company's ad researchers believed.

There's a flip side to the color question. When everyone else is also using color, its relative advantage diminishes, so much so in some cases that black-and-white might be more attention-getting, not to mention more efficient at lead generation. Cahners' specialized business publications charge an average of 24 percent more for four-color advertising full pages than for black-and-white. General business publication prices average 50 percent more, Cahners claims.[53]

Use your own judgment about whether color makes a genuine contribution to a message, builds its visual magnetism, and adds to its response. You probably won't need color to make a literature offer, unless your photo of the literature is particularly stunning. Color used just for the sake of it, because some art director is bored by black-and-white, is likely to be a waste of money.

Text vs. Graphics

Many advertisers have found that an all-text approach—often called an *editorial format*—pulls more inquiries than the standard headline/illustration/copy block advertisement, particularly when offering literature. In product tabloids with their pages of new product releases, the average editorial item pulls 25.6 percent more inquiries than the average ninth-page ad, *New Equipment Digest* reports.[54] Text apparently attracts information-hungry readers.

But that doesn't mean illustrations or photographs are trivial. They play a necessary supporting role. Only two percent of the top-readership ads in Cahners' database—ads tending to be larger units—had neither a photo nor an illustration.[55]

Again, use judgment. When you employ a graphic device as the main focal point of an ad or as an attention-getter secondary to the headline, make sure it's relevant to the selling proposition and that it works with the headline to drive home that key message. As eye-tracking researcher Ms. Treistman explained, "The key difference between strong and weak performances is the extent to which they link a strong visual to a message that's relevant to the reader. . . . Attention dissipates when the reader finds the visual unrelated to the copy message."[56]

Copy Length

The best answer to the evergreen question, "How long should copy run?" is: "Write it as long as it needs to be." A well-written, relevant message will rivet the qualified prospect's attention even when long. And copy that's off target can't hold a reader no matter how short.

The available advertising statistics don't shed much light on the question. Cahners reports that 65 percent of its best-read ads had 100 or more words of descriptive text, while 27 percent had 200 or more words.[57]

Information-hungry readers want facts, but the advertiser seeking an inquiry should give readers just enough to encourage them to inquire for more. Unlike direct mailers writing long, rhapsodic letters to make a sale on the spot, your objective is getting the inquiry.

Keep your ad free of unnecessary copy. Flourishes of corporate pride (e.g. "A leading supplier since . . .") and unsupported superlatives look great to the advertiser, but turn readers off. Lengthy "warm-up" copy that oh-so-slowly eases the reader into your message wastes time and exhausts the reader's patience. When reviewing copy after it is written, cut any and all phrases, sentences, and paragraphs that do not contribute directly to the selling proposition and generate a response. Apply the same ruthlessness to graphic elements. Everything in an advertisement must pull its own weight.

Typography and Design

Unfortunately, too many advertisers fail to pay enough attention to the readability of their type. They reverse white type out of black backgrounds, or, even worse, run light-colored type against four-color backgrounds, for no apparent reason other than to be different or to highlight a key selling proposition. Advertisers use uninviting, even ugly, typefaces that inhibit readability, printing it too small to see easily. And then they complain that their ads don't work.

Making it harder for the reader to stick with your message encourages page turning—and no response. Reading white-on-black type is 10.5 percent slower than reading equal size black-on-white type, according to psychological research.[58] And as *New Equipment Digest* points out, few of the top lead-producing ads it has run indulge in reversed type. Even fewer have type reversed against a multi-color photographic background.[59] Not only is such type hard to read because the letters don't stand out, the slightest problem with press registration (the alignment of different colors to compose a photo) renders such copy totally unreadable.

White-on-black type can be useful in certain situations, such as when a layout demands it (e.g. a short copy block appearing in a full-page photo of a nighttime scene). But the type must be large enough to read easily: at least two points larger than black-on-white type of equivalent readability.

Capital letters. All-caps type, frequently used to add emphasis to headlines, nonetheless detracts from readability, comprehension, and reader comfort with an ad. Type set in lower-case letters reads 13.4 percent faster, research says.[60]

Typefaces. Serifs, those design elements added to the strokes of printed letters, were designed as aids to readability. Hence the enduring popularity of serif typefaces (e.g. Garamond, Century) for body copy, as compared to sans-serif faces (e.g. Univers, Helvetica). Art directors often use a sans-serif face for the large type of a headline, however, to contrast it with the serif face of body copy.

But the distinction between the two types of faces probably isn't critical. Asking separate samples of readers and art directors to rank their typeface preferences, Cahners found readers choosing a serif face first for headlines and a sans-serif face for body copy. Art directors favored the serif face for body text and the sans-serif for headlines.[61]

There is much wider agreement that italic type is harder to read than roman. Use italics only for emphasis in body type, and sparingly, if at all, in advertising headlines.

Typesetting. Most advertising body text, and increasing amounts of editorial text, run with ragged-right margins, with or without hyphenation. Does that help or hinder comprehension, compared to right- and left-justified type? Psychological research says no.[62]

Your Advertising Response Formats

In Chapter 3, we examined in detail how buyers collect information and make purchase decisions. They turn to a variety of response devices to meet their needs, some of which greatly facilitate inquiry sight qualification.

Reader Service Cards

The workhorse of advertising lead generation is the ubiquitous reader service card publishers bind into their issues to facilitate response. By circling numbers (hence the common reference to reader service cards as "bingo cards") or otherwise recording their requests, readers complete the card, write in their addresses and perhaps other classification information, and mail or fax the card back to the periodical's publisher. The publisher in turn sorts the inquiries by advertiser and sends the readers' names and information requests to each advertiser by mail, fax, or electronic mail.

The reader service card is a low-cost, high-yield source of raw leads, easy for prospects to use and important to a publisher's ability to serve advertisers. But they have their drawbacks. Reader service cards are slow; the many days or weeks required to get responses back to advertisers can frustrate the reader. The hottest inquiries increasingly travel by phone and fax.

Evidently, readers also fear their response card requests don't allow them to ask for what they really need. In focus groups conducted by Thomas Publishing's *Industrial Equipment News,* participants expressed "feelings that the format contributes to inaccuracy. That is, because you cannot explain your need, you often don't get the kind of information you need." Participants complained that the cramped spaces with small numbers led to errors processing their inquiries.[63]

Write-in cards overcome that problem, but the extra work they require can depress the response an advertiser might have liked to receive. *Industrial*

Equipment News focus groups found that inquirers like it in concept, but in practice consider it "busy work." Advertisers tend to ignore the extra information anyway, focus group participants complained. Advertisers often fail to provide requested price lists, and they send general catalogs even when inquirers specified a narrow application.[64]

Reader service card formats. *Industrial Equipment News* says it invented the reader service card in 1933. Back then, readers mailed letters requesting more information about a product. To make that easier, the magazine's founder introduced "brevity numbers" for each advertised product. Shortly thereafter, the publication printed the numbers on a business reply card.

Since then the concept of the reader service card hasn't changed, but it's format has been varied. Exhibit 6-5 shows a typical publication reader service card aimed at a general business or hobbyist market. *PC Computing* magazine puts two cards on the same sheet of card insert stock so more than one reader can respond. The magazine carries the insert adjacent to its advertiser index pages. The card offers "free product information" and separates the reader service card numbers keyed to advertising from those referring to editorial product news.

PC Computing's card also asks where the inquirer uses a computer, his or her type of computer, the hardware and software used, and where the inquirer buys personal computer products. Of course, whether or not that information is useful is up to the advertiser.

Note, however, that it's a crowded card, unable to gather much information about the inquirer or the need involved. Nor does the typical reader service card allow the inquirer to indicate the urgency of the request.

Homing in on a more specialized audience, Gordon Publications' *Laser & Optronics* product tabloid collects more extensive information with a huge reader service card that the inquirer is to fold before mailing. (See Exhibit 6-6.) Like many publications serving focused industrial audiences, *Laser & Optronics* seeks information about the inquirer's job function, technological involvement and media exposure, company size and industry, pass-along readership and—very important to advertisers—product purchasing plans for the next 12 months.

The card is, however, a crowded information-gathering environment. And while it gathers some key category buying intention information, it does not indicate the urgency of a specific request to a specific advertiser.

The reader service card of *New Equipment Digest*, shown in Exhibit 6-7, illustrates one way to address that need. It invites inquirers to circle a number "for more information," to draw a line through the number if they "urgently need information" and to draw an X through it to "have a salesman call." Being a

Exhibit 6-5:
PC Computing RSC

FREE PRODUCT INFORMATION **PC WORLD**

NAME

TITLE

COMPANY

ADDRESS

CITY   STATE   ZIP

PHONE (   )   FAX (   )

INFORMATION FROM ADVERTISERS

Circle the number corresponding to the product or product category you need to know more about. Mail or fax the completed card today. Manufacturers will send product information directly to you. Fax to (413) 637-4343.

PRODUCTS FEATURED IN EDITORIAL

PRODUCT CATEGORY INFORMATION   03/94

For information on all of the products mentioned in an article or an entire category of advertised products, circle the appropriate number below.

Editorial Features (see article for numbers)

Advertised Products
951 Desktop computers   955 Accounting software   959 Multimedia products
952 Notebook computers   956 Draw/paint software   960 Utilities
953 DTP/Presentation software 957 Network/sharing products 961 Mail order companies
954 Monitors and video boards 958 Printers   962 Storage devices

Check this box for your subscription to PC WORLD. You will be billed $19.97 for a 1-year (12 issue) subscription (U.S. only).

March 1994   This card expires July 14, 1994   L1

Free Product Information

For quicker response, fax to (413) 637-4343.

BUSINESS REPLY MAIL
FIRST CLASS MAIL   PERMIT NO. 758   PITTSFIELD, MA

POSTAGE WILL BE PAID BY ADDRESSEE

NO POSTAGE
NECESSARY
IF MAILED
IN THE
UNITED STATES

PC WORLD

Product Information Center
P.O. Box 5330
Pittsfield, MA 01203-9871

FREE PRODUCT INFORMATION **PC WORLD**

NAME

TITLE

COMPANY

ADDRESS

CITY   STATE   ZIP

PHONE (   )   FAX (   )

INFORMATION FROM ADVERTISERS

Circle the number corresponding to the product or product category you need to know more about. Mail or fax the completed card today. Manufacturers will send product information directly to you. Fax to (413) 637-4343.

PRODUCTS FEATURED IN EDITORIAL

PRODUCT CATEGORY INFORMATION   03/94

For information on all of the products mentioned in an article or an entire category of advertised products, circle the appropriate number below.

Editorial Features (see article for numbers)

Advertised Products
951 Desktop computers   955 Accounting software   959 Multimedia products
952 Notebook computers   956 Draw/paint software   960 Utilities
953 DTP/Presentation software 957 Network/sharing products 961 Mail order companies
954 Monitors and video boards 958 Printers   962 Storage devices

Check this box for your subscription to PC WORLD. You will be billed $19.97 for a 1-year (12 issue) subscription (U.S. only).

March 1994   This card expires July 14, 1994   L3

Exhibit 6-6
Laser 7 Optronics RSC

TEAR OUT THIS POST- CARD NOW!

As you review each page in this issue, circle the numbers corresponding to the products and equipment you'd like to learn about. Please be sure to complete all items on the card.

TEAR HERE

April 1994 Card Expires August 1994

USE THIS CARD FOR
FREE
INFORMATION/ SUBSCRIPTION

Lasers & Optronics®

Please sign here if you wish to receive (continue to receive) LASERS & OPTRONICS — FREE.

Signature _____ Date _____

Print Name _____ Phone _____

Title _____ Fax _____

Please make corrections on printed address. If none appears, fill in below.

Is this your company address? ☐ Yes ☐ No

1. ☐ Please indicate your principal job function: (insert one letter only)
Management Related Functions
(A) Technical
(B) Production & Manufacturing
(C) Corporate
(D) Purchasing
(E) Other Management Function (specify)
(K) Other Science or Engineering Function:
Science & Engineering Related Functions
(F) Research & Development
(G) Design
(H) Application
(I) Production
(J) Measurement (Testing, Quality Control, or Safety)
(L) Consultant
(M) Educator
(S) Other (specify)

Other Functions: _____

2. ☐ Please indicate the primary end product or service of your company at this location: (insert one letter only)
Research & Development
(41) University Level
(42) For-Profit Corporation (Not Product-Oriented)
(43) Federally Funded Laboratory (Military or Civilian)
(93) Government Personnel Not Elsewhere Classified
Materials, Supplies, or Services for Optics Fabrication
(34) Data Processing and Storage Equipment
(35) Data & Information Display & Output Equipment
Equipment
(51) Finished Optical Components and Systems
(52) Electro-optical Components
(53) Lasers/Laser Systems
(54) Support Equipment for Categories 50, 51, 52, 53
(87) Consulting
(60) Other (specify)

(30) Manufacturer Incorporating Optical, Electro-optical, Laser, and Fiberoptic Components in the End Product Not Classified above.
(39) Industrial End-User Using Optical, Electro-optical and/or Machine Vision Equipment in Manufacturing and/or Materials Control Activities.
(40) Commercial User of Optical, Electro-optical, Laser, or Fiberoptic Products.

3. In the course of your work, I'm involved in the following areas of technology: (check all that apply)
(A) Lasers ☐ (B) Fiberoptics ☐ (C) Optics ☐ (D) Electro-optics ☐ (E) Other (specify)
(F) Photonics Spectra (G) R&D
(H) Mini-Systems (I) Laser Focus World
(J) Lightwave

4. Which publications do you receive personally?
(A) ☐ Yes ☐ At home ☐ At work

5. Number of employees at this site: (insert code number)
(1) 1–19 (2) 20–49 (3) 50–99 (4) 100–499 (5) 500–999 (6) Over 1000

6. How many other individuals do or will regularly read your copy of *Lasers & Optronics*? (write number in the next 12 months)

In your work, do you use: A ☐ PCs B ☐ Mini-Systems C ☐ Mainframe D ☐ In home
Do you currently have CD ROM capabilities? A ☐ Yes B ☐ No

A

Circle the number for product information desired

101 102 103 104 105 106 107 108 109 110 111 112 113 114 115 116 117 118 119 120 121 122 123 124 125 126 127
128 129 130 131 132 133 134 135 136 137 138 139 140 141 142 143 144 145 146 147 148 149 150 151 152 153 154
155 156 157 158 159 160 161 162 163 164 165 166 167 168 169 170 171 172 173 174 175 176 177 178 179 180 181
182 183 184 185 186 187 188 189 190 191 192 193 194 195 196 197 198 199 200 201 202 203 204 205 206 207 208
209 210 211 212 213 214 215 216 217 218 219 220 221 222 223 224 225 226 227 228 229 230 231 232 233 234 235
236 237 238 239 240 241 242 243 244 245 246 247 248 249 250 251 252 253 254 255 256 257 258 259 260 261 262
263 264 265 266 267 268 269 270 271 272 273 274 275 276 277 278 279 280 281 282 283 284 285 286 287 288 289
290 291 292 293 294 295 296 297 298 299 300 301 302 303 304 305 306 307 308 309 310 311 312 313 314 315 316
317 318 319 320 321 322 323 324 325 326 327 328 329 330 331 332 333 334 335 336 337 338 339 340 341 342 343
344 345 346 347 348 349 350 351 352 353 354 355 356 357 358 359 360 361 362 363 364 365 366 367 368 369 370
371 372 373 374 375 376 377 378 379 380 381 382 383 384 385 386 387 388 389 390 391 392 393 394 395 396 397
398 399 400 401 402 403 404 405 406 407 408 409 410 411 412 413 414 415 416 417 418 419 420 421 422 423 424
425 426 427 428 429 430 431 432 433 434 435 436 437 438 439 440 441 442 443 444 445 446 447 448 449 450 451
452 453 454 455 456 457 458 459 460 461 462 463 464 465 466 467 468 469 470 471 472 473 474 475 476 477 478
479 480 481 482 483 484 485 486 487 488 489 490 491 492 493 494 495 496 497 498 499 500 501 502 503 504 505
506 507 508 509 510 511 512 513 514 515 516 517 518 519 520 521 522 523 524 525 526 527 528 529 530 531 532

Please help us with our market research and tell us what your organization's purchasing plans for optical detectors over the next 12 months.

Which of the following types of detectors do you expect to purchase in the next 12 months (check all that apply)?
01 ☐ Silicon Photodiodes, Avalanche
02 ☐ Silicon Photodiodes, p-n, p-i-n, etc.
03 ☐ Photomultiplier Tubes
04 ☐ Thermal Detectors (bolometers, thermopiles, etc.)
05 ☐ Lead-Salt Detectors (PbS, PbSe, etc.)
06 ☐ III-V Photodiodes, Avalanche (InGaAs)
07 ☐ III-V Photodiodes, p-n, p-i-n, etc. (InGaAs, InSb, etc.)
08 ☐ Germanium Photodiodes, Avalanche
09 ☐ Germanium Photodiodes, Other
10 ☐ Pyroelectric Detectors (TGS, LiTaO₃, etc.)
11 ☐ HgCdTe or MnCdTe Detectors
12 ☐ Far Infrared Detectors

In which of the following do you expect to make measurements (check all that apply)?
13 ☐ Ultraviolet (<400 nm)
14 ☐ Visible (400 - 700 nm)
15 ☐ Near Infrared (700 - 2000 nm)
16 ☐ Middle Infrared (2 - 8 μm)
17 ☐ "Thermal" Infrared (8 - 14 μm)
18 ☐ Far Infrared (>14 μm)

What is the fastest rise time to which these detectors must respond?
19 ☐ 1 ms or longer
20 ☐ 100 μs
21 ☐ 10 μs
22 ☐ 1 μs
23 ☐ 100 ns
24 ☐ 10 ns
25 ☐ 1 ns
26 ☐ <1 ns

What is the minimum power these detectors must reliably detect?
27 ☐ 1 W or more
28 ☐ 100 mW
29 ☐ 10 mW
30 ☐ 1 mW
31 ☐ 100 μW
32 ☐ 10 μW
33 ☐ 1 μW
34 ☐ 100 nW
35 ☐ 10 nW
36 ☐ 1 nW or less

In the next 12 months, how much do you expect to spend on optical detectors of all types? Include built-ins such as preamps and dewars, as appropriate.
37 ☐ <$1,000
38 ☐ $1,000 - $3,000
39 ☐ $3,001 - $5,000
40 ☐ $5,001 - $8,000
41 ☐ $8,001 - $12,000
42 ☐ $12,001 - $16,000
43 ☐ $16,001 - $20,000
44 ☐ $20,001 - $25,000
45 ☐ $25,001 - $30,000
46 ☐ >$30,000

Which companies first come to mind when you are considering the purchase of pyroelectric detectors (check your top four only)?
47 ☐ Coherent
48 ☐ Coherent Infrared
49 ☐ Delta Developments
50 ☐ Edo Corp. (formerly Barnes Eng.)
51 ☐ EG&G Heimann Optoelectronics GmbH
52 ☐ Eltec Instruments
53 ☐ Gentec
54 ☐ Graseby Infrared
55 ☐ Hamamatsu
56 ☐ InfraRed Associates
57 ☐ International Light
58 ☐ ISI Group
59 ☐ Laser Probe
60 ☐ Microwatt Applications
61 ☐ Molectron Detector
62 ☐ New England Research Center
63 ☐ Ohel
64 ☐ Scientech
65 ☐ Sensor/Physics
66 ☐ Servo Corp.
67 ☐ Siemens
68 ☐ Spiricon

Do you plan to use general-purpose instrumentation control software in the next 12 months with your photodetection systems?
69 ☐ Yes, already have
70 ☐ Yes, plan to write or sub-contract custom software
71 ☐ Yes, plan to use commercial package
72 ☐ Yes, plan to purchase commercial software
73 ☐ Uncertain at this time
74 ☐ Do not plan to automate at this time

general-interest new product tabloid for many manufacturing industries, *New Equipment Digest* doesn't collect buying plans information via its reader service card.

Industrial Equipment News, another major manufacturing product tabloid, asks readers to expend more effort. Instead of providing numbers to circle and check-off boxes, its reader service card asks inquirers to prequalify themselves for a limited number of specific information requests. (See Exhibit 6-8.)

The *Industrial Equipment News* card asks inquirers to write the reader service card number on the card, indicate if their "need is current," and provide an original-equipment manufacturing application. The card also allows inquirers to request one or more of five actions from the publisher or the advertiser: "have tech rep call;" "name nearest dealer;" "send price list;" "send literature;" and "have advertiser fax info." There also is room to indicate the applications they have in mind. Below the space allocated for 10 of those detailed requests, the reader has 9 boxes in which to write the reader service numbers of advertisers who should "send literature only."

Seeking even more information to pass along to advertisers, the "Request for Quotation" full-page questionnaire printed in *PC Week* invites readers to complete a detailed questionnaire about their product needs and the systems on which products will run. (See Exhibit 6-9.) Readers fax the form to the publication which distributes it to the vendors specified by the reader.

Multiple bingo numbers. There is a simple way to use virtually any reader service card format to collect prequalification information from inquirers: use two or more reader service numbers in your ad. Publishers are usually willing to accommodate the request from an advertiser in good standing. But you do have to ask for it.

The approach that works best in most situations is the dual-bingo option. Give the inquirer a specific, unambiguous choice. We recommend this wording, which experience shows works best.

- "Send free literature."
- "Call me. I'm interested."

Tell inquirers to circle one reader service number if they only want literature, or circle the other if the need is urgent and your salespeople should call. Obviously, inquirers choosing the second number are high-priority inquiries ready to send to the sales force without delay!

Salespeople pounce on the lead when they know the inquirer has specifically asked for the call. And their excitement carries over to the entire program. At Zero Corp., the 10 percent of inquiries circling the "call me now" number turned out to be such hot leads that energized salespeople personally followed up on 40 percent more of the "send literature" inquiries as well.

Exhibit 6-7
New Equipment Digest RSC

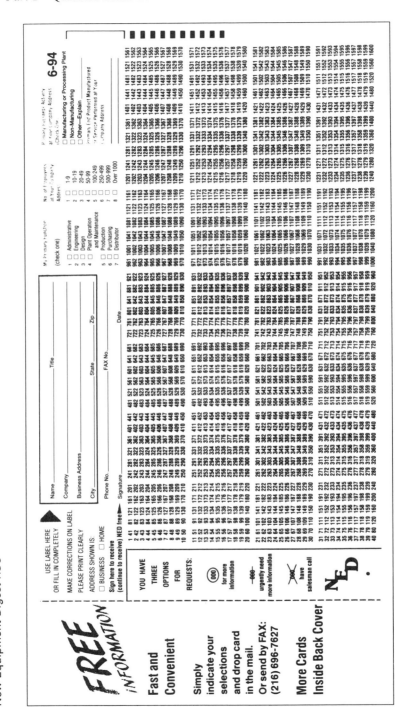

Exhibit 6-8

Industrial Equipment News RSC

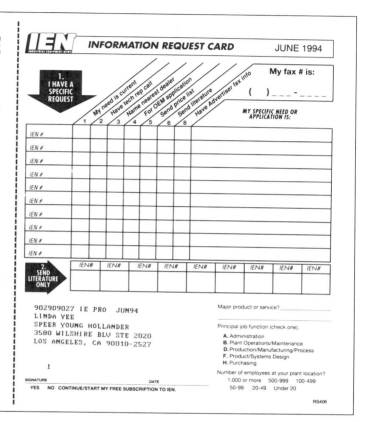

Exhibit 6-9
PC Week Page

PC WEEK'S REQUEST FOR QUOTATION

PC WEEK now has a way to simplify the process of gathering product pricing information with its Request for Quotation. By filling out the form below you will receive price quotations from equipment vendors through the support of PC WEEK. Just follow the instructions on the Request for Quotation form below.

PCWEEK RFQ REQUEST FOR QUOTATION

For your FREE demo disk of Relay/PC Gold Release 6 just check here. ☐

(Please allow 4-6 Weeks for delivery)

For The Personal Attention Of:

Please fill in all the information requested. IMPORTANT: Include your fax number so detailed information can be returned to you as fast as possible.

Vendors will respond to your RFQ directly.

PCWEEK

Name ____
Title ____
Company Name ____
Division/Mail Stop ____
Address ____
City ____ State ____ Zip ____
Phone ____ Fax ____

Your function in this purchase? ☐ VAR/VAD/Reseller ☐ Internal System Integrator ☐ Other ____

When will you be purchasing these products? ☐ Within the next week ☐ 7 to 14 days ☐ 15 to 30 days ☐ 31 to 60 days

System Vendors

☐ Acer ☐ AST ☐ Digital ☐ Hewlett Packard ☐ Texas Instruments
☐ ALR ☐ Compaq ☐ ExpoTech ☐ IBM ☐ Toshiba
☐ Ambra ☐ Dell ☐ Gateway ☐ NEC ☐ Zeos International

PCs (D= Desktop, S= Server, N= Notebook)

Type	# of units	Hard Drive	RAM	Monitor	Other
EXAMPLE 486/33	10	120MB	4MB	SVGA	Tower Case
386/20	5	80MB	4MB		

Software (App. Dev., Graphics, Databases, etc.)

Type	# of units	OS	Host/Standalone
Database	4	DOS	Host

Peripherals (Printers, Modems, Fax, etc.)

Type	# of units	Configuration
Laser Printer	3	10-12 pages per minute

Networking (NICS, Hubs, Bridges, etc.)

Type	# of units	Topology	Configuration
Hub	5	Ether Net	

9345

FAX THIS COMPLETED FORM TO 1-800-800-0880

For more RFQ information call 1-800-451-1032 ext. 3756

PCWEEK RFQ REQUEST FOR QUOTATION

FREE DEMO DISK!

Relay/PC Gold for Windows

The one communications package that can solve all your corporate communications needs. Now with TCP/IP Telnet, TN3270, and LAN gateway support.

To get a free demo disk simply check the box on the RFQ form and Fax it in today.

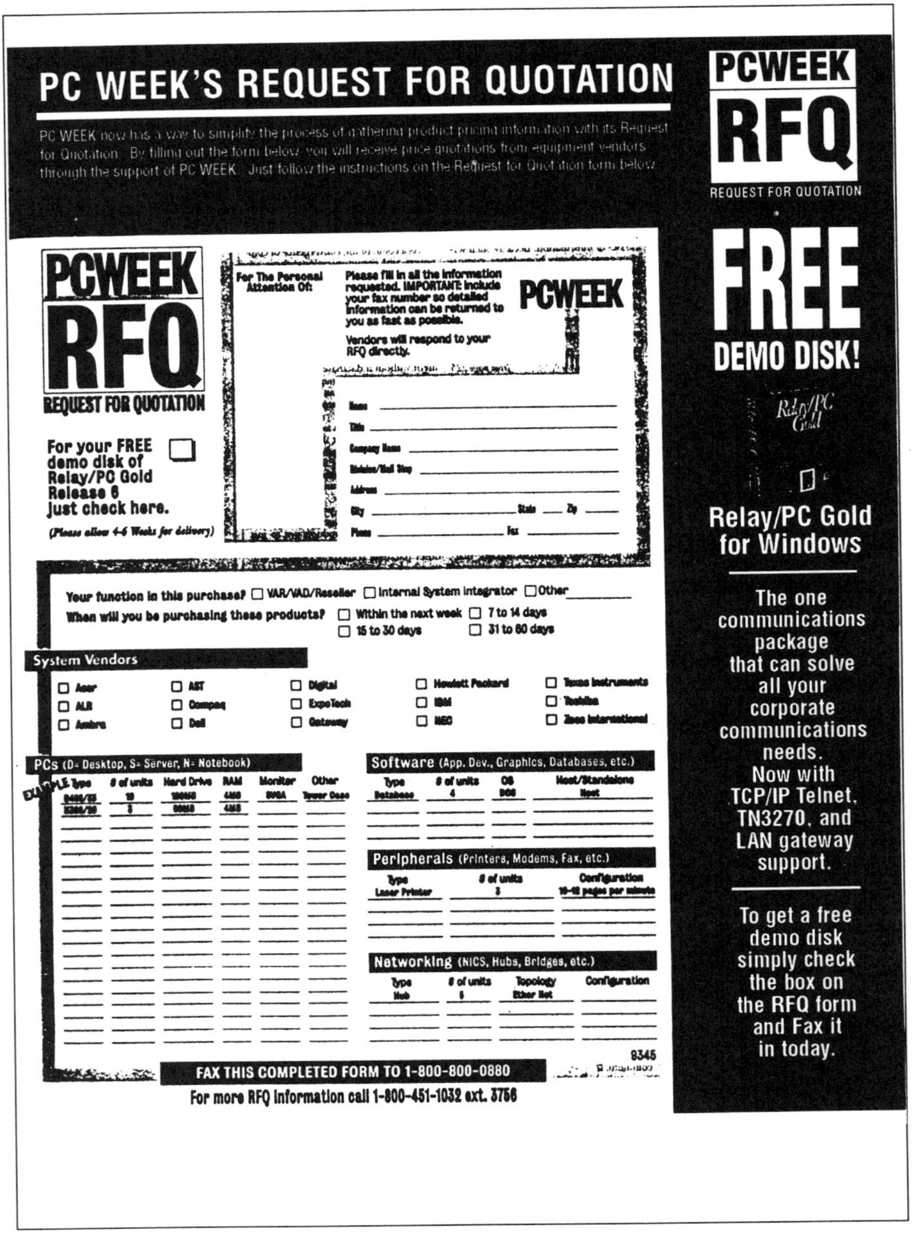

Skeptics sometimes do not believe it until they see it, but readers actually do check the "call me, I'm interested" option. We've seen upwards of 30 percent of inquiries making that request of well-written advertisements. The advertiser has nothing to lose by at least testing the dual-bingo option.

Using more than two numbers usually is not worth the effort, however, unless you are making some sort of multiple presentation in an advertisement, such as technical literature offers. Fine gradations of response can confuse readers and leave you tracking multiple databases that have little practical difference.

To avoid confusion in your lead system, be consistent with bingo number assignments in all your ads. Make all "send literature" numbers even, for instance, and all "please have a salesperson call" numbers odd.

Alas, dual reader service numbers aren't foolproof. Sometimes readers seeking only literature check the more urgent option nevertheless, particularly if it is an ambiguous invitation, thinking that will help them get a faster response. Although that shouldn't be the case, with some advertisers it will! And some readers with an urgent need might not want to call an 800-number nor circle the "call me" number, fearing a sales visit for which they are not quite ready.

Publisher responsiveness. Details count when publications transmit reader service inquiries to advertisers. How quickly does a publication receive, sort, batch, and transmit reader service card inquiries? Does the publisher send inquiries to advertisers weekly? Biweekly? Monthly? Fulfillment and eventual sales will suffer the longer the publisher takes to process reader service cards. We've seen companies that have fast in-house fulfillment programs nonetheless suffer a 60-day lag getting information to prospects because of publisher delays. With today's computer and scanner technologies, there's no excuse for lengthy sorting periods.

How much information does the publisher provide about each inquiry, and are the data easily integrated into your inquiry management system? You should not expect the publisher to prequalify leads for you, but you should be able to rely on receiving information that makes your qualification job easier.

Reply Coupons

Adding a reply coupon to your advertisement can be a powerful response builder, increasing both the number and quality of inquiries you'll generate, and which come directly to you. A sample appears in Exhibit 6-10.

There's also some evidence that coupons can increase the readership of your ad. Eye-tracking research finds reader involvement with an ad increases 34 to 93 percent with coupons, as long as they stand out and aren't overshadowed by

Exhibit 6-10
Sample In-Ad Reply Coupon

strong visuals elsewhere in an ad.[65] Readership studies meanwhile found that ads with coupons average 13 percent greater recognition scores than ads without them, says Cahners Publishing.[66]

Some advertisers generate as much as 40 percent more inquiries by adding a reply coupon to their ads. We've even heard claims that response doubled. The coupons encourage a response, often by phone.

Anyone taking the time to fill out a reply coupon is likely to be a genuine self-qualified prospect whose name can be sent directly to the field. Use check boxes on the coupon, asking if the inquirer wants a sales call or literature only. You can also collect additional qualification information such as company size, type, etc. But don't make it too hard for readers to inquire. Because the real estate on advertising pages is expensive and because writers are tempted to cram as much sell copy into an ad as possible, many in-ad coupons wind up ridiculously small. Even worse, some advertisers have printed coupons in reverse type, white lines on a black background!

Always print reply coupons in black on a very light, preferably white, background. Separate lines by at least a quarter-inch to make them easy to write upon. And be sure the coupon contains your phone number (preferably a toll-free number), and then your full company name and address. If the coupon becomes separated from the ad, the inquirer still knows where to send it.

Note that we suggest printing the phone number prominently, ahead of the address on the coupon, just as you would do in the main body of the ad. That's because you really want your interested prospects to call rather than mail a coupon, so you can get to them as soon as possible ahead of the competition.

And make it clear what you expect readers to do with the coupon. Put a heavy dashed line around it. Adding a little scissors symbol at a corner helps to get the point across. And be explicit: ad copy should say something like, "For more information, please fill out and mail the coupon below."

Business Reply Cards

Limited ad space, getting attention, gathering qualification information, and ease of response are benefits that often argue for using bound-in business reply cards (BRCs) adjacent to your ad. The card jumps out from the publication when the reader turns to your message; the card helps the publication open automatically to your page. Depending upon the product and the specific offer made to inquirers, we've seen BRCs nearly double response to an ad. In terms of readership, the average ad accompanied by a BRC achieves 29 percent more readership than the average ad without, says Cahners.[67] Publications often claim that BRCs in their pages generate proportionally more leads for the dollar than a full-page ad without the card.

Readers appreciate the no-postage convenience of a card they can fill out, rip from the issue, and drop in the mail. The size of a card, larger than a coupon, allows you to collect additional qualification information from the inquirer. And few things motivate a salesperson to follow up an inquiry as does a business reply card with the prospect's own writing asking to see a rep.

Publisher's rate cards usually specify extra charges for BRCs, but as a practical matter they should be a negotiable item provided as part of the ad schedule. You might get the BRC bound adjacent to your page very inexpensively. With saddle-stitched magazines and newspapers, a publisher often has a card scheduled either for another advertiser or for circulation promotion; your BRC runs on the other half of the card at negligible additional cost to the publication.

Electronic Response

Modern technology puts inquiries into advertiser's hands quickly, if not immediately, providing a critical advantage to a lead program. For example, service bureaus processing reader service cards for publishers cut an advertiser's inquiry-receipt time by one to three weeks through a special service option. Rather than wait for inquiry names to arrive in the mail, advertisers call remote computer databases to download the latest batch. Buyers, meanwhile, like the instant gratification of fax-back responses and toll-free telephone numbers. While adopting electronic response mechanisms might not provide a competitive advantage, operating without them in today's markets is a competitive disadvantage.

The range of electronic tools available for on-line response promises to grow with the "information highway" discussed earlier. Buyers will routinely access catalogs, periodicals, and advertisements on-line via computer, an area where computer magazine publishers Ziff Communications and International Data Group have been natural pioneers.[68]

Toll-free telephone numbers and fax are diminishing publisher involvement in the advertising-lead process. When *Industrial Equipment News* asked inquirers in 1992 about their most recent information requests, slightly more than half, 56 percent, said they used a reader service card, nearly all of them saying it was their usual method. About 40 percent telephoned the company, and just one percent of respondents said they had faxed their most recent requests.[69]

To keep pace with change, enlightened publishers help advertisers generate phone and fax leads. *Industrial Equipment News,* for example, includes "Express Fax" cards in issues, making it easier for readers to fax an inquiry with their name and address to an advertiser or to the publisher. Growing ranks of publications now list advertisers' inquiry phone and fax numbers alongside reader service numbers in back-of-the-book advertiser indexes.

Evidently, receiving information *from* advertisers by fax is more widespread than using fax to solicit inquiries. The same *Industrial Equipment News* survey found about a quarter of inquirers asking the advertiser to fax information back to them. Among those who needed information fast and called the advertiser, 40 percent asked for fax-back information, compared to just 11 percent of reader service card inquirers. Incidentally, 29 percent of inquirers who called advertisers bought within a month of their inquiry, according to that survey, compared to 9 percent of those using reader service cards.[70]

Fax-on-demand service completes the electronic-response loop by providing instant fulfillment of information requests. Inquirers call the advertiser on their fax lines, request information by punching in a code, and let the advertiser's fax send the data back, all in one call. One software company, for example, said it cut fulfillment costs from $5 per inquiry to 25 cents with fax-on-demand.[71]

Fax-on-demand service isn't a panacea, however. Facsimile of any stripe is superb for sending the latest specifications and technical drawings (having a spec sheet with a time and date stamp is important to some inquirers), but it's a poor way to transmit photographic art, multiple-page documents and the color promotion pieces important to building a professional, substantive corporate image. Although automated fax-back captures the caller's fax number, it often fails to record name, company, voice phone number, and other vital lead information without human intervention. We will discuss this important medium further, in the chapter on fulfillment.

More Response Tips

In the category of little things that sometimes get overlooked in the preparation of an advertisement are the following.

- Mnemonics work well for toll-free phone numbers, such as 800-GO-SLUGS for a pest extermination service, particularly for outdoor and broadcast advertising. But in an ad or brochure, put the associated numerals (800-467-5847 in our example) underneath the mnemonic in smaller type. Some people hate to hunt for letters on the telephone dial. And many phones no longer carry the letters in the first place. Avoid the letter *O* if you can. People tend to confuse it with the zero key for the operator.

- Use different 800-numbers for different lead sources. Then you can evaluate each source's productivity, in creative ways, if necessary. For example, a television advertiser that had used one number thought inquirers were calling at the time the ad aired. But using different numbers for commercials airing at different times of the day, the advertiser learned that inquirers often waited until the weekend to call even though they had seen the commercial during the week. Weekend viewing, once thought to be a strong time for the advertiser's commercials, proved to be a weak one instead.[72]

- Be attentive to the needs of special media audiences. In-flight magazines, for example, are very popular with business product and service advertisers because they reach a mobile, reasonably affluent business audience. But individual copies of an airline publication get used and abused with each reader handling them. To take advantage of in-flight pass-along readership, use BRCs adjacent to your ad, and gang several BRCs on one card insert, perforated so they can be ripped out separately.

- When designing your coupon or BRC, ask for the inquirer's phone number first, before the address. You'll need the phone number for telequalification and for the salesperson attempting to make an appointment. If you ask for the phone number after the address, the inquirer often thinks you've got enough information, and leaves the phone number space blank.

The Untapped Potential of Publicity Leads

Closely related to advertising because it primarily uses the same mass communications media to reach the same audiences, publicity can be a very effective and efficient inquiry generator. It's a part of the public relations function and a complement to communications effects a company tries to achieve with paid-space advertising. On average, publicity provides companies with 24 percent of their inquiries, in our experience. And in a Cahners publishing survey, two-thirds of business advertisers rated publicity as "extremely" or "somewhat" effective, compared to a 78 percent rating for advertising. (See Exhibit 5-2.)

Myths and Realities

Publicity doesn't get the respect it deserves. Advertisers apparently do not understand the medium. Treated carelessly by advertisers and their salespeople, publicity leads receive less follow-up, which makes them appear to be weaker than they are. Used correctly, however, publicity inquiries represent untapped potential that competitors let slip by.

Myth #1—Publicity is free advertising. Unfortunately persistent and widespread, the belief that publicity is somehow "free" stems from the fact that news service publications don't charge a fee when they write about a company, its products or services in their editorial columns. A few people even equate advertising and publicity space, claiming, for instance, that an inch of favorable editorial mention has the same marketing value as an inch of advertising in the same publication. It does not.

Actually, publicity could have more value than an equivalent amount of advertising space. Objectivity—favorable reviews, or just the evidence that a publication considers a product newsworthy—can provide a strong boost to your awareness and reputation advertising cannot match. No one has figured out a reliable way to directly compare the marketing effects of advertising and publicity.

Furthermore, publicity is not free to begin with. Writing and placing articles and news releases requires marcom staff or agency effort, and the time of executive and engineering personnel. The investments might not pay off; companies cannot control what legitimate publications and broadcast outlets say editorially, whether or not they advertise.

Myth #2—Publishers owe advertisers the extra marketing support. Publishers and space salespeople naturally portray themselves as the advertiser's marketing partner, always willing to help. But, dedication to the advertiser's well-being usually isn't shared by the editors of quality publications, whose job is to attract and hold the interest of the readers who make those magazines and newspapers worthy advertising media in the first place.

Some space salespeople mislead unsophisticated advertisers by implying that buying space also buys the attention of editors—which might be true at publications desperate for revenue. Or, publishers may succumb to pressure from a manipulative advertiser who understands just how far the size of his advertising budget will allow him to push for what editors sneeringly call "puff" coverage. Some amateurish advertisers try to pander with a press release come-on such as, "We may advertise if our editorial item generates sufficient reader response." Legitimate publications ignore such baloney.

Yet, even in legitimate publications with complete editorial independence, advertising can help an advertiser receive publicity. Editors read, too, and advertising educates them about a company, its products and what it stands for, making it more likely they will spot the company's press releases amidst the blizzard of announcements flooding editors' desks.

Myth #3—Publicity leads aren't worth following up. This is mainly a self-fulfilling prophecy. Without follow-up, who can know the overall quality of publicity inquiries? Obviously, it will vary by source and portal of entry. A phone call from the prospect asking about a product in an article certainly represents a lead worth checking.

Reinforcement and Reconnaissance

With its unique strength as communication bearing the implied endorsement of independent editors, publicity can reinforce your ad program and serve additional marketing objectives. For example, publicity campaigns can test the potential appeal of your product or service to new markets. If editors in publications serving those markets think you have something to offer, readers are likely to think so, too.

A protective coatings manufacturer, for example, enjoyed a brisk business in the utility and oil refinery business selling a anti-corrosion material used on underground pipes. Experimenting one Friday afternoon, the marketing manager studied *Bacon's Publicity Checker*—a reference list of U.S. publications—looking for oddball places to send some press releases. Three months later, she started receiving leads from mortuaries. She called the publisher of the publication providing the leads, and learned that the law had changed in some states, allowing undertakers to use coatings on burial caskets rather than enclose them in concrete vaults. She uncovered a genuinely new market for the company's product.

Publicity can also promote company news and market leadership issues that are not appropriate to product advertising. For instance, while a product ad might attract an engineer, an article about your company's customer partnering program could interest purchasing or manufacturing executives. When they inquire, be sensitive to their unique needs; don't send a bounceback card tailored solely to engineers.

Product News

Strive to acquire publicity leads from product tabloids and other consumer and industrial publications stressing new product news. Usually, the announcements are little more than product descriptions—a few paragraphs of information without the hype—typically accompanied by a product photo. It's not unusual for product-news publications to charge modest fees to run announcements and photos. Some attach reader service numbers to the announcements. And if asked, most publications (we've seen cooperation as high as 80 percent in some markets) will give a manufacturer's product news item "dual bingo" reader service numbers (the first number says "Call me, I'm interested;" the second says "Send free literature").

But even product tabloid publicity apparently doesn't get the attention marketers devote to advertising in the same publications. Just 77 percent of *New Equipment Digest* editorial inquirers received the information they sought, compared to 87 percent for advertising inquirers, according to the publication's Did-You-Buy? surveys. Salespeople follow-up is also worse for publicity: 14 percent vs. 19 percent for advertising inquiries.

Those studies, across 1,000 product categories, point out that fewer editorial inquirers than ad inquirers eventually purchased: 20 percent vs. 36 percent. And advertising leads outpaced editorial leads in terms of those "considering purchase." Yet, two-thirds of editorial inquirers said they had a specific application in mind (compared to 77 percent of advertising inquirers), signifying a market potential companies should not ignore.

Interestingly, the average editorial inquirer is more likely to be a hidden buying influence who lacks information about the manufacturer; 88 percent said they'd never seen a salesperson from the company receiving their inquiry, compared to 80 percent for advertising inquirers, *New Equipment Digest* said. And 69 percent said they had not known that the company of which they inquired made the product of their interest, compared with 59 percent of advertising inquirers.[73]

Publicity Techniques

Publicity is but one part of the broader public relations function ranging from sports and event marketing into corporate communications and investor relations, through philanthropy and government lobbying, to customer and community education and goodwill. Not all PR programs intentionally seek sales leads. But many do, including company newsletters and magazines designed to provide a subtle direct mail sell. Here, we focus on generating leads from independent media.

Publicity opportunities abound, and companies recognize that a variety of approaches can serve them well, as shown in Exhibit 6-11.

Press releases. The backbone of the typical publicity program, press releases should concentrate on news of potential interest to readers and viewers. Otherwise, editors will not use them. Product news releases are the kind most likely to generate inquiries; personnel releases are the least likely. But that does make staff changes or other company news unimportant. Every industry is a small-town community, in a sense. Its vendor and buyer companies are neighborhoods, their employees the residents. The specialized business publications serving those markets are the local newspapers. "Names make news," editors like to say, and personnel releases are a simple method for keeping the company name in print in a favorable context.

Technology is making the press release more versatile, with new services appearing ready to expedite your release. Distribution by diskette and on-line, for example, not only gets releases to editors quickly, it provides instant computer text the editor (the lazy editor, critics complain) can send directly to the publication's typesetter. Similarly, local broadcast stations will use all or part of audio and videotape press announcements.

Exhibit 6-11
Most Beneficial Public Relations Activities*

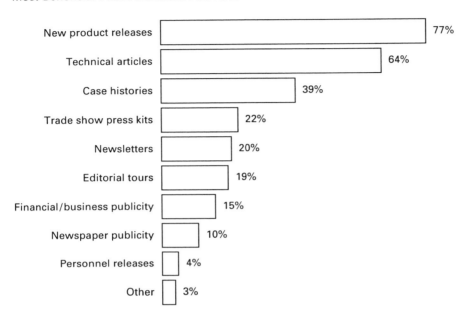

* Percentage of a sample of business-to-business marketers rating an activity as beneficial.

Source: *Here's What Really Matters to Today's Business-to-Business Marketer* (Chicago: Starmark, Inc. and *Business Marketing* magazine, 1988), p. 12.

Use press releases to pitch a feature story to editors, and to maintain a presence for industry-wide "round up" stories. Editors often toss news releases into files for later reference when they decide to cover a subject in depth.

Remember that releases are by definition announcements to everyone. Sometimes you can engineer in-depth coverage by promising an "exclusive" to a key publication in your field and not releasing the news to others. Publications, like marketers anywhere, love to beat the competition. Deciding when to try for an exclusive is not an easy decision, however. It risks angering competitive publications on which your long-term publicity plans also rely. The gamble has to be worth it, so make sure you get your quid pro quo before agreeing to an exclusive release.

Technical publicity. In many consumer and business special interest publications, technical publicity is the single most powerful public relations tool. Whether it's aimed at technical peers of your staff experts or directly at your customers, well-crafted technical publicity addresses reader problems and opportunities head-on, putting your company and its skills at center stage. It shares knowledge selflessly, claims the intellectual high ground of the true expert, and produces highly qualified inquiries. In technically oriented fields such as electronics, savvy companies offer incentives to staff experts writing technical articles.

Study publications serving your target audience well before attempting to place what inevitably must be an exclusive article. Strive to get reader service numbers attached to the article, and be sure readers know where they can call or write directly for more information. The better publications might even have an editor work with your technical author to ensure the article appeals to readers.

Strategically, the article's purpose is to position your company as *the* expert on a topic. It cannot be a sales pitch, which readers won't read and good editors won't publish. When readers feel they are well served and learn something useful from an article you've placed, they will ask you for expertise they feel they can trust.

Case histories. A subset of technical publicity, case histories report "how we did it," or, if written by an outside writer, "how they did it." Even better, write about how your customer did it with your product or service. The objective served is the same: positioning the company and its staff as the experts in solving a problem.

Of course, to have any impact, case histories must be read. So avoid the self-serving "aren't we great?" sagas that turn readers off. Make the case history honest, like real life, revealing some of the fits and starts that bedeviled your search for a solution. And share some of what you learned with readers; they'll come to you for more.

Editorial adjacencies? Advertisers frequently think that if an article mentions them, their ad running in that same issue should appear nearby, if not directly adjacent to the coverage. It's faulty thinking for two reasons.

First, adjacency subtly implies that you might have "paid" for the editorial mention with your advertisement. Perhaps you did and had no choice, but do not let readers think that. You want them to believe you received the coverage because sagacious editors think you deserve it.

Second, although your ad might elaborate on and reinforce the value of the editorial coverage, running adjacent to the article increases the likelihood that those who didn't read the story also missed your ad. On the other hand, you don't want your ad appearing in some section so unrelated to your product that it will only be seen by non-prospects.

Use judgment in working with the publisher to request a position with high prospect visibility that nonetheless gives you two separate shots at customers. Purchasing a premium position for your ad might be worth the extra expense.

Or, if you are not an every-issue advertiser in the publication, and the issue in question is not a "must be in" special, you could shift your ad to another issue to improve your cumulative exposure to the publication's readers over time.

Editorial tours. Inviting key industry journalists to tour the plant, visit the lab, come by and chat with the corporate brass, and otherwise hob-nob with your company is a popular technique, but hardly foolproof. The key to attracting the best editors and actually seeing your story reach print is—no surprise—newsworthiness and reader value. Without it, your expensive press tour will be a low-yield press junket: more an opportunity for an editor to reward a junior editorial staffer with a free trip than a serious mission requiring the attention and effort of the publication's best and busiest journalists.

Your objective is press goodwill, better understanding on the press' part of difficult technical subjects, and the final payoff of a good article heralding your virtues. The editorial tour is expensive, however. Invitations may not impress, and might even offend some journalists whose sense of professional ethics, and possibly publication policy too, prohibit trips unless they pay their own way. Be sure, when you announce the tour, to provide all the information they will need to judge the trip a valuable news-gathering investment.

Sometimes the tour takes you and key technical specialists out to visit the press one by one at editors' offices. Stay relaxed, and rather than try and force a particular story on each publication, suggest ideas casually and let editors find their own angles. They will expect you to answer every question they have, save for confidential information and trade secrets. But editors should not ask you to report what you discussed on your visits to other publications. If you hint that others might be interested in your story, don't be so blatant that editors dismiss it as cheap press agentry.

Press conferences. Conceptually an editorial tour that takes you to all press outlets simultaneously, the press conference is probably the most misused publicity tool. It is easy to stage a poor one, and many companies do, embarrassing corporate brass and endangering the survival of erring publicists. Ask any journalist who's been working in that field for more than a month, and the press conference question draws a snicker.

Despite relentless corporate aspirations to the contrary, a press conference will not generate coverage or inquiries unless you have genuine news to announce. Real news. Big enough news to entice the busy reporters who can do you the most good to show up. And at your industry's big trade show, where dozens of exhibitors vie to stage press conferences, the competition for reporters' time doesn't allow them to go anywhere except to those events with legitimate news. If you refuse to tip reporters off about the content of your announcement in advance, reporters won't show up.

If they do, they're likely to have plenty of questions, so have key technical and management personnel on hand to answer them. Have detailed documentation on hand for those technically minded reporters who need it. When you promise to send out follow-up information, give it your highest priority.

Press conferences often fail because the companies staging them mistakenly treat them as one-way communication sessions. The press expects to establish a dialogue, else why take an hour or more to collect only as much information as a minute of press release reading provides?

Financial publicity. Pitching your company story to investors and the general business community through the general business press (e.g. *The Wall Street Journal, Business Week*) usually is not sales-lead oriented. But it is an important part of building and maintaining a business reputation that's likely to affect the interest potential customers have in your organization. General business publications do report technical stories, told in non-technical terms. Those can be very important in reaching non-technical management corporate buying influences.

Newspaper publicity, typically the daily business sections of regional and local newspapers, aren't major lead producers, but they communicate with key constituencies: governments, local communities, and the like. In some fields, however, newspaper publicity is critical for maintaining an image with customers. In California's Silicon Valley, for example, vendors and buyers live side by side.

Trade show press kits. Business marketers should be especially attentive to the editorial opportunities before, during, and after a major industry trade show, whether or not they exhibit. The key is making sure publicity serves the objectives of your exhibiting strategy. Or, if you don't attend the show, design publicity to tap into the heightened market interest and reportage at the time of the show, and to keep you from disappearing from view while show exhibitors hog the limelight. Vertical publications often struggle to find enough editorial material to fill voluminous show-special issues, giving your news release or article a good chance of appearing in print.

Chapter 7

Mining Inquiry Gold at Trade Shows

An old joke in exhibiting circles, told with innumerable variations, taunts the sales manager who so highly prizes the daily harvest of inquiries at his booth that he locks them in a special steel box each night of his industry's big annual show. At the end of the event, he even takes the box back to his office as personal luggage. But the next year, when he opens the box for the first time, what does he find inside? Last year's leads, just where he'd left them.

A silly little story, it parodies a sorry truth at many companies. Exhibiting is a powerful medium, where buyers and vendors meet under one roof for the show and sell. Yet, despite the considerable investment and effort exhibiting requires, many organizations treat trade show inquiries cavalierly, if not apathetically. Few are shocked by a well-known exhibiting maxim: *70 percent of trade show leads aren't followed up!*

What should you expect from a medium that many companies still treat as a junket, complete with bikini-clad models hawking industrial wares to hungover conventioneers grabbing fistful of key chains to take home to the kids? Old practices die hard; seamy images linger even longer, despite growing professionalism of exhibit managers at many companies.

Closer to the truth about trade shows, however, is that even today, our experience indicates that 70 percent of trade show leads are not handled *properly.* It is an astounding statistic, considering the overall high quality of those leads, and the fact that obtaining them is the overwhelmingly most important reason companies exhibit in the first place. Even if not ignored, show leads are poorly fulfilled, haphazardly nurtured by salespeople, and inadequately tracked and analyzed. Many companies mistakenly believe that the literature they've distributed, the sales they may have made on the floor, the sales appointments lined up with the hottest prospects, and the competitive intelligence gleaned from walking the aisles make the total show experience. But, a show doesn't really end until every lead is handled properly.

Exhibiting is a lot like selling; but instead of you seeking out customers, interested prospects come to visit you. It's not all that easy; not everyone ambling down the aisle is qualified. Yet, you want to be sure you don't miss seeing those who are, particularly if they are also visiting competitors' exhibits. You've got to maximize the selling value of those precious few minutes you've got with a good prospect before he or she moves on.

Add to that the stress trade show selling imposes on field reps commandeered for in-booth duty. Field people usually work independently. They keep score with new orders and call reports. But at the show—often presented as a reward for superior performance in the field—the emphasis switches to teamwork and collective selling, including working with prospects from other reps' sales territories. Without adequate lead follow-up, notes consultant Allen Konopacki, "The team is not scored and it doesn't know if it is winning or losing. . . . they are frustrated and confused about their role; is it to sell, is it for awareness, image, goodwill or just to be nice people?"[1]

In this chapter, we'll look quickly at the big picture of exhibiting and show selection, and concentrate on show lead-generation strategies that will give you an advantage over less disciplined competitors. Remember that successful exhibiting, like successful marketing overall, must include a comprehensive sales lead management system or you are flying blind.

Your Industry's Fundamental Medium

About 85 million visitors troop through the roughly 4,300 shows staged annually in the United States and Canada, says the Trade Show Bureau, the exhibition industry's promotional organization.[2] Show attendees spent a collective $56.6 billion on travel and incidentals in 1991,[3] suffering sore feet, too little sleep, and too much bad food shopping for business products and services. And shop they do. As we saw in Chapter 3, 78 percent of first-time attendees and 85 of the veterans wield buying influence.

The average exhibitor, meanwhile, spends $185 per visitor reached, making leads from bona fide prospects expensive, indeed. Considering, however, that those exhibition contacts are real, face-to-face selling encounters, the trade show industry compares that figure to the $292 cost of the average personal sales call.[4]

Exhibitions are the third most productive source of business-to-business inquiries, behind advertising and publicity sources, providing nearly 12 percent of all inquiries in 1993.[5]

The Trade Show Bureau also points to research saying 54 percent of show leads do not require a follow-up call to close, and that the average sale to a trade show contact therefore closes in 0.8 calls. Considering the number of field sales calls required to complete the average business sale, the Trade Show Bureau reasons that closing the average show lead is 60 percent less expensive: $419 compared to around $1,080. Shows are efficient too; the average booth sees four to five potential buyers in an hour, compared to the four to five sales calls a field salesperson makes daily.[6]

Furthermore, trade shows generate a qualified lead for every 13 contacts, substantially fewer than the 790 impressions the average advertisement must make to develop one qualified lead, or 58 impressions per lead in direct mail and 4,990 impressions per lead from publicity, the Trade Show Bureau contends.[7]

And because show visitors have buying on their minds, they tend to be higher-volume prospects than the average purchasing influence in the field. A survey at the 1993 International Electrical Exhibition and Congress, for example, found attendees planned to purchase 11 times more equipment than similar professionals who did not attend the show.[8]

It's not surprising that such a powerful selling tool keeps expanding. While the pace of growth will slacken a bit through the 1990s compared to the 1980s, says *Tradeshow Week,* the trade show industry is expected to grow 35 percent during the 1990s.[9]

Attendees at today's shows are busier because of corporate restructuring. Not having as much time to see salespeople in their offices, what they seek at trade shows has changed. They are more likely to buy than in the past, making shows more a place to close prospects than they once were, and less a place to simply show the flag, build awareness, and make a statement.[10]

Some 1.2 million companies exhibited in 1992, spending 18 percent of their marketing budgets on show appearances.[11] In a fast-paced industry such as computers, for example, 42 percent of exhibitors had increased their show participation and 60 percent had increased their budgets during the two years preceding a 1991 survey.[12]

Not for Everyone

Of course, those data are industry averages based on exhibition industry-sponsored research and broad trends. Individual exhibitor experiences vary widely. Nor do most companies participate. By the late 1980s just 30 percent of companies that could exhibit actually did, the Trade Show Bureau reckoned.[13] Smaller companies tend to pass the medium by.

Superior marketing can overcome the disadvantages of being small, yet firms that try exhibiting for the first time tend to be poorly prepared. They don't get the payoff they had hoped. About 40 percent of first timers don't return to a show, the Trade Show Bureau has estimated. "A lot of them just go, stand around not doing much, and then swear they're never coming back," said Trade Show Bureau president E. Jane Lorimer. "They don't realize the effort it takes before and after to make a trade show work."[14]

For many, the trade show experience goes wrong at the start, with participation at the wrong show with the wrong audience. As a general rule, small companies should choose so-called *vertical* shows that appeal to a relatively narrow buyer interest and attract fewer casual visitors, rather than broad *horizontal* shows at which many different types of prospects jam the aisles in search of the hugh exhibits of major corporations. The small exhibitor, whose marketing should be focused on customer niches in the first place, gets lost at the large horizontal show, wastes money on exhibiting fees to reach a larger audience than needed, and pulls in less focused, less qualified inquiries.

But even if the show is right, the inexperienced exhibitor's approach may be weak. We repeatedly see companies "going to the show" without setting adequate objectives, particularly the specific number of qualified leads they expect to collect. Then, they do not collect lead profile information or follow up their leads, so they cannot determine how much value they received from an exhibit. Inadequate pre-show promotions and poorly designed booths cause additional problems. The people staffing the exhibit might be poorly trained, unable to separate genuine prospects from tire-kickers. Nor does it help when first-time exhibitors get the less desirable show floor locations. Typically, a show manager's best customers—the larger, repeat exhibitors—get the first pick of choice real estate, as they should.

Some companies have legitimate reasons for not exhibiting, or at least for avoiding the megashows in favor of more focused exhibiting opportunities. One recent study of telecommunications trade shows found that lead efficiency—the proportion of potential leads which an exhibitor captures—for horizontal shows is substantially less than the level achieved at vertical exhibitions.[15] That prompts some companies to take their own mini-shows on the road where they can invite key prospects to hotel suite exhibits. And, when enough marketers in a field complain that the giant show is more than they can afford, entrepreneurial show managers are likely to take the risk of launching new vertical or regional exhibitions.

Also, exhibiting isn't the right medium for every marketing strategy. Firms with a narrow base of known, potential prospects might not need to generate show leads. However, a show appearance could serve other marketing goals, such as maintaining a market image.

Finally, some marketers just cannot stand the effort, confusion, and potential disorder of exhibiting. Coordinating exhibits, space, shipping, contracting services, union labor, drayage (moving materials within the exhibition hall), and endless minutiae may not seem a price worth paying, particularly if an exhibitor doesn't receive enough qualified leads, doesn't follow them up properly, or doesn't really know how much return it is getting on its investment.

Making decisions based on impressions, or simply on the basis of gross inquiry volume, is a sign that the show program is vulnerable to senior executive whim—a trim-the-budget decision rooted more in gut feel ("Our booth never gets busy") than hard data. Bosses see lots of people and a tremendous burst of effort with few tangible results beyond a shoe box full of business cards. And bosses lose patience when marketing people describe the value of exhibiting only in vague terms: "The show was great; we got lots of leads." Management expects to hear about accountability: "Our experience suggests that the show will produce $7 to $9 million additional sales for us." The aphorism, "If you can't measure it, you can't manage it," is never more true than at trade shows.

Who Shows Up

According to the exhibition industry, 84 percent of show visitors have some degree of buying influence,[16] and 61 percent plan to buy something exhibited at a trade show. Yet, in the same way that other media also reach "hidden prospects," 83 percent of visitors say they have not been called on by an exhibitor salesperson in the previous 12 months. That's partly because 34 percent of show-goers are top and middle management,[17] a group not likely to see salespeople routinely.

Hidden buying influences. Trade shows' ability to reach hidden buyers hasn't varied significantly over 10 years, the Trade Show Bureau states, adding that it has held steady within industries. The ratio varies from 71 percent in Standard Industrial Classification 38 (measurement, control, photographic, optical and medical equipment, watches, and clocks) to 91 percent in SIC 357 (computer and office equipment), where falling prices have cut industry selling activity.

Nor does the percentage of hidden buyers vary dramatically for the type of industrial product sold. The proportions of buying influences who did not receive sales calls were 81 percent for capital equipment in the $5,000-plus range, 86 percent for less expensive capital goods, 79 percent for components and materials, and 69 percent for consumable products.[18]

Show attendance is serious business; visitors do not wander the aisles aimlessly. The average attendee spends 13 minutes at each of 26 exhibits, and over the course of a two-day visit, a third of attendees spend more than eight hours at exhibits.[19] One high-tech show survey found 44 percent of attendees plan their booth visiting schedule in advance.[20]

Chief executives who attend shows are not necessarily there to buy; they treat shows as a gathering of their industry where they can assess the competition and contact customers. Their staffers come to buy, or at least collect vendor information to pass along to the bosses. Therefore, shows are not likely to be the best way to reach senior corporate officials. Half say they never attend multi-industry shows, and 29 percent never go to shows specific to their own industry, the Trade Show Bureau acknowledges. Their major source of industry news is the press, although they do claim an interest in the educational opportunities a trade show seminar might offer.[21]

What Attendees Want

Not surprisingly, businesspeople attend trade shows to stay abreast of their industries and find better ways of doing their jobs. They credit shows with a variety of benefits, as noted in Exhibit 7-1, primarily because shows bring vendors together under one roof. They take action at shows that advance the purchasing process, as in Exhibit 7-2.

Exhibit 7-1
How Decision Makers Perceive Trade Shows

Perception	% "generally agreeing" with statement
Save my company time and money	85
Bring me up-to-date	83
Allow me to be very productive	82
Provide an invaluable opportunity	80
Help me decide what to buy	79
I am relied on by my company to keep up with industry developments	70

Source: "Trade Shows Provide Business Opportunities," *The Power of Trade Shows: Report PT2* (Denver: The Trade Show Bureau, 1992).

Exhibit 7-2
Action Taken at Last Show Attended

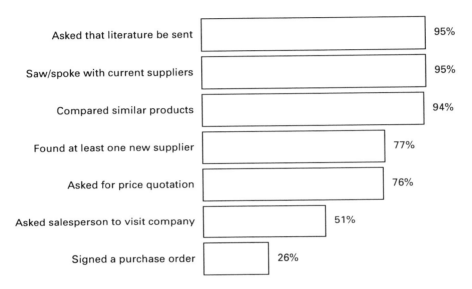

% of Sample Reporting

Asked that literature be sent	95%
Saw/spoke with current suppliers	95%
Compared similar products	94%
Found at least one new supplier	77%
Asked for price quotation	76%
Asked salesperson to visit company	51%
Signed a purchase order	26%

Source: "Decision Makers Take Buying Actions at Trade Shows," *The Power of Trade Shows: Report PT3* (Denver: The Trade Show Bureau, 1992).

Specific agendas. Among all show attendees, three-quarters have specific tasks to accomplish at a show, the Trade Show Bureau states; about half of all attendees come to see products and services, as shown in Exhibit 7-3. Research also suggests that when many people from the same company (or large corporation business unit) attend a show to examine available technology, they have an imminent purchase in mind, making them highly qualified sales leads.[22]

Evidently, veterans as well as first-time show visitors share that buying interest. All-industry statistics reported by the Trade Show Bureau point to similar distributions of job function and buying influence in each group. Slightly more than half of either group attend only one show a year. First-timers, however, do spend less time at the show, and word-of-mouth plays a much more important role in attracting them, compared to those who've attended before.[23]

It's important to know specifically why your target prospects attend a show. The reasons can differ by industry. A Trade Show Bureau survey found, for instance, that medical trade show visitors attend to learn about the latest technology and products, while manufacturing and computer show visitors have problem-solving in mind. In contrast, gift and apparel show attendees seek to cultivate trade relationships.[24]

Exhibit 7-3
Reasons People Visit Trade Shows

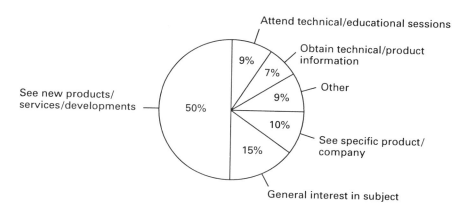

Source: Trade Show Bureau composite data published in *Trade Show Bureau 10-10: Ten Years of Trade Show Bureau Reports in Ten Minutes,* vol. 2 (Denver: Trade Show Bureau, 1991), p. 15.

In general, the average show attendee is a pretty warm, if not hot, prospect. High-technology product and service buyers with specific purchase decisions on their minds, for example, usually are well along in the information-gathering process. Half those surveyed at computer shows said they were "evaluating options," a quarter were closer to a decision, and about 13 percent said they still were at the "need recognition" stage early in their buying cycles. Nearly half of those surveyed recommend purchases, and 23 percent approve them.[25]

Visitors prefer hands-on demonstrations. They want spontaneous discussions with the technical people behind the product, not sales reps. They also prize technical specification sheets and hard-to-find price lists. More than 50 percent of high-tech show attendees file such literature for future use. Magazine article reprints—a handout popular with exhibitors—don't fare as well; as many attendees throw them out as file them. Interaction among show attendees and vendor-guided equipment demonstrations also rate well with high-tech show visitors. They consider more passive forms of involvement, such as lectures, watching videos, and witnessing unmanned continuous demonstrations as less informative.[26]

Show visitors also cite the value of gathering competitive intelligence and strategic ideas at a show. They often expect new product introductions to be announced, particularly in advanced technology fields. And, not surprisingly, a major show with the social and educational events surrounding it create a physical sense of community for an industry.

Room for improvement. Overall, however, high-tech show-goers in the Trade Show Bureau's survey said just 10 percent of the information they receive from all sources is "good."[27] That squares with complaints we often hear about vendor literature, and it is consistent with research throughout the trade show field that brands insufficient product knowledge on the part of booth personnel as attendees' main grievance. Evidently, an exhibitor with a well-planned and crisply implemented presentation has a substantial opportunity to delight buyers hungry for better information.

Picking the Right Shows for You

Useful Research

Audience "quality" is what counts most to exhibitors picking a show. The exhibition industry frequently uses three statistics, popularized by trade show research specialist Exhibit Surveys, Inc., to measure the audience quality of a given show:

- *Net buying influences,* the percentage of the audience that can recommend, specify or approve the purchase of an exhibited product;
- *Total buying plans,* the percentage of visitors planning to buy an exhibited product or service within 12 months of the show;
- *Average audience interest,* the percentage of the audience visiting a given number of exhibits.

Show surveys reveal other dimensions of a show's performance. Exhibit Surveys, Inc., for example, reports the average time attendees spend at exhibits and the number they visit, and the traffic density on the show floor, which indicates the intensity of show activity—how easy it is to buttonhole attendees in the aisle, for instance.

Research also reports data specific to a single exhibit: how well it attracts attendees interested in the exhibitor's product, the exhibit's memorability, and the performance of booth personnel, for instance.[28] No one measure is itself the definitive yardstick for an exhibit's performance, however.

Unfortunately, such data are not available for most shows. Exhibit Surveys, Inc. and other companies conducting post-show surveys only get to a handful of the nation's thousands of exhibitions. As a result, exhibitors generally have little more than audience head counts and basic attendee demographics to describe a show's past performance. Some progressive show managements and associations provide verified audits of registration records; inflated audience claims hardly are unheard of in the industry. That dearth of survey research and auditing provides yet another reason why a marketer must rely on sales lead tracking and analysis for trade show program planning.

Both lead tracking and diagnostic research are important for fine-tuning a trade show program. Absolute lead counts only tell part of the story. What counts more, in terms of fine-tuning your booth effectiveness, is your *lead efficiency*: your share of all potential qualified leads at a show. Surveys, combined with your qualified inquiry records, can indicate that share. Your inquiry records alone cannot, particularly because research suggests that as many as two of every three attendees who stop to talk with a booth's salespeople do not leave their name, yet many are valid prospects.[29]

Recent research sponsored by the Trade Show Bureau and a giant telecommunications firm with extensive exhibit activity attempts to bridge the gap and combine lead yield and floor performance measures into a single, still-theoretical trade show performance model. It uses Exhibit Surveys, Inc.'s statistics to rate a booth relative to others at a show. A pilot test with actual data from 28 trade shows was able to calculate how much each show- and booth-effectiveness factor contributed to lead generation.[30]

Rough and ready research. Certainly, we're not saying that you need expensive surveys and statistical models to measure a show by more than inquiry volume. Even the smallest of exhibitors should monitor booth and show activity. E. Jane Lorimer, president of the Trade Show Bureau, offers "six tips" for simplified exhibit performance measurement, one of which is counting leads and rating their potential. The others:

- Count passersby every hour, those who look at your booth and those who stop to talk. A person walking by and looking receives exposure to your message equivalent to a 10-second television commercial. Count for a minute and multiply by 60 to estimate the rate of hourly traffic.

  To calculate the number of visitors in the booth, count the number of people in the exhibit during a one-minute time period, and multiply that number by 60. Adjust the count by noting the average time a visitor spends with you. If four people are in the booth during a given minute, for instance, and they average 10 minutes each with your rep, watching a demonstration, etc., on average you are reaching visitors at a rate of $4 \times 60 \div 10 = 24$ per hour.

- Document your paid and unpaid exhibit-related media coverage and translate that into gross impressions and/or dollar value.

- Count the entries in your participative events, such as a business card drawings.

- Count the volume of literature and promotional specialties given away. Studies show visitors trash 64 percent of trade show literature handouts; 36 percent is retained.
- Get much of the same information about your two major competitors.[31]

Set Your Objectives

Nearly nine out of ten exhibitors set some sort of objective for their show participation.[32] Certainly, generating sales leads to identify new prospects is the prime reason for exhibiting for most companies—see Exhibits 7-4 and 7-5. And lead counts are the most popular method of measuring show performance, as shown in Exhibit 7-6.

Exhibit 7-4

Reasons for Exhibitor Participation in Domestic Shows

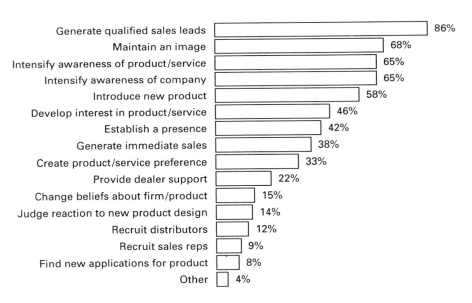

Generate qualified sales leads	86%
Maintain an image	68%
Intensify awareness of product/service	65%
Intensify awareness of company	65%
Introduce new product	58%
Develop interest in product/service	46%
Establish a presence	42%
Generate immediate sales	38%
Create product/service preference	33%
Provide dealer support	22%
Change beliefs about firm/product	15%
Judge reaction to new product design	14%
Recruit distributors	12%
Recruit sales reps	9%
Find new applications for product	8%
Other	4%

Source: Gary G. Young, *Managing the Exhibit Function: 1991 Survey of Exhibit Management Practices,* survey report conducted for the Trade Show Bureau, June 18, 1992. (Some statistics from that report, although not the data here, appear in: *Managing the Exhibit Function: Survey of Exhibit Management Practices; Report MC26A* (Denver: Trade Show Bureau, 1993).

Exhibit 7-5
Primary Corporate Trade Show Objectives

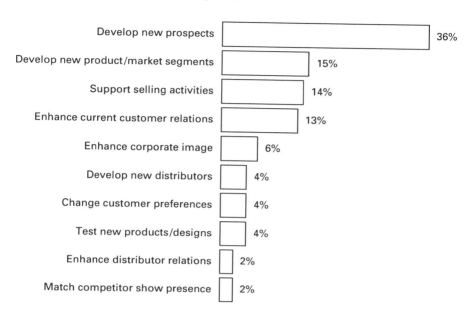

Develop new prospects — 36%
Develop new product/market segments — 15%
Support selling activities — 14%
Enhance current customer relations — 13%
Enhance corporate image — 6%
Develop new distributors — 4%
Change customer preferences — 4%
Test new products/designs — 4%
Enhance distributor relations — 2%
Match competitor show presence — 2%

Source: Valerie Kijewski, Eunsang Yoon and Gary Young, "How Exhibitors Select Trade Shows," *Industrial Marketing Management* vol. 22 no. 4 (November 1993): pp. 287–298.

Pursuing inquiries, don't simply set "more leads" as your goal. Forecast how many leads—better yet, qualified leads—you'll receive from a show and estimate when they will convert to sales. Otherwise, you will not know whether you achieved your goal, nor will you have estimates to guide your budgeting. Use the return-on-promotional-investment (ROPI) formula presented in Chapter 5 as a planning tool, and use sales lead tracking and analysis to assess your performance and indicate what goals are appropriate for the next planning cycle.

The same criteria—validity, measurability and timing—apply to any other objective you might set for an exhibit. If you plan to build attendee awareness of a new product, use survey research to determine pre- and post-show levels. Signing a target number of new distributors certainly is a valid goal. If your objective is of more modest purpose, such as "being there" to maintain awareness in a marketplace, that too is a valid, measurable, and time-dimensioned goal accessible through survey research.

Exhibit 7-6
Show Participation Measurement Methods

Measurement Method	% of Exhibitors Using
Number of qualified leads produced	72
Show attendance	55
Visitors to your exhibit	50
Profile of attendees	42
# of inquiries for information	36
Cost per qualified lead	31
Attendee awareness of company and/or products	30
Media coverage received	22
Activity at competitors	22
Evaluation of booth personnel	22
Evaluation of booth personnel performance	18
Evaluation of exhibit attributes	18
Amount of literature distributed	15
Cost per visitor to your exhibit	13
Memorability of your exhibit	12
Number of product demonstrations given	11
Reaction of attendees to the show or conference	11
Cost per inquiry for information	10
Attendees' evaluation of conference program	9
Attendees' purchase preferences	8
Cost per attendee	8
Cost per demonstration given	2
Other	8

Source: *Managing the Exhibit Function: Survey of Exhibit Management Practices; Report MC26A (*Denver: Trade Show Bureau, 1993).

Do not, however, hold an exhibit to invalid objectives such as "increasing sales" (unless it's orders written on the floor), "boosting market awareness," or other targets which rely on other marketing tools in addition to your exhibit. Vague paeans to growth may be fine for press releases, but they don't help you evaluate and improve your trade show marketing performance.

New product introductions rank highly as an overall corporate exhibit priority. New product or service marketing aspirations will influence show selection, booth size, and other factors. Shows can be a high-impact medium to showcase a product launch with hoopla and publicity; news usually attracts a crowd.

In some fast-changing high-technology markets, unveiling new products—or at least announcing their availability at sometime in the future—has become the critical competitive factor. Stories abound about engineering departments flogged to get a working prototype ready for display at a key trade show. Even if the prototype isn't ready, companies have been known to display a "box" that does not actually work, but simulates key features of the soon-to-come breakthrough. Engineering-oriented companies fear that if they do not promise the new product, they'll be dropped from buyers' consideration in the technology derby. But companies risk generating a lot of smoke and sales frustration, and hurting their credibility, when they collect show leads they can't close and deliver.

Timing is a critical question for exhibiting, particularly if you rely on just a few seasonal shows a year rather than an even year-round schedule. Can your sales and marketing systems handle a large bump in your inquiry volume from a show without letting some leads go stale? Considering the generally high quality of show inquiries, letting them sit around is a crime. Also, will exhibit inquiry volume match your selling and sales incentive patterns?

Program objectives can differ among individual shows. An active marketer exhibiting at several shows a year must be sure to pursue the right objectives appropriate to his or her marketing plan and each show's audience. At a user-oriented computer trade show, a computer software company, for example, doesn't expect to get many qualified leads for its sophisticated network operating systems. Information systems experts are its target market, not end-user "hackers." But the company exhibits anyway, using promotional devices that tie it to other exhibitors at the show (e.g. a "passport" requiring "stamps" from other booths at the show) in order to build awareness of how its software supports other vendors' products.

Geography and scope. Objectives vary with the type of show considered. Research finds that exhibitors tend to increase their interest in horizontal shows, those serving many industries, to introduce new products to existing markets or to develop new distribution. When the mission is developing new product market segments, interest shifts more toward vertical shows. Managements also favor vertical shows when they want to counter the presence of a competitor.[33]

Companies tend to increase their interest in regional trade shows when they exhibit to support selling activity, boost image, and match competitive presence. National shows attract above-average interest when marketers seek new prospects in existing markets. Developing new distribution is a much more important objective when exhibiting internationally, compared to domestically, research indicates.[34]

Your own industry may offer a number of national and regional exhibiting options. Depending on your marketing strategy and structure, both types can be attractive. Lead efficiency research does not find a difference between regional and national trade shows.[35] In a given field, The Big Show, if there is one, is likely to be national. But even national shows tend to pull the heaviest attendance from their surrounding region.

Regional trade shows might provide a more congenial selling environment with a more relaxed pace for attendees. And they may be broader in scope. That can make regional shows well suited to sales forces deployed by geographic territory selling to several industries. A regional show will attract local distributors or dealers, increasing your effective presence on the floor. And, when you press salespeople from a region into service at a show for their territories, they've got greater motivation to sell and generate leads than they might have at a national show with attendees they'll likely never see again.

Generating Your Show Leads

Enticing Visitors

A variety of related factors lure prospects to specific exhibits. The exhibitor can control some, but not all of them. An interesting study from 1980 by a group of newspaper graphics supplies manufacturers, reported 13 factors that visitors say influence their choice of booths.

Although the specific percentages shown in Exhibit 7-7 reflect the reasons cited by attendees at a major newspaper industry show, they imply the relative importance of each variable. The exhibitor can control most of the effect: in the case of the show profiled in Exhibit 7-7, 45 percent of the pre-show factors and 76 percent of the at-show influences.

Exhibit 7-7
What Determines Whose Booth to Visit?

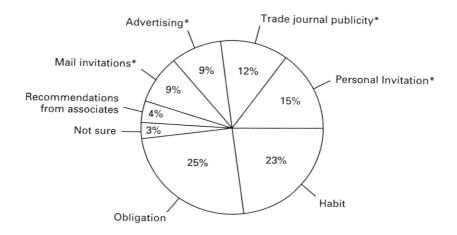

Influences before Show

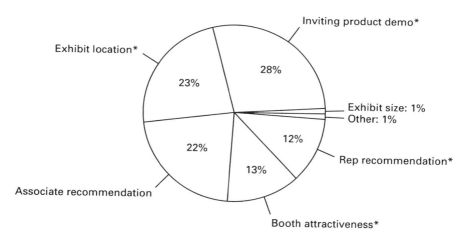

Influences at Show

* Indicates factors an exhibitor can control.

Source: Robert T. Wheeler Jr., "How to Boost Your Exhibit's Prospect Appeal," *Industrial Marketing* (July 1982): p. 75.

Location and the booth. Register for your show as soon as possible and read the show manager's exhibitor materials thoroughly. The sooner you pick space, the better. Remember that your location objective is maximizing the number of potentially qualified visitors passing by. That's why being close to a high-profile exhibit with live demonstrations and other audience lures will draw crowds, but not for you. The competition will distract them from noticing you.

Locations near seminar meeting rooms can work well; passersby have business on their minds. They don't when heading toward rest rooms, phones, or food concessions, so avoid being near them.

Research confirms common sense; the center of a hall is best for traffic, while dead-end aisles are the worst. Propinquity pays; locations near industry leaders draw better-than-average traffic. Narrow aisles bring prospects closer to your booth than wider aisles, all other things equal.

As a rule of thumb, rent at least 100 square-feet of space for every 800 visitors you expect to reach, says exhibit designer Robert Firks.[36] Remember that exhibit personnel need breaks, particularly because they should not be sitting in the booth just waiting for prospects to amble in. Keep in-booth duty shifts to four hours or less, with a short break every couple of hours. Ensure that the booth remains adequately staffed for the traffic expected at a particular hour.

Once you've got the traffic, you need to attract the people you want to see, minimizing the number of merely curious folk cluttering up your space and wasting booth personnel time. Your exhibit design, its signage and lighting, your offers, and, most of all, booth personnel accomplish that task.

Everything you can do to help the attendee remember visiting you is important. For the average show visitor, there's so much to see, so much to do, and so little time that confusion reigns. The busy attendee forgets the faces and the conversations linked to the jumble of business cards in pocket or purse. The plastic bag bulging with literature at the end of the day is likely to be discarded entirely, or heavily culled in the hotel room to save weight on the trip home. Booth personnel quality is the most critical factor in securing the lead. And it's the booth that provides a frame for that performance.

The physical booth's actual contribution to the exhibitor's ability to attract qualified prospects, engage them in meaningful conversation, and obtain a solid lead is not clear from general survey research. A booth's memorability is most heavily affected by the attendee's product interest, then whether the product was demonstrated live. Exhibit color and design rank third as a factor in memorability.[37] But just 13 percent of attendees rated booth attractiveness the main draw, according to the survey results in Exhibit 7-7. And, noting how booth attractiveness failed to show up as a significant contributor in their lead efficiency model, researchers for the Trade Show Bureau speculated that too attractive a booth draws too many non-prospects, cluttering up booth space and depressing the qualified inquiry yield.[38]

Managing traffic. Trade show lore argues that even details like the color difference between booth and aisle carpets affect traffic flow. A sharp contrast, a fortress-like booth design, for example, chases traffic away, while an open, almost nonexistent structure invites passersby in, the reasoning goes. Too much bright color and large busy signage will, says exhibit designer Robert J. Francisco, "overstimulate" the would-be prospect.[39]

Buy or rent all or part of a new or refurbished exhibit; they range from custom design work at the high end to "portable" models with folded backwalls or pop-up walls. Whichever configuration you choose, it should promote interaction between visitor and exhibitor. That's why passive displays, continuous video and film loops, unattended demonstrations, and other impersonal communication devices can attract attention and hold the interest of a visitor waiting to see a booth person, but they can't sell nor can they qualify a visitor. On average, just 42 percent of show attendees say they wait three or more minutes to see someone in a booth before leaving.[40]

Visitors prowl the aisles searching for new ideas and solutions. Be sure your signage tells them why they should stop to speak with you. Use lighting and design to draw attention to create a dominant focal point in the booth: a demonstration, a prototype, or a waiting booth person, for example. Use colorful graphics meaningfully to promote your key selling message. But avoid generalized art that may look spectacular but doesn't say anything; it's just wallpaper to the visitor scrambling to find ideas. Finally, don't try to get away cheap with blow-ups of your ads pasted to the backwall. Ads are not effective display elements because they are designed for reading up close. Would you use an ad as an outdoor poster?

Booth staffers are the primary agency of traffic flow control, separating the prospects from tire kickers. But the booth's design plays a role too. Decide what you want visitors to do before designing your exhibit's traffic flow. Booth design can encourage visitors to follow a predetermined path of exhibits and demonstrations.

Unless you want to keep interaction to a minimum, avoid the table spread across the front of a linear booth entrance. It creates a wall between "us" and "them" which fails to inspire salespeople and certainly won't impress passersby. At the other extreme, a "collector" design—ushering people through a formal entrance into a large room walled off from the rest of the show—gathers an audience for your sales pitch and demonstration. Conference rooms to the side provide a place to work with the hot prospects. Or a thoroughly open "random access" display, such as a peninsula or island exhibit without walls or counters, gives prospects and booth people complete freedom to walk amid demos and display elements.[41]

Promotion

Research and individual exhibitor experience invariably credits promotion with a hefty contribution to trade show selling success. But for it to support the show meaningfully, you must promote your exhibit specifically.

Your general marketing communications activities—the advertising, publicity, mail, and telemarketing that supports you year round and provides a steady flow of inquiries—builds market awareness and preference and will help make your name recognizable to the show's passing traffic. But that's not enough. You must entice the right prospects to visit your booth. Promote your show participation through advertising and publicity. Invite customers, known prospects and past exhibit visitors with personalized direct mail and phone calls. Mail to the show-sponsoring association's membership. Independent show managements often make attendee advance registration lists available. And use your standard direct mail list sources, especially reliable ones, such as publication circulation rosters and response lists.

A detailed statistical study of a major business-to-business trade show, the 1991 Annual Food Exposition of the Institute of Food Technology, found that heavy pre-show promotion boosted visitor traffic to the average booth by 15 percent.[42]

Concentrate on prospects most likely to attend: about 46 percent of show attendees travel 200 miles or less to a show. Use specialties, premiums, contests, and other inducements to make sure they'll be there (e.g. "Stop by to pick up the key to this little box with the treasure inside.") Research has found that a pre-show gift mailed with an invitation can boost an exhibit's traffic nearly three times, compared to an invitation without a gift.[43]

Set up appointments to meet key prospects at the booth, so your best people will be there, ready for them. Don't risk missing that 44 percent of show-goers who plan their booth visits in advance. Technical seminars at a show can be an even better way to bring hard-to-reach buying influences within your reach.

Invite bona fide prospects to more relaxed venues and events: hospitality suites or parties you'll throw for customers, distributors, prospects, and reps. If you ask them, they'll come or at least feel good about your thoughtfulness. But on or off the floor, give your invitees a business reason to be there: not that you want to meet them, but that they can "learn the newest numerically controlled technology," for example, or "meet the new distributors serving your area."

Advertising. Use advertising to reach lower-priority prospects and to supplement your invitation campaign. If you can afford it, run a special ad touting whatever you're featuring at your exhibit, rather than simply slapping a "snipe" saying something like "See us in booth 1473" in the upper corner of your standard ad. But a snipe is better than nothing, and publishers often will give you the snipe free if you advertise in a show issue. Giving prospects a business-like answer to their "What's in it for me?" question is the key factor.

Don't overlook advertising during the show, but don't assume that a "show daily" or other concurrent-exposure vehicle automatically draws attention. Does it attract an audience? Why? For some shows, dailies are important reading. For others, show publications are little more than republished press releases thrown together haphazardly. Check to see if advertising in a show's official publication earns you extra benefits, such as a better chance to reserve prime floor space.

Don't overlook opportunities to run television commercials on closed circuit hotel networks, or even convention-city cable and broadcast outlets. The credibility of the promise you make, not the production values of those one-use spots, is the critical element. Outdoor advertising near the exhibition hall and in-airport advertising also represent productive media options.

Additionally, a trade show's status as a community gathering for an industry provides an efficient way to reach other promotion targets besides prospective buyers with press conferences, analyst meetings, distributor forums, and technical discussions with lead users.

Exhibit 7-8 reports the popularity of different pre-show promotion techniques, according to a major cross-industry survey.

Exhibit 7-8
Pre-Show Promotion Techniques

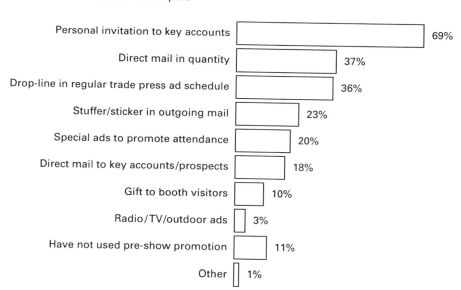

Technique	%
Personal invitation to key accounts	69%
Direct mail in quantity	37%
Drop-line in regular trade press ad schedule	36%
Stuffer/sticker in outgoing mail	23%
Special ads to promote attendance	20%
Direct mail to key accounts/prospects	18%
Gift to booth visitors	10%
Radio/TV/outdoor ads	3%
Have not used pre-show promotion	11%
Other	1%

Source: *Exhibitors—Their Trade Show Practices: Report No. 2050* (Denver: Trade Show Bureau, 1988).

Publicity. A story related to your exhibit may be newsworthy enough for publications to run before the show. Send short but informative press releases to publications, inviting their reps to visit you. Follow up with key publications before the show, offering more information for special show roundup articles they may be producing. You might also be able to set up appointments at the show with key publication reporters.

Check around and think creatively about what might help publications cover you better. For instance, trade magazines and newspapers sometimes sponsor drawings and contests to build their own competitive advantage at shows. Offer your product or service as a prize, generating extra publicity for you.

Be sure that you have a designated spokesperson on hand at all times to meet with reporters who have appointments and those who wander by unannounced. To handle the kinds of questions reporters usually have, the spokesperson needs to understand your technology, products, how they are sold, and how your industry is structured, being able to discuss all that in lay terms. A saintly patience helps, too.

Reporters will appreciate a spokesperson who can also discuss your competition—tastefully, of course. That will help them better understand the superiorities you claim for your product, and they'll be less inclined to accept uncritically competitors' assertions.

Unless you have got a strong story or a competitive thrust to overcome, don't waste your money sending lavish press kits to publications before the show, unless they ask. Just be sure that material you distribute to the press generates interest by succinctly stating the benefit you are selling. An engaging graphic accompanying releases will help get you attention.

An exception is the group of one or more publications producing special issues on the show for distribution on the floor. They specifically seek show-related material and plenty of it from which to choose; editors will appreciate receiving a detailed press kit they can reference if they wish. Those specials often have early editorial deadlines, so be sure editors receive your material in time.

Save the weighty documentation for those who visit the booth or attend your press conference. Many shows also have areas adjacent to press rooms where you can leave literature for reporters grazing for a story. Good ones do take time to explore.

After the show, follow up with your major press contacts, offering more information. But don't apply pressure. It's a genuine disappointment when your chief engineer spent an hour educating a reporter on your latest technology, only to have the reporter fail to produce a story. A helpful attitude might win you a concession elsewhere, such as a technical publicity placement.

Budgeting

As you plan the shows, booths, personnel, demonstrations, etc. that meet the objectives of your trade show plan, you'll need to budget the program to ensure the plan will provide a reasonable cost-per-expected qualified lead.

Exhibit space averages about a quarter of exhibitor's trade show budget. Contracting for installation and dismantling services, plus other services on the show floor, takes another 22 percent of the budget, according to Trade Show Bureau surveys. Add 15 percent for exhibit construction and 10 percent for ongoing exhibit refurbishment, 11 percent for transportation and the rest for all other expenses.[44] Exhibiting presents challenging budgeting problems because so many different types of services and equipment must be brought together on the show floor. Mistakes in timing, exhibit complexity, inadequate pre-planning and the failure to anticipate contingencies can ratchet a budget skyward in no time.

To get started on budgeting, Exhibit 7-9 provides a checklist of the types of costs your budget probably will accommodate.

More Than a Sales Call

Garnering leads at trade shows is a disciplined process that's different from the typical sales call. Spotting the truly live prospect on the show floor isn't a routine exercise. In one well-reported instance, a machine tool manufacturer checked his booth-qualification procedures by recontacting all booth visitors by phone after the giant International Machine Tool Show. Three-quarters of the booth-qualified leads turned out to be "not qualified" when recontacted. Although 40 percent of all booth visitors qualified on the phone, just a quarter of them had also qualified at the exhibit.[45] Perhaps qualification criteria changed between the booth visit and phone follow-up, or visitors' buying plans had changed. Then again, it could be a matter of exhibit personnel training.

Insisting that trade show booth staffs receive three hours training before each show, a self-confessed "tyrant on training" at a major telecommunications company says it took field salespeople a while to adjust to receiving quality leads. "There used to be a perception when you see a lead that came from a trade show to dismiss its validity as potential revenue," she explained. That thinking is changing at her company, and coming more in line with most other organizations where field reps give priority to trade show leads.

A Tale of Contrasts

Consider two fairly well-matched competitors with booths of comparable location, size, and quality at their industry's Big Widget Show in Las Vegas.

Exhibit 7-9
Trade Show Budget Form

Trade Show Budget Form

Show: _____

Date: _____ Location: _____

Size, Booth# & Description of Space: _____

_____

_____

_____

_____

_____

Costs:

Advance Planning $_____
  (Rough concepts, schedules)

Administrative $_____
  (Typing, forms, etc.)

Exhibit Construction $_____

Peripheral Supplies
  (Badges, materials, literature) $_____

Advertising & Public Relations $_____

Packing & Shipping Exhibit: $_____

                                       To show: $_____
                                     From show: $_____

Transportation, Lodging & Meals $_____

Cost of Products to be Displayed $_____

Insurance $_____

Installation $_____

Booth Space Rental $_____

Staff Time
  (Booth duty) $_____

Entertainment $_____

Services & Rentals

                                     Furniture: $_____
                                      Electric: $_____
                                 Telephone/Fax: $_____
                                        Copier: $_____
                                         Other: $_____

Hospitality Room & Related Expenses $_____

Dismantling & Refurbishing Exhibit $_____

Post-Show Evaluation $_____

                                                          Total: $_____

Source: R. E. Clark Advertising and Inquiry Handling Service, Inc.

Alpha Widget Co. brings the heavy-producer salespeople in its recognition-oriented Bandolier Club to the show. Attending is a matter of prestige, and not inconsiderable fun. Reps so honored earn extra "Vegas Vacation" time and savor the annual Customer Appreciation Gala that Alpha produces on The Strip. The Big Widget Show is respite for those who've slaved faithfully in the field all year.

The travel is pleasant, the meetings interesting, and the hospitality suite congenial for the Beta Widget Inc. salespeople and distributor reps at the show. But the hours are long, the training relentless, and the paperwork an inescapable chore, they say. Nonetheless, all reps prize the "Beta SWAT Team" caps they earn when they've finished the ordeal. (Not even the company chairman's wife can get one.) Beta reps joke about surviving their *rite de passage.*

Affable Alpha. Assigning the newer Bandolier Club members to morning booth duty, Alpha lets its veterans sleep-in and enjoy the perk of a relaxed recovery from the Customer Appreciation Gala the night before. Recognizing the dues they must pay as new sales club members, the Alpha morning staffers in crisp business suits sit primly in their booth, facing the passing crowd and scrutinizing those who stop to drop their business cards in a large goldfish bowl for a prize drawing.

Every 15 minutes, another salesperson takes his or her turn standing near the bowl, behind the table at the edge of the booth ready to spot an important account or answer any questions that might be asked of him—or of the gowned female model handing out one-page sales brochures. Alpha's sales manager insists that reps get a second business card from every visitor to the booth, and turn them in at the end of the day when they will be shuffled and redistributed by appropriate sales territory. The cards in the bowl will go home with the sales manager who'll mail a mini-catalog to every visitor.

Salespeople on duty quickly become involved with booth visitors, particularly their favorite customers stopping by for coffee and a chat. It solidifies a lot of relationships, the sales manager says, as long as reps don't ignore new visitors stopping to ask a question. For salespeople themselves, it certainly is easier than cold calling in the field. At the show, the prospect takes the initiative and opens the conversation. "Can I help you?" is a favorite opener among Alpha reps. Some visitors appear with specific technical questions, which the rep promises to refer to the Alpha lab for an immediate reply.

Businesslike Beta. Beta Widget salespeople meanwhile joke about the "Beta blue" blazers each wears as they jam into the Beta booth a half-hour before the show opens for a pep rally. Last minute questions, a review of the latest product specifications, a run through the booth-supplies checklist, a reminder on how to use Beta's lead qualification form, and the sales manager's funny story about getting lead information from an irascible booth visitor quickly fill the time before the first visitors appear. Before leaving to prowl the aisles themselves, Beta reps tease those remaining to work the first shift about "the chair." The only chair in the booth, no one but a visitor is to sit in it.

Morning booth duty is considered a dues-paying experience for Beta reps, yet management always assigns at least one seasoned veteran to every shift. No one thinks booth duty is easier than working the field. It is different, with its scripted activity and daily qualified lead quotas. Salespeople even have dress rehearsals.

"Catchers," younger Beta reps seemingly chatting amiably among themselves in the aisle, actually scout the passing traffic carefully. Spotting someone glancing at them or at Beta's exhibit, they make their move with a cheery hello and an offer to personally "show you the industry's most versatile widget designs." They ask what widget application the passerby might have in mind.

The catcher leads attendees who show interest into the booth for a close-up view of a cutaway widget model and polite discussion of visitors' applications and buying plans. Beta offers a chance in a prize drawing, and a "handy" widget-impedance slide rule mailed "tomorrow" directly to the visitor's office, as long as the visitor leaves his or her name, business card, or show-badge imprint. At shows where the system is available, Beta reps swipe the visitor's card through a magnetic stripe reader tied to the show's attendee database.

The catcher dutifully takes notes on a tiny pad of lead qualification forms, and mentally sizes up the visitor's qualifications against specific criteria drilled in pre-show training sessions. The catcher introduces visitors—qualified as A leads (big order soon) or B leads (big order later *or* small order soon)—to either the senior sales manager or the technical expert assigned to that booth shift. Beta trains its catchers to probe for signals about which type of executive will serve the visitor best.[46] Catchers encourage visitors who should hob-nob with corporate management to visit the booth at a time senior managers are available, or visit Beta's hospitality suite.

C-quality leads (small order later) will be thanked for their interest; they will receive a follow-up brochure mailing and telephone call in a month to reassess their interest and buying plans. The catcher is supposed to spot a D lead (casual interest) quickly and collect just basic information about the visitor and his or her need—then move on with the polite promise to send information and enter the person in the prize drawing. The name will go on Alpha's "priority 2" mailing list for occasional brochure and newsletter mailings.

Catchers know that wasting time with poorly qualified leads earns them less booth performance points than roping in highly qualified prospects. But every contact earns some points in Beta's exhibit performance incentive system. Reps enjoy getting something extra for their efforts, even when it's with prospects in other reps' territories.

Daily appraisal. At day's end, while attendees shuffle out of the hall and maintenance crews begin their assault on the trash left behind, Alpha's booth staff has already headed for the door and the evening ahead. Somebody is cajoled into taking responsibility for all the business cards collected.

Meanwhile, the Beta staff reconvenes. Everyone returns, to share pointers and swap stories and pat the day's best performers on the back. Their camaraderie and sense of "SWAT team" mission renewed, Beta reps will perform even better on the morrow.

Beta's exhibition manager or sales manager collects lead forms, examines them for completeness, then passes them to a typist who enters the data in a laptop computer and sends the names to the home office or to the lead-handling service that night by modem. In the morning, Beta's marketing department is putting follow-up information in the mail so it will be on prospects' desks when they return to their offices.

Training Is Critical

Alpha and Beta have substantially different attitudes about exhibiting. Alpha Widget suffers from outdated approaches that treat a trade show casually, as a reward for the troops and loyal customers. Waiting for the world to come to you guarantees that your trade show dollar will underperform. "Can I help you?" and similar closed-end questions merely invite a "no" response from the attendee who ambles past.

In contrast, Beta Widget isn't embarrassed about selling and prospecting. The prospects wouldn't be on the floor, of course, unless they, too, had serious business in mind. Otherwise they'd be late-brunching alongside Alpha's grizzled sales legends.

Beta sets daily targets for each booth person, awarding points for different levels of activity—more points for spending time with an A lead than with a C lead, for example—and publicly commending the best performers.

Another key operational difference is the product and boothmanship training Beta insists upon: an essential every bit as important as basic sales training for field representatives. "You could have the best exhibit in the world, the best location and the hottest product. But if you haven't trained your staff you're going to have a dismal failure," says a large corporation's exhibit manager. At her mandatory training sessions for booth personnel at each show, she recalls, "Many will say with amazement, 'No one ever told me that before.'"

The question of training also extends to the company's exhibit manager. The role is poorly defined; exhibit managers range from clerks keeping track of paperwork and shipping, to experienced marketing and sales strategists operating at a senior level in the organization. There's little excuse for putting inexperienced, junior-level people in charge of major show expenditures, which, unfortunately, has been a widespread problem.[47] Then again, high-priced senior talent is more firepower than the average exhibitor needs. Trade show industry groups, particularly The International Exhibitors Association, can provide guidance and training for the exhibit manager who is right for you.

It's important that the exhibit manager be an active member of the sales lead-management team. Without a clear understanding of the trade show role in your company's marketing program, an exhibit manager is not properly equipped to contribute to the inquiry-handling process.

Capturing Information

Getting hot leads is critical to show success, of course. But collecting business cards, which hold no more information than a directory listing, do not make useful inquiry documents. Of even less value are the ones dropped in Alpha's goldfish bowl. At best, they are from people interested in winning a prize, but Alpha knows nothing more about them.

Here's an ironclad rule of exhibition lead management: *never sacrifice lead quality for quantity.* Trade show leads are expected to be the cream of the crop. But if you drop a load of poor leads from a show on an unsuspecting sales force, the entire lead program, and your management of it, is very likely to be called into serious question.

The lead form designed for the exhibitor's specific purpose harvests critical information, ensuring that you capture data useful to the downstream selling process when it is easiest to do so. For instance, the form can record:

- Company name, address and phone, size, products/services sold;
- Inquirer's job function and decision-making status (specifier, approver, recommender);
- Specific product interest;
- Prospect's application;
- Buying time frame (e.g. three months, six months or longer);
- Potential purchase volume;
- Need for demonstration;
- Installed base, yours or competitors';
- Previous experience with your company.

A sample lead form appears in Exhibit 7-10.

The form gathers qualification information for the field, inquirer data for the sales lead master database, and summary data for show evaluation, planning, and management reports.

Exhibit 7-10
Trade Show Lead Form

TRADE SHOW LEAD FORM

Requestor Profile
NAME _____
TITLE _____
COMPANY _____
DEPT./MAILSTOP _____
ADDRESS/PO BOX _____
CITY/STATE/ZIP _____
DAYTIME PHONE aa (_____) _____
FAX ab (_____) _____

Who other than you should receive lit?
NAME _____
TITLE _____
COMPANY _____
DEPT./MAILSTOP _____
ADDRESS/PO BOX _____
CITY/STATE/ZIP _____
DAYTIME PHONE aa (_____) _____
FAX ab (_____) _____

Do you access LANs remotely?
☐ba Yes   ☐bb No

How many individual users are accessed?
☐ca 1–15   ☐cc 51–100   ☐ce 251–500
☐cb 16–50   ☐cd 101–250   ☐cf 501 +

Product of interest?
☐da Z Got   ☐db U Got   ☐dc V Got

Organization's primary business activity?
☐ea Aerospace   ☐eh Manufacturing
☐eb Communications   ☐ej Retail
☐ec Education   ☐ek Legal
☐ed Finance/Banking/Accounting ☐el Telecommunications
☐ee Government   ☐em Transportation
☐ef Healthcare/Medical   ☐en Utilities
☐eg Insurance   ☐ep Wholesale/Retail Distribution
☐ez Other_____

Company is a:
☐fa End user   ☐fd Reseller   ☐ff Distributor
☐fb In-house developer   ☐fe OEM   ☐fg Var/System Integrator
☐fc Commercial developer ☐fx Other _____

Purchasing time frame?
☐ga Immediate   ☐gc 4–6 mos.   ☐ge Info. only
☐gb 1–3 mos.   ☐gd Longer

Role in the purchasing decision?
☐ha To recommend   ☐hc To approve   ☐he To use
☐hb To specify   ☐hd To purchase

Budgeted?
☐ja Yes   ☐jb No

Would like a sales consultant to contact?
☐ka Yes   Best Time: kc_____AM_____PM
☐kb No

Note: Each answer as an alpha code to facilitate data entry and future retrieval.
Source: Inquiry Handling Service, Inc.

Using the lead form discreetly yet effectively is an important part of booth personnel training. To aid discretion, some companies favor printed forms with little check-off boxes for qualification data. They design the forms to fit unobtrusively in the palm of the hand.

Conversation with the booth visitor is not an interrogation, however, but a dialogue, a consultation. Pre-show training helps booth people learn how to take notes while conversing with the prospect. Notes based on later recall aren't as accurate. Few visitors will be offended if the booth person says something like: "What you're telling me is really important, and I want to be sure I get every one of these points down. Do you mind if I take a few notes?"

Proper training and your team's uniform use of a well-understood lead gathering approach will eliminate the need to treat trade show leads as if they were advertising reader service card leads. One way to diagnose your staff's lead-gathering skill is to telephone a sample of show inquiries and requalify them. Normally, there should be little reason for telequalification personnel to phone booth-qualified leads after a show to requalify them. It's redundant. Marketers with flabby booth qualification procedures may find, however, that visitors deemed to be prospects aren't as qualified as originally thought. Use phone follow-up as a diagnostic tool for improving weak in-booth performance.

Skeptics argue that too many booth visitors lie about their buying plans and status. That really only happens in a small proportion of cases, however. What is much more likely is that overenthusiastic or sloppy booth staffers hype the quality of the contact. A lead management system linking specific shows to specific sales will indicate if your booth personnel training and incentives are accomplishing what they should: energetic yet accurate identification of genuine prospects.

Technical advances. Collecting booth visitor information is undergoing dramatic change. For many years the credit card-type of show badge with raised lettering, provided by show managements, has reigned as the primary method of automating name, title, company, and address capture. It saves booth personnel some pencil work, but the small lead forms used with the cards and imprinters, sold to exhibitors by show managements, leave little room for qualification information. Because of that limitation, many companies continue to use their own lead forms, and some write their own software for in-booth computer use.

Technology, however, is creating new ways of gathering visitor information. Three methods now vie for supremacy: badges with magnetic strips, cards with bar-coded information, and "smart cards" with built-in microchips. Each method encodes cards with substantial information about the booth visitor, taken from his or her registration documents.

Exhibitors can access the information in each category in an infinite variety of ways and download the data to their in-booth computers. They are not limited to summary information collected with check-off boxes. Exhibitors can tailor their face-to-face dialogues with visitors to expand on the basic information provided on the cards.

Those identification methods eliminate the need to re-key data into the exhibitor's computers and lead-management systems. That lends accuracy to databases and allows for even faster literature fulfillment as visitor qualification information moves with the speed of light to the exhibitor's home office or inquiry fulfillment house. Although occasional formatting and compatibility problems bedevil the new systems, they are proving to be popular with exhibitors who know how to use the information collected.

Dispensing Literature

Inexperienced exhibitors frequently treat the trade shows primarily as a product literature distribution tool. Considering how much marketing power a well-designed exhibit can provide—demonstrations, product displays, face-to-face contact with buyers and the chance to collect extensive qualification information—distributing literature, at most, should be just a small part of the exhibit objective.

Many attendees throw away as much as three-quarters of the stuff they pick up even before they leave the exhibition hall, we've found. And few cart more than just a few selected pieces with them when they fly back to their offices. It's no surprise that hotel maids routinely complain about the brochure garbage left behind in hotel rooms.

The waste prompts growing numbers of exhibitors to *avoid* passing out brochures and other printed materials to booth visitors. They prefer to get the visitor's name and send the literature later as a follow-up. If they can pick up what they want at the booth without giving their names, prospects cannot become sales leads, the reasoning goes. Not distributing brochures at the show can actually improve sales lead productivity. As Allen Owen, a marketing communications manager at Hewlett-Packard Co., explains, "You lose the name if you hand the literature out. If they want the literature they have to give you the name." He doesn't even bring literature to a show, preferring to mail it after the event.[48]

Deciding what, if anything, to pass out at the booth shouldn't be treated as routine. Be sure that you employ literature strategically, as a tool to reinforce face-to-face salesmanship and to begin the sales lead conversion process. Simply leaving brochures out on a table for passersby helps the curious visitor stock a literature file, but it makes little sense for a sales lead program.

Nor do you further the selling process appreciably when your post-show activity mails inquirers only the same brochures they have already picked up at the booth without adding new information. After-show fulfillment in the mail—just like any follow-up mailing to someone contacted previously—should offer additional information.

Try to minimize the cost of handouts, avoiding the routine distribution of catalogs and other expensive literature. A salesperson could customize a simple handout by writing product specification or configuration information on it, for example. An added benefit is that the attendee is much more likely to keep it, refer to it, and be receptive to a post-show sales call. Or if traffic volume, your booth size, booth staffing or other reasons demand that you pass out something to visitors with whom you cannot speak, give them a simple brochure with a tear-off business reply card they can mail to you for specific information. Those are likely to be important leads you can sight qualify and pass directly to the field.

Promotional products such as advertising specialties or samples can be a better handout than literature. The ad specialty such as an imprinted pen, coffee mug, or pencil holder—let creativity be your guide—has intrinsic value and is less likely to be discarded. Using it will remind visitors of your company. Giving it to the prospect after an in-booth discussion is a tasteful way of ending a conversation on a high note, so a rep can turn to the next visitor awaiting attention. Research at the International Food Technology show found that distributing free food samples and premiums increased booth traffic an average of 33 percent.[49]

Research published by the trade show industry says a promotional product can boost a vendor's goodwill with prospects by up to 80 percent. But, cautions trade show marketing expert Dick Miranda, "You cannot accomplish this by simply handing out a 25-cent giveaway. A lack of planning is probably the number one reason ad specialties have been misused and abused by so many for so long. It's no wonder they are considered 'trinkets and junk' by some people."[50]

Follow-up

Trade show lead follow-up is straightforward. Get your fulfillment mailing into the mail as soon as possible; overnight delivery to your lead-handling center each day of the show makes it impossible for competitors to beat you in fulfillment.

Then follow the *30–40–70 Rule*. Distribute booth-qualified leads to field and distributor sales representatives immediately. They should follow up each contact within about a week; that gives visitors a chance to clear off the stuff that accumulated on their desks while they attended the event. *But do not take longer than 30 days to follow up;* by then they will have forgotten you.

Within 40 days after the show, those leads not already serviced with a sales call or reclassified unqualified should receive an additional follow-up by mail: a letter with reply card and additional information, for instance, to restimulate the contact process.

Unless the prospect has requalified or become an active contact for field sales or distribution, send another mailing 70 to 90 days later to gain bounceback card qualification information.

Other types of follow-up to lesser-quality inquiries might prove fruitful. For example, shows often provide exhibitors with lists of attendees sorted by product interest. Besides determining why some of those interested in your category did not stop by your exhibit, use those names in a post-show mail campaign or put them on your direct marketing lists for a limited time period if and until they return a bounceback card.

Keep in mind that a major rule of efficient sales force deployment also applies to those hot show leads. A sales rep shouldn't make a live (that is, expensive and time-consuming) call on a prospect until the prospect is ready to talk about an order, be closed, put out a bid, or take other substantive action furthering the sale. Both the booth rep and the field rep need to keep an accurate record of the prospect's timing.

But trade show lead quality being high, keep exhibit inquiries "warm" even if they are not poised to buy soon. They deserve high priority among inquirers in your sales lead master database.

Additional Tips

In addition to your mail and telemarketing pre-show promotion activities, provide your salespeople with invitations to extend to customers and prospects they visit each day. It is an inexpensive way to create one more opportunity for a sale and to let valued customers know you are active in the industry.

Once in the booth, be sure the lines of responsibility are clear. Designate a "booth captain" for each shift.

Also be sure that technically knowledgeable people are in the booth at all times, or quickly available in order to address what inevitably will be some detailed questions from some of your best prospects.

Maintain an identity that separates you from competitors and which helps attendees recognize your reps. This can be as simple as sporting colorful, matching boutonnieres, scarves and ties, or as elaborate as wearing uniforms that represent a booth theme (western, space, nautical, etc.)

Exhibiting well gives smaller firms a chance to level the playing field. Although they usually cannot match the lavish booth designs and massive spaces the corporate behemoths enjoy, smaller firms can exploit the weak spots in most companies' trade show tactics and follow-up. Preliminary evidence also suggests that exhibitor size is not a critical factor in converting a booth visitor into a qualified lead.[51]

Chapter 8

Put Your Sale in the Mail to Generate Leads

Direct mail is hot and getting hotter for lead generation. As we have pointed out, two-thirds of business marketers rate direct mail an effective medium, which generates 10 percent of the inquiries they receive. We expect future surveys will show dramatic increases from those levels, however. Direct mail has exploded as a prime medium for business and consumer product and service marketers alike. The growth comes not just from mail-order firms selling directly, but also from inquiry-minded marketers using mail as a surgical medium to smoke out qualified sales leads in discrete market segments, and to maintain active prospect databases.

In a bygone era just a few years ago, account-driven strategies dominated business-to-business marketing. Selling was a matter of sales prospecting and closing, and many marketers dismissed the notion of selling their product by what they considered "mail order." Makers of high-ticket business and industrial goods, in particular, routinely expected their sales forces and distribution channels to handle the full selling load, aided by trade show appearances and advertising leads sent directly to the field. Of course, they used direct mail in a supportive role each time they mailed a sales letter, catalog, price sheet, or whatever. However, they didn't think in terms of using direct mail as a distinct marketing tool.

During the 1980s, beginning a trend continuing today, the cost of keeping a salesperson in the field ballooned, forcing marketers to find more efficient ways of locating prospects who are ready to see a salesperson, and less costly ways to service small and routine reorder accounts. Advanced computers and improved database management techniques certainly helped, spawning the growth of database-oriented marketing information systems. The payoff has been a dramatic boost in sales efficiency. In our experience, using direct mail at the start of the selling process to identify prospects ripe for a sales call cuts selling costs by as much as 25 percent compared to cold-call prospecting.

By any measure, direct mail to consumers and businesses constitutes a giant medium. Ad agency McCann-Erickson says marketers' direct mail spending totaled more than $27 billion in 1993.[1] The direct mail industry itself says third-class mail alone captured $25 billion of U.S. marketing budgets in 1992.[2]

Mail order, meanwhile, has grown into its own as a business marketing tool. Buyers seem to like it. A Cahners survey of buyers found only 27 percent reporting they had not purchased items by mail over the course of a year; 55 percent said they bought by mail three or more times during a year.[3]

And, as direct mail has grown more popular with business marketers, so too have the now-ubiquitous postcard decks available from publishers and list compilers for nearly every industry. Low-cost lead generators, postcard decks cast broad nets for capturing inquiries. We recommend them as a regular adjunct to all but the most tight lead-oriented communications programs. Because of the scant space on postcards, they generally do not allow asking many sight qualification questions and gaining more information about the inquiry. Hence, postcards are a loose-lead medium.

Consumer durables similarly provide fertile markets for greater use of direct mail. Now, even packaged-goods manufacturers are embracing similar approaches to their markets. In recent years, the growing costs of sales promotion and greater inefficiencies of mass media advertising have prompted consumer packaged-goods marketers to consider database-oriented strategies, with mail as the main communication tool for reaching core heavy-user segments.

But with the average consumer database maintenance cost-per-record edging close to $2—$1.74 was the estimate bandied about by the industry in 1992,[4] substantially more than the profit on the average sale—relatively few packaged-goods makers actively use database marketing so far. Those few who do either have special marketing needs and problems, such as cigarette marketers (who someday may not be able to advertise in mass media), or they've made a leap of faith and budget their database efforts with an eye on the lifetime value of customers.

Like most everything else in marketing communications and sales, using direct mail remains a persuasive art married to the sciences of mathematics and modern data-processing technologies. To stand on its own without the help of a salesperson delivering the pitch, the mail piece must prevail against hostile forces such as corporate mail rooms that discard bulk-rate mailers and secretaries trained to screen their boss' mail even before it gets to its target audience. If it survives that far, the mailer must demand attention and create interest in order to overcome the common tendency of executives and everyday consumers alike to dismiss it as junk mail. To break through the mail blizzard, it's not unusual for marketers hoping to impress key prospects to mail elaborate "dimensional" mailings, and costly gifts to grab attention, get opened, and be remembered.

Generating Mail Leads

Mail excels at delivering a personalized, elaborate message at a precise point in time to a well-defined audience. That justifies its higher cost-per-contact compared to media advertising. Mail favors a tight-leads strategy of relatively high-cost, high-quality lead generation in which media advertising and publicity play supporting marketing communications roles.

A mailing can produce a faster response than a publication advertisement, arriving at a recipient's desk in a more or less predictable number of days after it is dropped into the mail system. It does not wait for a publication subscriber to get around to reading a specific page in a magazine she might pick up many times during a month. The ability to give the sales force extra leads when really needed can be critical to building sales department support for a lead-management program.

Your lead-producing mail campaign consists of a list or database of people to whom you mail the package—the letter, enclosures, reply device and envelope to hold them—that presents your offer. Successful direct mailers typically credit list selection with 50 to 60 percent of the response, and the value of the offer with another 25 to 30 percent. The package that goes in the envelope get 25 percent or less of the credit.

Set Objectives

This first step is no less important for mail than for any other type of lead generation program. But it is easier to set mail program objectives properly, with relevant, measurable, and time-dimensioned criteria.

A point we've stressed earlier bears repeating: only hold the medium accountable for what it can accomplish on its own. If you are selling mail-order products or services, increasing sales is a relevant objective. But if your mail produces inquiries for field follow-up, your objective is just that, generating qualified leads.

Measurability is particularly straightforward with mail campaigns. You know how many pieces you mailed and how many recipients responded. Naturally, the objective exists in a time frame and should be stated, for example, as "Generate 1,000 new-prospect inquiries during the first quarter." Timing is particularly critical for mail-program objectives because of the control the mailer has over mailing dates. When used correctly, mail produces leads exactly when salespeople need them, according to your "promotional window" schedule.

Set objectives for your overall mail program, and for each of the campaigns or subprograms within it. For example, you might require that your mail activity "produce 5,000 qualified sales leads during the calendar year." An individual mailing aimed at a well-defined target might have the sub-objective: "produce 1,000 qualified dealer referral inquiries from $100 million-plus companies east of the Mississippi in SIC XXX, during the first quarter." To satisfy that sub-objective, the next steps are developing the list, designing the offer, and devising a budget.

Planning the Expenditure

Ideally, you'll set your direct mail program budget *after* you've determined the kind of offer and the amount of list (database) management required to meet your communication objective. Most companies, unfortunately, start the process backwards, first setting a budget, then figuring out how to spend it.

The most practical approach sets a budget concurrent with offer design, list management, and the testing that should accompany program development. Using the return-on-promotional-investment (ROPI) formula in Chapter 5 and the performance analyses we'll discuss in Chapter 14, you will be able to make accurate estimates of your upcoming program's lead production and adjust your budget accordingly.

Exhibit 8-1 lists the cost elements of the typical direct mail budget. Notice that the costs listed include a healthy 15 percent add-on for testing offers and lists.

The budget form also illustrates how to calculate the campaign's net profit, a useful statistic when you've designed a program to sell merchandise directly. Profit is not, however, relevant for lead-oriented mail programs where the appropriate bottom-line number is the cost-per-qualified inquiry.

Building Your Database

List is the time-honored word for the database of names and addresses that go on the envelopes carrying your mail offer. Databases serving modern marketing—or Power Profiles™ as we call them—are much more than lists of names, addresses, and phone numbers. They contain valuable background and selling history information about customers and prospects. When they are developed properly, they are built rather than merely rented or bought, as are lists developed by others. No matter how powerful the offer or creative your spiel, if the message doesn't get to the right prospect, it's wasted.

Sales lead management is an important part, arguably the most important part, of building the databases that effectively guide marketing communications, selling, and distribution programs. But powerful marketing databases include information from a variety of sources.

Exhibit 8-1
Direct Mail Budget Planner

Direct Mail Budget Planner

Description: _____

Quantity: _____

General Expenses:

Planning/Administrative/Operating		$_____
Salaries (hours × hourly rate)		
Creative Costs/Preparations		
Copy	$_____	
Layout	$_____	
Artwork	$_____	
Photography/retouching	$_____	
Printing preparation	$_____	$_____
Printing/Paper/Materials		$_____
Other Enclosures		$_____
Envelopes		$_____
Mailing List Rental/Purchase		$_____
Mailing List Maintenance		
Handling (folding, collating, inserting, labeling, addressing, metering, sorting, tying, etc.)		$_____
Postage		
Outgoing	$_____	
Return	$_____	$_____
If selling merchandise:		
Cost of merchandise	$_____	
Packaging/Handling	$_____	
Postage/Shipping	$_____	
Royalties	$_____	
Refunds/Cancellations	$_____	
Refurbish/Returns	$_____	
Bad debts	$_____	
Storage	$_____	$_____
		$_____
Other:		$_____
_____	_____	_____

Total campaign budget:	$_____
Plus 15% for testing:	$_____
Adjusted campaign budget:	$_____
Gross profit from merchandise:	$_____
Net profit from campaign:	$_____

Source: R. E. Clark Advertising and Inquiry Handling Service, Inc.

In-house Databases

Most companies swim in data. The trouble is, the information usually is squirreled away in different places, under the jealous control of different functions and fiefdoms, such as finance and accounting departments. Databases relevant to marketing include shareholder and creditor lists, and customer transaction information about orders, shipments, receivables, and returns. Then there are databases maintained in different parts of the marketing and sales operation, such as customer service requests, warranty card registrations, sales call reports, sales rep field reports, and the sales lead master database with its inquiry and lead-status information.

Unfortunately, the typical marketing department often finds those databases inaccessible. Other departments won't allow you to "mess up the files." More likely, record formats differ among databases. Merging them is a science and practiced art in its own right.

The ideal, something a new business can design at the start, is a database containing information about all interactions a customer or prospect has had with the firm, be it a single inquiry or a lengthy sales, service, and credit record. That facilitates planning. For example, ranking customers by the recency, frequency, and size of their orders indicates who deserves the most attention from the sales force or outbound telemarketing. A complete database allows you to determine if an inquiry has come from a customer or a prospect on whom the sales force is already calling. The inquirer might be a new purchasing influence at a prospect firm, making the lead particularly important to the salesperson working that account.

Outside Databases

Varying widely in quality, outside databases include compiled and response lists. Savvy marketers, therefore, keep updating their own databases with outside lists on a regular basis, spawning the relatively new business discipline of *marketing information systems* (MKIS).

MKIS specialists are the alchemists of database construction, combining lists to improve database accuracy and depth. It's science and art combined, they say, where a duplicated-name match rate of 75 percent is considered exceptionally good. MKIS managers then make the information available to marketing users— brand managers, regional sales managers, economic forecasters, marketing communications directors, production planners, etc.—in ways that will encourage use of the data.

Compiled lists. Compiled lists are lists put together from other lists and, at times, spruced up with some value-added information that updates and enhances their value. Compilers might combine information from a variety of sources—

Yellow Page listings and industrial directories, for example—to construct a special, narrowly defined database of interest to certain types of marketers. Some compilers, for instance, will develop a single industrial list by combining and reorganizing the information in several different industrial directories. Yellow Pages list compilers specialize in combining different Yellow Pages directories.

Compiled lists run the risk of being "dirty"—with many outdated names—because the compiled lists themselves are products of other lists that have been aging. Time is the great enemy of list accuracy. Database expert Todd Gibson of Unibase Direct, Inc. estimates that the average compiled list becomes outdated at the rate of 1.5 to 2 percent a month. Nonetheless, some compiled lists are remarkably accurate and up to date, giving them substantial value for loose-lead exploratory mail campaigns.

Compiled lists carry many names, typically sorted by SIC code and usually available in many other segmentation formats, as well. Often, they are the closest one can get to a publicly available census of the executives in a given field. One might feel put off by a high rate of "nixies" or duplicates showing up in a test of the list, when you've paid the Postal Service to return undeliverable mail. But what really counts is the hit rate: the number of qualified inquiries the list provides for your offer. A dirty list that is nonetheless productive on a cost-per-lead basis is still worth using.

Some list compilers go to extra lengths to improve the accuracy of their lists. The largest available list of all U.S. businesses is the 10-million-name D&B-Dun's Market Identifiers from Dun & Bradstreet Corp. D&B also vends the list on-line in abbreviated form, and in Canadian and International versions. D&B uses its extensive credit reporting information system to keep the list information updated, and to add information that allows substantial list segmentation. The American Business Lists division of American Business Information is the second largest list of U.S. businesses, kept current by periodic telephone calls verifying list information. That is also available for automated searchers, either on-line or via CD-ROM.

Each compiled database has its unique strengths and concurrent weaknesses, however. Some lists based on major corporate data will not have strong coverage of small business, for example, or of government buyers. Other lists may be weak in linking corporate parents and subsidiaries. So it is not surprising to find different names on different lists purportedly of the same universe. Gibson reckons that if you compare two large lists of the same kinds of businesses, as many as a fifth of all names might not appear in both lists.

Response lists. The other basic form of external databases, response lists, also varies widely in character and quality. But response lists share a critical common denominator: all are based on actual consumer or businessperson behavior.

Specialized business publication circulation lists of paid or *request controlled* subscribers, for example, are very popular response lists for industry-focused mail campaigns. They tend to be current, based either on paid subscription renewals or readers specifically asking to receive copies. Advertisers in those publications demand accurate circulation estimates, and the leading publications even ask publishing industry auditing services to attest to list accuracy. Circulation databases can segment markets by company type and size, reader job function, purchase involvement, and other criteria useful for lead generation programs, for example. Business association membership lists also help to define the extent of a particular industrial field. Compared to compiled lists, response lists are more useful for reaching targeted audiences with a tight-lead program.

Response lists can originate almost anywhere. In consumer marketing, recent catalog shoppers, mail-order buyers, and credit-card customers comprise the hot lists most prized by mailers. Those relying on mail marketing for business survival test such lists constantly, always looking for productive new ones characterized by high *RFM values* (the recency, frequency and monetary value of purchases). In turn, they create their own hot lists of customers which, typically, they'll put on the market.

Publication circulation lists are an interesting option for consumer marketers, because consumer publications tend to accumulate audiences of people with similar outlooks and interests. Association membership lists offer the same dimensionality.

The widespread use and availability of response lists has become a sensitive privacy issue in the 1990s. Computers enable some services to combine many response lists into virtually complete dossiers on individual households reporting their purchasing, credit, and income behavior, plus other purchasing behavior peccadilloes that critics argue should remain private from business or government scrutiny.

However, business response lists from other marketers tend to be much more jealously guarded than consumer response lists. Business market lists are smaller, average order sizes are far larger, and the individual names of each customer, prospect, inquirer, etc. are therefore far more valuable than consumer records.

A relatively new business-to-business marketing technique has shown how to capitalize on the value of response lists. Mailers, typically independent direct marketing agencies, send specialty premiums and questionnaires to large compiled lists. As many as a third of recipients might respond with a completed questionnaire about their businesses, which the mailer sorts into highly segmented databases for narrowly focused mailings.

For example, they could offer a specialty item to 500,000 forklift owners, seeking responses to very specific questions such as:

- Age of the forklift,
- Brand of forklift,
- Have they bought the current unit(s) or do they lease?
- Gas or electric?
- Do they have a service contract?

The mailer segments the respondents into separate, highly focused databases. Manufacturers use those lists to aim personalized letters and offers to owners of competitive brands, lessees, or, say, electric model owners. Service firms can target operators with expiring leases, or operators without service contracts, for instance, again with messages tailored to the recipient. Subsequent responses, often in double-digit percentages, provide highly qualified leads for sales and distributor follow-up.

Address accuracy. To maintain list integrity as you combine and compile your own lists, the United States Postal Service provides a number of list correction services to mailers that are particularly helpful to consumer marketers. Using their own personnel, such as route carriers or licensed services, the Postal Service can apply a variety of options to ensure that lists comply with stricter addressing and discount criteria.[5]

Crafting Your Campaign

There's an old expression in direct marketing that isn't repeated enough: A brochure in an envelope isn't direct mail; it's a brochure in an envelope. Far too often, mailers fail to achieve their potential because they've merely sent a piece of collateral to a prospect, not a message that attempts to replicate how a good salesperson, armed with knowledge of his or her customer's needs, would approach a prospect. They've instead used mail as if it were media advertising.

The mail medium owes its true power, however, to the letter accompanying the brochure and other materials in the package. Actually, those other elements—be they a simple price list or "deal sheet," or an elaborate free gift—support the letter, not the other way around. The letter is the message that teases, excites, and convinces the recipient. The best letters are true works of art in persuasive writing.

The brochure accompaniment is hardly unimportant, of course. What you mail in the way of information, premiums, teasers, and gifts draws the recipient into your offer, reinforces it, and lends memorability and persuasion to the selling message delivered by the letter.

The nature of the message—the offer—can employ virtually every type of salesmanship and appeal appropriate to the target audience and the action you seek. Direct mail experts caution that each element of the package should make sense to recipients if, in their fumble-fingered eagerness to read through the package, some pieces get lost. In particular, the letter and brochure/enclosure should carry the complete selling message and indicate how and where to respond.

The Envelope

The initial impressions your envelope creates should be appropriate to your campaign strategy. Or, to put it another way, the envelope will produce recipient expectations that should match how you want your offer to be perceived.

Teaser copy on the outside of the envelope conveys a different message than a personally addressed plain business envelope. Each type has its virtues: a benefit-oriented teaser may grab the attention of qualified prospects, but isn't as dignified as the business-letter look appropriate to personalized executive letters. Similarly, using a window envelope—the kind that carries checks and account statements as well as direct mail pitches—can grab attention with recipients who open their own mail. Then again, windows don't create the same personalized impression as a plain business envelope with individually printed (not labeled) address. Some envelope and addressing formats, such as labeled addresses, immediately denote direct mail advertising to recipients, even without teaser copy on the envelope.

You can resolve format questions empirically with testing, but only after you've tested the most important elements in your campaign: the list and the offer. If your audience is large enough, and you don't feel confident that judgment alone will lead to the right format decisions, run tests. Unfortunately for many business-to-business direct mail efforts, the potential audience isn't large enough to sustain much testing activity. Getting statistically meaningful test results may require mailing to nearly the entire list.

The Letter

Direct mail letters need not be personalized to be powerful marketing tools. Personalization helps substantially, however, and it is easily available in modest quantities to anyone printing a string of letters on a computer. Technology also allows a personal-letter look even for mailings in the millions.

But what really makes a letter zing is the way its major elements reach out to a single reader to address his or her concerns, generate interest, and motivate a response in a way no brochure or piece of collateral stuffed in an envelope can.

The letter should be a message from a single writer to a single reader, crammed with facts proving why the offer benefits that individual. It talks about what the reader wants, not what the mailer is selling. It immediately addresses the prospect's inevitable question: "What's in it for me?"

Some will argue tactical niceties, such as whether to insert subheads in the letter text to reinforce the development of the selling arguments. Others suggest that subheads be avoided because they detract from the personal business-letter look. Again, judgment, your objectives, the nature of your offer and the kind of impression you wish to make dictate how to proceed. If your budget and market size allow it, testing will indicate what works.

The key issue, however, is not design, subheads, margin sizes, flush- vs. ragged-right type, etc. as much as it is the progression of the selling message. Bob Stone, the dean of direct mail, recommends these letter-writing pointers.

- Promise a benefit in your headline or first paragraph.
- Immediately enlarge on your most important benefit.
- Tell the reader specifically what he or she is going to get.
- Back up your statements with proof and endorsements.
- Tell the reader what she might lose if she doesn't act.
- Rephrase your prominent benefits in your closing offer.
- Incite action, now.[6]

It's important to make your letter a true letter, addressed and signed like any other. That adds to the personalized feel, even if the salutation is a non-personalized greeting such as "Dear Systems Manager."

The Enclosure

Playing a supporting role to the well-crafted pitch in your letter, each enclosure—be it a brochure, floppy diskette, videotape, ad reprint, catalog, price sheet, etc.—should stand on its own to repeat the selling message and encourage the response. Enclosures might also be product samples or premiums and advertising specialties that cannot carry much more information than your company name. But don't ignore even that opportunity to reinforce the "where to get it" message.

Incidentally, know in advance how postal regulations will affect different types of premiums and fulfillment items. Tales abound of companies pouring thousands of dollars into premiums—razor blades, flammable materials, and other items that could conceivably injure postal workers—only to find out too late that the U.S. Postal Service would not accept them.

One popular form of direct mail doesn't require enclosures: the self-mailer serves as the envelope as well as the letter and brochure. Similarly, catalogs can be mailed without an envelope and letter.

Keep two caveats in mind when considering what, if any, brochure or enclosure will supplement your direct mail letter. First, avoid using an enclosure that's not suitable for the mailing. Mailers understandably trying to stretch a dollar often overlook this rule, stuffing in the envelope whatever promotional items happen to be lying around. More is not necessarily better if it fails to contribute to the message or confuses the recipient. The extra advertisement and article reprints the magazine publisher gave you may raise different issues and promote different products and services than the main thrust of your campaign, for instance.

Second, do not give the recipient too much information. If, say, you are generating leads with your mailing, you want to build the target audience's curiosity so that qualified prospects have a reason to respond for more information or a sales call. But be careful to avoid the other extreme—the literature loop—in which you fritter away the prospect's interest in a sequence of mailers, bouncebacks, more mailers, and more bouncebacks. The qualified response to the first mailing should receive a salesperson's follow-up call as well as your fulfillment.

The Reply Device

All mailings must solicit a response. And, short of asking the business prospect to write on her letterhead, your mail package to business and consumer prospects will need a reply device. But they receive short shrift from many marketers. Even if you only want phone or fax responses, you should include a card prominently telling the prospect "How to order," "How to receive your free information," etc.

We do not recommend relying solely on phone or fax responses, because some prospects, although qualified and very interested in your proposition, will prefer the relative anonymity of a reply postcard or questionnaire. Some will fear that a telephone call implies too much obligation on their part, and will lead to a sales pitch they're not ready to hear.

Also, print your inquiry phone number prominently on your response card, because what you really want are immediate responses from qualified prospects, not lots of cards moving slowly through the mail. Salespeople recognize the value of inbound phone leads and follow them up. And, offering an inquiry phone number will boost response. (Using an 800-number prominently throughout a mailing can increase response fourfold!)

In designing your response vehicle, keep in mind the response tips cited in Chapter 6. You want to gather as much relevant information as is practical to enable sight qualification. Typically, a postage-paid business reply card (BRC) with a few critical qualification questions will do the trick. Use a business reply envelope (BRE) and questionnaire for more involved or confidential information. Exhibit 8-2 shows the front and back of a well-designed mail package reply card.

Note how the card gets right to the point. The card asks first if the inquirer wants a sales call, then it asks for phone and fax numbers and the best time to call. Next, it lists basic qualification questions relevant to the services being offered (lead management, telemarketing, and fulfillment), and it offers three different types of literature. The inquirers' name, title, company, and address are less important than her phone number, so space for those data appears at the bottom of the card.

Exhibit 8-2

IHS Bounceback Card

ihs

NO POSTAGE
NECESSARY
IF MAILED
IN THE
UNITED STATES

BUSINESS REPLY MAIL

FIRST CLASS MAIL PERMIT NO. 112 SAN FERNANDO, CA

POSTAGE WILL BE PAID BY ADDRESSEE

INQUIRY HANDLING SERVICE, INC.
200 PARKSIDE DRIVE
SAN FERNANDO CA 91340-9976

Yes! I Need Some Answers

☐ja Call me. I'm interested.
My phone: (______) ________________ Ext. ________
Best time to call: jc ________ a.m. ________ p.m.
My fax: jd (______) ________________

Our need is: ☐ka Immediate ☐kb 1-3 months ☐kc 4-6 months ☐kd Over 6 mos. ☐ke Info only

We sell/manufacture the following type of products:
☐ba Medical instruments ☐be Electronic components
☐bb Pharmaceutical ☐bf Food services
☐bc Computers ☐bg General business/industry
☐bd Computer peripherals ☐bz Other: ________

Name/Title: ________________
Company: ________________
Dept. or M/S: ________________
Address: ________________
City/State/Zip: ________________
Please make necessary address corrections.

☐ Send me literature about your services.
☐ Send me The Three Sales Secrets.
☐ Start (continue) sending your free newsletter.

I'm a: ☐aa Business to business marketer ☐ac Media space rep ☐ab Advertising agency ☐ad Consumer marketer

I'm interested in the following sales & marketing support services:
☐fa Closed loop lead handling ☐fe Bulk literature distribution
☐fb 800 number services ☐ff Product fulfillment
☐fc Outbound telemarketing ☐fg Sales Projector software
☐fd Fax on demand ☐fh Direct mail services

The number of inquiries we generate per month is:
☐ca Less than 100 ☐cc 501-1000
☐cb 100-500 ☐cd 1001-3000 ☐ce Over 3000

The number of reps/distributors we have is:
☐cf Less than 50 ☐cg 50-100 ☐ch Over 100

If your need is immediate, please call 1-800-VIP LEAD or Fax 818-361-7286

20-30-294-50M

Source: Inquiry Handling Service, Inc

On the front of your reply card or reply envelope, be sure you meet the Postal Service's detailed printing regulations, including the size of the card itself, the required printing and notifications, and barcodes needed for automated mail sorting. Returns will cost you much more if you do not meet requirements. Postal Service representatives usually are happy to review your card design in advance.

Postage-paid reply cards and toll-free phone numbers are the most popular response formats. A survey of direct mail services and list brokers ranks reply devices as shown in Exhibit 8-3.

Co-ops and Postcard Decks
In direct mail, you don't have to go it alone. Consumer marketers frequently use "co-op" mailings which combine the coupons, brochures, etc. of several companies into one envelope. The most common form of the co-op in business-to-business markets is the postcard deck.

Exhibit 8-3
Most Effective Response Mechanisms

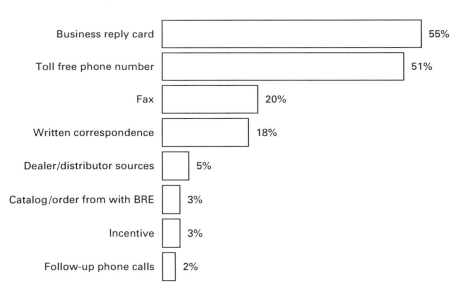

Source: *Cahners Advertising Research Report No. 560.1A* (Newton, MA: Cahners Publishing Co., 1992).

The postcard deck medium has enjoyed substantial growth among business marketers over the past 15 years, paralleling growing sophistication in inquiry generation and lead handling. Specialized business publications have found postcard decks to be a profitable way to offer access to their readers at rates substantially lower than standard advertising. And postcard deck advertisers enjoy a very lead-oriented medium: a business reply card with an ad on the other side. Unlike reader service inquiries requiring publisher handling before they get to the advertiser, the postcard goes to the advertiser or its lead-management service directly, cutting days, even weeks, off the fulfillment cycle.

Decks provide a fast and economical way to build extra inquiry volume, particularly when assessing the possibilities in a new market segment. And, while the card must compete with other cards in the deck, every advertiser has an ad the same size, leveling the playing field.

Nowadays, virtually every industrial field has one or more postcard decks serving it, either generating inquiries or soliciting orders for everything from paper clips to executive jets. The medium has become a valuable extra source of revenue for most special-interest business publishers. Decks provide marketers with economical access to high-quality, well-targeted circulation lists.

The trick is not what you promote, but how intelligently you approach the medium, in line with your lead program objectives. Postcard decks are not image- or awareness-building media. They are pure lead generators. Recipients like the ease with which they can flip through a variety of mail offers. Cahners Publishing claims that 91 percent of audiences receiving its publications' postcard decks say they are useful. About 89 percent said they look through them, with the average recipient mailing back 4.5 cards per deck.[7]

That points to one of the drawbacks of a postcard deck; unlike an advertisement with a reader service number, there's no pass-along readership for a card that's been returned. Another difficulty: the space on a 3- × 5-inch card is limited, and at least a third of it must provide room for the reader's response (name, phone, address, and some qualification information). Some advertisers ask inquirers to put their addresses on the front of the card, like a return address, to save room on the back. Make sure you get the phone number. It's more important than the address for follow-up purposes.

Give your inbound 800-number prominent display on your card, because you're really looking for hot leads, not lots of cards in the mail. But don't discount the cards mailed back with handwritten information. It's compelling proof to a salesperson that a real live prospect actually did ask for more information.

In choosing which decks to join, use the same criteria you would apply to direct mail lists. Recognize that while a thin, anemic-looking deck won't look important to the recipient, your card risks getting lost in too fat a deck. We recommend avoiding decks of fewer than 25 cards or more than 100.

Testing Your Campaign Response

Because direct mail allows you to trace replies and mail-order sales to specific pieces mailed, it's a medium particularly amenable to testing. Comparing the performance of different combinations of specific packages mailed to specific lists generally will indicate which combinations work best and, therefore, should be used for the complete mail campaign. Large mailers, such as consumer marketers, office supply companies, and the like, constantly test new lists and offers, always seeking the new combination that beats their reigning champion.

Yet, while simple in concept, testing is a discipline that requires careful controls and more attention to detail than many are willing to invest, particularly business-to-business marketers. Testing requires professional judgment. Many factors interact to make a mailing successful and testing them all is rarely feasible. Testing could exhaust the relatively small lists of business-to-business campaigns before the full campaign is ready to roll out, for example. So you usually must limit tests to the items most likely to influence response rates. According to direct marketing expert Lin Andrews, the list will affect 50 percent of your response rate, while creative elements in your mail package affect just 10 percent. Timing and the nature of your offer each influence about 20 percent of response, she says.[8]

Testing can be expensive, particularly if you produce two significantly different packages for comparisons. (Experts recommend that you avoid sinking money into testing minor variations of letters, brochures, envelopes, response cards, etc.) The vagaries of statistics suggest that even the best-crafted tests can easily produce results that could vary widely from subsequent full mailings. Make sure you mail enough test pieces to make it likely you'll receive stable test results.

To keep costs controllable, marketers do not actually test every candidate list paired with every candidate package; they test lists against each other and compare packages to each other, and infer the likely effect of pairing a winning list with a superior package. They are careful to run tests simultaneously to avoid the effects of seasonality and changed market conditions. They only test meaningful differences in packages and offers and they are alert to possible biases in the list samples they procure for testing.[9]

Response and Timing

One of the most frequently asked questions in direct mail marketing concerns response rates. What, everyone naturally wants to know, is a "good" response rate?

The answer isn't an easy one; it varies widely by market, product, season, economic conditions, etc. General business list mailings for business seminars that produce a half a percentage point response are considered winners. But the same response rate from a dimensional mailing seeking inbound phone and bounceback card leads from, say, a tightly defined list of specialist engineers, would be a colossal flop. (In the latter case, outbound telemarketing should follow up such a well-targeted, high-impact, high-cost mailing, no matter what the passive response.) Seeking leads produces more response than seeking firm orders, all other things being equal. Mailing to customer or inactive customer lists will produce more response than mailing cold to unknown individuals.

Watch your response closely day by day, because early returns hint at your eventual response total. As a rule of thumb for responses to lead-generating mailings, your first phone inquiries will occur within about five business days after the mail drop. Your first BRC responses will come about one-and-a-half weeks after the drop. The response will build over the next week-and-a-half to two weeks, then taper off. Additional responses will dribble in and, within five weeks of the drop, you should have received about 90 percent of the inquiries you'll eventually get.

But, rather than rely on someone else's numbers, use sales lead management to keep track of your raw inquiries and qualified leads, so you can beat your reigning champion.

Receiving too many inquiries at one time can overwhelm your qualification and follow-up resources, not to mention the sales force that will only cherry-pick the best and ignore the rest. When that's a risk, rolling out a mail campaign in portions fairly distributed among sales territories (such as an *n*th name draw) avoids a glut of leads.

Use multiple mailings to build response, sending follow-ups to non-responders, or distributing serial mailers. In a serial mailing, each drop includes a different piece of a set: for example, a teaser campaign or pieces of a premium. Serial mailings work well for getting a foot in the door to sell expensive business products and long-term service relationships. For instance, mail a set of drinking glasses one at a time, then offer a free rack to hold the glasses, to be delivered by a salesperson.

Finally, do not assume that everyone receiving your mail piece will see it. Do you, for example, read every piece of mail sent to your office and home? The need to break through the clutter prompts mailers to mail often, working a list several times until response trails off significantly. In other words, don't discard a productive list after just one or two passes at it unless you have firm evidence that most people on it saw your offer and rejected or accepted it, or that not enough new prospects have yet moved into the market to make another drop worthwhile.

Chapter 9

Telemarketing: Ignore It at Your Peril

Mention telemarketing in a room of marketing executives and mixed reactions surface. From pained expressions to subtle, knowing smiles, this not-so-new method of customer contact and relationship building still provokes strong opinions. Driven by companies desperately seeking new markets for which they have no channels of distribution, and employed by others hoping to trim soaring sales expenses, telemarketing is either grudgingly adopted or eagerly embraced as a savior or a panacea. Typically, firms dip a toe into the medium rather than take a plunge. One reason is that sales vice presidents steeped in field operations are reluctant to admit that there might be better, less expensive ways to sell a product or service.

Many companies nevertheless have learned that the phone can be the most economical way to service small accounts, with little or no loss in customer loyalty. Other companies have literally been saved by telemarketing handling virtually all their selling, in business as well as consumer markets. And many firms have thrived by making telemarketing their prime sales channel. One computer software maker, for instance, even designs products to fit the telemarketing medium, offering systems salespeople can explain easily over the phone.[1]

Telemarketing also attracts a loud chorus of critics from business, consumerist, and government circles concerned about telemarketing's unique intrusiveness. But it is a medium that is here to stay, and that can be effective without being offensive. Marketers who ignore telemarketing's virtues do so at their peril.

Seeking Leads Through Telemarketing

In seeking sales leads, telemarketing is a powerful tool in three ways. Telemarketing generates leads, it's an efficient inquiry tool popular with prospects, and it is the best mechanism for qualifying inquiries that can't be sight-qualified. According to our lead database, toll-free inbound telemarketing calls produced 8 percent of all inquiries in 1993, and toll-call inquiries added another 7 percent.

Technology and competitive pressures combined in the 1980s to propel telemarketing to explosive growth. By 1990, telemarketing sold $435 billion in goods and services annually, up from $72 billion in 1982. Entrepreneurs had launched some 450 telemarketing service agencies by then, with 300 of them in business less than four years.[2] By 1993, calls to 800-numbers totaled nearly 13 billion, compared to 11 billion the year before. More than a half-million companies offered 800-lines by the end of 1993, according to AT&T.[3]

Meanwhile, corporate "internal call centers" became increasingly popular until a soured economy and corporate "rightsizing" moved many companies to outsource telemarketing duties.[4] Wherever marketers initiated their calling, in-house or out-of-house, the $9 to $10 average cost per telemarketing call continues to be a very attractive alternative to the $200-plus costs of a person-to-person visit to an account, particularly when the order gathered is a modestly sized one or a routine repurchase.

The Right Medium for You?

Whether you should start a telemarketing operation inbound or outbound, in-house or outsourced, depends on your answers to several key questions:

- Could inbound callers to your company be better serviced?
- Will the product mix—and your gross profit—support the inbound and outbound call costs?
- Are your current sales and distribution channels unable to serve all prospects you would like to pursue?
- Can you make the commitment to manage the function and provide appropriate personnel and resources?
- Are your competitors using telemarketing, inbound or outbound, and why?

A *yes* answer to any of these questions suggests that some sort of telemarketing service can help you gain market share and reduce sales expenses.

The question about competitive activity is particularly important. If competitors telemarket heavily and they are gaining share at your expense, you might be underselling to your market, missing segments telemarketing can reach efficiently and effectively. If competitors are not using telemarketing, those same segments may represent unexploited opportunities waiting to be plucked from the vine before your rivals spot them.

Inbound Telemarketing

We discussed the critical nature of inbound telemarketing in Chapter 3. Increasingly, prospects expect to be able to telephone a company—particularly with urgent inquiries—and have those calls answered courteously and professionally. Typically, those calls are the first contact customers-to-be will have with your company. The quality of those first impressions will determine the future of your company.

Although toll-free phone numbers arguably are the hottest marketing tool around for both business and consumer marketers, the technology isn't new. AT&T introduced it in 1967. Call volume that year was 7 million. Today, AT&T has 500 competitors offering 800-number services. It still dominates the field, handling 13 billion 800-number calls in 1993,[5] out of an estimated 20 billion 800-number calls overall in the United States.[6]

Callers expect they will be able to get oral or printed information quickly, and speak with someone knowledgeable about the product or service offered. They want to find out where to buy the product, learn how much it costs, and be able to do that at odd hours and still get an answer. Perhaps they are the ultimate hot lead, calling to make an appointment to see a sales representative or to place an order.

To handle the inbound function correctly, you must treat it as a department in its own right, staffed by well-trained people aided by the right equipment for their mission. Your telephone service representatives (TRSs) might simply answer incoming calls and capture callers' names, addresses, products of interest, lead sources, and a few other bits of qualification information. Or, they might attempt to close the sale on the phone. They might work closely with outside sales representatives, or have a "territory" of their own.

Some inbound systems automate the process and automatically fax information back to the caller. Others automatically read the incoming call phone number, search a database, and bring an information record to the TSR's computer screen, if the caller has inquired or purchased before. Still other systems can transfer calls automatically to dealers, according to the location indicated by the caller's phone number.

Inbound numbers can link callers to on-line ordering services, computer bulletin boards, recorded information messages, and up-to-the-minute where-to-buy advice. The permutations for handling inbound phone inquiries are almost as limitless as the imagination and budget of the company employing them. If you think of inbound telemarketing not only as a live body on the end of the line, but strategically as a tool for convenient information access for your marketplace, then you are ready to adopt inbound telemarketing as a competitive weapon.

In contrast, not having a disciplined, professional inbound call-handling system makes a company look old-fashioned, unresponsive, and out of touch nowadays. Prospects demand gratification, and they've learned to get it from many firms. Whether the person calling is a purchasing agent, the recommender, or the final decision maker, an inbound telemarketing phone number—preferably a toll-free 800-number—is a must.

Timing and Convenience

Salespeople, whose livelihoods depend on shrewd judgments about prospects, consider the ones who call to make an inquiry to be the best leads for follow-up. Although inbound phone leads convert at roughly the same rate (50 percent) as all inquiries (45 percent), they are immediate, fresh requests for product information. They give salespeople an additional chance to beat the competition.

The best sales reps also know that even if their particular products take months or years to specify and install, providing an 800-number is simply good business. Inbound telemarketing satisfies the buyer's information-gathering process launched by your press releases, ads, direct mail, etc., regardless of where prospects are in their buying cycles.

Newly introduced products regularly seize attention and eventual sales from buyers might have chosen tentatively until your new product appeared. Buyers often change their requirements when a new whiz-bang product comes along with a better solution. The information access 800-number can greatly help their last-minute course corrections.

As we saw in Exhibit 3-8, the telephone (20 percent) and inbound 800-number telemarketing (12 percent) combined comprise the largest method of lead reception among business marketers. That's just the average, however. Some companies compete in markets almost completely driven by inbound telemarketing leads. A computer peripherals manufacturer, for example, uses 800-numbers to communicate with four different audiences in vertical and general consumer markets. About 90 percent of its inquiries arrive by phone, thanks in part to the company's memorable 1-800-4PRINTERS number.

While some CEOs and chief financial officers might not understand the importance of catering to telephone information requests with the extra convenience of a toll-free number, we have yet to meet a sales manager who did not believe in the value of an 800-number to advance the sale. Certainly the available research explains why. Nine out of 10 business publication readers use 800-numbers to inquire about products. And 92 percent said they would like to see more advertisements listing 800-numbers.[7] Ads with 800-numbers tend to be more frequently read, as well.[8]

If you want to find out if your marketplace would like you to have a toll-free number, just ask your receptionist how often callers have inquired about one.

Then call your own company from outside to find out how easy or difficult it is for prospects to receive information. Try at critical hours, such as around lunchtime and near the start and end of the business day. See how may rings it takes to get answered, how long you are on hold, and how competent is the response.

Then, if you think you will not receive enough calls to justify staffing an inbound phone operation—a frequent management reservation—investigate your outsourcing options.

800-number Benefits for You

The virtues of inbound telemarketing imply these specific benefits for marketers using the medium to gather inquiries via trained telemarketers capturing database input. 800-numbers can help you:

- Measure the results of different promotional tactics.
- Increase overall response to marketing communications.
- Immediately qualify a high percentage of leads: 15–40 percent.
- Refer caller to nearest dealer or distributor.
- Refer hot leads to the field faster.
- Make appointments on the spot for sales calls.
- Develop a database of profile information coming from different sources.
- Control the message given to callers if the inbound calls are centralized and don't simply go to a receptionist.
- Cover extended hours. Usually the service or in-house inbound department will work those hours needed to capture the greatest number of callers. With the time zone differences in the United States, that requires 12-hour coverage daily to catch the 8 A.M. callers in New York and the 5 P.M. callers in California. Add two more hours to include Hawaii. Longer hours usually are available from outside services at no premium.
- Drive the inbound caller directly into a fax-on-demand system.

One of the greatest benefits of the telephone is that it is an interactive inquiry management tool. The TSR can gauge a person's interest and qualification on the spot, and discard or filter those people who may be confused about the application of your product. For example, if a company advertises scanning microscopes, then a person from a biology lab may not be the ideal user. The scanning microscope is used to detect surfaces down at the atomic level, while the biology department may be more interested in frog livers.

Consumer popularity. On the consumer product marketing side, two-thirds of manufacturers offered 800-numbers for inquiries in 1993, up from 40 percent a decade earlier, according to the Society of Consumer Affairs Professionals in Business.

Consumer marketers consider inbound systems more a tool for building databases and keeping customers rather than finding new ones. And research found that 86 percent of consumers think an 800-number on a package connotes quality. It gives a marketer a human face.[9] Overall, consumers make 80 percent of all 800-number calls.[10]

Benefits for sales, too. Ask salespeople what they want from corporate regarding sales leads and the first thing they'll say is "I want more leads." Provide the leads and ask the question a second time. The response will then be: "Oh, no, you misunderstood. I don't need more leads; I need more qualified leads."

For salespeople, the 800-number provides:

- A large proportion of highly qualified leads.
- Inquirer profile information indicating need, desire, authority, budget, etc.
- A means of screening out unqualified leads.
- An opportunity to beat competitors who do not use 800-numbers.
- A means of making appointments for the sales force.
- A way callers can get where-to-buy information: the names of nearest sales reps or dealers.
- Faster literature distribution.
- A way of limiting information given by phone to carefully orchestrated scripts (rather than letting a caller reach an uninformed receptionist or someone in service who "tells all").
- Increased cash flow via credit card sales.

Benefits for inquirers. Remind skeptics that an 800-number builds goodwill with customers and prospects.

- They will receive fulfillment literature in days rather than weeks compared to other inquiry methods.

- They will receive critical information they need right on the phone.
- Inquirers can find the nearest place to buy the product.
- Inquirers willing to give profile information will likely get a faster follow-up.
- Inquirers can access other information services available from the company (fax-on-demand, etc.).

Maximizing 800-Number Benefits

Having worked with hundreds of companies, we have found that most that do have an 800-number often underutilize it. Those burying the 800-number in copy blocks or in signature copy will be lucky to get 2 to 5 percent of their response from the toll-free number. Readers are more likely to use instead the reader service number, delaying the information they seek by three to 12 weeks. By then, however, decisions to buy have often been made, and product has even been delivered by competitors.

But, those who aggressively use the toll-free number might receive 15 to 40 percent of their response through it. Here are some ways to use an 800-number to multiply the number of inquiries telephoned to your company several times over.

Call-handling tips.

- Automated call routing prequalifies inquirers and holds callers at peak hours. Make your message a friendly but sales-oriented one, and provide a live-operator "escape" for callers.
- If your phone number is one that spells a name or mnemonic (e.g. 800-USA-LEAD), provide the numerical sequence beneath it in smaller type. Not all phones show letters nowadays. And some people hate to study the phone dial. Be careful of the letter *O;* people confuse it with the operator key, the numerical zero.
- Avoid having tech service reps handling 800-number calls. They wind up giving out more information than they should, they won't fill out the forms, and they'll resent the imposition.
- Avoid the "call collect" invitation. It's old fashioned, and collect calls require an operator's intervention to accept the call.
- Test your system periodically by calling in yourself at peak times, to see if calls are properly handled, inquirer questions answered, and proper information collected from inquirers. Was referral to technical experts handled properly and promptly?

• When salespeople call accounts for appointments, have an 800-number for them to leave as a call back if the prospect isn't in.

In advertisements.

• Separate the 800-number from the signature block. Leave plenty of white space around it.

• Use a second color to direct reader attention to the number.

• Announce the call as "free." That word attracts plenty of attention.

• Increase the size of the 800-number typeface so it is as large as your logo.

• Print the 800-number prominently on coupons or tip-in reply cards. Don't bury it in small type. You really don't want the card returned, you want phone calls. Run it ahead of and more prominently than your address, to encourage phone inquiries.

• Provide separate response numbers depending on the service the inquirer seeks (e.g. send literature, have a salesperson call, etc.).

• List your service hours for the 800-number. Make sure a recorded message or answering service can field calls at other times.

• Use the TSR to receive fax-on-demand inquiries. The TSR can capture names and other vital information, then transfer callers to the fax system.

• Do not let your ad agency drop the 800-number from the ad because it allegedly makes the presentation ugly. That and other "reasons" are excuses for avoiding accountability. If the agency insists and is stubborn, find one that understands your needs.

• Do not drop your reader service card number from the ad, hoping that will prompt more phone response. That will hurt more than help in the long run. Give inquirers every possible response option, being sure that inbound phone inquiries receive the priority treatment they deserve.

In brochures.

• Print the 800-number in a prominent place, next to the signature block.

• Print it larger than the address line.

• Repeat it on reply cards placed within your literature.

In direct mail. You only want a returned business reply card as a last resort. Move the sale ahead two to six weeks by placing the 800-number:

• Above the signature block.

- Next to the call to action.
- Wherever a call to action appears throughout the direct mail package letter, brochure, etc.
- Repeat it on the reply card, at the top.

In newsletters. We have seen overwhelming response when an 800-number appears in soft-sell newsletters. Whether the newsletter is considered educational or a presentation for your products and services, an 800-number generates response throughout the life of a newsletter issue—three to four weeks for a monthly. One company expecting 500 calls from its newsletter received an astounding 5,000-plus inquiries on its toll-free number. Approximately 60 percent of the calls resulted in sales!

Use the 800-number in newsletters:

- At the end of each article that describes your product or service.
- Near the signature block.
- On loose or bound-in reply cards.

In press releases. An 800-number can be used as more than a convenience for the editor to call the person on the release listed as the "contact person." If it is cleverly designed into the release, and is tastefully executed, the editor might leave the number in the PR release body copy.

Outbound Telemarketing

Although its reputation suffers at the hands of annoyed consumers and unscrupulous "boiler room" operations, outbound telemarketing has year-by-year marched to the forefront as a major marketing and sales tool. Considering how often one calls customers and prospects for whatever reasons, telemarketing expenditures dwarf those of other marketing tools.

Still, when the subject of outbound telemarketing comes up at business marketing planning meetings, some hidebound corporate managers sing familiar refrains:

"One of those people interrupted me at dinner . . ."

"But our products are technical!"

"Our customers expect to talk to someone who can answer tough applications questions."

"Our salespeople don't want anybody talking to their customers but them."

Predictable excuses, they're usually mouthed by those out of touch with industry trends. While full-bore outbound telemarketing is not appropriate for every firm in every market, we have seldom found companies that can't use a trained TSR to sell product, qualify sales leads, book appointments for sales-people, perform valuable market research, render technical support, advance special promotions, and perform other precise communications tasks.

Powerful Field Support

Most outbound TSR applications support the established outside sales force. When done correctly, outbound telemarketing handles accounts the field reps have not serviced well, if at all. With three calls to each name on a list, the outbound telemarketer will, on average, reach 75 percent of them.

The TSR, as a sales rep who never leaves the office, speaks to 50 customers and prospects a day, and doesn't need a car allowance or expense account. Companies that have adopted outbound telemarketing out of frustration with an expensive outside sales organization often find their market is so huge that no direct sales organization can reach it, or dealer or distribution channels may be locked up with agreements that preclude newcomers.

They find outbound telemarketing can move capital equipment as well as consummables. One of the authors, for instance, sold $1 million in excess medical equipment inventory, at $16,000 per unit, in six months with four TSRs. Most good TSRs have one thing in common: they consider themselves to have greater skill for telephone selling and account penetration then outside sales representatives. Their verbal skills and "on-the-fly" ability to spar successfully with gatekeepers and hard-to-reach prospects can be awesome. Telemarketing consultant Richard Bencin describes the ideal TSR virtues as: "self-confident, resistant to rejection, clear communicators, good listeners, bright and creative, full of energy, reliable, thorough, able to handle an office environment, moti-vated by money, computer literate, and eager to excel."[11]

Relationship marketing. Outbound telemarketing in support of outside reps builds customer relationships at low cost. Outbound TSRs can help sales people immeasurably by beginning the customer contact process. A good TSR can make about 50 business-call dialings a day (or 75 to 100 consumer dialings a day). Armed with a good database (lists are as critical to telemarketing as they are to direct mail), the TSR can make 25 to 35 prospect presentations daily. Considering that it takes an average of 4.8 sales calls to close a sale, if one or two person-to-person calls can be handled by an outbound TSR, the savings can be significant.

Companies have even capitalized on outbound telemarketing by positioning it to prospects as a premier service superior to normal channels. For example, sales management in a medical instrument company had a problem getting salespeople to call on hospitals in a four-state area of North and South Dakota, Nebraska, and Kansas. Four telemarketers were assigned to those states, and the company spent $100 per hospital on premiums and incentives to introduce lab managers to their status as "priority" accounts. Telemarketers told the lab managers they therefore qualified for discounts and special binders of all literature on products they could buy. Each received specialty items mailed to them monthly to remind them of their "priority" status. They were told they would not be "bothered" with salespeople visiting unless they wanted an on-site demonstration. After sales for the four-state area doubled, field sales demanded the territory back.

Telequalify

One of the most important outbound telemarketing functions supporting sales is lead telequalification: gathering more information from inquirers whose quality (or lack of it) is not apparent on the face of the inquiry. We reviewed how telequalification fits into your lead system in Chapter 4.

Even the best sight-qualification effort can sort only 50 to 75 percent of inquiries properly. You can wait for the rest to mail their fulfillment package bounceback cards, a slow and usually unproductive process, or you can call them. The call is more expensive, but it's more immediate. And it will uncover more qualified prospects, for only 5 percent or so of inquirers will return a fulfillment bounceback card.

In effect, the telequalifier makes a preliminary sales call. But the mission is not to sell. The telequalifier shouldn't even try. The goal is educating prospects enough so they continue to the next stage of the selling process. Then, the telequalifier collects information to send to the highly trained sales experts in the field who know how to put the knowledge to use and close the sale.

Consultant and sales automation expert Richard Brock of Brock Control Systems, notes that, unlike the protocols for face-to-face sales calls, TSRs can use computerized scripts to guide their presentations. A rep on a call can't use a computer that way. In three to five calls, as Brock explains the process, the telequalifier maintaining contact with a prospect continues the education process at a low cost-per-call, until field sales is ready to move in with a live presentation and close.

Support Other Media

Outbound telemarketing will boost the success of your trade show exhibit. Invite prospects to visit the booth; call the ones within 200 miles of the show site and offer reasons they should stop to see you.

Use outbound telemarketing to bring salespeople up to speed in new territories, by getting them appointments every other day for the first two weeks. Companies that have tried it find new reps achieve almost the same productivity in the first month as seasoned salespeople.

Outbound telemarketing is a superb medium for gathering leads quickly if selling schedules or market conditions require a quick shot of adrenaline in the field.

Use outbound telemarketing to test the productivity of mailing lists. Calls to a random selection from the list, or a list test sample, can indicate quickly whether the list identifies the right kinds of people for your offer, and whether the offer needs some modification.

Seminars and group sales situations benefit greatly from outbound telemarketing to those prospects who did not respond to your mailed invitation. The call is an insurance policy for filling the room and covering costs. In the group sales/seminar situation, outbound and inbound telemarketing can serve together. Outbound can call in advance to test the mailing list and test the offer. Inbound can handle the response. Outbound comes back into the picture for reminder/confirmation calls prior to the event and to provide a final list of attendees. The outbound person can call after the event to survey attendees opinions.

Did-You-Buy? Research

Use outbound telemarketing to perform follow-up research with inquirers that's faster and more complete than a mail survey. Telephone inquirers three, six, nine, or 12 months after their request. You'll collect invaluable information about your closing rates, field follow-up, and market share. We'll discuss Did-You-Buy? studies in more detail in later chapters.

Telemarketing—Make or Buy?

The telemarketing explosion has spawned hundreds of independent telemarketing agencies across the country, operating locally, regionally, or nationally with varying degrees of skill and efficiency. Meanwhile companies of all sizes also maintain successful in-house operations. The question for anyone contemplating telemarketing in the marketing mix is whether in-house or outsourced services will best serve.

Shop carefully, and keep the suggestions that follow in mind.

The In-House Option

When we talk about "in-house," we refer to telemarketing managed as professionally as an outside service should perform it. Constant training and performance incentives, the use of approved scripts wherever possible, and comprehensive record-keeping are hallmarks of true telemarketing.

In-house telemarketing, as we consider it here, is not simply picking up the phone to call a customer. Nor is it letting the phone be answered by whoever is around. People charged with telemarketing "in their spare time" have other priorities that will command their attention. And forget the notion of "hiring a few college kids to make some calls." That, too, is an invitation to marketing chaos.

Nurture excellence. Consider the role telemarketers play as the first contacts your company has with customers, the future of your business. Actually, telemarketers are so important, TSRs are as critical to a company's health as its senior management—and more important than mid-level telemarketing department managers—according to recent research at a major telecommunications firm.[12]

Compensation is part of the formula for building such success. Because lead management plays such a critical role in presenting the company to its markets, pay the telemarketing staff well. We recommend that some portion be performance based, say 75 percent salary with 25 percent commission for outbound telequalifiers and outbound telephone service reps. Existing sales department and corporate personnel policies will dictate the right mix. On the other hand, don't over-entice people to rush through their duties in order to build volume.

In inquiry-handling departments, frequent praise, pedestals such as membership in an exclusive "200 Club" of high performers, the posting of results that highlight top producers, "caller of the day" awards, and the like help keep the staff in competitive trim. Reminding them of their critical contribution to the company, that they're the start of the selling process, and telling how much revenue and profit they produce will give them more pride, improving performance.

Strengths. A prime benefit of building your own telemarketing operation is tight on-site control of people and expenses. Your per-hour expenses might be about 60 percent of what the outside service charges.

Also, the in-house TSR can work closely with your field salespeople. And, if its possible for a TSR to replace a salesperson in the field, you can achieve significant cost reductions. For instance, a field representative requires a $75,000 to $95,000 investment per year for salary, commissions, car, benefits, etc. An inside telemarketing TSR can cost $50,000 to $60,000 per year, including salary, benefits, bonus and commissions.

Could an out-of-house telemarketer replace your in-house TSR? More than cost is at issue. Being fully immersed in your corporate culture and training, your in-house TSR undoubtedly becomes more technically competent selling your products, answering inquiries, etc. Some consider that to be both a boon and a curse, because you might not want too knowledgeable a TSR attempting to close an inquirer on the phone. Also, a technically knowledgeable TSR could give the qualified inquirer all the information sought, which could stall selling progress rather than pave the way for a salesperson's visit. The TSR's goal is to keep the lead hot.

Weaknesses. How would you like to speak with 60 people per day and only be able to have positive conversations with 20? The rest will be unavailable, abrupt, dismissive, and, on occasion, viciously rude. Regardless of the exciting nature of a company's products or its incentive system, the rejection rate can be devastating to all but the most iron willed. It takes its toll and adds to job burnout and turnover, a persistent problem in the telemarketing business. Unlike out-of-house TSRs who can vary their work among different products and clients, in-house people face what could be numbing predictability and an apathy that might be discernable to prospects they call. New products and promotional programs which alter the TSRs' routines can help their psyches considerably.

Then there's downtime: keeping reps busy when there are no calls to be made or answered. Make-do work is often needed to keep people productive.

We strongly recommend *against* assigning people to both outbound and inbound telemarketing duties. First, there's the timing problem. When working outbound call lists, a TSR cannot answer inbound calls. Then there's temperament; outbound TSRs face rates of rejection that will wilt the staffer used to handling inbound calls.

In-house people tend to generate larger phone bills than outsourced TSRs because they tend to talk more on calls. And in-house operations need special telephone equipment and reporting capabilities, the costs to be spread over however many or few calls are made.

The Outsourcing Option

Strengths. A major benefit in hiring a telemarketing service for outbound and/or inbound calls is that most services work on a project basis. You do not incur charges unless calls have been made or received. You buy the service by negotiating the rate per hour.

Services, experienced in their craft, maintain tight productivity schedules and controls on their TSRs. The best services train their staffers well.

Once you've established a relationship with a telemarketing service, it will have people on board who know your products. They will be able to respond quickly when you need a short-term burst of selling and lead management activity.

Weaknesses. The cost-per-hour of actual calling time for the outside service frequently is 30 to 50 percent greater than an in-house effort, depending on how you allocate in-house costs.

High turnover at outside services means they constantly retrain, decreasing the likelihood that veterans seasoned by working on your product will be available to service all your needs. Retraining a parade of new people eats into your marketing staff time.

Because they attempt to squeeze maximum productivity from their TSRs, outside service companies seldom have more people than absolutely necessary to answer the inbound call volume they expect. That means the call-abandon rate or call-waiting time might go up if a sudden client promotional blitz catches the outside service unprepared.

Some outside services specialize in certain industries, such as high tech or medical products. But many claim they can sell anything, an assertion as dubious as if a field rep says it.

Many companies, however, believe that they need their own people on the phone, particularly for inbound work, to answer technical questions that generalists cannot handle. The degree to which that's true depends on many factors, including your willingness to commit to TSR training. Remember, however, that out-of-house TSRs handle so many different products, that as time progresses their technical knowledge and ability to sound knowledgeable grows considerably.

A small company with modest call volume can get lost at a large telemarketing service used to handling clients receiving thousands of calls a month.

Predictable Failures

Both inbound and outbound departments within companies often fail for predictable reasons. When a manufacturer or service provider starts its telemarketing efforts with little forethought, minimal investment, and even less management, the scenario goes something like this.

The president tells the vice president of sales or marketing to "do this telemarketing thing ourselves. Hire someone to do it, put 'em in the vacant cubicle in the marketing department, and let 'em report directly to you."

The president has it all figured out. "Have the receptionist transfer the calls from the ads and such directly to that desk. When they're not takin' those inbound calls, have 'em call out and try to get appointments for the sales reps.

"When we get a lot of leads from PR and such, where we don't know anything about the inquirer, have 'em call those people in their spare time.

"Where do we find someone for this kinda job? Call the local college. Got to be some college kid that wants a job like this. Hey, even a part-timer would be good. We won't have to pay 'em benefits will we? Maybe two part-timers! Let 'em use the same desk. Let's make our outside sales representatives more productive!"

That company president violated every rule. He or she wants to entrust future sales to a part-time college kid. Mixing inbound and outbound duties is a recipe for trouble. And having the TSR report directly to the busy vice president never, never works. Get a telemarketing department manager; most vice presidents haven't had an hourly person report to them in years and now is no time to start.

Telemarketers need constant care and attention. They hunger for an almost daily affirmation of your confidence in them. They require a manager to keep them pointed at the right objectives.

Finally, plunking them down at a desk without the proper equipment— phones, computers, head sets, and direct lines that go around the company switchboard receptionist—will spell failure.

Telemarketing, whether inbound or outbound, can be a vital link to provide qualified sales inquiries for your distribution channel. Or it can be a distribution channel in its own right. When well organized and well led, with the proper equipment and solid objectives, it will be a powerful marketing tool and the source of decisive competitive advantage.

Part **3**

Managing Leads

Chapter 10

Qualifying and Profiling Hot Sales Leads

Quality exists in the eye of the beholder. That watchword of product and service marketing is no less true when it comes to sales leads. Depending on whom you ask, the same lead may be hot, lukewarm, cool to the touch, or tombstone cold.

The purpose of disciplined lead qualification is to remove biases from the lead-screening process. This means selecting leads not out of prejudice or hope, but objectively, based on the facts. A key reason why lead-management programs that depend solely on field sales qualification fail is the mix of emotions and preconceived notions salespeople bring to the task. Some might, for instance, summarily dismiss inquiries without telephone numbers or those from heavy circlers of reader service card numbers. Neither condition really correlates with an inquiry's actual "quality," but both are widely *assumed* to be signs of poor inquiry value.

Sometimes ingrained habits get in the way. We've heard of die-hard salespeople determined to make a personal call without telephoning first, who waste time trying to determine the street addresses of post office box number leads for which they had phone numbers. Others dismiss leads for less expensive line items as less qualified than those for more costly goods, regardless of the buyer's purchase likelihood. Some hate to acknowledge that leads from the home office are helpful, while others treat leads and follow-up requests as an imposition and resent the effort it takes to check up on them. At the other extreme, leads with some apparently very attractive qualities might be instantly—but erroneously— taken at face value.

Salespeople aren't the only ones using their emotions to screen leads. Branch and regional sales managers have been known to use leads as some sort of reward system for favored salespeople, while withholding them as punishment from those needing a slap on the wrist. Back at the home office, management wants to feel in charge of what's happening in the field, so it turns to lead follow-up as an enforcement mechanism. Marketing communications managers want lead performance to validate communications programs. And information systems management thinks first about the accuracy and completeness—not the quality—of a lead record so it can be worked into marketing databases smoothly.

Qualification Strategy

Facts, not emotions, must rule the lead management process. Objective qualification standards and procedures emphasize facts, and build teamwork in an organization by encouraging everyone to work with those same facts. Of course, each function brings its unique perspective to the inquiry qualification effort. Marketing, in charge of the company's market strategies, must determine if an inquiry offers potential within those strategies. Sales, meanwhile, provides field expertise, knowing the trends in territories and account-by-account activity.

Therefore, the model inquiry qualification system puts marketing in charge of the up-front stage of lead screening: using sight qualification, telequalification, and bounceback mailings to determine if a lead matches objective criteria of quality. It sends those to the field, tagging them "qualified" and worthy of follow-up. Sales also examines *all* the leads to see if any look interesting, for whatever reason or hunch salespeople wish to apply. Sales does not have to pursue every lead, but it must call the qualified leads and let the marketing department know the status of those immediately. If the company qualifies inquiries properly at the start, it has a right to *demand* that salespeople follow them up, even to the extent of making follow-up a condition of employment. In this way, sales and marketing work *together* to qualify leads.

You cannot eliminate subjectivity entirely from the process. Economics usually require the marketing department to sight qualify leads whenever reasonable. The very process of choosing which "objective criteria" to apply in your program inevitably requires judgment. For example, restricting sight qualification too tightly risks sending too many inquiries off to more elaborate and expensive qualification procedures, such as telequalification, which boosts individual lead-processing expense three or four times. Once managers see the expense of telequalifying, say, 30 percent to 50 percent more leads than should be followed up by central office telemarketing, they are tempted to loosen their sight qualification criteria too much and send too many weak leads, accompanied by a follow-up directive to the sales force.

The marketing department should also use inquiries for all they are worth, as pieces of marketing intelligence as well as a database of potential customers. For example, do not be too quick to move leads along to the field and then forget about them. Study the new inquiry database regularly looking for marketing patterns, festering problems, and emerging opportunities.

Balance Loose and Tight Leads

We examined loose- and tight-lead generation tactics in Chapter 5: the difference between gathering relative few leads of high average quality, or many leads of lesser average quality. Each inquiry source produces a different proportional mix of high-, moderate-, and low-quality inquiries.

At first glance, it seems that a tight leads strategy will allow you to send all inquiries to the field after minimal sight qualification because of their higher average quality. So you encourage trade show and 800-number inquiries, nearly all of which should be qualified, and direct marketing replies containing meaningful qualification information.

But too tight a policy—ignoring reader service card inquiries, for instance in hopes of saving money on upfront inquiry qualification—risks screening out too many leads that should be followed up.

Your main objective is not to minimize the number of weak leads going to the field, but to optimize salesperson time. Provide enough good leads that are worth a salesperson's attention, while minimizing time wasted on poor leads. Your lead program's contribution should meet your marketing needs and selling capacity, not the availability of a convenient lead qualification capacity.

An integrated circuit manufacturer, for example, now acknowledges that it has underutilized its inquiries by relying solely on self-qualification via fulfillment bounceback cards. It had not wanted to spend the extra money on telequalification, its communication manager says. The 3 percent of bounceback returns that eventually get to the field tagged as hot leads provide too few opportunities too slowly, compared to the competition, the manager now realizes.

Strategic factors. In addition to the quality of leads you receive from different inquiry sources, the balance between sight qualification and telequalification depends on your marketing strategy, market conditions, and method of distribution. For example:

- *Product life cycle* can affect qualification. Marketing a new product that seeks market penetration and early-adopter buyers is likely to require follow-up with more inquirers regardless of their superficial "quality," compared to selling in a mature product category where buying patterns are well established and literature library update inquiries are commonplace.

  Life cycle may also affect your choice of sales channels. For instance, as your product matures and faces growing price pressure, you might seek to shift sales toward less expensive, lesser-value-added dealers. Anticipating that shift influences your choice of dealers, distributors, reps, etc. receiving qualified inquiries for follow up.

- *Technical complexity* may require that you gather some key application information from inquirers in order to qualify and distribute leads properly for field action.

- *Value-added segmentation* strategies similarly require more knowledge about an inquirer and the application than do undifferentiated, price-competitive approaches to the market.

- *Competitive pressure* accelerates the need to get prioritized leads to the field for immediate follow-up.

- *Average profit per order, selling costs, and lead closing rates*—the statistics of the return-on-promotional-investment (ROPI) formula—influence how much you can afford to send lower-quality inquiries to the field.

- *Channel structure* will dictate lead-handling tactics. Selling high-margin products direct requires attentive inquiry qualification and field follow-up. But, if you sell through dealers or retailers that have few, if any, outside sales reps, leads probably have only secondary importance for you to begin with. Your advertising concentrates on getting the prospect to the showroom, and you fulfill inquiries with literature and dealer-locator information. A tight-lead strategy would be wholly inappropriate because, as a practical matter, you are not expecting retailers to contact prospects, but the other way around.

Note that we've said these factors influence the choice between sight qualification and telequalification. Those are the two most expeditious ways to handle leads. The old-fashioned reliance on the mail bounceback card in your fulfillment package is poorly suited to the compressed time frames of marketing today. And it suffers from chronically low return rates, generally in the 3 to 8 percent range, just a fraction of the 60 percent qualification ratio the average company should achieve through all approaches. Many desirable prospects do not return the cards, and, if they do, perhaps it is because your fulfillment material did not give them the right information the first time.

Having a formal program hardly requires conforming to the best practices, however. When Cahners Publishing surveyed 4,000 of its trade publication advertisers and prospects, 72 percent claimed a "formal program for qualifying inquiries/sales leads." Just 40 percent used telemarketing. Most, 68 percent, mailed literature with bounceback cards.[1]

Inquiry Quality Defined

What defines inquiry and lead quality?

> *The greater its quality, the more likely the lead will identify a previously unrecognized prospect with buying influence and a potentially high lifetime value to your company.*

The concept of customer lifetime value is important because it goes beyond the simpler notion of whether the prospect buys once or not. The longer and more often the customer buys, and the purchase volume each time, determines the customer's lifetime value. The notion is similar to the RFM concept—a customer's recency, frequency, and monetary value—embraced by direct mail marketers. It is the central concept behind the relationship-building strategies consumer and business marketers pursue so avidly.

As a practical matter, however, determining the likelihood of making a *single* sale, its timing, and its size is the goal of lead qualification. While it's valuable to predict an inquirer's potential lifetime customer value, it's usually enough for qualification to answer a straightforward question: Will this prospect buy, how much, and when? As we've seen, 45 percent of inquirers do make a purchase within a year, from you or a competitor.

Five Criteria, Plus One

The quality of a sales lead depends on five specific criteria, plus an additional grab bag of considerations that determine the lead's priority for sales follow-up. Typically, sales and marketing managers speak of the inquirer's *resources, desire, authority, need, and timing.*

Additional criteria pertain to the inquirer's accessibility, suitability for your sales operation, past inquiry history and other factors not conveniently pigeon-holed in the five main categories.

Somewhere in the lead qualification process—be it via telequalification, a trade show conversation, a field salesperson contact, a mailed reply card, or a faxed questionnaire—you should collect answers to the following questions.

Desire. Every inquirer has signaled a desire for something, of course. But is their desire to buy strong enough to justify your follow-up effort now?

At one extreme, the inquirer may have determined in advance that your product or service is his first choice and that he definitely will purchase it. Another inquirer may have only the vaguest of interests in your product or service category, much less you as a prospective supplier, as she uses reader service cards and other low-commitment response devices to graze for "whatever's out there."

Which inquiries are which? The qualification process must discriminate between the black and white extremes, and among the many shades of gray.

- What kind of information does the inquirer seek? General product knowledge, or specific application-related information. Is the inquirer seeking a price list? A specific quotation?

- How technical is the request? Does it require handling by your technical experts or can field sales personnel take care of it?

- How soon is the information needed? The type of inquiry will imply its urgency; fax and phone inquiries signal more urgency than mail or reader service card inquiries, for example.

- Does the inquirer wish to see or speak with a sales representative? Typically, the greater the desire to buy, the greater the willingness to see a sales rep immediately. Those with less ardor generally are reluctant to commit themselves to the interruption and perceived pressure of a sales call.

- Has the purchase been "approved?" Regardless of the approval mechanism (buying committee, the boss' orders, etc.), does the purchase have a green light or is the inquiry more casual, fishing for information?

- How did the inquirer learn about your product or service? If his or her only source of information is an ad, desire may be different from an inquiry based on a colleague's recommendation, a technical article, or the boss' demand.

Need. Just as with desire, the inquirer may recognize a strong need for your product or service, or have just the blurriest of inklings about what you could do for him or her.

Keep in mind that the inquirer may have a strong need for *information* rather than for a purchase at this time. Of course, that too signals a lead worth following up. The inquirer may not know what he or she really needs to buy in order to solve a problem. But the inquirer can tell you about the problem, providing the seller with an outstanding opportunity to propose a solution.

Finally, in high-technology markets particularly, the prospect may not even know he or she has a problem that can be solved with a new technology. The response-generating message in the advertisement, direct mail letter, etc. has to teach the prospect about the problem. How well the vendor's capabilities fit the appropriate solution will determine how strong the prospect's need can become with proper salesmanship.

Specific types of information addressing the need dimension that the qualification process can collect include:

- What does the prospect make and sell? Does the process typically use your product/service?
- What is the prospect's size and market position, particularly in product/service lines that would use your product?
- What is the application, use, or problem to be solved?
- How many or how much of the product or service is required?
- What complementary or competitive products/systems are installed now?
- What alternatives is the prospect considering?
- Can the prospect make do, or even be happier, with a smaller purchase? Or does he or she require a larger purchase than originally anticipated?
- What is the prospect's technical ability to use your product?

Resources. Does the prospect have the cash to make the purchase? Or is the prospect gathering information for a purchase "someday" when the budget is big enough?

- What is the company's size and market position?
- What are the growth trends in the industry? For the inquirer's technology? For the markets he or she serves?
- What is the prospect's financial strength reported in financial statements, analyst reports, credit reports, etc.?

Timing. Efficient sales lead management puts salespeople into the selling process when they are needed, and not before. Knowing when a prospect plans to buy determines how quickly you need to have the lead followed up by the field, and how you will maintain contact with the prospect until the buying process moves into high gear.

- When does the prospect plan to buy? How urgent is the need *now*?
- Does the prospect need or purchase the product or service often? How often?
- What is the next step in the purchaser's buying process after making the inquiry? Sharing information in the organization, soliciting quotations, interviewing vendors, making a purchase?
- Is the need urgent enough for the prospect to pay extra for expedited service?

- Should a salesperson (with general information) or a sales engineer (with application specifics) call?
- Should your marketing department stay in touch with the prospect via telemarketing or direct mail until the inquirer is ready to see your salesperson?

Decision authority. The inquirer's personal clout indicates a lot about the quality of a lead. Yes, a secretary or assistant may ask for information that will be passed along to a Mr. or Ms. Big, but if the executive or engineer makes the inquiry, quality on the authority dimension is unambiguous, paving the way for your salespeople to contact that important purchasing influence directly.

- What are the inquirer's title, job function, and responsibilities? In some companies, buying clout may not be obvious from a job title, or could be misleading because of general practices in an industry, organization politics and personalities, or other idiosyncracies of the buying firm.
- Who else is in the approval loop? Who else should receive information from you? Whom should salespeople see? When qualifying an inquirer and building your prospect database, particularly over the phone, avoid potential conflict and embarrassment. Rather than challenge the inquirer by asking if he or she has buying influence, ask "Who other than yourself is involved in the purchasing decision?" You'll invariably get the name of another individual who may be more important, or at least as important, as the person you're speaking with. Rarely will an inquirer name an underling who is less important.

Additional criteria. You'll probably want to know several other things about an inquirer, depending on your specific market and competitive conditions, before anointing an inquiry as qualified.

- Is the inquirer accessible? Can your standard marketing and selling programs reach that person, or should you concentrate effort on others in the inquirers' company?

    For instance, you should try to reach the president of a big firm whose name appears on a lead, but don't give up if you can't. Salespeople, in particular, can use "the president's interest" to justify attempts to set appointments with others in the firm. Using phony referrals is an old selling trick that can anger experienced buyers. But having a bona fide lead from Mr. or Ms. Big can open doors otherwise shut.

- Have you done business with this prospect before? Called on him or her before? Is the prospect firm already a customer of your company?

    Marketing information systems should reveal if the inquirer has experience with your company. The advantages in making sales appointments, quotations, etc. are obvious. But, oddly enough, companies often do not make the effort to check whether they've talked to a prospect before, or if the prospect has bought from another division or subsidiary. It's demoralizing to salespeople (and therefore harmful to the lead management system) to make what they thought was a virgin call on a current customer, or a past customer who had a problem unbeknownst to them.

- Does the inquirer have a multi-sourcing policy? Is it seeking a new single-source vendor?

- If your company has a strategy for developing key account strategic alliances, does the inquirer's firm appear to be the kind of company that would qualify for a close relationship? Or is it a company that would not respond to such overtures, or one not worth the effort to service except at arm's length?

- Is the prospect already a customer of your competition? If the cost of switching vendors is high in your marketplace, a prospect hoping to upgrade equipment may be predisposed to stick with the competitor. Then again, the prospect could be dissatisfied with the current supplier, something the salesperson needs to determine quickly.

- Is the prospect a customer of your distributors? Should the prospect be a customer of your distributors?

    This can be one of your most important questions about a lead. Your distribution policies and strategies for handling channel conflict will, or should, give clear direction about handling and refering the inquiry. But whatever the referral decision, add the inquiry to your database. It is always valuable to know who is buying from your distributors and dealers. Dealers frequently keep those lists to themselves; it's the core of their power in your distribution chain.

    Certain kinds of market feedback, such as warranty cards, provide exactly that information: highly useful data for customer surveys, which allows you to avoid leaving your markets totally hostage to your dealers. (Returned warranty cards also indicate likely prospects for product upgrades and accessories.)

Modern computerized database management techniques provide ample capability for checking new inquiries against your lists of past inquirers, active prospects, current or past customers, distributors' customers, etc. Ideally, your marketing information system will keep track of every inquiry that has even the slightest chance of someday becoming a qualified lead. Your database of "not currently qualified" inquiries, fed by home office and/or field evaluation of every inquiry, provides you with a list far more valuable than just about any compiled list you can rent on the market, because your message generated each inquiry, regardless of its current quality.

Keep It Simple

In describing the types of qualification criteria you should consider, we are not saying that you should ask every question suggested by our list. In certain circumstances, you might require more information. Most of the time, however, your list of important "need to know" questions will be reasonably short, sticking to the issues most salient to your marketing and sales strategies.

Asking too many questions over the phone discourages inquirers. When you collect information by mail, inquirers won't act like dutiful schoolchildren, compelled to complete every question on a lengthy form. And whether you collect information by phone or mail, make questionnaires easy to complete and code by using check boxes.

Even when your own employees ask the questions on the phone or face-to-face at the trade show booth, there are limits on how long they can keep the prospect's attention. As the selling process unfolds, you will collect the more detailed knowledge of customer needs and timing that you require to hone your sales approach. In the first-pass data collection needed for qualification, keep things as simple as possible.

The profile template. Exhibit 10-1 illustrates a sample *profile template.* It is a core set of standard questions a company probably wants to ask each inquirer at the start. You might want to add a few application- or market-specific questions. But, again, keep it simple. Depending on the inquiry's portal of entry and the depth of information each inquiry source provides, the questions you will ask an inquirer come from your template customized to your needs.

The template's prime value is making sure that different question formats among portals of entry provide consistent, comparable data. You do not want some inquiry records indicating one kind of data breakout, while other inquiries destined for the same database use a different breakout pattern. For example, if some inquirers are asked to choose among four time-to-decision periods, as in Question 1 of Exhibit 10-1, but a different source only offers three choices, combining the different responses in the same database becomes a record-editing headache.

Exhibit 10-1
Power Profile Question Template

Power Profile Question Template

1. Is your requirement:
   A. ☐ Immediate   B. ☐ 1–3 Months   C. ☐ 4–6 Months   D. ☐ 7–12 Months

2. Are you currently budgeted?
   A. ☐ Yes   B. ☐ No

3. Have you used our products in the past?
   A. ☐ Yes   B. ☐ No

4. Did you know that (company name) made this product?
   A. ☐ Yes   B. ☐ No

5. Has a (company name) salesperson called on you before?
   A. ☐ Yes   B. ☐ No

6. What is your application for this product?
   ☐ A. _____
   ☐ B. _____
   ☐ C. _____

7. Would you like a representative to call you?
   A. ☐ Yes   B. ☐ No

8. What is the best time to call?
   A. ☐ A.M.   B. ☐ P.M.

9. Would you like a no-obligation demonstration?
   A. ☐ Yes   B. ☐ No

10. Do you:
    A. ☐ Recommend   B. ☐ Specify   C. ☐ Have final approval   D. ☐ Purchase

11. What other companies have you contacted to supply this product?
    ☐ A. _____
    ☐ B. _____
    ☐ C. _____

Consistency also pays off when a specific prospect approaches a company through different portals, i.e. shows *and* direct mail. Each source will contribute to a complete data record on a prospect.

The Screening Process

Having collected relevant information about an inquiry, you must screen it according to criteria matching your strategy, and applied consistently across all inquiries. Consistency is critical; everyone working with your inquiries must have a clear idea of each lead's quality and what to do with it.

Coding

The typical approach assigns a letter or number code to a lead, indicating its likely value and required disposition. Sent to the field and entered in your inquiry database, it's a shorthand designation of a lead's overall value. For example, you might code leads as follows:

A leads: Prospects about to make a buying decision. Leads have first priority for *immediate* follow-up.

B leads: Prospects likely to buy within six months. Leads require immediate follow-up.

C leads: Prospects likely to buy within a year. Follow-up in no longer than a month.

D leads: Prospects with no firm buying plans. Retain on active mailing list.

E leads: Prospects not presently qualified. Retain record on appropriate database.

Of course, such a coding scheme assumes that the prospect's purchase time frame is the single most important factor in lead quality. And, note that the screening plan specifies that unqualified leads nonetheless be saved in an appropriate database for possible use later.

Depending upon your marketing program, your sales and distribution capacity, specific promotion program requirements, and other factors, you might want your screening system to reflect other lead quality dimensions. Or you might combine two or more critical dimensions into the plan. For example, a screening process emphasizing potential order volume as well as timing might look like this:

A leads: Prospects making a buying decision within three months for a $50,000+ order. Leads have first priority for *immediate* follow-up.

B leads: Prospects making a buying decision within three months for an order of less than $50,000. Leads have second priority for *immediate* follow-up.

C leads: Prospects likely to buy within a year for a $50,000+ order. Leads require immediate follow-up.

D leads: Prospects likely to buy within a year for an order of less than $50,000. Follow-up in no longer than a month.

E leads: Prospects with no firm buying plans. Retain on active mailing list.

F leads: Prospects not presently qualified. Retain record on appropriate database.

Or you might use an alpha-numeric code, marking leads *A1, A2, B1, B2*, etc. by combining two quality dimensions:

A leads: Prospects about to make a buying decision. Leads have first priority for *immediate* follow-up.

B leads: Prospects likely to buy within six months. Leads require immediate follow-up.

C leads: Prospects likely to buy within a year. Follow-up in no longer than a month.

D leads: Prospects with no firm buying plans. Retain on active mailing list.

E leads: Prospects not presently qualified. Retain record on appropriate database.

1 leads: Prospects likely to buy a $50,000+ order (if they buy at all).

2 leads: Prospects likely to buy a $25,000 to $50,000 order (if they buy at all).

3 leads: Prospects likely to buy an order of less than $25,000 (if they buy at all).

Then coding options would appear as A1, A2, A3, B1, B2, B3, etc. And the follow-up priority plan for the field could specify which leads have priority, such as A1, B1, A2, A3, B2, C1, B3, C2, C3. Obviously, F leads do not require a qualifying numerical code, and you probably would not ask the field to follow up D or E leads.

Multidimensional coding better reflects the multifaceted reality of inquirer quality. The more dimensions you add to the coding process, however, the messier it becomes for both the field sales organization and the marketing department. Generally, there is seldom a need to go beyond the two most important lead-quality dimensions for coding purposes.

Of course, you should capture all relevant information about the inquiry in your database. But, most organizations are likely to find very simple coding schemes work best for them. First, complex codes could require more hair-splitting than it's worth for the average company's inquiry handling. Second, the more complex the system the tougher it is to run, particularly if the key staffer adept at handling complex codes quits or goes on vacation.

Notifying the field. Exhibit 10-2 shows a sample generic field notification multi-part form sent to the salesforce. Note that the code, marked in a box at the upper right, supplements information on the form that will help reps estimate the value of leads for themselves. The salesperson is supposed to follow up, of course, and provide additional information in the space provided at the bottom of the form.

With effective field follow-up, you will have critical information for refining your coding and follow-up priority plan. You might learn, for example, that even purchases planned a year from now require immediate attention because customers start narrowing their vendor lists that far in advance. Or you might find that a prospect's estimated purchase size, told to a telequalifier or indicated on an inquiry form or postcard, bears little resemblance to the size of the purchase eventually made in your marketplace.

Collecting lead follow-up information and tracking which prospects eventually buy from which vendors provide a database rich enough for more sophisticated analysis. You could weight several factors and sum them into single overall code. For example, experience might suggest that imminence of purchase determines half a lead's overall quality, size of purchase 35 percent of its quality, and the presence of a competitive installed base 15 percent of quality.

Some database specialists have claimed success building multivariate statistical models out of lead qualification information. They use follow-up and eventual-purchase information (or Did You Buy? studies) to statistically profile the prospect's likelihood of purchase.[2]

Adding external databases. Modern computing hardware and database management software has spawned explosive growth in marketing information systems. Dramatically reduced costs for processing power put database management in just about anyone's reach, right from their desktops. Commonly called

Exhibit 10-2
Sample Generic Field Notification Form

ATTENTION - IMPORTANT SALES OPPORTUNITY

FROM

947
NATIONAL INDUSTRIES
12345 MAIN STREET
YOUR TOWN, CA 91606

TO

TERR: 132
ELLEN BARBER
DATACAM SYSTEMS
SUITE A
5339 CHESAPEAKE DR.
SAN DIEGO, CA 92123

CONTACT THIS PROSPECT USING THE INFORMATION BELOW
947-01420GENMED951005-030-132
BILL MEDERIOS
GENERAL ELECTRIC CO
166 BOULDER DR
FITCHBURG, MA 01420-3168

508/343-1467

NEW INQUIRY

PRODUCT	SOURCE TYPE
DYNO-MITE SOFTWARE	800LIN

SOURCE OF THE LEAD
PC WORLD

ISSUE DATE	RSN	CODE	PROCESS DATE
SEP '94	801	C2	05OCT '95

DO YOU USE NATIONAL INDUSTRIES PRODUCTS?
NO

WHAT WORKSTATION PLATFORM DO YOU HAVE/OR ARE YOU ACQUIRING?
HP/APOLLO

WHAT TYPE OF INDUSTRY IS YOUR COMPANY IN?
ELECTRONICS

IS YOUR NEED FOR OUR SOFTWARE:
OVER 10 MONTHS

HOW MANY SOFTWARE SEATS WILL YOU NEED?
1-2

IS YOUR SOFTWARE BUDGET:
UNDER REVIEW

INTEREST IN BUILDING OR ACCESSING MATERIALS INFO. DATABANKS?
BOTH

DO YOU HAVE AN IN-HOUSE PHYSICAL TESTING LAB FOR MATERIALS?
YES

WHICH IS YOUR PRIMARY AREA OF RESPONSIBILITY? (ALL THAT APPLY)
SELECTING MATERIALS

COMPLETE AND RETURN TO NATIONAL INDUSTRIES
COMPLETE AND RETURN AFTER INITIAL CONTACT

marketing information systems (MKIS), they allow wide-ranging analysis of marketing and sales activities, combining a company's many internal databases (inquiries, orders, receivables, shipments, etc.) with information available externally from mailing lists, industrial databases, and government records. Sales lead database management is both a contributor to and beneficiary of an MKIS.

Much of what you may want to know about an inquirer may be available from other databases. Finding and matching records from other databases for, say, an inquirer's company, can fill in much of the information you might otherwise need to gather by telequalification, by sales follow-up, or go without. For example, what and how much does an inquirer's company buy? Commercial databases combining government business census information with proprietary research can provide an estimate for each standard industrial classification. Who are the senior executives at an inquirer's company? To which publications do they subscribe? Where are their plants located?

The database-building possibilities are enormous, at least in theory. Actually matching records from different databases is still as much a programming art as a science; 75 percent correct match rates are considered extraordinarily good. You must understand the hidden biases and shortcomings lurking within any large database, particularly compiled lists that are themselves the product of database combinations.

Screening Competitors

Obviously, you would not consider an inquiry from a competitor or its distribution channels to be a qualified lead for follow-up. The real question is how much effort to expend in identifying inquiries from competitors, and if identified, what do you do with them? Send the requested literature?

Some would argue that competitors will be able to get your product literature anyway through phony inquiries or through friendly buyers. Do the right thing, they say, and be professionally proactive. Send the requested literature and ask the competitor to send his or her new literature in return. It's all honest and up front, in the noblest traditions of a competitive economy, they insist.

We agree with the other side of the issue, however, one perhaps a bit less munificent but a lot more practical. We recommend that you cull competitors from the inquiry list and send them nothing. Why make it easier for them to build their competitive intelligence files, or get their hands on your materials faster than they would otherwise? They might even be too lazy to collect your literature the hard way. On battlegrounds, marketing and military, good commanders never let the enemy learn anything if they can prevent it. Besides, literature kits are expensive.

One high-tech marketer's experience illustrates the potential danger of not weeding out competitive inquiries. A small company appearing at the Federation of American Societies for Experimental Biology show introduced a radically new product that was cheaper yet better than the established technology. Basking in the attention the booth received at the show, the company's president handed out literature to all comers, without qualification.

The show opened at 10 A.M. Within a half hour, a faxed copy of the literature kit sat on the desk of the president of the small company's major, and much larger, competitor. By noon, every one of the competitor's engineers was poring over the information. The next day, the giant competitor had photographs of the upstart company's product, acquired you know where.

On the third day of the show, competitive engineers swarmed around the small company's booth for friendly chats. They exploited a once-a-year opportunity to look closely at the upstart and get a jump on countering the new product introduction. If the small company had not distributed literature at the show but sent it only to qualified visitors after the show, as we recommend, it would have had a better chance to exploit the excitement it generated at the show.

Qualifying Special Cases

Some types of inquiries are special cases. Some will appear to be duplicates, but perhaps only at first glance, and therefore should not be ignored. Also, we discussed the hidden value of heavy bingo circlers in Chapter 3, but they are not the only kinds of inquirers who are frequently ignored when they shouldn't be. A number of inquirers exist in most markets and deserve more respect than they generally receive in the qualification and fulfillment process.

Duplicate inquiries. It is almost impossible to have a true duplicate inquiry unless an inquirer is responding more than once to a specific publication, a specific issue, a specific advertisement, and on a specific date. We believe you should not consider inquirers responding to your advertisements as duplicates if:

- They are inquiring about different products in the same publication.
- They are inquiring about the same product but at a different time.
- They are inquiring about the same product but from a different publication.

It is important to the overall marketing plan to keep these inquirers in the database, send them more literature and, at the same time, notify your field sales force. There are six reasons why.

1. They might not have heard from your salesperson. A red flag may be raised when a second inquiry is received on the same product. This could be because the sales representative has not called to follow up, and the inquirer does want a call.

2. Same name, different product. The inquirer may be requesting information about a different product. If this product is handled by a separate channel of distribution, there is all the more reason to send more literature and notify the field sales force. This also gives your company the chance to sell a family of products, not just one product line.

3. They need a second set of literature. Sometimes inquirers are asking for more information because they've given the literature to someone else (boss, fellow designer, engineer, specifier, etc.) and they need the data for themselves. Therefore, they may be your hottest leads. The need for more specific data may also indicate intensity of buying plans.

4. Building a history. Maintaining the same inquirer from various sources and product interests builds a history. That is important because it enables the marketer to know which publications are being read and responded to by inquirers, and which are producing requests for quotations and ultimately sales. This statistical data allows a scientific approach to marketing communications.

   Also, marketers learn the percentage of duplicates between publication audiences, which may enable adjustment of the media schedule to broaden the marketing reach. Perhaps the publication with a high degree of duplication can be replaced by one reaching a different audience.

5. The first fulfillment package didn't get to the inquirer. In some instances, the inquirer asks for more information because the first package of literature was not delivered. About 7 percent of all mail is undeliverable. Or perhaps the inquirer's mail room or secretary screened the mail and discarded the literature.

6. Each inquiry is credited to the appropriate source. Linking an inquirer to various communications sources enables the marketing department to analyze what their inquirers are reading, what trade shows they're attending, what direct mail lists they're on, etc.

If your reason for wanting duplicates not to appear in your database is to prevent having more than one package mailed to the same person in the future, never fear. It is a simple matter to identify the duplicates and produce only one label per inquirer.

Librarians and others behind the scenes. In searching for those big management and engineering titles characteristic of heavy-hitter purchase influencers,
companies frequently ignore inquiries from others with hidden, indirect, yet
potent ability to tilt a vendor search in their direction.

Corporate librarians, for example, don't specify, influence, recommend, or
approve purchases outside the library. But they often maintain the literature files
to which direct buying influences turn for building a lists of candidate vendors.
Not only should you send literature to those libraries, send a salesperson, too,
who can help the librarian make sure literature files on your products are up-
to-date and in good condition.

Purchasing agents, whom salespeople often treat as obstacles between them
and the real buying heavyweights, are another mistreated breed. Typically, they
keep track of vendors' day-to-day performance and pricing rather than choosing
vendors for technology-sensitive products and services. Get on their wrong side
and they can make a salesperson's life miserable and jeopardize a supplier's hold
on an account. Stay on their right side and they can help a salesperson learn more
about the account. Purchasing agents' importance and clout is growing as
corporations downsize and outsource more of their processes and materials.

Home addresses. Once routinely treated with disdain, home address inquiries
are becoming increasingly important for several reasons. Corporate mail rooms
coping with the explosion in business direct mail marketing frequently shun
third-class and other non-first-class mail, prompting some executives and engineers to have their business publications delivered to their homes. Or, they
might prefer to read those publications at leisure. That home address is on the
label the publisher provides for reader service cards, and the address attached
to the reader service inquiry.

In many fields, significant buying influences might actually be working out
of their homes. That trend is growing as downsizing corporations shed full-time
staff professionals and turn their specialized service needs over to consultants,
many of whom work from home and wield substantial authority with their
clients. We've known consultants of renown, widely quoted experts able to
make or break a new product, on whom salespeople refuse to call. If they haven't
already tossed the lead with the residential address, the salespeople see the neatly
trimmed residential shrubbery and station wagon in the driveway, and conclude
the inquiry was all a mistake.

Students collecting information for term papers or job hunting will provide
home or campus addresses, and it's usually not worth it to send them an
expensive literature kit, much less to follow-up with sales activity. But a student
may be a significant purchasing influence in the future. An abbreviated literature

kit might be appropriate; a courteous letter thanking the student for the inquiry and providing information designed to build goodwill about the company can be an investment in the future.

Government and institutional inquirers. Buying influences in the $630 billion government market obviously should not be ignored. But neither should inquiries from research-oriented organizations, even if they don't seem to indicate an imminent purchase. "Think tanks," independent research firms, university laboratories, and government agencies asking about your products may be writing specification and performance benchmarks that will have a tremendous impact on accepted standards in your marketplace. Ignore such opportunities at your peril. Qualify the inquiries and attempt to find out what prompts their interest. That could point you toward new applications and markets you had not considered.

Power Profiling™

We recommend what we call the Power Profiling approach to organize inquiry information to maximize its usefulness throughout the organization. It allows companies to develop and maintain comprehensive profile histories of prospects and customers. It makes salespeople better informed of the inquirer's buying intentions before they make follow-up calls. And Power Profiling enables an analysis system in which marketing managers can retrieve statistical data to appraise prospects, products, buying time frames, market trends, etc. age of product, etc. Power Profiling™ embodies concepts discussed in this chapter, providing users with the ability to capture virtually unlimited amounts of information about an inquirer, collecting the information via inbound and outbound telemarketing, trade show interviews, direct mail bounceback cards, postcard deck returns, and advertising coupons, BRCs and reader service cards.

Salespeople receive a lead report form, as shown in Exhibit 10-2. It provides plenty of space to inform reps about the inquirer's "state of purchase possibilities," information that greatly facilitates pre-call planning. (Some firms use shorter forms for those inquiries without profile information to relay to the field.)

Handling the Paperwork

Printed on paper, fully computerized on diskette, or mixed among several media, lead information is a business asset. It's essential to handle it quickly and orderly. Sadly, companies frequently forget that. Booth visitor contact cards are mistakenly tossed into the garbage during the confusion of departing a trade show. Returned BRC cards languish in a figurative, or literal, "shoe box" somewhere in the marketing or sales department. Stacks of reader service card inquiry printouts rot, forgotten in a file drawer.

Those are common sins repeated many times over in marketing and sales circles. Considering that 45 percent of all inquirers on average will eventually buy something from a company or its competitors, lackadaisical physical lead handling borders on the criminal. It literally is the destruction of information assets a company has purchased!

Whoever controls the lead-management process *must* draw a formal plan for physical lead handling and insist that it always be followed by subordinates. The person in charge should be the only one who can authorize variations from the plan. Otherwise, you risk chaos as telequalifiers, exhibit managers, sales managers, product directors, and who knows who else starts handling inquiries in creative and mysterious ways.

Telequalification

Telequalification is the process of using primarily outbound phone calls to collect more information about an inquirer who has inquired through other means than an inbound call. The reasoning is unambiguous: Why sqaunder an expensive salesperson's time to do the same thing a relatively lower-paid telephone service representative can accomplish quickly and easily?

According to surveys by *New Equipment Digest,* 66 percent of that product tabloid's advertisers telequalify leads,[3] they being a particularly lead-oriented group by virtue of their media choice. But their telequalification programs evidently include informal "pick of the phone" type calling as well as the formal, disciplined programs we described in Chapter 9. Telequalification solves a number of lead-management problems for both marketing and sales. Rather than relying on sight qualification alone to determine if an inquiry should be referred to field follow-up, it provides a middle-ground of response. Telequalification is an economical way to collect accurate information about an inquirer's intentions without having to burden expensive sales talent that should be concentrating only on bona fide prospects. Telequalification also keeps that important information-gathering process at home, ensuring that marketing will have the information it needs to feed its marketing database, rather than leave things at the mercy of field sales reporting.

Some have even argued that all inquiries should be telequalified, even those qualified at a trade show, because other qualification methods cannot be as precise as a well-scripted telemarketer interviewing an inquirer. That strikes us as a wasteful overkill that squanders valuable marketing dollars.

Qualify, Don't Sell

Do not forget a cardinal rule of telequalification: *telequalification gathers information, it does not sell.* Notwithstanding the confusion and anger you might cause among salespeople by, as they see it, calling on "their" accounts, when you try to "sell" an inquiry on the phone, you risk losing both the information you seek and the opportunity to make the eventual sale. Of course, if your marketing strategy is to close sales over the phone and that's a workable approach, your telephone people will be trained as salespeople. But if your objective is to gather qualification information for the field, avoid the temptation of trying to shortcut your established selling process.

Technically trained people who can close sales over the phone are expensive, more so than the salaried telequalifiers. You don't want novices trying their hand at closing when they don't know what they are doing. And, you don't want anyone giving the inquirer a chance to say "No, I guess I'm not interested in your offer." The telequalifier's job is to gather *information* about prospects, not *commitments* from them, and pass that along to field salespeople adept at asking for commitment, and finessing the prospect's objections about price and terms, product features, competitive benefits, etc.

The telequalifier who addresses objections and provides product data is using the wrong setting to give information the prospect can use to make a decision, often before the prospect gets to see the product literature requested in the first place. In many fields, a face-to-face presentation is the proper way to approach the buyer. Most people don't mind answering a few routine questions posed by the telequalifier, however. They infer a quid pro quo, where those who inquire share information two ways. They aren't as challenged as they'd be if the telequalifier attempts to close.

Also, recognizing that the telequalifier is definitely not a salesperson nor a technical expert renders moot one of the debates surrounding do-it-yourself qualification vs. out-of-house services. Many in-house proponents argue that outside service employees who serve many clients simply cannot know enough about the marketer's product line to handle telephone contact with prospects. They might be right about the out-of-house telequalifier's technical knowledge, but what really counts is the telequalifier's ability to elicit information. Very often, the out-of-house person has honed that skill while the in-house person who telequalifies only part of the time is not as adept at eliciting qualification data.

Reasonable Throughput

Telequalification does add a time-burden to your system. You don't want it to become a bottleneck for hot leads that obviously should receive immediate attention in the field. On average, you can expect telequalifiers will be able to reach 45 percent of inquirers on the first try, in our experience. You will contact about 20 percent more on the second try, and perhaps an additional 10 percent on the third try. So, to reach 75 percent of a 100-inquirer list will require about 190 calls. If a telequalifier can handle 35 to 40 prospect interviews a day, that's a week's work.

The 25 percent or so that you cannot reach in three calls probably is not worth the extra effort unless you have enticing knowledge about them. Some will be disguised competitors, some will be students. There's always a certain percentage that have left their companies since they inquired, and some are genuine duplicates. Others among the unreachables will refuse to speak with anyone until *they* are ready, and some will already have bought, lost their budgets, or simply will have lost interest. Calling such people is more trouble than it is worth, and usually only adds to the rejection telephone service representatives have to endure in the first place.

Finessing voice mail. Today's business environment of downsized corporations, busier executives and exploding office automation technology has started to upset some of the typical call completion ratios, however. Voice mail answering equipment is become more the rule than the exception in corporate America. As one marketer of industrial sensor devices complained to us, "It's very difficult to make contact with the inquirer. It takes too many calls to try and reach the inquirer or get anyone to call you back. Once we reach him and qualify him, we may have to repeat the same procedure to set up a sales call. The sales rep is going to give up after one or two tries. We've wasted a lot of effort and expense."

To cope with that emerging problem, we recommend leaving a voice mail message that you will call the inquirer back at a certain time. Knowing the call is coming, the inquirer is more likely to answer it. Or, when encountering a voice mail message, escape to the receptionist and ask when is the best time to call back.

Qualification and the Field

Some salespeople harbor a persistent hostility for telemarketing, telequalification, and any other meddling in their territories. Lazy salespeople have a reason to hate *telemarketing.* Companies apply it very successfully to reordering and repeat sales while they expect their salespeople to do the tough part of face-to-face selling. The lazy reps lose their chance to lope along with old reliable accounts that provide enough volume to keep them afloat.

Oddly enough, when they confuse telemarketing with *telequalification,* as many do, they distrust your very efforts to help them! When you sell the lead management program properly to the field force, good salespeople will embrace telequalification. It saves them valuable time and brings them more closable business per week. Even the skeptics can be won over when they see the benefits of telequalification.

At one high-tech company, marketing installed an experimental four-person telemarketing group to, among other duties, telequalify inquiries that used to go directly to the field. One group of veteran salespeople—affectionately and appropriately dubbed the "old buffaloes" of the firm—prided themselves on their product knowledge and ability to deal on an equal level with their leading-edge professorial and research Ph.D. customers.

Vociferously resisting the new phone operation, they complained that: "You can't possibly contact my accounts for me;" "We have highly technical customers and you can't call them and satisfy them;" "You can't really find out their needs cause it took me 20 years in this business to talk their language;" "I don't want anyone messing with the buyers in my area;" and the classic "I know all of the people who buy in my area."

Tempers simmered for a few weeks. After a month, however, the old buffaloes started to remark about the increasing quality of inquiries they received. They started to enjoy receiving bona fide leads with phone numbers and information about buyer identity and needs attached. Had the company offered to end the telequalification "experiment," a new uproar would have followed.

Share Information

Again, we recommend sending all inquiries to the field and to the salesperson responsible for the account. Mark the obviously hot ones "hot leads," and send them in a special attention-getting envelope if mailed, or with "urgent" designations if delivered on your fax and e-mail systems. Whatever it takes to encourage reps to pounce on them. Mark all the other leads "FYI." You are not expecting all of them to be followed up, only some as your lead qualification report will indicate. But reps may spot valuable inquiries before your qualification system can. They are expected to know their territories, after all, and most reps will claim they know it better than anyone else.

Some inquiry managers still argue from the perspective of the 1950s. They say salespeople should not receive all leads, but only those qualified at the home office or, worse yet, only those inquirers who qualify themselves by returning the fulfillment kit bounceback card asking for a sales call. The slow-motion logic of that old-fashioned approach escapes us, and smacks of a marketing department attitude that treats the field more as a competitor than as a partner. In some industries, particularly those with a heavy consumer lead flow, salespeople may not want the leads *until* someone else has vetted them. That's not the usual case, however.

Field notification form. The inquiry information you send to the field will include basic information such as name, address and phone number, application, product interest, and other details germane to a sales call. The system should require reps to return follow-up information within 60 days of receiving the lead. Make the lead form easy to complete, with check-off boxes as in the generic field notification form in Exhibit 10-2.

The form features valuable inquirer profile information collected by a telequalifier on either an outbound call or an inbound 800-number call. The field rep makes the initial contact and completes the check off boxes and spaces for comments at the base of the form. The top copy goes back to the central office after the initial follow-up. The rep returns the second after completing the sale and adding additional information. The third copy stays in the rep's files.

Beneath the header area with the respective company and rep names and addresses, the computer-printed form lists the inquirer's name and address below the database code assigned to the inquiry.

To the right of the inquirer's name and address, several fields indicate basic lead information, as shown in italics:

- Inquiry status: *NEW INQUIRY*
- Product: *DYNO-MITE SOFTWARE*
- Source type: *800LIN* (inbound 800 line)
- Source of the lead: *PC WORLD*
- Issue/date: *SEPT '94*
- Reader service number: *801*
- Code: *C2*
- Process date: *05OCT '95*

Most of the form consists of questions asked by the telequalifier, and the answers, printed from the computerized sales lead database. Notice that the telequalifier asked a few specific questions about application, need, budget, buying time frame, and installed facilities. Just enough questions, tailored to the product, to enable both sight qualification and sales call preparation. The lead in the exhibit is coded *C2,* in line with the coding system discussed earlier, reflecting its relatively modest size and 10-month buying horizon.

Sharing telequalification information encourages field follow-up. One manufacturer of electronic equipment, for instance, sends what it calls "conversation reports" to the field. The company's group vice president claims the practice has boosted the firm's already admirable 50 percent field follow-up rate to the ability to track virtually all leads through to the sale.

Make follow-up reports easy to return. If they are on paper and not computerized, provide business reply envelopes for lead reports only. Also, design a system that encourages salespeople to maintain their own territorial databases. They report to you and keep a copy of the form or e-mail report for themselves on file, should they ever need information about the inquirer again.

Finally, remember that your system is designed to facilitate the selling process, not to second-guess salespeople. If the rep's estimate of a lead's value conflicts with your qualification system's assessment, go with the rep's rating. Your system can be confounded by the inquirer who thinks he or she is the most important lead you could have. Closer to the territory, your salesperson will know, or soon learn, the real score.

Distributors and Dealers

When the field consists of independent businesses—dealers, distributors, jobbers, manufacturers' reps, resellers, integrators, whomever—lead qualification becomes an even more important process. They aren't employees of your company. They handle many kinds of products or services besides yours. They might even handle your competitors. Anxious to make sales and keep their customers satisfied, they might even sell a competitive product to your inquirer. That is a breach of faith matched only by a manufacturer's urge to sell direct to accounts distributors thought were theirs.

Dealer and distributor relations have become one of the more fascinating subjects in marketing management in recent years, as technology has allowed them to know more about ultimate customers and take greater "ownership" of the customer base. Consumer product fields have witnessed a profound shift in that direction. Business-to-business marketers increasingly find that the ultimate buyer and user seeks solutions from the dealer, not necessarily a particular manufacturer's brand.

Sending distributors only qualified inquiries necessarily must be part of the alliance a manufacturer needs to form with its channels. The manufacturer–distributor partnership uses training, merchandising, promotion support, and pricing terms to create trust and a sense of mutual destiny. Dumping poorly qualified inquiries on the dealer detracts from the relationship and hardly encourages follow-up or lead-status reporting. Frequently, it's the feedback that the toughest area of cooperation.

At one manufacturing company, for example, the corporate advertising manager says he expects salespeople to encourage lead follow-up by dealers. "When I say not following up, I mean they're not returning the form to me to let me know they followed up," he complains. "But I also realize that if you start pressing them hard enough, if they're reluctant to do it and you threaten them, they're going to send in something that they've just fabricated just for the sake of sending a piece of paper back, to get me off their backs."

Lead qualification is a visible and very important part of channel relations strategies, with your own salespeople and distributors alike. Actions speak louder than words when your distributor wants to know if you care about his or her business success.

Chapter 11

Fulfillment: The First Step in Closing

It might seem that inquiry generation and qualification are among the real arts of sales lead management, while fulfillment—sending the inquirer what he or she requested—is a no-brainer. Inquiry fulfillment isn't rocket science, but companies that treat the process cavalierly do so at their peril. Not simply stuffing literature in an envelope, fulfillment delivers on your promise to provide something of value to continue the selling process.

It hardly makes sense to try and cut corners on inquiry fulfillment. It's a critical finishing touch to a program, yet takes only a small portion of overall sales lead handling costs. Lead generation media expenses typically comprise 60 to 70 percent of overall costs; media advertising production costs add another 15 to 20 percent, and collateral (envelopes, reply cards, letters, etc.) 3 to 5 percent. The fulfillment costs of postage, literature, and handling are just a few percentage points each.

If your literature package arrives after the inquirer has made a purchase decision, or the package doesn't contain the right information or is incomplete, you might have wasted all you investment to generate the sales lead. At the very least, you have made follow-up and closing tougher for salespeople. (They frequently complain about literature arriving late.) If the information you send is incomplete, or doesn't advance the selling process, you demotivate the inquirer. If it doesn't contain a response card, or it neglects to say where the inquirer can purchase your product, your fulfillment fails at its mission.

Fulfillment Planning

In the 1950s, when marketers could afford a leisurely approach to fulfillment, they received raw advertising leads, mailed literature, casually mailed the leads to the field, and waited to hear back from inquirers. Four to eight weeks delay between registering a reader service card inquiry and receiving literature wasn't unusual, nor was it a matter of concern to inquirers or marketers. But, trading bounceback card and literature back and forth in the mail ensnared prospects in a "literature loop" going nowhere.

Old habits die hard, and even today many a company still plays the literature loop game despite the competitive urgency of today's inquiries. Rather than wait for inquirer self-qualification via the bounceback card, the competitive firm sight qualifies and telequalifies leads immediately. At the same time, it fulfills inquiries with literature that advances the selling process, not the literature loop.

Fulfillment provides the additional information you promised to send, prepares prospects for the sales close, allows inquirers to ask for even more information, and gives them the opportunity to be kept abreast of future developments at your company. The fulfillment method must match the typical inquirer's need for speed, using fax and e-mail if necessary to stay ahead of competition.

Options such as fax-on-demand service—also known as fax-back and interactive fax—meet those needs superbly for certain applications. Otherwise, marketers have to ensure that potentially slow-moving printed literature fulfillment doesn't dawdle. At the worst, it should take no more than 72 hours, or three business days, to get the newly arrived inquiry's fulfillment package out the door. Two business days should be your target, however.

Stay Atop the Process

Performing fulfillment properly takes planning and constant monitoring by the head of the sales lead management program. You must stock fulfillment items in sufficient quantities, and make them physically accessible to your mail room or shipping personnel. It must be clear to them exactly what each inquirer should receive. Meanwhile, your salespeople and distributors must be kept posted of available literature and changes in what you offer. You must keep accurate records to facilitate lead tracking and analysis.

Write a complete guide to the fulfillment system and a style manual for all literature. Bind it loose-leaf for easy changes. Such an operations manual is essential when regular fulfillment personnel go on vacation or leave, and part-time and backup staff get involved. Cover every step of the system.

Flow-chart the fulfillment process, including putting timelines in for the various steps. Do it by hand or with computer software, The exercise will indicate where your program bottlenecks are likely to occur, and which steps must be completed on time lest the system bog down.

Take nothing for granted. Human error and unforeseen bottlenecks are inevitable. We've known dozens of situations where a marketing manager assured us, mistakenly, that his or her department fulfills all leads within the target deadline. For example, visiting one electronics manufacturer's headquarters, we toured the lead-handling facility with the company president. Meeting "Suzy," one of the employees there, we had a conversation something like this:

VISITOR: What do you do with the inquiry when it comes in?

SUZY: I usually enter it into the database, notify the sales rep of the hot ones, send out the lead to the salespeople, and send the lead to shipping to pull the literature.

VISITOR: You said "usually." What do you mean?

SUZY: I mean I usually do it right away, but I am a bit behind now.

VISITOR: How far behind are you?

SUZY: (pulling a box of leads from under her desk) I usually do it every day but right now I'm a couple of weeks behind.

The key danger sign there is the word "usually." Employees assigned to fulfillment chores "in their spare time" wind up handling more pressing matters, particularly in today's downsized companies. There's no spare time left. A week's delay here and there results in handing business to your competitors, sales that might have been yours. On average, companies spend less than a month investigating possible vendors, according to Penton Publishing research.[1]

Over the years since those leisurely 1950s, marketers have improved their ability to get mail pieces out the door, setting new standards for all firms to meet or exceed. Eight out of 10 inquirers now say fulfillment literature arrives "in time to be helpful with current projects." On average, inquirers surveyed by Cahners Publishing received the material they sought in 3.4 weeks; two-thirds of them got the material in two to four weeks).[2] Among industrial product tabloid readers surveyed by *Industrial Equipment News,* 56 percent said they generally received information within one to two weeks of sending in a reader service card; 85 percent received information within four weeks.[3] Those are the time frames inquirers have come to expect. Fail to meet them lets swift competitors get to prospects first.

Response Media

Proper planning means matching the fulfillment method to the mission.

Mail. The traditional and least expensive way of sending printed literature, ad specialties, diskettes and tapes, and other fulfillment items, is the U.S. mail—in the opinion of many deserving of the "snail mail" sobriquet. Mail's several days delivery time is usually acceptable if your up-front operations fulfill incoming inquiries immediately.

Use first-class mail, not third-class. Timely delivery of each piece is what counts, not delaying in order to accumulate enough volume for a third-class mailing. Third-class (bulk) mail provides its own delays; the postal service is not obligated to delivery it until it's convenient to do so. Mailers frequently contend that 10 percent or more of third-class mail never gets delivered in the first place. Also, corporate mail rooms groaning under the weight of direct mail solicitations often discard third-class mail.

Use special envelopes for inquiry fulfillment, prominently marked "Here is the information you requested!" That will help get the package through the gauntlet of mail rooms and secretaries, and prompt its intended recipient to open it. Window envelopes are easy to handle and look professional. Does it matter if you use a stamp on the envelope for that personal touch, or businesslike metered postage? Probably not; affixing the stamp isn't worth the effort.

Fax. Instant response to an inquiry implies that your company is just as responsive to a customer's every need. With a fax machine in virtually every business large or small, fax is the ideal fulfillment medium for urgent inquiries, particularly those seeking up-to-date information on prices, technical specifications, etc. According to a Cahners Publishing reader survey, 64 percent said they use the fax for immediate information needs; 11 percent use fax for non-immediate needs.[4]

Marketers share the enthusiasm. About 18 percent of *New Equipment Digest* advertisers use the fax to follow up their hot leads, that product tabloid learned in a 1990 survey.[5] No doubt fax usage has increased dramatically since then, particularly because of automated fax-on-demand service. In fast-paced fields such as electronic engineering, inquirers prefer a fax response that shows the date and time they received it, proving the information is timely.

Fax is not a suitable medium for lengthy fulfillment packages or brochures with color artwork, detailed halftones, spreads and gatefold presentations, and other design elements that contribute to a complete image of your company and products. No-frills typesetting, and simple line art drawn large enough to survive the fuzziness of fax transmission is what works best, at least until fax technology improves. Sending graphics directly from computer files helps to sharpen the fax image the inquirer gets, particularly if the receiver is a laser fax machine. Still, the emphasis in fax fulfillment is not prettiness, but speed.

And, just in case anyone asks the question, fax is not at all a suitable medium for cold-call lead generation. Sending such "unsolicited fax" messages to people with whom you do not have a relationship is considered rude in business circles, and even illegal in many jurisdictions. That doesn't apply to press-release distribution, however, which many argue is protected by the First Amendment. Fax has become a routine tool for the buy and sell sides of the news business.

Electronic mail and EDI. Rapid advances in wired and wireless transmission media, new software technologies, and the widespread use of powerful desktop computers should spur electronic mail to the forefront of business communications by the turn of the century. Fully integrated corporate systems linked by global, public and private networks will put buyers and sellers together with a couple of mouse clicks. In technical jargon, "We will have access to a reasonably priced public switched broadband network which will allow us to have real-time multimedia interactions with our customers and partners," telecom strategist Huntington D. Lambert of US West declared in 1993. In other words, "You'll have personal presence without being there."[6]

Electronic mail and its more sophisticated cousin, EDI (electronic data interchange) will include video, sound, and data transmission capability, eliminating, for those taking the plunge, the need for mail, sales calls, and the routine ways of doing business on which we concentrate today. But like the "paperless office" ballyhooed 20 years ago and the "information superhighway" someday to come, the reality will arrive much later than the hype.

Until technology catches up to the sales pitches, comparatively hum-drum technology nonetheless moves communications several orders of magnitude faster than the typical forms of inquiry fulfillment used in the 1980s. Companies routinely maintain bulletin boards from which customers or prospects can download posted information, or upload their information requests. Intercorporate workgroup software running over public phone lines or wireless via satellite will deepen strategic alliances between vendors and customers. Human inertia is perhaps the biggest problem, however. It's still easier for most users to dial an 800-number to request information. Comfort levels run high when a live service representative answers the phone.

Fax-on-demand. With its automated instant-response capabilities, fax-on-demand adds a powerful option to sales lead management. Typically, marketers use fax-on-demand to send sales literature, technical support documents, price lists, order forms, dealer information, specifications, and drawings to the "need it now" inquirers who are the likeliest buyers. Some systems can charge a caller, asking for a credit card number and confirming it before returning information. By reading the caller's telephone area code, some fax-on-demand equipment can select information about dealers and repair centers in the caller's locality.

Fax-back is simple in concept and does not rely on exotic technology. An inquirer telephones a special number and, through voice prompts (see Exhibit 11-1), enters on the telephone keypad the codes designating the documents sought. The caller also enters his or her name and other qualification information, plus, of course, a fax number. A personal computer then immediately sends the requested information, stored on disk, to the inquirer's fax, without operator intervention, 24-hours a day, seven days a week. And it transmits graphics and illustrations, something an operator cannot send over voice phone.

Fax-on-demand is catching on among specialized business publications as an additional service for advertisers and readers. At *Computer Design,* for example, an Instant Fax Response Service sends fulfillment literature to advertiser's inquiries. Publisher David Allen quips that callers who dial in on their fax lines have the option of "getting a response immediately, or in 15 seconds if they can wait."

We have found the quick response of fax-on-demand improves the likelihood of a sale dramatically. And, of course, it reduces printing, postage, and document handling costs by about 30 percent. (Depending on lead quality, you might choose to follow-up a fax-back reply with a more extensive mailed package.) Running a fax number in an ad or mail brochure ensures that many inquirers will use the system.

Fax-back automates routine information exchanges at substantial cost savings. For example, software publisher Symantec Corp. saved $60,000 in labor costs over six months by handling 25,000 product literature requests through fax-back. The market for fax-back services has been expected to hit the $100 million mark by 1995.[7]

Exhibit 11-1
Fax-on-Demand Flow Chart

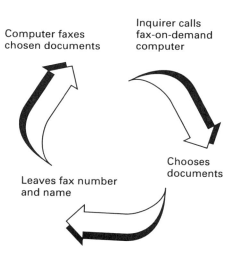

Computer faxes
chosen documents

Inquirer calls
fax-on-demand
computer

Chooses
documents

Leaves fax number
and name

Service options. Specialized software on the market enables extensive system customization. All-inclusive turnkey systems cost $12,000 to $30,000 to purchase initially, depending on equipment (computers, scanners, etc.). Add the annual cost of a system administrator and phone lines to your monthly maintenance charges.

If the number of documents your company enters is large, and the call volume heavy, the system will need an administrator: part telephone wizard, part draftsman and designer, part computer expert. If the system is going to be used for large broadcast-faxing chores, you'll need at least a half-time, more likely a full-time person to run the system, update documents, take the names off the recording system, run monthly reports, etc. Fax-on-demand is somewhat labor intensive; it's not the kind of plug-and-play automation some proclaim it to be.

Nor is it easy to plan the right size system. One company we know almost bought a system but at the last minute realized that handling the traffic and the technology would require an extensive upgrade of its old phone system. Another company, anticipating a world eager to get its product specifications, squandered more than $60,000 on an overbuilt fax-on-demand system that could handle more then 100,000 documents a month. Volume after the first few months— once all the salespeople, dealers and distributors tired of sampling the service— totaled just a few thousand documents a month, traffic that a $12,000 system could have handled adequately.

Outside fax-on-demand service suppliers are an alternative. They generally charge a set-up fee and a monthly rate based on transactions and computer storage costs, subject to a volume minimum. Some offer the option of a live operator intercepting incoming calls. Services should advise clients about fax cover sheet design and the right kinds of documents, technical drawings, product specifications, and other documents to use in the system. They will scan documents into computer storage for you.

Data capture shortcomings. Fax-on-demand systems attempt to capture caller identity, qualification, and lead source information, but their record is spotty on that dimension, particularly for fully automated systems without an operator on hand. In automated mode, fax-on-demand asks callers to state their name, company, and address, so the equipment can capture that data. Only about a third of callers leave that information, in our experience, although some system vendors claim greater capture rates. However, that's not a problem for applications where name capture is not critical.

Many inquirers seem to like the way fax-on-demand allows them to call and receive information quickly, while remaining anonymous. Unless inquirers take the time to enter data on a telephone keypad—a laborious process—or return the bounceback form sent as part of the faxed fulfillment, the marketer never finds out who called. Even Caller ID-type services that capture the caller's phone number and company name cannot provide the inquirer's personal name, essential for your sales force follow-up. Maintaining live-operator contact at the start or finish of a call overcomes that problem—at significant additional cost.

The Fulfillment Package

Naturally, inquiry fulfillment must deliver whatever it is you promised in order to snare the inquiry in the first place: the offer, as discussed in Chapter 5. You want to generate action and greater receptivity to your sales presentations, and project a quality image. Carefully designed fulfillment packages serve those goals, tailoring fulfillment as much as is feasible to the inquirer's particular need.

We have seen, and you probably have, too, miserable response packages with no message on the envelope, a photocopied letter, photocopied literature with no "where to buy information," and no reply card. Who would you buy from: the company that doesn't "care enough to send the very best," or the company that takes all parts of its relationship with you, the inquirer, very seriously? Most marketers, however, evidently provide satisfaction at some level; 95 percent of business inquirers polled said "almost all" information they received "has clear and easy-to-understand" text; 78 percent said the material contains enough technical information.[8]

Some fulfillment media have practical limits to the amount of information one can send, fax-back for example. Mailed fulfillment packages provide the most freedom in choosing what to send, so let's examine what could go into a mail package.

The Offer and Letter

The cover letter that accompanies the literature you send is the heart of a fulfillment package successfully performing as a selling tool. Without a strong letter that orchestrates your presentation to the inquirer and delivers your key selling message, your package is not working hard.

Despite that common sense, most companies settle for sending brochures, product sheets, catalogs, etc., and a cover sheet that's designed more to guide the stuffing of the envelope than sell to the prospect. Even companies spending lavishly on their original direct mail solicitations and painstakingly persuasive letters, kiss off the fulfillment package with a slipsheet containing a few lines thanking prospects for their interest, and inviting them to call if they need more information or a sales call. Perhaps the computer will have typed in the names of some local dealers near the bottom of the cover sheet.

Our quibble isn't with the format, however, as much as it is the limp selling proposition such cover sheets provide. Like weak advertising and flabby brochure copy, the matter-of-fact, as-if-you-didn't-care cover sheet is a sales opportunity foregone.

The key is to remind the inquirer—and many of them will have forgotten when your package arrives—why they inquired and what you can do for them. The cover letter's mission is to regenerate and heighten interest in your product or service, particularly what it can do for the prospect. It's nice that you are pleased that he or she inquired. And it's nice that you're polite and thank inquirers for their interest. But it's essential to steer them into your package. If the inquirer merely files the material or sends it to someone else without studying it, the package has failed to exploit a key selling opportunity. And, it might be doomed to obscurity, particularly if a more engaging fulfillment package from a competitor grabs the inquirer's attention.

Keep the fulfillment letter short and sweet, because it has a different, more abbreviated mission than the direct mail letters we discussed in Chapter 8. But the fulfillment letter should be just as persuasive, written by a professional direct response copywriter. Following what should be a personalized greeting, here's the basic structure:

Tell the reader what he or she has received, and why, in a professionally friendly way:

Here is your copy of the Widget Applications and Specifications Guide you requested.

Then tell the inquirer why he or she should be interested:

With energy costs facing long-term increases nationwide, companies like yours are searching for ways to squeeze more power from each kilowatt they consume. Widgets provide the only proven and reliable method of improving electric power productivity for existing plant and office locations.

Please see page 4 of the enclosed guide for a table of the latest widget specifications. It will also show you why Acme widgets lead the field in terms of critical widget characteristics:

— Size to output ratios permit installations in tight spots.

— Output purity and consistency under all input conditions maximizes your equipment protection.

Then invite the inquirer to take action:

Our technical staff will be happy to discuss your widget needs, or arrange an on-site consultation for you with one of our dealers in your area.

For more information, please give me a call at 1-800-WIDGETS (1-800-943-4387), or return the enclosed reply card. You can also reach us by fax at 1-800-555-2222.

Finally, say thanks . . .

Thank you for asking about Acme Widget.

. . . and add a postscript with an additional reason to buy:

We offer an extended three-year warranty on all widgets purchased by April 1st.

It's not an elaborate missive, but the cover letter acknowledges that the inquirer might have a problem and it proposes a solution. The letter can appear on heavy stock and have a tear-off reply card attached. Whatever the format, the letter should look clean and neat.

Personalize the letter if possible, as long as it doesn't cause delays or significantly greater costs. Although it's a customer-friendly touch, there's no hard proof that personalization increases response. Personalization includes a real or simulated signature at the close of the letter, printed in blue ink to add to the personal look. If it's the signature of a senior company officer such as the president,—a good idea for a small or medium-size company projecting a personal touch—be sure the letter gives a name of someone the inquirer can call if necessary: a "sales representative," "customer service manager," or other operating-level person.

Don't try to recreate the fulfillment brochure and all its selling points in the fulfillment letter! Cite the most important user benefits quickly, tailoring them to the inquirer's industry, if possible. Add the local dealer's or salesperson's name to the cover letter.

Also, tell the inquirer what the next step in the process should be and how to take action, clearly and unambiguously.

Certainly, keep the letter to one page maximum. Avoid stilted phrasing that sounds more like a stuffy lecture than the way real people talk. And never talk about how you feel, gushing on with paeans to "how wonderful it is to serve the widget field for, lo, these many years, etc." Concentrate on how wonderful *your prospect* will feel.

Dealer Locators

The names, addresses, and phone numbers of dealers close to the inquirer, are essential to the fulfillment package if you sell through those channels. Telling the inquirer the name of your salesperson for his or her location or industry is a good idea, too. Moreover, the fact that you provide the information builds rapport with your dealers. Whenever you provide the dealer's name, inform him or her of the lead.

Be careful not to overpromise about services the dealer will provide. Saying the dealer gives free application assistance, for instance, only antagonizes the dealer who does not. Don't tell inquirers that all resellers, even non-stocking ones, give demonstrations. Such gaffes will only hurt what is probably already a poorly coordinated distribution structure.

Various software programs that work with telephone area codes, zip codes, or even longitude/latitude data simplify the process for complex distribution networks. Information about dealers, nearby salespeople, and manufacturers' reps, etc. can also be included in the sales letter that must accompany all fulfillment literature.

Ignore the temptation to send a "salesperson list" or roster of dealers to inquirers. It reveals your coverage to competitors who'll inevitably get a copy from somewhere, and lists become outdated quickly as reps and dealers turnover. Also, by listing all dealers you have no control in routing leads where you'd like.

Because of mobility and financial weaknesses among some dealers, you need a dealer locator system that is highly flexible. If a dealer is out of business today, you do not want to refer inquirers to that dealer today or tomorrow. So printed lists and literature imprinted with individual dealers' names—obsolete as soon as they are off the press—should be avoided. The best method is one that takes locator information from an up-to-date database. When packages are mailed the nearest dealer or distributor is designated by the files maintained in the computer at that point in time.

Reply Vehicle

Inbound telephone and trade shows are likely to provide your highest quality leads because you can qualify them on the spot. Making it easy for inquirers to call is essential in sales lead management. Apply the same logic to fulfillment kits; make sure every document you send indicates where the prospect can call for more information or to ask to see a sales rep.

Relatively few inquirers, just 3 to 8 percent on average, self-qualify themselves by using the bounceback card in fulfillment packages. Inquirers do not respond because field sales has already caught up with them, or they've received enough information. Those who do return bounceback cards might not have received what they thought they'd get, might not have received enough information, or may want more material to share with colleagues.

Still, the extra expense of including a reply card or a reply form and postage-paid envelope is worth it to get bona fide leads with information about application, time frame for decision, and other critical qualifiers. Boost your bounceback response about 50 percent by preprinting the card with the inquirer's name and address. Ask for the prospect's telephone number before asking for the address; the phone number is more important. Rather than ask if they want a sales call, encourage a response by asking prospects the best time to call. And do not forget to put your inbound telemarketing phone number on the card. You really want phone calls from prospects, not snail mail. Exhibit 8-2 illustrates the correct format for a business reply card.

You can seek more than buying information, of course. The fulfillment package can include an application questionnaire, and offer some sort of technical reply if the prospect returns it. An attention-getting variant is a computerized questionnaire on diskette, inviting the user to configure exactly what he or she would like to buy, then return the diskette to you for a sales and engineering quotation.

Finally, for products that you sell directly, don't forget to include an order form!

Product/Service Information

Sales literature can take a multitude of forms. Among the options to include in your package:

- Brochures and product specification sheets. Give literature extra value by calling it "product selection guide," "planning kit," or other label promising usefulness.
- Catalogs and downsized "catalogettes" tailored to particular applications or types of customers, providing an overview of your line.
- Technical data and application notes.
- Published technical papers.
- Trade press article reprints.
- Current press releases and ads, to supplement more substantive information.

- Corporate communications information about the company, its background, what it stands for, etc., can help to cross-sell products.
- Applications questionnaire, often a strong device in highly technical fields, is both an information dissemination and response device.
- Literature indices.
- Newsletters and other regular, periodic mailings such as new product announcements and brochures, company magazines, news releases, upcoming trade show appearances, technical seminars, executive appointments, etc. Customer-oriented letters from your president or other senior executive keeping the prospect informed work well for some companies.

  Give the recipient a chance to elect to stay on your active promotion mailing list, that being a good qualification indicator. Each mailing is what we call a "soft-touch" contact with the prospect, not so much a hard-pitch sales message as a friendly reminder of how helpful a company can be as a supplier.

  How many prospects will stay on the mailing list also depends on the quality of what you send. Too many companies seem to forget that simply owning a desktop publishing program doesn't make one a publisher. Good newsletters that break through the clutter and win ongoing reader loyalty are not easy to produce. They face the same challenges as full-scale periodicals, albeit on a smaller scale. Graphics and headlines must grab reader attention. Articles must sustain interest while, at the same time, serving the sponsor's promotional objectives.

  One evergreen approach to sponsored-newsletter journalism is the customer case history. Make your customers the stars and you'll look great by association. Share interesting "news you can use," thoughts, laughs and friendly observations in your newsletter as well as the serious stuff. Don't use the newsletter to flog the same sales pitches in your advertising and news releases. No one will read it and you'll waste money. A few promotional letters become so popular they convert into paid-circulation periodicals.

  Custom-published magazines about a company's products and services have grown in popularity; a few consumer product marketers are able to charge for circulation.
- Electronic data, diskette, and CD-ROM catalogs, including programs that allow prospects to design their own application of your product. Basic catalogs on diskette cost about the same to produce as printed catalogs, but distribution costs are a lot lower. CD-ROM data disks offer tremendous capacities, about a half-million pages of typewritten text.

Personal computer use in business is nearly universal, and CD-ROM drives are being installed on more desktop machines and system servers. Make the medium's special power work for you; include a subroutine, for instance, that lets the prospect print product choices or configurations automatically on an request-for-quotation form to fax directly to you. Don't eliminate the printed version of the catalog, however!

Adding snappy graphics, games, and quizzes will send prices soaring. Automobile company diskettes have included race-car video games, for instance. Production costs range from $10,000 to $50,000 or more for exotic effects.

As one commentator described a valve maker's "intelligent electronic catalog:" "As the valve opens, the fluid in the valve begins to flow. The sound of the fluid flowing heightens the sensation. The computer then asks the user several questions about the valve's applications and makes a recommendation about which size valve to specify. The latest data sheet on the recommended valve can be printed."[9]

- Audio and video tapes. Promotional videotapes hit their stride in the 1980s with nearly universal ownership of videocassette recorders. Production costs vary widely; $1,000 per minute for long programs is not unusual. Use the medium to advantage, to show action and dynamism, not just talking heads. And unless you've got a compelling message, keep it short: four to six minutes. Some experts contend that tapes longer than 14 minutes will lose their audiences.

  Audio tapes might be more productive. They are cheaper to produce and distribute, and inquirers can play audio tapes in their cars.

- Syndicated material relevant to the prospect's interests and industry, such as economic service reports, independent newsletters, etc.

- Advertising specialties designed to elicit a response such as a phone call to order a critical "missing piece." A variant is to have the salesperson deliver the missing piece. Or, stage a serial mailing of several pieces of a set (e.g. glassware, desk accessories), with a sales call required for delivery of the final piece.

- Your list of offices and maps.

What to avoid. Do not send inquirers a blizzard of every sales brochure and deal sheet you can cram in an envelope, or material about extraneous products and services that will confuse the inquirer. Concentrate on what the recipient wants and needs to know. Never forget that prospects do not really care about your company, they only care about what your product or service can do for them!

Design your literature so it is easy to file. Cahners Publishing readers reported that just 70 percent of the inquiry fulfillment literature they received had an easy-to-file format.[10] Some companies think that odd-sized material will discourage literature collectors. Perhaps, but it also frustrates legitimate prospects, presents a poor quality image, and motivates prospects to discard material that's hard to handle.

Price Lists

Whether to include a price list in your fulfillment package continues to be a subject of spirited debate—and serious senior management attention. Some buyers consider price lists important. In a Cahners Publishing survey, inquirers' greatest disappointment was the price information they received; only 24 percent said they got enough of it. Then again, eight out of 10 inquirers rank product specification information as most important, compared to just 14 percent citing price information as the most important part of the information they receive from advertisers.[11]

Companies generally do not promote price unless they have an advantage. They usually want salespeople to deliver the quotation in person, at the same time stressing the benefits of purchase to overcome objections. Their prices might not be competitive. And, keeping prices close to the vest and out of public circulation gives them more negotiating room with individual accounts. Trade secret experts often consider price lists to be privileged information.

Another problem is the way the term "street price" has crept from the computer field to other industries. Prospects expect to find actual prices lower than list, particularly if purchased form a dealer. So publishing a list price defeats the purpose of promoting an advantage, and of motivating prospects to visit their dealers.

If you publish a price list at all, you could fudge, wording your information such as: "Under $5,000, depending on configuration." Safer yet, simply offer a "quotation" as an option on your bounceback offer.

Fulfillment Segmentation

Obviously, you want to be sure you send the inquirer information about the product or service asked about. Code every inquiry coming in the door, specifying which pieces of literature or other items go into the envelope, out on the fax machine, etc.

Depending upon your consumer product or service, different prospects may require different treatment. You might want to send certain items to readers of technical publications, but not to management readers of industry newspapers, for instance. Industries, job functions, decision-making role, inquiry source, method of lead acquisition, and how you follow up are among the characteristics that might allow you to tailor fulfillment to each inquirer. Different cover letters could emphasize different benefits described in your product literature.

You certainly should consider whether to send your standard fulfillment kit to the special kinds of inquirers we discussed in Chapter 10: purchasing executives, corporate librarians, research institutions, students, and other atypical inquiries that you spot through sight qualification. Most likely a stripped down or other altered version of the package, with a special cover letter, will be more appropriate.

Marketing Follow-Up

In addition to the field follow-up essential to proper sales lead management, marketing has a follow-up obligation as well. Marketing must reawaken prospects' initial interest and make sure they received what they requested. They must also make sure that the field made appropriate contact and find out whether leads converted to sales.

Storing inquirer names in your database for direct mail, newsletters, trade show announcements, etc. is a sound idea, particularly the names of those who say they want to be on your list. But, you should also follow up in a more formal manner, with a regular feedback program. Mailing to inquirers some weeks after your initial fulfillment can increase your yield of bounceback-qualified leads dramatically. A doubling is not unusual. *New Equipment Digest* says one of its advertisers tripled the response with two mailings after the initial fulfillment.[12]

On average, about 15 percent of your sales from a lead-generation program (ad campaign, direct mail drop, trade show, etc.) will occur within the first 90 days after you acquire them. About 10 percent of all sales will occur in each of the following three quarters. You want to maintain the momentum of the interest you initially generated.

Besides, from 5 to 10 percent of U.S. mail isn't delivered, postal office critics contend, so some of your fulfillment packages will not arrive at their destination. When they do, corporate mail rooms will screen some percentage of them into the trash.

Therefore, send a follow-up mailing—an important soft touch—to inquirers who have not yet responded or bought 30 to 40 days after your initial fulfillment. Send another at 70 to 80 days. The 30- to 40-day window is good for all but immediate inquiries, and it is not too long after the inquiry if your initial fulfillment package didn't arrive. Some companies selling products with long buying cycles wait three of even six months after initial fulfillment before dropping the second follow-up mailing. Considering that so few leads receive personal follow-up to begin with, mailings help substantially.

Offer Help

Follow-up mailings should exude a helpful attitude. A good salesperson does not call a prospect after the first sales call and demand to know, "Ready to buy yet?" The rep calls to "offer more information," in order to maintain contact. Follow-up mailings serve the same objective.

A personally addressed and signed letter and a reply card can accomplish the task. A short brochure about the product of the inquirer's interest, article reprints, newsletters, press releases, etc. will remind the prospect of his or her interest. It conveys the message, "You are important to us."

Such mailings are extremely efficient, given the improved results they generate. The average raw inquiry typically costs somewhere between $25 and $150 to generate and another $2, minimum, plus literature, to contact. The few pennies required to send a follow-up letter—10 cents to 13 cents plus postage—to a name already in your database hardly is an obstacle to improved qualification rates.

Copy can read something like this:

Hello again!

You recently inquired about Acme Widget products. We hope you received the information you're seeking. Perhaps we can provide additional information or assistance.

Please take a moment to complete and return the attached, postage-paid reply card. Of course, you can always call us at 1-800-WIDGETS (1-800-943-4387), or fax us at 1-800-555-2222.

We would like to hear from you. We appreciate your interest in Acme Widget.

Exhibit 11-2 shows reply cards from two high-technology electronics manufacturers. Each asks about the adequacy of the initial fulfillment mailing, and collects additional qualification and application information.

Knowing that follow-up letters regularly go in the mail to inquirers will motivate reps to contact leads themselves and report the lead's disposition. Whether or not field sales contacted them, those leads should still receive follow-up mail. Considering that it might be difficult to know whether your sales rep has already contacted the prospect, send the follow-up mailing to all inquirers. Helpful additional information cannot hurt if your salesperson is working with the account, nor can it hurt if the account is not yet ready to buy. Even if the prospect has already purchased from a competitor, your follow-up mailing might lay the groundwork for a switch in supplier later on.

Exhibit 11-2
Dummy Reply Cards

Tell Me More...

If the information you received was not adequate, please specify additional information: _____
_____
_____

Your SPM need is:
- ☐ CA immediate
- ☐ CC 4-6 months
- ☐ CE over 12 months
- ☐ CB 1-3 months
- ☐ CD 7-12 months
- ☐ CF info only

Name _____
Title _____
Department _____
Address _____
City, State, Zip _____
Country _____
Phone _____ Fax _____

Would you like to receive a quote? ☐ Yes ☐ No
On which product(s)? _____
_____

☐ Have a sales engineer contact me.

Best time to call _____ AM PM

Would you be interested in attending a TopoMetrix SPM seminar? ☐ Yes ☐ No

Where? _____

How else can we help you? _____
_____
_____

TopoMetrix
VISUALIZING THE MICRO WORLD
6-0293 003

Yes! Tell me more about Everywhere Networking™

Are you: Reseller:
- ☐ VAR/Dealer (ka)
- ☐ Retail Dealer (kb)
- ☐ Distributor (kc)
- ☐ Systems Integrator (la)
- ☐ Consultant (lc)

End User:
- ☐ Data/Telecommunications Manager (ja)
- ☐ LAN Manager (jb)
- ☐ Government User (le)
- ☐ OEM (lb)
- ☐ Other (jz)_____

Would you be interested in a no-cost, 30 day evaluation unit?
☐ Yes (ma) ☐ No (mb)

Name/Title _____

Company _____

Dept. or M/S _____

Address _____

City/State/Zip _____

Your Phone # (___) _____ ext. _____

Best time to call: _____ A.M. _____ P.M.

If your need is immediate, please call

If a Reseller: Do you resell wide area network (WAN) products?
☐ Yes (aa) ☐ No (ab)
If yes, how many sales offices do you have?
☐ 1-5 (ba) ☐ 6-10 (bb) ☐ 11+ (bc)

End Users and Resellers: What are your purchase plans for remote access solutions?
☐ 1-3 months (na) ☐ 4-6 months (nb) ☐ 7-12 months (nc)
☐ Reference only (nd)

Do you or your customers currently access LANs remotely?
☐ Yes (da) ☐ No (db)
If yes, how many branch offices are accessed?
☐ 1-10 (ea) ☐ 11-50 (eb) ☐ 51-100 (ec) ☐ 101+ (ed)

How many individual users are accessed?
☐ 1-10 (fa) ☐ 11-50 (fb) ☐ 51-100 (fc) ☐ 101-500 (fd)
☐ 501-1000 (fe) ☐ 1001 + (ff)

If the information you received was not adequate, what additional information would you like?
_____

Ask for Reseller sales or End User sales. **BRC-1**

Did-You-Buy? Studies

By surveying leads some time after they inquired, you can learn if they eventually did buy, from whom, whether they received a sales call and the fulfillment package sent to them, and the answers to other questions. Such Did-You-Buy? studies are essential for lead tracking and analysis. And, by polling recent buyers of competitive products, you collect valuable information not accessible through customer-service contact reports or customer satisfaction surveys.

Did-You-Buy? polling gives you an additional view of lead disposition, sales force and distributor effectiveness, and market share, a picture that does not rely on sales force reporting. Did-You-Buy? studies give you data for your return-on-promotional-investment (ROPI) calculations and lead program diagnostics. Chapter 14 will examine how you can interpret data from a Did-You-Buy? study. Here, we dwell on the importance of Did-You-Buy? surveys and some key points about conducting them.

We recommend regularly surveying inquirers by telephone six months after you received their inquiries. Then you will build a database with consistent benchmarks for your lead system performance. On occasion, call them 12 months later to gain perspective on purchases taking that long to close. As a rule of thumb, figure a telephone survey will be completed with fully tabulated data in about two weeks.

You can also conduct Did-You-Buy? studies by mail. Although the timing between inquiry and survey response is not as precise, and it takes longer to get results, mail survey data are less expensive to procure and are certainly better than no information at all. We suggest you drop mail survey questionnaires 90 to 120 days after receiving the inquiry, and maintain consistency as you build your survey results database. Timing consistency obviously is important if you are to build a time-series database of buying behavior in your market.

Response rates will be higher for telephone surveys—around 75 percent if you make three calls to everyone in the sample—than for mail polls. And telephone surveys are more resistant to response bias than mail surveys. But we've also seen responses as high as 28 percent with mailed studies, a level adequate to the task.

Sensible Information Option

Considering that a company is doing very well if its salespeople contact more than two-thirds of the leads sent to the field—even 40 percent is competitively superior—you cannot wait for the sales force to embrace universal follow-up and reporting before you start building your program performance databases to learn who bought. "Salespeople don't know from databases," as a friend aptly puts it. Marketing wants the data, but sales wants to close orders. Getting follow-up information from dealers typically is impossible.

A sound marketing information system (MKIS) will match lead data to order-entry records, but an MKIS won't normally be able to link leads to purchases made by others in a large company, particularly those at other locations than the inquirers.

The easiest option to learn how well your lead generation and sales follow-up efforts are paying off is surveying a representative sample of inquirers. As in most marketing surveys, you cannot reach everyone who should be a respondent in a Did-You-Buy? poll. But you do not have to, particularly if you have a large number of inquirers. Remember, however, that inquirers who like your company and have bought are more likely to respond to your survey, biasing the results, particularly in mail surveys.

Diagnostic Power

Surveys asking consumers and business buyers about their purchases and buying intentions are not unusual in most industries. Often, you can get data for free. Business and industrial publications frequently provide their own form of Did-You-Buy? studies to illustrate the value of the inquiries they generate. But in having to serve all their advertisers, the information they collect is perforce limited.

Industrial product tabloid *New Equipment Digest,* for example, publishes Reader Action Reports based on mail surveys of inquirers to particular ads. Exhibit 11-3 shows the average results from all Did-You-Buy? studies the publication conducted from 1968 through 1989.

Conducting your own study can be fancy or plain. An outside service, for instance, will charge around 12 to 15 cents per questionnaire simply to put a Did-You-Buy? study in the mail, printing, postage, and tabulation charges not included. A serviceable telemarketing survey requiring about 30 hours phone time to contact 100 inquirers with two calls will cost about $2,500 from an outside service, including data reporting.

Exhibit 11-4 shows a basic Did-You-Buy? questionnaire designed for telephone interviewing. Each response field has a unique code, facilitating tabulation. Note how the telephone format allows the interviewer to probe for answers to open-ended questions.

One way of customizing the basic questionnaire is probing for where a customer purchased the product, a valuable insight for products sold through distributors and dealers who do not report lead dispositions back to you. Another probe that might be valuable is checking the adequacy of fulfillment literature. One electric motor advertiser, for instance, forgot to include an essential specification, speed, in the technical data sheet. The advertiser couldn't understand why its latest leads were converting so poorly, until a Did-You-Buy? study revealed the gaffe. Once the company fixed the literature, sales took off.

Additional Tips

Put those in charge of the ad program—an advertising department if you have one—in charge of fulfillment. They have a vested interest in the success of inquiries.

Exhibit 11-3

New Equipment Digest Did-You-Buy? Study Results, 1968–1989

% that received fulfillment info	86.3%
% followed up by salespeople	20.7%

% that normally see salespeople from advertiser:

Regularly	1.1%
Occasionally	16.5%
Never	82.4%
% purchasing product	35.6%
% purchasing advertisers product	19.2%
% considering purchase of advertised product	52.9%
% purchasing competitors	16.4%
% with specific application in mind	73.8%
% that did not know advertiser made product	61.0%

378,523 inquirere surveyed with a 33% return

Source: *Reader Action Report: 22 Years of Advertising Effectiveness Research* (Cleveland: New Equipment Digest, 1990), p. 47.

Avoid obvious but common fulfillment sins, such as:

- Failing to personalize correspondence.
- Failing to thank the inquirer for his or her interest.
- Sending the wrong literature.
- Failing to provide clear product/service information, or enough to aid decision making.
- Failing to tell the inquirer where to buy or how to order.
- Sending cheap-looking photocopies of literature that's out of stock. Keep a three-month literature inventory on hand; it generally takes that long to write, design, and produce new literature.

Exhibit 11-4
Did-You-Buy? Questionnaire

Did-You-Buy? Questionnaire

Hello, my name is _____.
I am calling from _____.
You recently requested information from _____ magazine.
We are conducting a brief marketing research survey. May I have a
few minutes of your time?

1. Do you recall inquiring about _____ system/product/service?
   ☐ a. Yes   ☐ b. No
2. Did you receive the information that you requested?
   ☐ a. Yes   ☐ b. No   ☐ c. Don't Remember
3. Do you recall being contacted by a company rep?
   ☐ a. Yes   ☐ b. No
4. Did you contact someone after receiving the information that you requested?
   ☐ a. Yes   1) Whom did you contact? _____
   ☐ b. No   ☐ c. Don't Remember
5. Did you make inquiries to other manufacturers about similar products?
   ☐ a. Yes   1) Which other manufacturers? _____
   _____
   _____

   ☐ b. No   ☐ c. Don't Remember
6. Since making an inquiry, have you purchased any products?
   ☐ a. Yes   1) What products did you purchase? _____
   _____
   _____

   ☐ b. No   ☐ c. Don't Remember
7. If you haven't purchased since receiving the information, which
   manufacturers are you considering?
   _____
   _____
   _____
8. Why did you buy those products instead of (company name) products?
   _____
   _____
   _____
9. Are you still in the market for the product?
   ☐ a. Yes   1) When do you plan to buy?   ☐ a) Within 3 months
                                             ☐ b) 4–6 months
                                             ☐ c) 7–12 months
                                             ☐ d) Longer than 12 months
   ☐ b. No
10. What is your intended application _____
    _____
11. Would you like to have a rep call on you?
    ☐ a. Yes   ☐ b. No
12. When is the best time to call?
    ☐ a. A.M.   ☐ b. P.M.   Specific hour? _____
    Comments:

Name _____ Title _____
Company _____ Telephone # _____
Dept/Mail Stop _____
Address _____

| Street | City | State | Zip |

- Not having literature for a new sales program ready to go the day you begin receiving inquiries.

Puzzled by the honorific—Mr., Ms. etc.—to use in a cover letter salutation to a "J. Smith," a "Chris Johnson?" Using a "Dear J. Smith" greeting gives a letter that mail-merged look, killing its personalization. Your letters could drop the "Dear so-and-so" greeting, however, and simply start your letter with a cheery "Good morning!"

If space allows, use the bounceback card to collect industry trend information from prospects—opinions and observations not directly related to the product sale.

Be sure to make it easy for prospects to correct wrong addresses, titles, phone numbers, etc. appearing in the fulfillment package.

"Shop" the competition, so to speak, by replying to their ads, and see how well and how fast they fulfill your inquiries. Do salespeople follow-up? Of course, if you aren't careful in hiding your identity, they might screen you out, just as you should do if they inquire of you. Try to learn the answers to the following:

- How long does it take to get the competitor's literature?
- What did they send?
  - Letter or cover sheet?
  - Where-to-buy information?
  - What is the literature quality?
  - Business reply card?
  - An 800-number for fast service?
  - A fax number for fast service?
  - Does the delivery envelope have a message to get it through the mail room (e.g. "Here's the information you requested!")
- Do they send follow-up mailings?
- Do they telemarket?
- Do they announce new products to past inquirers?
- Will their sales rep call?

Color code bounceback cards to link them to their specific programs: white for the direct mail campaign, light blue for the trade press ad campaign, etc.

Add barcodes to bounceback cards and to sales lead notification forms sent to your field personnel. Coding can ensure that the additional data the inquirer or the field salesperson add to the forms are attached to the correct records in your database.

Use computerized mail-merge to customize bounceback cards for laser printing, rather than printing one-size-fits-all cards in large quantities.

Chapter 12

Selling Your System to Sales

Sales and marketing teamwork is essential for the sales lead system to maximize revenue and customer satisfaction. When sales representatives don't follow up leads or report inquiry status as they should, marketing management probably shares the blame, either by perpetuating flawed practices or by failing to earn the confidence of salespeople.

But salespeople often do not express their misgivings well. Instead, they simply complain that they do not receive enough "good leads." Often, they suspect management is not delivering on its lead qualification promises. Part of the reason is the difference in perspective people bring to the party. Marketing communications departments, for instance, take pride in the volume of inquiries they generate. Marketing management, meanwhile, wants to analyze performance and build databases. Sales reps are paid to know territories and close orders.

When they do their jobs right, of course, salespeople already know a great deal about their territories. They have productive sources of information they've developed and nurtured on their own. Their sales managers expect this. But even if a large portion of the qualified leads they receive from the home office are prospects of which they're already aware, they'll scan leads for hidden gold. In our experience, some territories receive as much as half their sales from leads, the other half from referrals and salespeople's own prospecting.

It's in the interests of salespeople not to overlook promising prospects, and they'll appreciate it if marketing makes it easy by sending only qualified leads with related information. For example, about 75 percent of salespeople and distributors in one ad industry poll credited advertising-generated inquiries with frequently or at least occasionally helping them find new sales opportunities. About 71 percent said inquiries have helped them identify new customers in their present markets; six out of 10 credited inquiries with finding new prospects in new markets. And two-thirds of salespeople and distributors surveyed said inquiries have helped them identify new product opportunities within their existing customer base.[1]

A unique five-city, year-long field experiment by a heavy equipment manufacturer revealed how salespeople will publicly dismiss the importance of leads even though they recognize their value. Telemarketers called lists of potential industrial users, sending the names of those planning a near-term purchase to the field for follow-up by direct and distributor salespeople. The company carefully tracked each lead. It discovered, depending on the territory, that 10 to 28 percent of prospects planning to buy within 12 months were previously unknown to salespeople. And 7 to 19 percent were already known, but salespeople were not aware of their return to the market.

When researchers interviewed them in front of sales managers and peers, territory reps claimed to know about prospects they really hadn't known. "Sales reps don't get paid for not knowing," explains Howard L. Gordon, the researcher. Once peers and managers left the room, however, salespeople were more forthcoming about the telemarketing program's value. "But even then, it took a combination of hand-holding and interrogating them like attorneys," Mr. Gordon recalls. "There's a reluctance to admit that somebody else helped."[2]

Two Principles

Keep two thoughts in mind to avoid the frustration of an apathetic sales response to your lead-management system.

- Maintain a high quality lead flow to the field.
- Remember that most salespeople must be sold, not told.

Quality Lead Flow

One of the prime goals of sales lead management is making the selling process more efficient: reducing the chance of missing genuine prospects, reducing the time wasted in the field chasing non-prospects, and trimming the duration of the selling cycle. The better the quality of lead flow, the better a program meets its efficiency objective.

Most companies, unfortunately, still send raw inquiries to the field. They fail to qualify inquiries, at least objectively. Some insist that qualification is part of what salespeople are paid to do anyway. When management acts as if inquiries are solely the field's responsibility, it fails to build a sense of teamwork and common purpose. Salespeople feel no need to report the status of "their" leads. They believe that if the leads are theirs alone, they can take them or leave them as they see fit.

Reps know that even batches of unscreened inquiries contain some golden leads. But, emotionally, they don't want to acknowledge that they don't already know everything about their territories.

Also, piles of unscreened leads overwhelm salespeople. If the quantity is too large—more than 25 to 35 leads a month—follow-up suffers, potential sales slip by the sales person, and guilt sets in. They become defensive over inquirers not contacted. Unqualified leads dumped on the field imply to reps that management isn't very sophisticated, hard working, or on top of things. If salespeople work on full commission—they get paid only when someone buys—asking them to handle what could be done better centrally incurs an opportunity cost of foregone income for reps and the home-office alike.

Sell 'em, Don't Just Tell 'em

Actions speak louder than words, but the words are pretty important, too. In addition to providing quality leads, marketing must actively sell the lead management system to its salespeople. It requires full-scale internal marketing on a constant basis, using media such as sales meeting presentations, newsletters, and envelope stuffers. Marketing must merchandise its success stories as avidly as it promotes case histories to prospects.

Salespeople are optimists by nature, preoccupied by near-term goals and buffeted by lots of rejection in the field. Action-oriented rather than abstract thinkers, sales reps need to stay pumped with enthusiasm, the thrill of the chase, and the taste of success right around the corner. They gravitate toward the places where they *think* they're most likely to get the business—existing customers and prospects they already know. Thirty percent of a reps calls are on new clients or customers, and 10 percent are on new buying influences at existing customer firms.[3]

As one wag put it, "They practice Labrador retriever marketing: they go where they get petted." It takes a mix of education, incentives, building partnerships, and constantly communicating to overcome comfortable old habits. Reps, too, ask that most important question: "What's in it for me?"

Hit the hot buttons. To illustrate how an engaging, friendly lesson can help accomplish that goal, see the sidebar on the next pages. We have found it to be an effective low-key lesson, particularly for salespeople new to the field who most need to get "lead follow-up religion."

Three Sales Secrets That Successful Salespeople Hide

When you were new in sales, the old-timers didn't talk about them. They were helpful in telling you all you wanted to know about the products; they even helped with closing techniques.

But when it came to the topics that would really help you compete with them, secrets that would make you stand above the rest, well, these simply weren't discussed. If you asked how they had become so successful, top salespeople simply smiled and said, "There are some things you have to learn for yourself." Nobody told them the secrets. Until now.

We'll take the risk and tell you.

We told a top salesperson at a medical instrument company what we were going to do. He just shook his head with a look of disgust, and, while backing away, said, "You don't have the right to do it . . . a lot of top performers are gonna be mad at you." And with a parting sneer, he said, "They won't believe you anyway."

Regardless of the gamble we're taking, we will reveal to you three secrets. If you know them and act on them, you can be in the top 10 percent of your sales organization within six to 12 months.

Getting to the top in 12 months!

When you took your job, one of the first questions you asked your manager and the other salespeople was, "Where do we get our prospects? Does the company give us sales leads?" Just like a magician who misdirects you, your manager said, "Yeah, we get leads, but a lot of them are no good. You'll have to prospect on your own."

Misdirection. They steered you into the idea of cold calling (even though you were getting sales leads from the company). The old hand believes you have to "earn your stripes" the hard way. But there was some hope in what was said. "You will get sales leads," your manager admitted. And that is the beginning of your trip to the top. Which brings us to Secret Number One.

Secret Number 1

The Rule of 45 says that 45 percent of all leads turn into a sale for someone.

Within one year, 45 percent of all the leads you receive will turn into a sale for you or your competitor. Of the leads, 22 to 25 percent will convert within the first six months.

Marketing research studies have proven this for more than 20 years. Nevertheless, only 10 to 15 percent of top salespeople admit (usually in whispers) that there is a predictable closing ratio for sales leads. This could be because many salespeople are skeptical of marketing research or because the salesperson hides the facts from the green recruit.

Many salespeople know about the Rule of 45 because so many of them say that half of the sales leads they get are no good. They're right—half are no good. But the up side is that half do turn into a sale. It's up to you to determine which half of the sales leads are good, and which half won't be buying.

If you get 50 sales leads a month, there is a potential for you to make 23 sales (within the coming year). If there are 10, you can make four to five sales. If you don't make the sale, someone else will.

Once you know the Rule of 45 and that nearly half of all sales leads turn into a sale for someone, you understand that the someone can be you. But to make the Rule of 45 work for you, you have to know Secret Number Two.

Secret Number 2

Great salespeople follow up every sales lead, until the prospect buys or dies.

Great salespeople don't give up. They call and call until the prospect answers. They visit, write, and follow up until the person says they bought another product or they are no longer in the market.

You must overcome the temptation to believe that only 10 percent of the leads turn into a sale. The reason some salespeople believe this is that they stop following up on most leads after the first 90 days. For them, only 10 percent may turn into a sale. The fact is, to get your fair share of the sales that can occur in your territory, you have to act on Secret Number Two.

The salespeople who don't know Secrets One and Two will very often believe that if a lead doesn't turn into a sale within a month or two, they've lost the sale. They dump the lead, and go on to the newer, fresher, most recent inquiries.

Remember, everyone has a different schedule for buying a product. For some, it is a comparatively short time; for others it takes months, a year, or longer. If you get a lead that is a few months old, there is still an 80 percent chance the buyer hasn't made a decision yet.

When the lead is six months old, there is a 50-percent chance that the decision is still pending. At nine months, you have a 25-percent chance to make the sale. Some documented facts:

- Seventy-six percent of the people who inquire intend to buy.
- Forty percent of the time the person doesn't approach your competitor.
- More than 50 percent of the sales leads are not followed up. Some research indicates the number could be as high as 87.5 percent.

True, as leads age, some begin to fall into the sold category, but the most interesting fact of all is that there is less and less competition for the sale for those prospects who are taking time to make their decisions.

Follow-up for many salespeople is weak initially, and almost non-existent as time goes by. To be in a less and less competitive position, don't give up simply because the person hasn't bought in the first few months. Take courage from the fact that as time goes by, the less disciplined salespeople will stop calling on the prospect.

The person with the discipline to have a follow-up system for their prospects will win more often than they lose. *The odds are always with the salesperson who continues to work the prospect when others give up.*

Which brings us to Secret Number Three.

Secret Number 3

The older the sales lead, the less the competition.

These three secrets seem almost too simple, too easy to be true. Plus, you've probably noticed that if you believe in them, you needn't be the glibbest, slickest salesperson in your outfit. But you do have to be the most persistent.

In organizations where you are overwhelmed with sales leads (more than 30 to 50 a month), you can probably live off the sales leads that convert if you follow up each lead. If you only get five to 10 leads a month, then your sales leads can provide the core of your business; referrals, cold calls, etc. will still be a part of your routine (although a much smaller part than if you had no leads).

Regardless, whether you work directly for a company, or whether you're a dealer or a distributor, if you get sales leads, use the three secrets that the best salespeople in the business hide and you too will be in the top 10 percent of your sales force.

Source: © 1991 by Inquiry Handling Service, Inc.

The three secrets address the salesperson's desire for recognition as a savvy operator and a master of knowledge others do not possess. At another level, it offers that elusive "secret to success" that entices many to sales careers. It's the notion that shortcuts unknown to the average person will unlock wealth and success. The Rule of 45, for instance, is an estimation for lead program planners. But to salespeople, the "half will buy" promise becomes a talisman promising success in a chaotic world of rejection, rude prospects, and angry customers. And by presenting the Rule of 45 as an unrevealed truth those in the know want to keep hidden from others, "Three Secrets" encourages salespeople to embrace their leads enthusiastically. Instead of pandering to dreams of easy street, however, the message convinces its target readers that hard work and persistence will pay off; the statistics prove that effort wins the day.

Your Merchandising Campaign

Start building the aura of teamwork around the lead program by enlisting representatives of the sales department—managers and foot soldiers alike—into the lead program planning process early.

Sales can provide important input. Salespeople certainly know customers better than anyone else in the company, and know which inquiry qualification criteria will work best for them. They can spot problems and contribute ideas to telequalification script development, indicating the prospect information they'd like to receive before they follow up.

Emphasize to salespeople that the lead handling system is not designed to monitor their performance, but to provide a report card on marketing's ability to serve the sales department's needs. Vow that if they find the lead quality is not good, *you will fix it.* All they have to do is report back regularly.

Ask for Feedback

Reversing those timeworn "big brother" suspicions about lead management paperwork works wonderfully. Experts offer a variety of theories to explain the celebrated indifference salespeople show for paperwork. Whatever the cause, when home office "checking up" is turned on its head to become an evaluation of home office performance, salespeople can't resist the opportunity to keep those pencil pushers at headquarters on their toes.

Use informal polls—an envelope stuffer in with the lead notification forms, for instance—to keep track of sales force attitudes toward the lead management program. Questions might include:

- Do you receive the proper number of leads?
- How well are leads being qualified before you receive them?

  ☐ I receive too many unqualified leads.

  ☐ Qualification seems about right.

- Are leads easy to follow up?

  Why? _____.

- How do you judge the following type of leads?

  — From advertising

  ☐ good   ☐ okay   ☐ bad/unproductive

  — From trade shows/specific shows

  ☐ good   ☐ okay   ☐ bad/unproductive

  — From direct mail campaigns

  ☐ good   ☐ okay   ☐ bad/unproductive

  — Others

Other multiple-choice questions could probe specific aspects of your marketing program, and questions such as:

- How much awareness do prospects have of the company's advertising and direct mail?
- How well does the home office/outside service handle the lead program?
- What do customers think about the company? The product(s)?

Running such a survey, make it easy to respond with check-off boxes and use few, if any, open-ended questions requiring a written response. Do not, in your zeal to make sales a lead program partner, risk alienating salespeople with so much additional paperwork they fail to appreciate your collegial purpose.

Use Showmanship

Introduce the new sales lead-management program with hoopla, preferably at an annual sales meeting or similar gathering where sales enthusiasm rides high. Don't be bashful; make an elaborate presentation, just as management would introduce a new sales contest. Don't present simply a lead management system, but "the key to greater selling success." Give your program a distinctive logo and name so it has a life of its own.

Just as with any sales program, contest, or incentive plan, the excitement you generate when you introduce the new lead system at a sales meeting has to be kept fresh, with frequent and engaging communication to the field. You want salespeople to feel confident they are fully informed about what's happening to "their" customers in "their" territories.

Also, report how well your best programs are translating to sales in the field. At one company, once salespeople realized that inbound phone inquiries converted to sales 25 percent better than other inquiry response types, they jumped on such leads with relish.

Use a motivational speaker to pump up the success aspect of the plan, stressing what's in it for sales. Inquiries help salespeople learn customer needs in advance, get appointments with specifiers and hidden decision makers, open doors to prospects at the best time in the buying cycle, keep informed of changes at customer firms, etc.

Tell salespeople about the effort and planning behind the lead handling plan: the search for the most efficient and effective inquiry generation methods, the details of fulfillment, and the effort expended in sight qualification and telequalification.

And tell them how much it costs to generate and process an inquiry. Salespeople who think leads are throwaways will change their attitude when they learn inquiries cost the company from $10 to $500 each.

Share the Promotional Window concept with them, illustrating how you plan marketing communications and lead generation timing to serve their best interests. Show how inquiry management can help to rationalize and balance sales quotas, making sales forecasts more realistic. Don't get hung up on describing the program's success serving communications strategies reps may not understand. News that "The new widget advertising campaign complements an across-the-board corporate communications thrust," is only of secondary interest, compared to "Your prospects will be seeing the new widget advertising campaign just as they begin their capital budgeting meetings in the fall." Even better: "Your prospects will be seeing the new widget advertising campaign just as the Widget Your Way to Hawaii contest begins."

To encourage a more productive attitude, the positive motivators generally work best. Recognition, merchandise, or travel awards work better than cash, the prize value of which tends to be forgotten quickly. Strive for a bit of creativity: generating the excitement of a sudden windfall as well as rewarding the long-haul performance. For instance, give sales incentive contest points for consistent lead follow-up, but salt the information sent to the field with "mystery leads" that, when called, award an instant prize or a chance in a lucrative sweepstakes.

Involve senior management, particularly when positive recognition is in order. For example, at a giant telecommunications company, the motivation program includes a corporate vice president personally telephoning his thanks to reps doing an outstanding lead follow-up job each month. The vice president also signs letters mailed to salespeople who are tardy with their follow-up.

Set Standards

Give each salesperson a loose-leaf binder with information about the program, how and why it works, and what they can rely on from the home office. Loose leaf allow frequent updating via newsletters, copies of new ad and mail programs, etc. Keep reminding them how the program contributes to their success. And include a hot line for reps to call for a cheerful answer to any questions that might arise.

Present system procedures from a rep's perspective. Provide, for example, advice on how to organize the lead flow coming from the home office. Explain everything that's on the sales lead notification form you use. (See Exhibit 10-2 for a sample form.) How should reps sort the forms? Should they take all forms on the road? What are the best telephone calling patterns for hot leads and for leads of lesser priority? Anticipate all the questions they will have about inquiries from prospects they hadn't known before.

At the same time, don't be bashful about seeking information. If the prospect has told you he or she is ready to buy, and has the money, and qualifies, you've got a right to ask salespeople what happened to the lead and insist that it be followed up. Don't pick fights with sales, but do stand your ground once you've developed a system that serves company needs without making unreasonable demands on sales.

The first question is who receives the leads. Make sure it's clear to all concerned how information will flow through the system. The preferred method is to send leads directly to the person responsible for following them up. Sales managers should get a list each month of the leads sent to each territory. Tread carefully, however. Some managers, jealous of their prerogatives, like to use leads as favors and rewards to dole out to deserving reps. Such behavior tarnishes the lead program, making it look like an exploitative device and not a partnership between sales and marketing.

Explain to reps how you will mail leads at least weekly, in an envelope emblazoned with the words "HOT LEADS INSIDE!" or similar attention-getters in big red type. But why rely on 400-year-old postal technology? Send leads to the field by fax or, electronic mail if you've equipped the sales force with computers.

Intelligent Motivation

Motivating a sales force to perform certain tasks requires meeting the three goals shared by every successful sales incentive plan: encouraging the right behavior, energizing the mediocre performers, and keeping excitement and goal-orientation high. Of course, the sales leader must recognize that asking for new or more intensive activity toward one goal is likely to steal time from other objectives.

Make sure you are motivating the right behaviors. If it appears, for instance, that salespeople are following up leads, but not reporting back—a common problem—use incentives to encourage reporting. Don't ask salespeople to intensify their activity prospecting among the more marginal inquiries they receive.

Field reps, by the way. are not the only staffers worth motivating. Lead program personnel, such as telequalifiers, should be rewarded with recognition or material incentives for exceptional performance.

Recognize, too, that output from the top 20 percent of your sales performers will not be affected by incentive programs. They keep on plugging regardless. The bottom 20 percent will not perform better either. Your target for motivation is the middle 60 percent of your audience. Those maybe-hot, maybe-not producers need the full-court press: training, education, and incentives, positive and negative. You must, for example, make them believers of the Rule of 45. Stars implicitly know the phenomenon behind it. Losers cannot believe it because it challenges their treasured rationalizations for their poor showing.

Promote success stories prominently. Spread the recognition, Make it "their" lead handling newsletter. Let salespeople write for it, particularly with inspirational stories. One rep we know, for instance, loudly resisted his company's new lead program. He was doing just fine without the useless intrusion, he bragged at sales meetings. Yet, as he admitted in a story that inspired his peers, he became a believer when he broke his leg skiing. Confined to the phone to work his territory, he started calling the leads sent by the home office and made a huge sale to a prospect he had not called before.

In addition to the newsletter, put all reps on your regular promotional mailing lists. Then they see exactly what their prospects receive. And when you send fulfillment material to an inquirer, send a copy of the cover letter to the local rep. The value of that small gesture is more motivational than informational; you build the teamwork attitude as they're assured their territories are not being worked behind their backs.

You can also get your suppliers into the act. A popular technique for merchandising a new advertising campaign is to have the publisher of the campaign's prime vehicle mail a letter and copy of the campaign kickoff issue to each field rep. The letter explains how the campaign serves sales objectives with the publication's core readership. That helps the salesperson refine the sales call presentation.

When necessary, also send the reality-check material to the field. Without being ham-handed about demanding follow-up, nonetheless remind salespeople of overdue lead reports. Just send each a list of those leads the rep has had for more than a month. The evidence that marketing, and hence sales management, knows what's going on (or not going on) has clear implications. We've heard managers recommend that you withhold sending new leads to tardy reps to get their undivided attention. That it might, but it strikes us as a shortsighted solution, punishing a salesperson who might be following up though not reporting, letting good leads languish, and ignoring inquirers' needs.

Take a more positive approach. Periodically, tell the field about how your regular Did-You-Buy? studies independently track inquiry quality and follow-up performance. Don't tout your surveys as a check-up. Simple matter-of-fact statements have obvious implications.

Cooperation Killers

Out in the field, fear of being left out of the information loop runs high. Feed that fear and you hurt attitudes about the lead program. One of the most potent cooperation killers, for example, occurs when a sales rep hears about a new program from the company for the first time from a customer or, perish the thought, a competitor! It happens, because someone "forgot" to coordinate field communications properly and get a memo out on time. Humiliated, the rep loses faith that the company will do what it says.

What's more likely, however, is that your lead system will perk along and you'll assume that enough communications are getting out to the field. Or, that you can avoid preparing a newsletter issue just because you have no "news" to report. To the field, the "real news" is that lead management is proceeding, serving reps without a hitch. Simply sending a message with a lead program update delivers that real news.

Avoid overload. Sending too many inquiries to the field will frustrate sales-people, even the ones capable of sorting leads out for themselves. Relationship selling, referrals, and salespeople's territory longevity will allow a salesperson to reach a comfort level in the territory.

High comfort levels result in a failure to follow up new leads. The salesper-son must not get so many leads that they cannot be followed up, nor so few that the rep will starve for some time until referral relationships can be built.

Having studied sales reactions to industrial lead programs, market researcher Howard Gordon quips, "Field salespeople will only take so many inquiries a week. It's like taking a drink from a fire hydrant." In a major industrial equipment study, Mr. Gordon found that reps could handle just four or five qualified leads a week without cutting into their current account service duties. "You give a guy 20 leads a week and he says he just can't handle it." You have to modulate him like you do a knob on a stereo set." Mr. Gordon advises. "You have to make a judgment about how many new inquiries a sales rep can follow up each week. You must be very careful of that because it's no big trick to get inquiries today."[4]

"One of our largest manufacturers' reps, calling on those big accounts, feels it knows everything going on in its territory," says the communications director of an integrated circuit manufacturer. "They probably don't spend a lot of time doing missionary work, going through and looking through those leads.

Avoid sloppiness. Home office lapses on lead program details can imply a lackadaisical attitude that tarnishes your program. Sending incomplete inquiry information to the field is inexcusable. Little details, such as inquiries without phone numbers, incomplete addresses and names, cumbersome paperwork and other botched essentials hardly imply that you think the leads are important.

Leads as a Training Tool

Sales leads can be a tool to help new reps get up to speed in their territories quickly. We call it the Fast Start approach. It works particularly well in challenging high-technology fields. Many sales managers will claim that it takes up to six months for a new salesperson to become productive on a predictable basis. We, instead, recommend a three-step plan that's easy to implement and gets a rep started within the first week or two, instead of months.

Many sales training courses take a few weeks, or even longer. When they're done, new reps are exhausted and go home to relax for a few days while they "get ready to do business." That allows valuable knowledge to slip away and "first call" fears to creep in.

Step One: Guaranteed Calls

The new salesperson's first business day back in the field should start with a *guaranteed* appointment made for the rep by your lead system telemarketers.

The new person should have a guaranteed appointment every other day for two weeks—six appointments preferably within 25 miles of home. Considering that guaranteed appointments have two or three times the closing rate of random sales leads, the new person will usually make at least one or perhaps two sales in the first two to four weeks.

Obviously, the high closing rate is more likely when selling low- to medium-priced equipment; sales of supplies or service may fare even better. When that happens, you develop super-confident salespeople who will be unstoppable. They've made their first sale, and immediately start using the information you had just given them in training. They're on their way to the top 10 percent of your sales force.

Step Two: List Sales Leads

As we've seen, the vast majority of leads aren't followed up. Once you're confident your sales trainees will graduate, give them lists of all leads from the past six months. Have them call and make appointments, beginning with the first day after they finish their training.

Statistics cited in earlier chapters indicate that at least 35 percent of the leads less than six months old will still be in the market. During their last week of training, every salesperson can be on the phone during coffee breaks and lunch hours, with the goal of filling in open times between guaranteed appointments. If they're having problems getting appointments, what better time to find out and correct them than while they're still in training.

Step Three: Fresh Leads Close to Home

Step three is very easy if you have a prospect database. Two weeks before graduation, drop 200 to 500 direct mail pieces into territories within 25 miles of each new salesperson's home base. At about the time they complete training, the new, incremental leads start coming in.

The mailing doesn't have to be a new direct mail piece. When you create direct mail programs, always overprint a few thousand which can be used for this purpose. The overrun can also be used to support weak territories and special dealer promotions.

Six guaranteed appointments will probably cost from $150 to $300, depending on who does it for you: in-house vs. outsourced. Direct mail costs vary widely; figure a cost of 75 cents on average for each mailer. That will add $150 to $375 to the new salesperson's launch cost.

When a high-tech company implemented the program, the first month's productivity from 10 new salespeople came within 10 percent of the national average for that sales force. Those new salespeople had their ups and downs just like others, but at the end of six months they had out-produced every sales class before them and their failure rate was non-existent. Several of them climbed to the top 10 percent of the sales force.

You can probably accomplish significant results with at least two of the three steps listed here. You'll not only make heroes of the newcomers, they'll become the lead program's most ardent fans and your best promoters.

Selling the System to Distributors

When the factory manages inquiries poorly for its channels—distributors, dealers, retailers, manufacturers' reps, jobbers, resellers, etc.—it reaps something worse than a grumbling sales force. At its mildest, the manufacturer sets a poor example when it should be encouraging channel partners to be the best marketers they can be. At its worst, it hurts channel relationships, encouraging intermediaries to look elsewhere for vendors more attuned to their marketing needs. Freedom gives channel members substantial leverage.

They, too, must cope with change sweeping their fields, as markets mature and different resellers scramble to specialize and control market segments. Price competition, demanding customers, and competitive pressure to provide more service with the sale conspire to make channel members a nervous lot. The dealer's lead problem usually results from inertia back at the factory: a manufacturer's unwillingness to invest in more dealer support. Dumping leads on the channels is the result. Another gaffe: sending dealers only those "leads" the company's own sales force does not want.

If follow-up is a problem, or even if it isn't, the manufacturer should enlist the dealer's participation in the lead program. The factory can explain what might not be obvious. Follow-up and status reporting allow a marketer to improve inquiry value and fine tune qualification procedures, all to the dealer's benefit. Brought to the center of problem-solving, dealers see the wisdom in helping out.

For example, Sony Dictation Systems applied some creativity to its dealer lead follow-up program, and more or less created lead generation in reverse. It used a contest and recognition program to improve dealer salespeople skills and product knowledge. It got dealer reps to develop prospect lists which they turned over to Sony for fulfillment, and for contest points. Sony scored some competitive coups with the program against archrival Lanier.

Chapter 13

Computerizing Your Lead Management Edge

Desktop and portable computing have revolutionized the way business creates and handles marketing information—including the management of sales lead databases. Marketers now take control of their own information rather than rely on centralized corporate data processing departments. They replace paper-based systems piecemeal as their needs and all the costs associated with computerization change. Perhaps they ramp up a marketing information system (MKIS) for their databases this year and automate sales force activity the next; in the meantime, fax, phone, and mail communication with the field suffice.

Increasingly, computerized sales lead management becomes less a matter of state-of-the-art and more the everyday process for the average company. Industry pundits have predicted that marketing and sales computerization will boost productivity 15 to 20 percent and account for a quarter of all corporate computerization expenditures by the turn of the century.[1] Computerizing lead management might not provide a competitive advantage, but trying to make do without it is very likely a competitive disadvantage.

The old ways, struggling to manage inquiries intelligently without a dedicated computer system, are still a vivid memory to one marketer. She recalls comparing by hand inquiry databases of engineers with order-entry records listing purchasing executives. "We had 50,000 inquiries. The printout with 100,000 records to match was three feet deep!" she remembers the ordeal.

"Next I asked the computer department to generate the names of all new customers we acquired in the last 12 months, and those who had not purchased for the previous three years. It took me four months of every spare minute I had going through that horrendous list of new customers to see if they had inquired. I only did that once. I couldn't handle it!

"Again, I went to the computer department and asked, 'Can you help me?' They said they had priorities: payables, receivables, payroll, all this other stuff. I got nowhere." Six months later, she was still waiting for her report, she complained.

Promises and Realities

New Equipment Digest, surveying its advertisers in 1984 and 1990, found the proportion using computers to track inquiries increased from a third to nearly two-thirds of its sample. That large, new product tabloid credits desktop computing growth for the increase.[2]

But, as many companies approach the automation process, they confuse automating sales paperwork with properly handling prospects. Only the customized, upper tier of sales force automation systems—the software category most closely related to lead management—can provide the in-depth reporting capability which allows back-end analysis of the promotional dollars spend to drive the sales force.

Amid all the computer hoopla, managers mistakenly believe that the high-tech wizardry putting prospect names in the sales person's computer will automatically result in a closed-loop lead-handling system. It seldom works that way, however. Particularly in terms of shrink-wrapped software sold at retail or by mail, and advertised in computer and sales management magazines, few if any packages are flexible enough to handle the whole lead-management task. Some are good at reporting. Others are superior sales trackers. It is difficult to find one good at both.

Sales force automation is a great communication tool, effective and efficient for delivering names and qualification data, call reporting, order placement/status, etc. But, sales force automation is sales oriented. Few packages address the quarterly analysis essential to closed-loop marketing. Most are several years or more away from satisfying the marketing analysis needs for most corporations. With the great majority of U.S. companies having fewer than 25 employees, and virtually all upper-end sales force automation software written for organizations with 50 or more salespeople, there's a wide gap between the promise and reality for the average company. Contact management programs, popular for their ability to keep reps organized, help the small sales force. But they do not offer much in the way of inquiry management capability.

Nonetheless, today's shortcomings will not persist indefinitely. Computerization continues to be a fast-moving target for marketers at companies of all sizes. Because they usually deal with so-called "soft decisions" that are difficult to quantify, marketing and sales applications have been an elusive last frontier of business computer use. In 1986, for instance, a group of Fortune 500 company executives convened to ponder what looked then like the future of business personal computing. They predicted productivity gains driven by the technology would approach 1,000 percent for large organizations like theirs. But it hasn't happened, authors of that prediction acknowledge, not because the technology isn't there, but because organizations aren't ready for it.[3]

For some firms, however, marketing and sales technologies have proved to be the most exciting computerization challenge. They make the effort to learn how to use new data sources and advanced software. The leaner, flatter organizations of the 1990s put a premium on workgroup productivity solutions, expert systems, and the like. In the hardware arena, early adopters wrestle with advances in miniaturization, wireless data transmission and personal digital assistants, networking, and data storage.

Technology promises a world where no salesperson is ever out of touch. Press reports trumpet spectacular productivity claims by users, such as SmithKline Beecham's pharmaceutical division crediting laptops for an additional 1.5 calls per day average among its 1,800 salespeople.[4] A computer trade magazine article illustrates the technological capabilities vendors promote to corporate buyers:

> SalesTrak (by Aurum Software Inc.) is designed to run on Windows-based laptop computers and to communicate with a back-end database sitting on top of Unix-based Oracle or Sybase databases. It is aimed at making field sales personnel and engineers more effective by letting them download up-to-the-minute information on price quotes, potential customers, and leads from headquarters . . .
>
> With SalesTrak, field salespeople can download leads relayed to the database by other field salespeople wanting to share information or by telemarketing personnel who prequalify leads. Downloading and uploading of data can be done in an unattended mode at night.[5]

A widely quoted 1989 article by Harvard University researchers piqued top management interest by reporting that companies achieve 10 to 30 percent sales increases from advanced sales and marketing technologies, often achieving 100 percent return on investment. Those researchers acknowledged, however, that very few companies had achieved that magnitude of automation benefits.[6] More recent assessments insist that despite the wide use of computers, the potential automation holds for sales and marketing remains unexplored,[7] with an estimated 85 percent loss from inadequate customer, market, and competitor information.[8]

Pricey glamour. The sales automation bag of tricks doesn't stop with communications. Mapping software allows sales managers to reallocate territories at the touch of a button, and telemarketers to find instantly the dealer closest to an inbound inquirer. Expert systems allow salespeople to customize presentations on the fly, and configure complex orders and bids instantaneously in prospects' offices. The bill for all the fun of full-scale sales force automation, according to the 1992 estimate of consultants Todd Schofield and Donald R. Shaw, runs $7,000 to $15,000 per salesperson in hardware, software, training and support over a project's three- to five-year life.[9] According to a 1989 Conference Board survey, the initial sales automation tab comes to a median price of $5,000 per salesperson outfitted with computers plus the requisite software and training, with prices in the top quartile running $10,000 or more per rep.[10]

Grasping for the glamour raises new risks. "There is the danger that marketers will forget that all the information in the world cannot substitute for their vision, creativity, and intelligence. Information is no substitute for those qualities," wrote marketing information systems expert Charles W. Stryker.[11]

Yet information surely will change how vision, creativity, and intelligence are deployed. Computerization changes the culture of the marketing function, sometimes with unintended effects. Applying an industrial revolution-type notion of worker productivity to computerized selling, some systems—including some lead management programs—merely try to push clerical tasks downward from the home or regional office staff to the field. That is what systems vendor Richard Brock calls one of the worst causes of sales automation failure.[12]

Setting Objectives

Many obstacles impede the speed of sales and marketing automation, not the least being the different objectives of the departments most directly served. Salespeople want systems to help them meet their quotas and stay on top of their accounts and territories. Marketing, however, wants to manipulate decision-making data and attain organization objectives, based on sales feedback, requiring follow-up reports to plan and adjust marketing programs.

Management must position automation as a time-saving, sales-boosting tool for sharing information that helps reps look like heroes to their customers. Simply automating old, inefficient paper-based processes will not allow you to achieve justifiable returns from your investment.

All parties should recognize that "Automation doesn't automate sales, but it does automate the flow of information in a timely manner, in a complete manner, in an accurate manner throughout your organization," says Brock, whose Brock Control Systems is one of the leading high-end computerized sales systems. "Automate only if you want to know the results, what's going on. If you want to stay in a dark hole," he quipped, "keep on going without it."[13]

Designing the Lead-Management Solution

A symposium on the subject by the Business Management Association (formerly the Business/Professional Advertising Association) concluded that automated lead management should serve these objectives:

- Respond quickly to an inquirer's request.
- Qualify hot prospects for immediate transmittal to the field.
- Reduce selling costs by helping to concentrate sales efforts on the most promising prospects.
- Ensure timely personal meetings between sales and hot prospects.
- Evaluate and increase the effectiveness of advertising and communications programs.
- Monitor progress of the selling effort.
- Relate the sale to the initial inquiry.
- Serve as a marketing research and planning tool by providing information on prospects, product applications and new ideas.[14]

At the start, unrealistic expectations can lead to problems and the unrealistic assumption that everyone on whom the system's success depends will understand and endorse its "obvious benefits." But all the advantages are not obvious to everyone; each functional department has its own agenda. Computer system planners must design from conflicting advice while avoiding a least common denominator result. Each constituent of the sales lead management system must be consulted, better yet represented, on an interdisciplinary system design task force. "Make sure both foot soldiers and commanders sign on, because the resulting system must serve both," says consultant Shaw.[15]

Step-By-Step Process

The critical first step is determining the exact problem to be solved or opportunity to seize. Is current fulfillment and qualification too slow? Is the sales force unable to keep track of leads sent to the field? Has a large new market opened up? Is the qualification system swamped? Is follow-up reporting and other communication with the field too slow? Is the inquirer database a mess, with outdated contacts, incorrect addresses, and other frequent inaccuracies? Is program analysis rudimentary? Then, the task force builds the system step-by-step, remembering that the goal is creating better salespeople, not better computer users.

Knowing the objectives, identify required system features, those that are nice to have but not essential, and those that can wait or are not needed. Exhibit 13-1 provides a checklist of potential system capabilities.

Exhibit 13-1
Lead Management Automation Checklist

Data Entry

- Receive inquiries from publishers via modem or electronic mail.
- Enter leads directly into database at trade show.
- Receive inquiries direct from inquirers via electronic mail.
- Enter printed inquiry and database lists into computerized database.
- Inbound telephone service operator inquiry data entry.
- Download and merge external computerized databases (e.g. directories) into lead database.
- Download and merge internal computerized databases (e.g. customer lists, receivables) into lead database.
- Combine internal and service bureau inquiry databases.

Inquiry Qualification

- Sort inquiries by geo-demographic characteristics (e.g. location, industry, company size or household income, application, previous contact/sales history, planned purchase date).
- Provide branched scripting to outbound/inbound telequalifiers.
- Automatically sort inquiries by sight-qualification criteria.

Inquiry Fulfillment

- Determine fulfillment package content by inquiry classification.
- Provide immediate response to requests for faxed information.
- Get literature in the mail within 24 to 48 hours of inquiry data entry.
- Customize bounceback card questions.
- Customize fulfillment package cover letter.
- Issue follow-up letters.
- Automated dealer-locator service (where-to-buy information).

Lead Distribution to the Field

- Electronic distribution of inquiry data to the field.
- Automatic assignment of lead to sales rep/territory/distributor.
- Provide telequalifier/trade show qualifier background information on inquirer with the lead.
- Automatic addition of lead information to salesperson call-plan database.
- Provide a host system/database to field sales software.
- Lead information sharing among sales territories/branches.

Lead Tracking

- Issue follow-up tickler to salespeople and/or sales managers.
- Receive electronic lead follow-up reports.
- Enter paper follow-up reports into database.
- Assign leads to Did-You-Buy? study samples.
- Add Did-You-Buy? survey findings to individual lead records.
- Merge order-entry records into inquiry database.
- Merge customer service records into inquiry database.

Inquiry Database Enhancement

- Regular addition of lead data to larger marketing information database.
- Provide for future expansion of inquiry record data fields.

Sales Lead Program Analysis and Reporting

- Analyze lead generation performance by medium.
- Analyze lead generation performance by medium type.
- Analyze inquiry trends by product.
- Analyze sales follow-up.
- Cross-reference sales follow-up by product.
- Cross-reference lead-generation media performance by product.
- Capture sales follow-up reports in product/media/territory analyses.

- Capture sales conversion reports in product/media/territory analyses.
- Prepare return-on-investment analyses.
- Track inquiry trends over time.
- Prepare management program summary reports.
- Calculate ratios for ROPI analysis and forecasting.
- Add returned warranty card data to database.
- Analyze Did-You-Buy? study data.
- Prepare statistical models of sales conversion likelihoods.

Next, determine what system users will expect and will accept. But, warns Brock, "Don't let them dictate to you. It's kind of like asking children what they want for dinner. They don't know what they really need."[16]

Also, be careful not to overpromise or oversell the system. An overenthusiastic fascination with "how good it's gonna be" will raise expectations too high, particularly among people who don't know they'll inevitably face some "no pain, no gain" frustrations learning the system once it's installed. In our experience, they will be the first ones to undermine computerization, by word or even deed. On balance, it is probably better to underpromise a bit.

Experiment with software and then hardware, if possible, only after you have determined what your system must accomplish. A period of experimentation, even playfulness, with various software packages or custom solutions can precede pilot testing of a candidate system.

As the design process continues, it needs champions—partisans who'll welcome the new tool and encourage others. "The ambitious regional manager who wants the vice-president of sales job is a favorite vendor target," says Clare Gillan, a senior analyst at International Data Corp., "because a successful implementation means high visibility."[17]

Closing in on your system design, try to find inexpensive software that simulates at least part of what the contemplated system will accomplish, consultant Shaw advises, so users can try it out.[18] What might have seemed important at first, say a feature like autodialing capability in field software, might turn out to be unneeded and unloved by its intended users. Testing prepares you to write better specifications and design a better pilot test for a full system. Testing should assess ease of use, as well as what a program actually accomplishes.

Whenever possible in those trial runs, automate those tasks with the most dramatic near-term payoff. Benefits will be apparent, contributing to organization enthusiasm.

Next comes pilot testing before full system installation. But don't assume, Shaw cautions, that the pilot is an experiment which "doesn't require massive preparation and a full-court press when it comes to introduction and training. If anything, the pilot is *more* important than the subsequent roll-out with regard to those elements."[19]

Prepare yourself for staff training; it might cost more than the hardware and software combined, experts caution. They also advise that you not scrimp. Says Shaw, don't try to teach everything at once—let lessons sink in—and don't assume that anyone is totally free of computerphobia. There's always something that will bother someone. Remember that the user has to know what's in it for him or her. Don't be concerned if some slow starters want to keep using their paper-based methods for a while, Shaw adds. Laggards will catch on once they see others using the system successfully.[20]

Hard Software Choices

Hundreds of marketing and sales-oriented software packages compete for attention in what was estimated to in 1991 to be a $200 million fast-growing marketplace.[21] And that's just off-the-shelf programs—either at retail or via mail order. It does not include the custom software better suited to lead tracking and analysis, as we noted above. *New Equipment Digest* estimates that two-thirds of business advertisers use custom solutions to manage inquiries.[22] Some degree of customization seems to be inevitable; a Conference Board survey found that nine out of 10 companies modified packages to better suit their needs. Respondent marketing managers said a vendor's willingness to make alterations is a critical purchase criterion.[23]

When shopping for a software supplier, also evaluate its training and support capabilities and policies, its willingness to tailor a package to the buyer's precise needs, and its policies and prices for upgraded versions in the future. Be attentive to the vendor's track record, and whether it and its technical experts will be around if something goes wrong. A penny blithely saved on software could lead to massive headaches and bigger expenditures in training and system corrections down the road.

Lead-Management Applications

Basic information about vendors isn't hard to find. By the early 1990s, marketers could choose from among some 500 personal computer-based software packages, sales lead management among them.[24] For example, the *Sales & Marketing Management Software Directory* published in the December 1993 issue listed nearly 500 sales force automation packages from 400 vendors, 19 of them listed as lead-tracking applications. On occasion, computer enthusiast and trade magazines run announcements or reviews of new marketing and sales automation products. Because it's a fast-growing field, make sure you check up-to-date sources when you search for candidate packages.

Some of what's on the shelf is quite inexpensive—less than $100 per copy. Those tend to be relatively unsophisticated contact managers, with basic database, mail, and word processing, activity reporting, and telephone dialing capabilities. They're often suitable for individual salespeople and small companies, however. And, adds consultant Shaw, they're inexpensive enough to be "throw away items" suitable for experimentation.

"The only way to get a tailored system that meets your precise specifications will be to build it or hire a systems house to do so," Shaw maintains, pointing to specialists in the category. But he cautions: custom programs, which cost more, "entail a certain 'pig in a poke' risk. When you get the result, it may not be as good as it looked on paper."[25]

Price-performance tiers. A 1991 study of the sales automation software field by International Data Corp. found the market dominated by single-user applications, but noted that multi-user, multi-function systems have been growing in popularity. International Data Corp. segments the software field into three price-performance-service tiers. The mix of those three characteristics most appropriate for a company in general depends on its size, says International Data Corp.'s Gillan, the report's author.

- First-tier vendors typically sell to companies with more than 50 salespeople. Their complete solutions stress customization, support, networking, and training. They integrate all of a major corporate marketing department's clerical, database, and communication processes. Prices start around $40,000, International Data Corp. said, and systems typically are sold direct by the developer.

- Small and medium-sized companies may find second-tier products appealing, International Data Corp. continues, but levels of service vary widely among them. They are designed to integrate both field and home office with database, activity planning, mailing, communications, and other sales activity modules. Prices run in the $1,000 or higher range, International Data Corp. says; typically resellers handle the products, sometimes bundling them with consulting, training or hardware.

- Third-tier products in International Data Corp.'s classification scheme are the under $1,000 small company and individual salesperson packages mentioned above. They're sold direct, by resellers, and through retail.[26]

In the fast-developing field of computerized sales support, it's difficult to classify software to a finer degree than International Data Corp.'s broad categories. So many applications perform different mixes of multiple tasks—contact management, account management, activity planning, communications, etc.—making it hard to assign them to discrete classifications.

As automation has caught on, software publishers keep making their packages more complex with more features, hoping to retain a one-package-does-all status in the marketplace. But time is running out on that strategy, says Russell Thomas a former Hewlett-Packard Co. marketing engineer-turned-consultant. New operating environments and software standards will enable users to mix and match modules from several software products to build their own quasi-custom applications—a spreadsheet from one publisher, a word processor from another, a contact manager from a third, for instance.[27]

Inquiry Databases for Management Decisions

The back-end analysis that simple, stand-alone software applications do not address concern the sales lead master database, the heart of your sales lead-management system, as depicted in Exhibit 4-1. Information about inquirers, prospects, and buyers constantly flows in and out of the database, updating records and guiding lead fulfillment, qualification, follow-up, and analysis.

To recap the short-term benefits, a company's inquiry and lead database provides:

- Maintenance and control over customer and prospect inquiries.
- Lists for direct mail, telemarketing, and other customer and prospect contact.
- A structure for inquiry qualification.
- A system accepted throughout the company for monitoring sales performance and lead follow-up.
- A method for avoiding missed sales opportunities.

- A means of preventing the sloppy fulfillment and follow-up that will mar a lead program, and a company's image.
- Communications coordinated with selling programs, quota periods, and customer buying cycles.
- Effective and equitable sales territory allocation.
- More efficient selling activity.
- A scorecard for comparing the performance of different media options, communication strategies, and selling tactics.
- A mechanism for maintaining sales activity in temporarily vacant sales territories.
- An early warning system monitoring changes in product appeal, sales territory potential, and market segment strength.
- A means of automating multiple follow-up letters to prospects.

In the long run, the sales lead database produces more efficient, orderly, and accurate marketing and marketing communications programs by:

- Broadening the customer base with improved list management.
- Enabling better dealer information and dealer relations programs.
- Adding otherwise unknown customers to the customer list.
- Maintaining data critical for long-term customer relationships.
- Feeding useful data into market and competitive intelligence systems.
- Producing more accurate sales forecasts.
- Providing a common platform for marketing and sales data presented to top management.
- Assisting the marketing budgeting process.
- Contributing a reliable historical base for brand valuation modeling.
- Fostering productive teamwork among marketing and sales people.

Finally, and perhaps most important, the sales lead database provides hard evidence, not inference, of the value of marketing and sales programs, ending guesswork about which part of the marketing dollar is fat and which is muscle.

Database Dimensions

The individual record eventually could contain the following information, as collected from inquirers during initial lead acquisition and subsequent qualification and follow-up steps.

- Inquirer name, title, job function.
- Company name and address, phone and fax numbers.
- Company primary business or businesses.
- Company size (sales, number of employees).
- Date of inquiry.
- Source of inquiry.
- Inquiry method employed (reader service card, inbound phone, fax, etc.)
- Kind of information sought.
- Immediacy of need for information (mail literature, send a salesperson).
- Asked to see a salesperson?
- Request to stay on mailing list?
- Definitely plans to buy?
- Likely timing of purchase.
- Size of anticipated order.
- Anticipated use/application for product or service.
- Inquirer's role in purchase decision (adviser, specifier, final approver, etc.)
- Best time to call.
- Ever before called on by a company salesperson?
- Purchased from the company before?
- Currently used or installed products.
- Expect to lease or purchase?
- Purchased product?
- Purchased which brand, and why?
- Reason for purchase.

Certainly, you should also include any other information of special importance to your unique marketing needs.

The database system should be able to match records within its own files. Ideally, it should also match records from other databases within the company such as customer files, orders pending, credit records, sales call reports, shipments and returns, etc. That is, however, an ideal that's tough to attain, for reasons we noted in Chapter 8.

Armed with customer records, qualification information, and sales follow-up reports, the well-designed lead management database allows innumerable decision-support analyses. For example, the inquisitive marketer can compare:

- Sales/distributor territory performance vs. potential.
- Lead sources ranked by overall effectiveness and cost-per-inquiry or cost-per-qualified lead in various target market niches.
- Intramedium options, such as high-frequency vs. large-page advertising strategies, different mail packages, different trade shows, alternative telemarketing scripts, optional creative approaches, and different promotion schedules.
- Types of offers, such as product literature, free consultation, sample, etc.
- Comparative product appeal.
- Why an inquirer bought your product vs. a competitor's, or vice versa.

Plan, Then Slice

Designing the database before you collect information is critical. And it is essential that decision makers control the planning. Data entered into a misconceived database often cannot be retrieved in a more useful form. Flexibility is the key to a well-designed database. Users must be able to combine facts their way and spot relationships easily.

Handling inquiry data. As an example, we have used 14 basic sorting and selection criteria in simplified databases of initial inquiries. Fourteen distinct data fields for each inquirer record strikes a balance between having too much expensive information and too little information. Users determine how much information they want to employ in a specific application.

The best system for you as a minimum might collect more or fewer than 14 types of data, depending on your current and future needs. We show the 14 here just to illustrate the contents of a representative inquiry record. Extensive inquirer profile information—need, authority, budget, timing, etc.—will add additional information to each record. In choosing system hardware and software or in outsourcing your database management, make sure you will have more than enough room to add additional data fields if you need to.

1. Zip code.
2. Sales territory.
3. Product of interest.
4. Qualification level.
5. Date processed.
6. Date status last changed (e.g. by sales follow-up report).
7. Magazine or other source.

8. Issue or trade show date.

9. Whether from an ad, publicity, show, direct mail, etc.

10. Reader service number.

11. SIC (Standard Industry Classification), when provided by the publication.

12. Profile code.

13. Coded response to open-ended qualification question.

14. Special field available for specific product-use data.

Here are some examples of ways a marketer might "slice, dice, and drill" the database to create special-use lists.

• Print labels for a mailing to qualified prospects in the New England area.

• Print labels for a mailing to all qualified prospects in California, introducing the new sales manager for that state.

• Provide a list of all inquirers who responded to the June issue of *Electronic Design*, sorted and counted by sales territory.

• Make a mailing to qualified prospects in territory 173 who are interested in Models 200 and 7200.

• Provide a list of people who qualified themselves but who have not yet been seen by salespeople. Sort the list by company within territory.

• Prepare a report to show how many qualified leads are in the data bank by state.

• New features have been added to Model 300. Print a set of labels of all prospects who were interested in that product at last year's conference in Pittsburgh. Send a mailing inviting them to see the new model at this year's conference.

• Make a mailing to all prospects in the seven midwestern states reminding them who the sales reps are in their areas. Print a card on the computer showing the phone number, name, and address of the reps. Send those reps a list of the names in their area who are getting that mailing.

• Prepare a report showing how many leads were sent to each sales office in the past 12 months and how many of those they followed up and reported the results.

• Send our new salesperson in Chicago a list of all qualified prospects in that area and a set of peel-off labels for all names so that the rep can do a mailing to them.

- The in-house telemarketing department is going to try to contact as many inquirers as possible. Each week, print a set of peel-off labels for that week's inquiries. On the top of each label, show the phone number (if available) and the product the prospect inquired about.
- Send an invitation to people in areas around the attached list of cities inviting them to a seminar to be held in those cities.
- Print a list, in zip code order, of all inquirers from any IBM office or plant in the United States, Canada, and Europe.
- Make a mailing to all of our inquirers from last year's Comdex show.

Exercising marketing options like these without a computerized inquiry database would be tedious, if not impossible. Considering the chaos of making seat-of-the-pants decisions, any step taken to organize sales lead data is going to yield benefits.

Chapter 14 shows a list of basic reports a sales lead-management system should produce for marketing decision making.

Additionally, information from inquirers and marketing and sales programs can be combined with transactional data from within the corporation. For example, are any inquirers on the company's credit watch list? Are any former customers? Has sales called on this inquirer before? Was his or her last order a direct or distributor sale?

Then, spice the growing database with outside source material: competitor and customer financial information, market research reports, government registration records, rented lists, business census statistics, etc. At that stage, the inquiry begins its transition to its highest calling, as the heart of a genuine marketing information system.

Chapter 14

Insights from Inquiries: Closing the Marketing Loop

What if your company president asks, "Why should I give you more money for advertising? Our sales manager claims that by adding one or two reps we can increase sales by five percent."

If you've done your homework, you can reply authoritatively, "From each ad we place, we get 50 inquiries. Within six months, about a quarter of them will be closed at an average sale of $60,000 each. We will get about half of that, more or less in line with our overall market share. In a year, nearly half of those leads will have bought, and we will have about $750,000 in sales we probably would not have made otherwise.

"If we invest in another 10 insertions, at $5,000 each, we can expect an added 60 sales within six months, and 100 to 110 within a year. The $50,000 investment gives us the leads to roughly $7.5 million in new business."

Sound like fiction? Hardly. Proper sales lead analysis will support your marketing budget for advertising, trade shows, direct mail, and other inquiry-generating activities with proof that leads *do* become sales.

Total Quality Lead Management

Analyzing inquiry generation and follow-up data, and integrating them into your company's overall marketing information system (MKIS), provides the finishing touch to sales lead management. It solidifies the link between marketing and sales. And it provides the "closed loop marketing" system that allows you continuously to improve the effectiveness and efficiency of your entire marketing process.

From a strategic viewpoint, sales lead analysis also helps a company succeed with its core mission: providing superior value to customers based on knowledge of their individual needs. Whether you market to consumers or to businesses, a customer orientation is essential in a worldwide economy that prizes the loyalty of profitable customers as a firm's most important asset. The ability to learn from sales leads where to find your best prospects has become an essential business skill in the 1990s. The ability to learn faster than one's competitors might be the only competitive advantage that's sustainable in today's information-intensive marketplace, says Arie De Geus, corporate planner for Royal Dutch/Shell.

Knowing your customer better than anyone else could well be your firm's most important asset, the marketplace advantage that's hardest for competitors to reproduce, says Gary T. Lilien, president of the Institute of Management Sciences. The best marketers in the information age are "learning organizations" which tie everything they know about a customer—often spread around a corporation is disparate databases—into a single record, the building block of what Lilien calls the Market-Driven Customer Information System (MCIS).[1]

Your sales lead master database, as described in the previous chapter, is the place to begin. But you must follow through and close the loop. You need to analyze lead performance to measure and improve your marketing performance. For example, a revealing study of "winners" and "losers" among business-to-business marketing communicators found that just 28 percent of the winners, those large company managers with communications results that exceeded expectations, relied on counting the number of inquiries as their prime performance measurement. About 39 percent said they tracked their inquiries to measure their contribution to sales and profit. In contrast, 42 percent of the losers—those acknowledging that their communications fell short of goals—relied on raw lead counts for performance measurement, while just 25 percent linked inquiries to sales and profit.

Pointing to "an all too common problem in business marketing," the survey report chided managers for measuring the wrong things. "We say we want awareness and sales, then all we measure is 'leads,' often without regard to whether these leads are qualified or result in sales. The program is deemed a failure based on that incomplete, inconsistent measurement and placed in jeopardy."[2]

MKIS Advantage

How a company will use its marketing information is limited only by its decision-making creativity. Many MKIS reports will be standard fare in just about any company: tracking sales by product and customer category to forecast future sales; clustering customers with similar characteristics into discrete market segments; measuring sales, distribution, and communications performance; tracking the causes of customer complaints; tracking profitability per account, . . . the list goes on.

Beyond sorting the information in MKIS databases, marketers can apply statistical models to the information, replicating market segments and creating prospect-based profiles useful for market planning, forecasting and "what if?" decision testing. For example, a company can use qualified lead data to identify the characteristics of its best market segments, use commercial databases of business establishments to identify the most likely prospects in those target segments, and estimate the potential purchases of each using government-generated economic data broken out by industrial classification. That approach generates powerful lists for sales development and qualification of leads generated by traditional sources.

However, surprisingly few companies even try to harness MKIS to anywhere near its full potential. According to research at Harvard University, fewer than 20 percent of companies attempt to develop any sort of large-scale system. Complexity, and management's inability to use traditional capital budgeting to assess the "soft" benefits of MKIS stand in the way.[3]

Or, as MKIS consultant Charles W. Stryker explains, the problem is with the way marketers work. Companies cannot use an MKIS. "If you gave them a list and said here are people who will buy your product if you communicate with them effectively, they couldn't do anything with it."[4]

Among the sins are sloppy inquiry handling: slipshod inquiry qualification and follow-up, a failure to maintain inquirer records, an unwillingness to link inquiries to sales. For instance, companies often collect qualification data in different formats depending on the source. They use one classification scheme for advertising, another for trade shows. They should have planned their information capture with an eye on combining records, using a common qualification profile template as shown in Exhibit 10-1. Carefully choose the data you will need to make decisions, then begin collecting it even if you can't use it right away.

Clearly, there's a great opportunity to achieve a competitive advantage for companies getting their marketing information and sales lead management systems in order. Your competition might be napping. The inaccuracies plaguing business data are "scary," according to a survey by the researchers at the Massachusetts Institute of Technology. Half the information officers polled said they thought their data were less than 95 percent accurate. "Almost all of them said that databases maintained by individual departments weren't good enough to be used for important decisions." One major manufacturer, for example, found that its customer database listed the same company under 7,000 different customer numbers. Because they received bonuses for opening new accounts, salespeople were entering new customer numbers for every order.[5]

Use Your "Sales Finder"

Squeezing marketing and sales insights from inquiries benefits from a process we've dubbed the Sales Finder™ and have used with our clients.

It doesn't take abstruse knowledge, tremendous amounts of labor, or lots of money to exploit the potential of the sales lead master database. What marketers need is proof that their budgets produce a return on investment. The evidence can include the products sold as a direct result of advertising, the publications in which advertising produces a payback, the inbound inquiries signaling otherwise unknown prospects, etc. Of course, salespeople get the credit for closing orders. But in today's economy, marketers must prove they are finding the right prospects for sales reps to pursue.

One way to get the proof is to compare the sales order database with the inquiry database to identify new customer sales. This is a simple process of matching the company names and addresses. (Do not try to match individuals' names; often engineering people inquire while purchasing people buy.) Be sure you examine the inquiries old enough to have led to the sales; if it takes six months to close the average sale, examine inquiries six months or older against current sales, for instance. Then, analyze the inquiries that converted to sales. The Sales Finder reveals how wisely marketing has spent its budget, and how the marketing communications that generate leads must run continuously to keep the lead pipeline stocked.

A true story. Company A has a comprehensive sales lead-management program. It profiles all leads received from trade shows, 800-numbers, and direct mail. It employs a team of telemarketers to call advertising reader service inquirers and glean vital profile information. The company enters all the information into the database and forwards it to the sales force each week.

Even though Company A's sales force reports back on the quality of leads, the marketing department uses the Sales Finder to gather additional proof of the actual closed sales that began with marketing programs. Out of 3,000 orders for one product line, Company A traced nearly 700 new customer sales directly to marcom.

Company A also learned:

- Which of 33 inquiry sources produced the most leads.
- Three publications produced more than 100 new customers each, with one publication topping out at more than 250 matches.
- Eighty percent of the new sales came from four sources, with the remaining 25 sources producing only 20 of the sales.

- Sales from marketing efforts far and away exceeded their expectations.
- Trade shows produced excellent sales as compared to other source types.
- Additional downstream sales of supplies and accessories to new customers made the marketing payback even better.

When companies compare their inquiry database to the sold-product database they can adjust and tweak their marketing communications plans and accomplish closed-loop marketing. While the idea of comparison isn't new, it is more easily performed today with advanced record-matching software.

Valuable Information Assets

You bought them, so to receive full value from your inquiries, use your inquiry database to provide:

- Names, addresses, and related inquirer data sorted by product, market segment, etc. for direct mailings, telemarketing, Did-You-Buy? surveys, pre-show promotions, etc.
- Automatic publication of sales lead notification forms, for distribution by mail, fax or e-mail.
- Sales lead follow-up reminder notices to the field.
- Follow-up mailings to inquirers.
- Regularly scheduled computerized management reports on communications, sales, and distributor performance.
- Cost-per-inquiry analysis of inquiry sources, products, territories, etc.
- Conversion-to-sales data by inquiry sources, products, territories, etc.
- Analysis of why some inquiry sources work better than others.
- Regular customer-activity profiles.
- A means of setting communications and promotion budgets required to meet sales targets (as in using the return-on-promotional-investment [ROPI] model explained in Chapter 5).
- Sales forecasting and quota-setting, by product, territory, etc. Today's inquiries are tomorrow's sales.
- A means of geomapping accounts and sales territory design.
- Input to statistical models.
- A way to test the inquiry yield from different target markets defined by industry, geography, application, distribution channel, etc.

- Information about selling successes you can promote to the field to encourage inquiry follow-up.

- A means of matching new inquiries with old, by person and/or company.

- Immediate identification of customers inquiring about other products. Spot cross-selling opportunities.

- A means of matching inquiries to purchase orders, despite different names on each (engineers inquire, purchasing agents handle orders).

- A "buying-influence profile" of a prospect firm by examining the patterns of multiple and duplicate inquiries over time, and among a prospect company's plant locations.

- A way to profile best-customer qualifications: need, desire, authority, budget, time frame for a commitment, applications, installed products, etc.

- A means of tracking new customer relationships: longevity, lifetime value, retention and defection rates, and repeat inquiries.

- A means of tracking order volume per customer over time. Do those who buy prototyping quantities buy production quantities from you or the competition?

That's just a typical list of what's possible. Unique circumstances probably will prompt additional database uses at your company.

Power Report Examples

While there are many ways to examine data, combine them, sort them and display them, we show one system here of the lead analysis "Power Reports" you can generate to monitor your sales and marketing. Power Reports also produce information to pass along to the sales force, to give reps the big picture and encourage their cooperation and follow up. The example comes from Inquiry Handling Service, Inc., and is typical of the reporting used by its clients. This is not the only way to present inquiry database information. But, in the spirit of a picture or printout being worth a thousand words, the samples for pseudonymous National Industries illustrate the points we've been making throughout this book.

Exhibit 14-1 shows National's "Database Listing" form.

- At the left, the printout lists the tracking codes assigned to the inquiry (customer and prospect coding should be consistent throughout the entire company's information systems) and the date of inquiry processing.

Exhibit 14-1
Database Listing

```
                    N A T I O N A L   I N D U S T R I E S
                            DATABASE LISTING                                    5 FEB 94

94748824  PATRICK RUMLER, CHEMIST        ANIMAL HEALTH DIA LAB   CARIBBEAN T & L              ISS:93JUN   RS#:666    TYP:PUBLCT
MICRUM    MICHIGAN STATE UNIVERSITY                              STATUS: PROSP RESPND-QUAL      PROD:GENERAL           TERR: 225
93-07-01  E LANSING, MI 48824            TEL: 517/355-0281       SIC:    UPDATE:9312          SPECIAL CODES:026

94754923  DAVID PRITZL, MGR COMP SVC     242 S PEARL ST          CHEM PROCESSING TECH         ISS:93MAY   RS#:252    TYP:ADVERT
SOUPRI    SOUTHWESTERN ENGRG                                     STATUS: IMMEDIATE NEED         PROD:MULTI 8           TERR: 210
93-05-30  BERLIN WI 54923                TEL: 414/361-2220       SIC:    UPDATE:              SPECIAL CODES:

94760181  P. MCKERNIN, PROD. MGR.        442 WEST ST CHARLES RD. CHROMATOGRAPHY               ISS:93NOV   RS#:      TYP:LETTER
ATOMCK    A TO Z TOOL, INC.                                      STATUS: NEW INQUIRY            PROD:SYSTEM II         TERR: 213
93-07-08  VILLA PARK, IL 60181           TEL: 312/279-4118       SIC:3549  UPDATE:           SPECIAL CODES:

94763128  RANDY J KOOPMAN                4730 MCILROY DR         CHROMATOGRAPHY               ISS:30NOV-93RS#:582   TYP:ADVERT
93-12-12  SAINT LOUIS, MO 63128          TEL:                    STATUS: NEW INQUIRY            PROD:HI SPEED          TERR: 215
                                                                 SIC:    UPDATE:             SPECIAL CODES:

94771301  SISSY FRANKS, ED COORD         P O BOX 30101           CHEM PROCESSING TECH         ISS:93MAR   RS#:423   TYP:PUBLCT
RAPFRA    RAPIDES REGIONAL MED CENTER                            STATUS: NEW INQUIRY            PROD:MATRIX            TERR: 310
93-04-03  ALEXANDRIA, LA 71301           TEL: 318/473-3814       SIC:    UPDATE:             SPECIAL CODES:

94777027  LARRY T GRISSETT, STS MGR      2200 WEST LOOP SOUTH    CHROMATOGRAPHY               ISS:20JUN-93R#:339    TYP:ADVERT
LANGRI    LANDATA SYSTEMS                #500                    STATUS: NEW INQUIRY            PROD:PREMIER           TERR: 310
93-08-29  HOUSTON, TX 77027              TEL: 713/871-9222       SIC:    UPDATE:             SPECIAL CODES:

94779924  MRS LINDA MORTENSEN, DEPT HEAD TEXAS-OHIO SHIPPING DPT CHEM PROCESSING TECH         ISS:93MAY   RS#:252   TYP:ADVERT
WISMOR    WISCHER-AVERY DRUG COM, THE    10009 RUSHING ROAD/SUITE 15  STATUS: NEW INQUIRY       PROD:MULTI 8           TERR: 140
93-06-21  EL PASO, TX 79924              TEL:                    SIC:    UPDATE:             SPECIAL CODES:

94785203  ALEXANDER KOSTEN, RES CHEMIST  1866 EAST BROOKDALE     CHROMATOGRAPHY               ISS:13DEC-93RS#:103   TYP:ADVERT
ANOKOS    ANDRON COMPANY                                         STATUS: PROSP RESPND-FAIR      PROD:MICRO FAM         TERR: 100
93-11-18  MESA, AZ 85203                 TEL: 602/835-9253       SIC:8900  UPDATE:9308       SPECIAL CODES:AP

94790071  GIB HOXIE, SR CONS             2410                    CHICAGO SEMINAR              ISS:93SEP   RS#:1281  TYP:ADVERT
ARTHOX    ARTHUR D LITTLE INC            400 SO HOPE ST          STATUS: NEW INQUIRY            PROD:386 PLUS          TERR: 125
93-11-04  LOS ANGELES, CA 90071          TEL: 213/627-1000       SIC:                        SPECIAL CODES:GAADOD  B

94792011  GARY A GARDNER                 228 INKOPAH ST          CANADIAN SPECTROSCOPY        ISS:93OCT   R#:24     TYP:800LIN
GAR                                      SUITE 150               STATUS: NEW INQUIRY            PROD:PREMIER           TERR: 132
93-11-17  RANCHO DEL REY, CA 92011       TEL:                    SIC:    UPDATE:9204         SPECIAL CODES:

94793003  CHARLES PIERCE                 SUITE 150               CICC ATTENDEES               ISS:93NOV   RS#:532   TYP:PSTCRD
VENPIE    VENTURA REG SAN DIST           1001 PARTRIDGE DR       STATUS: NEW INQUIRY            PROD:CLASSIC           TERR: 125
93-12-05  VENTURA, CA 93003              TEL: 805/658-4639       SIC:    UPDATE:9204         SPECIAL CODES:                  U

94794538  LARRY EARL                     SALES ENGINEER          CHICAGO CRIT CARE SYMP       ISS:93SEP   RS#:632   TYP:ADVERT
MAGEAR    MAGNUM MICROWAVE               4574 CUSHING PARKWAY    STATUS: NEW INQUIRY            PROD:386 PLUS          TERR: 115
93-01-03  FREMONT, CA 94538              TEL:                    SIC:    UPDATE:9207         SPECIAL CODES:

94795814  K E SULLIVAN                   SUITE #600              CHEM PROCESSING TECH         ISS:93MAY   RS#:252   TYP:ADVERT
SU        SULLIVAN & WALSH INCORPORATION 801 12TH STREET        STATUS: NEW INQUIRY            PROD:MULTI 8           TERR: 115
93-06-14  SACRAMENTO, CA 95814           TEL: 916/444-8008       SIC:    UPDATE:             SPECIAL CODES:

94799163  CLIFF COOPER, MANAGER          P O BOX 546             CHEM PROCESSING TECH         ISS:93MAY   RS#:252   TYP:ADVERT
CHECOO    CHEM SAFE                                              STATUS: PROSP RESPND-HOT       PROD:MULTI 8           TERR: 105
93-07-27  PULLMAN, WA 99163              TEL:                    SIC:    UPDATE:9311         SPECIAL CODES:021               H
```

- The next two columns list the inquirer's name, company, address, and phone number.

- Next are fields for the inquiry source, in this example by publication name, issue, and reader service number for both advertising- and publicity-generated leads.

- Below the source information are fields for inquiry quality status, product of interest, sales territory to which the inquiry belongs, and fields for SIC, last-update code, and special codes as determined by the marketer.

Note that Exhibit 14-1 only lists the raw material that other reports massage into more meaningful comparisons.

Product Performance

Breaking out inquiry activity by product provides a useful comparison, particularly when products receive equal promotional exposure, such as ganged fractional ads on a product tabloid page. The critical step, however, is adding qualification and follow-up data to the report, basing comparisons on the leads that really matter.

Exhibit 14-2 is an example of a quarterly report showing total and qualified lead performance for the most recent three-month period, and for 12 months. It monitors the quantity and quality of all inquiries across the full product line, indicating possible problems at both ends of the inquiry process: generation and follow-up.

While the data categories shown in Exhibit 14-2 will serve the average company well, you should tailor them to meet your particular needs. Here, the sample shows data for a simplified lead-handling program using field contact and bounceback replies for qualification. The report would carry at least one additional column for companies telequalifying inquiries.

Data shown here are:

Three months:

- Total inquiries: All inquiries for a product from all sources, with the product's percentage of overall inquiries during the period.

- Total contacted: The number of three-month inquiries contacted by field sales and reported upon.

Because National Industries' marketing and sales managers want to see which products receive better lead follow-up, the report calculates the percentage of the product's inquiries, not overall inquiries, that are contacted. The

Exhibit 14-2
Sales Lead Qualification Report by Product

NATIONAL INDUSTRIES
SALES LEAD QUALIFICATION REPORT BY PRODUCT
FOR 12 MO PERIOD ENDING: JAN 94

PRODUCT SUMMARY	LAST 3 MONTHS TOTAL INQUIRIES	TOTAL CONTACTED	PRE-QUALIFIED	QUALIFIED BY INQUIRER	QUALIFIED LAST 12 MONTHS BY REPRESEN.	12 MONTHS BY INQ&REP	TOTAL ALL QUALIFIED	LAST 12 MONTHS NOT QUALIFIED	NO ACTION	TOTAL INQUIRIES 12 MONTHS
MATRIX	151 7.2%	15 9.9%	23 7.7%	37 12.5%	34 11.4%	8 2.7%	102 34.3%	8 2.7%	187 63.0%	297 6.0%
HI SPEED	389 18.5%	40 10.3%	25 5.9%	103 24.3%	38 9.0%	1 0.2%	167 39.4%	6 1.4%	251 59.2%	424 8.6%
GENERAL	307 14.6%	15 4.9%	69 14.1%	12 2.4%	29 5.9%	3 0.6%	113 23.1%	11 2.2%	366 74.7%	490 9.9%
PREMIER	616 29.3%	102 16.6%	159 14.6%	70 6.4%	111 10.2%	11 1.0%	351 32.3%	58 5.3%	677 62.3%	1,086 22.0%
CLASSIC	282 13.4%	22 7.8%	33 10.3%	27 8.5%	29 9.1%	0 0.0%	89 27.8%	2 0.6%	228 73.5%	319 6.5%
SYSTEM II	121 5.8%	9 7.4%	43 12.1%	10 2.8%	33 9.3%	16 4.5%	102 28.7	5 1.4%	247 69.8%	354 7.2%
*286 PLUS	0 0.0%	0 0.0%	13 6.0%	7 3.2%	9 4.1%	0 0.0%	61 28.1%	1 0.5%	155 71.4%	217 4.4%
MICRO FAM	65 3.1%	17 26.2%	4 3.5%	1 0.9%	27 23.9%	0 0.0%	32 28.3%	2 1.8%	79 69.9%	113 2.3%
MULTI 8	4 0.2%	2 50.0%	98 8.2%	120 10.0%	158 13.2%	41 3.4%	417 34.9%	31 2.6%	748 62.5%	1,196 24.3%
386 PLUS	164 7.8%	32 19.5%	46 10.6%	70 16.1%	57 13.1%	9 2.1%	182 41.9%	33 7.6%	219 50.5%	434 8.8%
TOTALS	2,099 100.0%	254 12.1%	513 10.4%	457 9.3%	548 11.1%	98 2.0%	1,616 32.8%	157 3.2%	3,157 64.0%	4,930 100.0%

average rates for all products combined appear at the foot of the table in the "totals" row. Of course, contact data will understate actual sales force follow-up if salespeople neglect to return lead follow-up reports.

12 months:

- Pre-qualified: Total inquiries for a product deemed qualified by the company's inquiry-generation strategy. Pre-qualified leads typically include bona fide trade show inquiries, letterhead inquiries, inbound and cold-call outbound telemarketing inquiries, plus post cards, coupons, dual-bingo number responses asking a salesperson to call, and other sight-qualified leads for which further qualification does not seem necessary. The percentage shows the pre-qualified proportion of all inquiries for the product.

- By inquirer: Inquiries self-qualified by bounceback card returns meeting qualification criteria.

- By representative: Inquiries judged qualified by field sales and distributors who have reported the status of the inquiry. It's a statistic that often causes considerable discomfort for marketing executives, because it plainly states the degree to which salespeople think the leads are any good. It can embarrass sales, too, when it shows many salespeople not following up or not reporting on leads.

- By inquirer and representative: Inquiries qualified twice, in effect, once by the inquirer's bounceback reply and once by the salesperson, indicating a high-quality lead.

- Total all qualified: The sum of all qualified leads for the product, showing the percentage of qualified leads among all inquiries for the product. Note how some products enjoy a larger proportion of qualified leads than others.

- Not qualified: Inquiries known to be not qualified, usually as determined by the sales rep's follow-up and report back, or a bounceback card indicating no further interest.

- No action: Inquiries not followed up or not known to have been followed up. Their quality remains a mystery. Large no-action percentages indicate a lead-management process that is not operating as it should.

- Total inquiries 12 months: The totals are by product, and the percentages indicate the product's portion of total inquiries generated. It suggests whether a product is receiving its fair share of marketing communications support.

Problems revealed. It's not a perfect world and, until it is, sales reps are unlikely to return paperwork on every lead they actually contact. Sometimes they purposely hold back reporting in order to keep a prospect name from the database hoping they can later claim to have "discovered" it on their own. If you log inquiries into your database, you'll be able to spot that deception, however. Failure to build teamwork and cooperation between marketing and sales winds up inflating the no-action statistic, making the qualification report a less than accurate management tool.

Complete field feedback is the key to qualification report precision. At least collect enough field follow-up reports to build a statistically valid picture of your inquiry quality. More than one manager has had to call reps individually asking them to send back the paperwork on accounts they'd already contacted. That approach often works best before sales meetings.

Marketing and sales should watch how many of the inquiries sales does follow up, by product. If the ratio is much lower for one product line than another, it could indicate that salespeople need more training to be comfortable with the product. It could also mean that the commissions on certain product lines are so low that field sales reps do not want to spend their time selling the product.

Poor follow-up by product also implies that the quality of inquiries from a specific ad is so low that the advertisement needs to be adjusted to make the call to action meaningful. If a high percentage of inquirers return the bounceback card seeking more information but not a sales call, it could also signal that fulfillment literature is deficient in product specifications, preventing the inquirer from making a buying decision based on the information at hand. That could lead to the competition getting the order.

Differences in inquiry yield among products also suggest that a product is not capable of producing enough leads to justify its claim on marketing communications dollars. In the exhibit, can the marcom manager justify spending 10 percent of the budget on product Micro Fam if it yields just 2.3 percent of the inquiries? Perhaps yes, if the typical Micro Fam order is much larger than the average for all products, or Micro Fam is a new product. It certainly seems to get proportionately more attention from sales reps than almost all other products. But perhaps spending cannot be justified, if Micro Fam is an established part of the line. Then again, maybe the problem isn't the budgeting, but some other factor, such as the publications in which Micro Fam ads appear.

Judging from Exhibit 14-2, National Industries is not setting the world ablaze. Unfortunately, the anemic follow-up ratios are not unusual, however. National's most egregious shortcoming is its laziness and inattention to the inquiries it has spent money to generate. National has contacted just 12.1 percent of its last-three-months leads—a pretty dismal record unless all those leads just came in a few days or so before National produced its report. The percentage shown probably is much lower than reality; salespeople probably are not reporting lead status back to the marketing department. Nonetheless, the company ignores a full two-thirds of its 12-month inquiry volume, according to the "no action" data. Management is letting new business literally slip though its system undetected!

Examining a product's contribution to total inquiry volume depends, of course, on promotional activity, as we will soon discuss. The product report suggests that product Multi 8 is for some reason not producing leads in the current quarter despite a relatively strong annual performance. Multi 8 has a decent qualification rate on its inquiries, so the decrease in recent inquiry volume might be accidental, requiring immediate correction. Promotional support for various line items seems to have varied, comparing the three-month to 12-month inquiry rates. But what other market or competitive forces might be affecting lead flow?

National's Hi Speed product seems to be the star with prospects and salespeople alike. Inquiry qualification is relatively high, and "no action" is moderate on a 12-month basis. Marketing and sales management should know why.

Territory Performance

National also sorts its inquiry database by sales territory, producing a "Sales Manager's Report" as shown in Exhibit 14-3. It lists all inquiries sorted and subtotaled by sales representative, dealer, or distributor. It provides a quick overview of sales lead distribution across National's sales operations, so managers can spot key prospects and point them out to sales reps and distributors.

Managers in a central office can compare inquiry activity among different areas, spotting trends and competitive activity and getting an early warning for any sudden changes in sales activity that inevitably will follow changes in lead volume. The Sales Manager's Report also provides information of value to distributors, enhancing relationships with them, and subtly letting them know that you know how much business you're sending their way.

The inside story. The diagnostic information explaining goings-on in the field and National's poor lead follow-up appears in the Sales Lead Qualification Report by Territory, in Exhibit 14-4. Using the same format as the product report, the territory breakout enumerates qualified and unqualified inquiries, and those of unknown value. It shows who is working the inquiries the hardest— for whatever reasons that become apparent with further investigation of market conditions and account closing rates.

The qualification by territory report is also an excellent tool for setting quotas. If a territory receives 10 percent of the inquiries, for instance, it is

Exhibit 14-3
Sales Managers' Report

```
                        N A T I O N A L   I N D U S T R I E S

                         SALES MANAGERS REPORT FOR JANUARY 1994
                                      BY TERRITORY

DONALD NIXON**BURNS & CO.**5110 KIFER ROAD**SUNNYVALE, CA  94086-5303

94795121   MICHAEL FORNALSKI       1977 CONCOURSE DR         VIDEO NEWS                          ISS:94JAN  RS#:338   TYP:ADVERT
SPAFOR     SPACE POWER INC                                   STATUS: NEW INQUIRY                        PROD:386 PLUS   TERR:  115
94-01-18   SAN JOSE, CA  95121      TEL:                      SIC:          SPECIAL CODES:00B0D E

94795134   JERRY D WARREN          PRODUCT MARKETING SPECIALIST  VIDEO NEWS                       ISS:94JAN  RS#:338   TYP:ADVERT
FUJWAR     FUJITSU AMERICA INC      3055 ORCHARD DRIVE        STATUS: NEW INQUIRY                        PROD:386 PLUS   TERR:  115
94-01-18   SAN JOSE, CA  95134      TEL: 408/432-1300          SIC:          SPECIAL CODES:0BCDYD E

94795152   R FENTON, PUB AFR REP    NOSC                      PLANT DESIGN & MGMT                 ISS:93DEC  RS#:511   TYP:PUBLCT
USGFEN     US GOVERNMENT                                      STATUS: NEW INQUIRY                        PROD:MATRIX     TERR:  115
94-01-30   SAN DEIGO, CA  95152     TEL: 619/553-2735          SIC:          SPECIAL CODES:

94795404   M G KOONCE, APPRAISED ANLST  585 FISCAL DRIVE      VIDEO NEWS                          ISS:94JAN  RS#:338   TYP:ADVERT
SONKOO     SONOMA COUTY ASSESSOR'S OFC                        STATUS: NEW INQUIRY                        PROD:386 PLUS   TERR:  115
94-01-18   SANTA ROSA, CA  95404    TEL: 527-3302              SIC:          SPECIAL CODES:JDADYD EHIJK

94795610   CARY REASE, SLS         8022 OAK AVE               PLANT DESIGN & MGMT                 ISS:93DEC  RS#:511   TYP:PUBLCT
INFREA     INFORMATION                                        STATUS: NEW INQUIRY                        PROD:MATRIX     TERR:  115
94-01-04   CITRUS HEIGHTS, CA  95610  TEL: 916/485-7366         SIC:          SPECIAL CODES:

94795616   E STEVE MCNIEL, ASST PROF   DEPT OF ENVIR DESIGN   VIDEO NEWS                          ISS:94JAN  RS#:338   TYP:ADVERT
UNIMCN     UNIVERSITY OF CALIFORNIA                           STATUS: NEW INQUIRY                        PROD:386 PLUS   TERR:  115
94-01-21   DAVIS, CA  95616         TEL: 916/752-7209          SIC:          SPECIAL CODES:P0B000 E

94795616   RAMIRO MERINO, RES      DEPT OF ENVIRON TOXICOLOGY  TELECOMMUNICATIONS TODAY ISS:93NOV  RS#:582   TYP:ADVERT
UNIMER     UNIVERSITY OF CALIFORNIA  MEYER HALL5-4422/1422 FASB  STATUS: NEW INQUIRY                      PROD:HI SPEED   TERR:  115
94-01-16   DAVIS, CA  95616         TEL: 916/752-1142          SIC:          SPECIAL CODES:

94795814   BOB HOWELL, ADMIN INFO SCI  721 CAPITAL MALL       VIDEO NEWS                          ISS:94JAN  RS#:338   TYP:ADVERT
STAHOW     STATE DEPT OF EDUCATION                            STATUS: NEW INQUIRY                        PROD:386 PLUS   TERR:  115
94-01-18   SACRAMENTO, CA  95814    TEL: 916/445-0774          SIC:          SPECIAL CODES:PAD0D HI

94795825   MARK THOMAS             425 UNIVERSITY AVE  120    PLANT DESIGN & MGMT                 ISS:93DEC  RS#:511   TYP:PUBLCT
PACTHO     PAC SOUTHWEST PLANNING GRP                         STATUS: NEW INQUIRY                        PROD:MATRIX     TERR:  115
94-01-03   SACRAMENTO, CA  95825    TEL: 916/920-1155          SIC:          SPECIAL CODES:

94796301   MR MARK C JOHNSON       1ST SIG HHC                PLANT DESIGN & MGMT                 ISS:93DEC  RS#:511   TYP:PUBLCT
ACAJOH     ACA FIELD SERVICE                                  STATUS: NEW INQUIRY                        PROD:MATRIX     TERR:  115
94-01-04   APO SAN FRANCISCO, CA  96301  TEL:                  SIC:          SPECIAL CODES:

TOTAL: 52
```

reasonable to expect it to return 10 percent of the sales. That's a more sensible approach than simply bumping up a territory's quota by a fixed ratio each year. Among the inferences National draws from the report:

- The Framingham rep has a qualification rate double the average. That territory also has the highest inquiry qualification rate and the lowest no-action rate, on an inquiry volume more or less in line with other territories. Is he the hardest working of the reps listed on the page? Or is the territory well endowed with "bluebirds" (business just flies in the window) or a high-concentration of high-volume prospects? The territory's three-month contact rate is hardly strong, so perhaps an industry event or trend, or a promotion or incentive program produced a boost sometime in the past 12 months.

We can learn more by examining other data from National's broader MKIS, such as Mitchell's account closing rates, the results of Did-You-Buy? studies in his region, and his track record expanding business with current customers rather than chasing new ones.

- Inquiry generation and follow-up seems to warrant further study in Austin and Maitland, where the reps—only slightly better-than-average performers over 12 months—seem to have turned into real road warriors during the past three months.

- Is the Atlanta rep coasting? Blessed with a large proportion of pre-qualified leads, her territory nonetheless has only an average inquiry qualification rate and an average no-action rate. Her rep-qualified inquiry rate is near the bottom of the pack. Maybe she feels she doesn't have to work hard. Or perhaps she has benefited from the traffic at an Atlanta trade show and has been killing herself servicing those pre-qualified leads.

Again, the inquiry database signals a situation bearing further investigation. Further probing should examine the territory's qualified lead-to-account closing ratio. Low closing rates relative to inquiry volume indicate coasting—or too large a territory for the rep assigned to it.

- Columbia, meanwhile has been producing well-above-average lead volume over the past year and the past quarter. Is there a marketing or competitive reason? It could be the territory is too large, a supposition supported by its significantly larger-than-average no-action rate.

Quarterly follow-up. National's Sales Lead Follow-Up Report, in Exhibit 14-5, reveals who is working the inquiries and when. Reps have no place to hide,

Exhibit 14-4
Sales Lead Qualification Report by Territory

N A T I O N A L   I N D U S T R I E S
SALES LEAD QUALIFICATION REPORT BY TERRITORY
FOR 12 MO PERIOD ENDING: JAN 94

SALES TERRITORY	LAST 3 MONTHS TOTAL INQUIRIES	LAST 3 MONTHS TOTAL CONTACTED	QUALIFIED LAST 12 MONTHS PRE-QUALIFIED	BY QUALIFIED INQUIRER	BY REPRESEN.	BY INQ&REP	TOTAL ALL QUALIFIED	LAST 12 MONTHS ALL NOT QUALIFIED	NO ACTION	TOTAL INQUIRIES 12 MONTHS
TOM WHITT AUSTIN, TX 78752	98 4.7%	34 34.7%	31 13.3%	26 11.2%	38 16.3%	17 7.3%	112 48.1%	4 1.7%	117 50.2%	233 4.7%
PAUL GALLANT RALEIGH, NC 29625	46 2.2%	6 13.0%	12 9.4%	17 13.4%	7 5.5%	0 0.0%	36 28.3%	6 4.7%	85 66.9%	127 2.6%
SHARON ROGERS MAITLAND, FL 32751	86 4.1%	35 40.7%	15 6.8%	41 18.6%	39 17.6%	3 1.4%	98 44.3%	10 4.5%	113 51.1%	221 4.5%
WAYNE GYSER ATLANTA, GA 30339	75 3.6%	5 6.7%	41 19.2%	11 5.1%	10 4.7%	0 0.0%	62 29.0%	7 3.3%	145 67.8%	214 4.3%
ED HANSON COLUMBIA, MD 21046	168 8.0%	2 1.2%	56 16.2%	19 5.5%	3 0.9%	4 1.2%	82 23.8%	8 2.3%	255 73.9%	345 7.0%
MARY BECK HACKENSACK, NJ 07601	84 4.0%	0 0.0%	26 12.0%	18 8.3%	22 10.1%	0 0.0%	66 30.6%	7 3.2%	143 66.2%	216 4.4%
SCOTT BADEN HORSHAM, PA 19044	89 4.2%	1 1.1%	40 18.6%	27 12.6%	22 10.2%	8 3.7%	97 45.1%	9 4.2%	109 50.7%	215 4.4%
ROBERT JAMES FAIRPORT, NY 14450	52 2.5%	0 0.0%	9 6.5%	14 10.1%	17 12.3%	1 0.7%	41 29.7%	5 3.6%	92 66.7%	138 2.8%
JOHN PIERCE HAUPPAUGE, NY 11788	84 4.0%	4 4.8%	35 15.2%	2 0.9%	9 3.9%	1 0.4%	47 20.3%	9 3.9%	175 75.8%	231 4.7%
CHRIS MITCHELL FRAMINGHAM, MA 01701	90 4.3%	2 2.2%	27 12.8%	19 9.0%	39 18.5%	1 0.5%	86 40.8%	6 2.8%	119 56.4%	211 4.3%
RALPH PHILLIPS SL6 8AE, ENGLAND	17 0.8%	0 0.0%	7 13.2%	0 0.0%	11 20.8%	1 1.9%	19 35.8%	0 0.0%	34 64.2%	53 1.1%
ALBERT THOMAS TEMPE, AZ 85282	29 1.4%	0 0.0%	10 10.9%	6 6.5%	1 1.1%	0 0.0%	17 18.5%	0 0.0%	75 81.5%	92 1.9%
TOTALS	2,099 100.0%	254 12.1%	513 10.4%	457 9.3%	548 11.1%	98 2.0%	1,616 32.8%	157 3.2%	3,157 64.0%	4,930 100.0%

as management possesses hard evidence of field activity. It reports leads sent to the field and returned in a given month, by salesperson, for each month of the latest quarter and by each quarter in the past year.

According to Exhibit 14-5, for example, Tom Whitt received 19 leads in January 1994, which comprised 4.1 percent of all the inquiries sent to the field that month. He reported back on three, which is 15.8 percent of the inquiries that he received in the month of January.

The December data indicate that Tom had received 46 leads in December and as of the January report, he has reported back on 48 percent, or 22 of those leads. The returned figure represents the number of leads reported back by the time the quarterly tally is issued. In November, Tom received 17 sales leads. Those are three months old at the time of the report; he has returned 53 percent of them during that time.

It is logical to expect that as time passes, salespeople have more time to follow-up and report on the leads mailed to them. Thus, over a 12-month span, the percentage followed up will increase as the inquiries age. Note that the return figures are only for those leads reported by the field sales force, not those qualified by outbound telemarketing, returned business reply cards, or pre-qualification.

The Sales Lead Follow-Up Report shown here is more evidence that National Industries is not getting the field cooperation that it should. The average for all companies in our database is about 40 percent better follow-up.

Accuracy and motivation. The precision of your sales lead-management system relies on cooperation and feedback from the field. And your system's accuracy and perceived fairness will motivate that cooperation. Inquiry monitoring that salespeople perceive to be a gun at their heads rather than a help to their efforts becomes a system for them to "beat."

So use your analysis data judiciously. Information can help you cut through fuzzy thinking and preconceived notions. We recall the experience described by the sales vice president of a California-based company. "The rep in Idaho didn't look like us, didn't talk like us, and didn't act like us. So we firmly believed that he wasn't very good. We were ready to fire him. Meanwhile, we thought the guy in New York was wonderful." But an analysis of the territories found that Idaho generated three percent of sales with one percent of the inquiries, while New York generated 15 percent of the sales with 35 percent of the inquiries. As a result, "Mr. Idaho didn't get fired, and we split the New York territory. Although Mr. New York was working very hard, he couldn't keep up with the volume."

Exhibit 14-5
Sales Lead Follow-up Report

NATIONAL INDUSTRIES

SALES LEAD FOLLOW-UP REPORT

FOR 12 MONTH PERIOD ENDING JAN 94

TERRITORY	JAN 94 RCVD	JAN 94 RTND	DEC 93 RCVD	DEC 93 RTND	NOV 93 RCVD	NOV 93 RTND	AUG-OCT 93 RCVD	AUG-OCT 93 RTND	MAY-JUL 93 RCVD	MAY-JUL 93 RTND	FEB-APR 93 RCVD	FEB-APR 93 RTND	FEB 93-JAN 94 RCVD	FEB 93-JAN 94 RTND
TOM WHITT AUSTIN, TX 78752	19 / 4.1%	3 / 15.8%	46 / 5.9%	22 / 47.8%	17 / 4.1%	9 / 52.9%	51 / 4.9%	16 / 31.4%	56 / 4.4%	20 / 35.7%	26 / 6%	8 / 30.8%	215 / 4.9%	78 / 36.3%
PAUL GALLANT RALEIGH, NC 29625	12 / 2.6%	0 / 0%	18 / 2.3%	1 / 5.6%	8 / 1.9%	5 / 62.5%	28 / 2.7%	8 / 28.6%	38 / 3%	8 / 21.1%	10 / 2.3%	2 / 20%	114 / 2.6%	24 / 21.1%
SHARON ROGERS MAITLAND, FL 32751	23 / 5%	7 / 30.4%	34 / 4.4%	19 / 55.9%	14 / 3.4%	9 / 64.3%	47 / 4.5%	6 / 12.8%	71 / 5.5%	10 / 14.1%	17 / 3.9%	6 / 35.3%	206 / 4.7%	57 / 27.7%
WAYNE GYSER ATLANTA, GA 30339	18 / 3.9%	0 / 0%	32 / 4.1%	2 / 6.3%	11 / 2.6%	3 / 27.3%	38 / 3.7%	8 / 21%	86 / 6.7%	20 / 23.3%	15 / 3.5%	2 / 13.3%	200 / 4.5%	35 / 17.5%
ED HANSON COLUMBIA, MD 21046	31 / 6.7%	0 / 0%	101 / 13%	2 / 2%	18 / 4.3%	0 / 0%	59 / 5.7%	12 / 20.3%	85 / 6.6%	18 / 21.2%	29 / 6.7%	5 / 17.2%	323 / 7.3%	37 / 11.5%
MARY BECK HACKENSACK, NJ 07601	19 / 4.1%	0 / 0%	31 / 4%	0 / 0%	14 / 3.4%	0 / 0%	44 / 4.2%	10 / 22.7%	60 / 4.7%	15 / 25%	16 / 3.7%	5 / 31.3%	184 / 4.2%	30 / 16.3%
SCOTT BADEN HORSHAM, PA 19044	20 / 4.3%	1 / 5%	45 / 5.8%	0 / 0%	13 / 3.1%	0 / 0%	50 / 4.8%	22 / 44%	57 / 4.4%	21 / 36.8%	14 / 3.2%	4 / 28.6%	199 / 4.5%	48 / 24.1%
ROBERT JAMES FAIRPORT, NY 14450	15 / 3.3%	0 / 0%	22 / 2.8%	0 / 0%	7 / 1.7%	0 / 0%	29 / 2.8%	8 / 27.6%	36 / 2.8%	11 / 30.6%	17 / 3.9%	5 / 29.4%	126 / 2.9%	24 / 19%
JOHN PIERCE HAUPPAUGE, NY 11788	20 / 4.3%	0 / 0%	33 / 4.3%	1 / 3%	15 / 3.6%	3 / 20%	61 / 5.9%	4 / 6.6%	60 / 4.7%	5 / 8.3%	15 / 3.5%	5 / 33.3%	204 / 4.6%	18 / 8.8%
CHRIS MITCHELL FRAMINGHAM, MA 01701	17 / 3.7%	0 / 0%	31 / 4%	2 / 6.5%	15 / 3.6%	0 / 0%	46 / 4.4%	26 / 56.5%	52 / 4.1%	22 / 42.3%	18 / 4.1%	9 / 50%	179 / 4.1%	59 / 33%
RALPH PHILLIPS SL6 8AE, ENGLAND	1 / .2%	0 / 0%	0 / 0%	0 / 0%	7 / 1.7%	0 / 0%	14 / 1.3%	4 / 28.6%	15 / 1.2%	8 / 53.3%	7 / 1.6%	2 / 28.6%	44 / 1%	14 / 31.8%
ALBERT THOMAS TEMPE, AZ 85282	3 / .7%	0 / 0%	7 / .9%	0 / 0%	7 / 1.7%	0 / 0%	22 / 2.1%	2 / 9.1%	29 / 2.3%	5 / 17.2%	12 / 2.8%	2 / 16.7%	80 / 1.8%	9 / 11.2%
TOTALS	460	35 / 7.6%	774	114 / 14.7%	416	105 / 25.2%	1041	416 / 40%	1281	833 / 65%	434	304 / 70%	4406	1807 / 41%

Inquiry Source Performance

The inquiry database also signals potential problems or opportunities in lead generation. National's Monthly Advertising Effectiveness Report includes several different views of inquiry volume: by source, source type, and product.

Exhibit 14-6 shows the monthly inquiry flow by source: individual advertisements, mailings, publicity, and a trade show. If the costs of generating those leads is known (not always the case for an out-of-house lead management service), the printout reports the cost-per-inquiry (CPI).

Exhibit 14-7 shows a summary by source type, which is useful information for strategic communications decisions.

Exhibit 14-8 shows the monthly lead yield and annual CPI broken out by product.

Note how the reports hold each lead-generating medium accountable for its inquiry flow. Typically, an advertisement or publicity placement will produce inquiries for three months, peaking in the second month. Postcard decks generate inquiries for two months, with the bulk arriving the first month and the balance in month two.

The number of inquiries per month provides critical information. Are you overproducing one month and starving the field the next? National's promotion program seem to be accomplishing that; failing to generate a steady stream of inquiries and allowing many to age too long because of volume.

The Monthly Advertising Effectiveness Report also indicates if publishers are processing inquiries in a timely manner. If an ad appears a January issue and the inquiries don't arrive at National until March, the inquiries are aging, potential business goes unrecognized, and buyers perceive National as unresponsive and lazy.

National also should compare the costs of different source and product leads, and watch for dramatic changes over time that might signal market and competitive dislocations, the threats of new technologies, market penetration and stalled growth, etc. Use the effectiveness report as an early warning to spot anomalies in trend data, then investigate. Also, beyond the quick performance snapshot in the Monthly Advertising Effectiveness Report, National will want to evaluate each source and product for its qualified lead yield, and leads converted to sales.

Cross-references. Exhibits 14-9 and 14-10 combine the source and product data into summary views: source performance subtotaled by product, and product performance subtotaled by source.

Subtotaling by source rearranges the Advertising Effectiveness Report information into an instant picture of each source's contribution to each product promoted. Marketing communications managers and product managers find the

Exhibit 14-6
Monthly Advertising Effectiveness Report by Source

947 - 1

N A T I O N A L   I N D U S T R I E S

MONTHLY ADVERTISING EFFECTIVENESS REPORT

BY SOURCE FOR PERIOD ENDING 31 JAN 1994

SOURCE OF INQUIRY	ISSUE	R/S-NO	TYP	ITEM/PRODUCT	TOTAL	COST	CPI	JAN	DEC	NOV	OCT	SEP	AUG	JUL	JUN	OTHER 4 MO.	OLDER
ARCHITECTURAL DESIGN	93JAN	307	TEL	386 PLUS	74								5	7	14	42	6
ARCHITECTURAL DESIGN	93SEP	28	PUB	MATRIX	73			5	10	12	46						
CHEMICAL AGE	93OCT	356	D-M	HI SPEED	45			8	25	12							
COMPUTER INTERNATIONAL	93MAY	145	ADV	GENERAL	311	2950	95.16	76	235								
COMPUTER INTERNATIONAL	93NOV	132	PUB	MATRIX	42	3615	86.07					2	7	33			
ELECTRONIC DIRECTORY	93FAL	413	ADV	MATRIX	104												
ELECTRONIC LIT NEWS	92NOV	350	PUB	PREMIER	36	1206	33.50		1								
ELECTRONIC LIT NEWS	93JUN	665	ADV	HI SPEED	113	2537	22.45										
ELECTRONIC LIT NEWS	93AUG	252	ADV	PREMIER	741				187	341							
ELECTRONIC LIT NEWS	93OCT	24	800	PREMIER				90			123	4					
ELECTRONIC LIT NEWS	93DEC	24	ADV	HI SPEED	41	2537	61.88	41				80					
FINANCIAL INDUSTRY	93JUN	666	PUB	GENERAL	45							6					
HOSPITALITY TIMES	93NOV	772	ADV	CLASSIC	45	2620	201.54	11	2								
HOSPITALITY TIMES	93NOV	773	PUB	SYSTEM II	18	2620	145.56	10	8								
MATERIAL DESIGN & HNDLG	93APR	132	ADV	MICRO FAM	11										11		
MATERIAL DESIGN & HNDLG	93MAY	307	PUB	*286 PLUS	55	1187	20.12							7	48		
MEDICAL LIT REVIEW	92NOV	691	ADV	MICRO FAM	59												50
MIDSTATE EXPO	DALLAS		SHO	GENERAL	103												
NEW PRODUCT DIGEST	93FEB	336	PUB	MULTI 8	117	3665	215.29									103	
NEW PRODUCT DIGEST	93MAR	378	ADV	MULTI 8	17	1475	16.21								11	106	
NEW PRODUCT DIGEST	93MAR	379	PST	*286 PLUS	91	2826	403.71								2	15	
OFFICE EQUIPMENT DEALER	92APR	225	ADV	MATRIX	7										11	80	
OFFICE EQUIPMENT DEALER	93MAY	423	PUB	MATRIX	20	1126	1.49								1	87	
OFFICE EQUIPMENT DEALER	93MAY	252	ADV	MULTI 8	756								145	201	270	19	
OFFICE EQUIPMENT DEALER	93NOV	378	800	CLASSIC	103											140	
OFFICE EQUIPMENT DEALER	93NOV	379	ADV	CLASSIC	16	2826	176.63										
PLANT DESIGN & MGMT	92NOV	176	PUB	MICRO FAM	65												
PLANT DESIGN & MGMT	93JUN	383	PUB	MULTI 8	321							9	29	180	96		
PLANT DESIGN & MGMT	93AUG	307	PST	SYSTEM II	273	1800	6.59				3	81					
PLANT DESIGN & MGMT	93SEP	632	TEL	386 PLUS	80					59	102	33					
PLANT DESIGN & MGMT	93NOV	511	PUB	HI SPEED	126					10	12						
PLANT DESIGN & MGMT	93DEC	511	D-M	MATRIX	269				269	15	96						
SERVICE MGMT MONTHLY	93SEP	1280	ADV	SYSTEM II	127	1500	115.38	62									
SERVICE MGMT MONTHLY	93SEP	1281	LET	386 PLUS	196	1500	7.65	8		67		5					
TELECOMMUNICATIONS TODAY	92DEC13	102	BON	SYSTEM II	72			1	31	3	6	36	7	5	4	24	12
TELECOMMUNICATIONS TODAY	92DEC13	103	ADV	MULTI 8	25						89	2				8	17
TELECOMMUNICATIONS TODAY	93JAN15	310	PUB	MICRO FAM	99	4688	47.35	17			5			65		33	66
TELECOMMUNICATIONS TODAY	93JUN20	339	ADV	*286 PLUS	136			5			11				51	103	33
TELECOMMUNICATIONS TODAY	93JUL17	730	PUB	PREMIER	142	4688	33.01										
TELECOMMUNICATIONS TODAY	93JUL21	147	PUB	CLASSIC	45							6	20				
TELECOMMUNICATIONS TODAY	93NOV30	582	ADV	PREMIER	116							11	29				
TELECOMMUNICATIONS TODAY		51	ADV	HI SPEED	51	4688	91.92	127	42	59		105	22	7			
VIDEO NEWS	93JUL	337	M-L	GENERAL	39			9	2			8					
VIDEO NEWS	93NOV	532	PST	CLASSIC	153	1610	10.52	30	64								
VIDEO NEWS	94JAN	338	ADV	386 PLUS	28	1362	48.64	28									
TOTALS					5418	53021	9.79	535	1020	578	531	389	280	568	536	699	282
12 MOS					5136												

Exhibit 14-7
Monthly Advertising Effectiveness Report: Summary by Type of Source

```
947 - 3                         N A T I O N A L   I N D U S T R I E S

                            MONTHLY ADVERTISING EFFECTIVENESS REPORT

                    SUMMARY BY TYPE OF SOURCE FOR PERIOD ENDING 31 JAN 1994
```

TYPE OF SOURCE	TOTAL	COST	CPI	JAN	DEC	NOV	OCT	SEP	AUG	JUL	JUN	MAY	APR	MAR	FEB	OLDER
ADVERTISEMENT	1678	48136	28.69	100	74	67	128	134	182	329	340	156	10	12	30	116
BONUS INQUIRIES	25			0	0	0	0	0	0	0	0	0	0	0	8	17
DIRECT MAIL	314			8	294	12	0	0	0	0	0	0	0	0	0	0
TELEPHONE	154			17	8	10	12	33	5	7	14	9	11	13	9	6
POSTCARD	517	4885	9.45	30	95	118	102	81	0	0	11	26	34	20	0	0
MAILING LIST	39			2	0	0	0	8	2	0	0	0	0	0	0	0
800 LINE INBOUND	844			152	228	341	123	0	20	0	0	0	0	0	0	0
PUB. RELEASE	1672			222	315	27	161	131	64	220	167	28	74	64	68	131
TRADE SHOW	103			4	6	3	5	2	7	5	4	4	7	103	4	0
LETTER	72													9		12
TOTALS	5418	53021	9.79	535	1020	578	531	389	280	568	536	223	136	221	119	282
12 MOS	5136															

Exhibit 14-8
Monthly Advertising Effectiveness Report: Summary by Item/Product

```
947 - 2                        N A T I O N A L   I N D U S T R I E S

                               MONTHLY ADVERTISING EFFECTIVENESS REPORT

                      SUMMARY BY ITEM/PRODUCT FOR PERIOD ENDING 31 JAN 1994
```

ITEM/PRODUCT	TOTAL	COST	CPI	JAN	DEC	NOV	OCT	SEP	AUG	JUL	JUN	MAY	APR	MAR	FEB	OLDER
MATRIX	300	9391	31.30	132	10	12	46	3	12	37	18	10	17	3	0	0
HI SPEED	442	8431	19.07	58	337	12	0	4	5	26	0	0	0	0	0	0
GENERAL	498			78	235	341	167	14	28	40	51	0	0	103	6	98
PREMIER	1216	7225	5.94	90	187	59	5	191	20	65	0	0	0	0	0	0
CLASSIC	330	7056	21.38	103	123	62	113	11	29	0	4	4	7	9	4	12
SYSTEM II	376	5920	15.74	14	47	0	0	88	7	5	5	7	34	61	62	33
*286 PLUS	282	1475	25.23	0	0	0	0	0	0	7	59	26	0	12	30	116
MICRO FAM	234	5875	23.11	8	57	0	0	9	0	0	11	174	67	20	8	117
MULTI 8	1236	4786	3.87	1	3	0	3	9	174	381	379	174	11	13	9	6
386 PLUS	504	2862	5.68	51	21	92	197	69	5	7	14	9				
TOTALS 12 MOS	5418 5136	53021	9.79	535	1020	578	531	389	280	568	536	223	136	221	119	282

Exhibit 14-9
Monthly Advertising Effectiveness Report: Subtotaled by Source

947 - 1

N A T I O N A L   I N D U S T R I E S

MONTHLY ADVERTISING EFFECTIVENESS REPORT

SUB-TOTALED BY SOURCE FOR PERIOD ENDING 31 JAN 1994

SOURCE OF INQUIRY	ISSUE	R/S #	TYP	ITEM/PRODUCT	TOTAL	COST	CPI	JAN	DEC	NOV	OCT	SEP	AUG	JUL	JUN	OTHER 4 MO.	OLDER
ARCHITECTURAL DESIGN	93JAN	307	TEL	386 PLUS	74								5	7	14	42	6
ARCHITECTURAL DESIGN	93SEP	28	PUB	MATRIX	73			5	10	12	46						
SUMMARY BY ITEM/PRODUCT																	
				386 PLUS	74			0	0	0	0	0	5	7	14	42	6
				MATRIX	73			5	10	12	46	0	0	0	0	0	0
				TOTAL ALL 12 MONTHS	147 / 141			5	10	12	46	0	5	7	14	42	6
CHEMICAL AGE	93OCT	356	D.M	HI SPEED	45			8	25	12							
SUMMARY BY ITEM/PRODUCT																	
				HI SPEED	45			8	25	12							
				TOTAL ALL 12 MONTHS	45 / 45			8	25	12							
COMPUTER INTERNATIONAL	93MAY	145	ADV	MATRIX	31	2950	95.16					1	5	4	17	4	
COMPUTER INTERNATIONAL	93NOV	132	PUB	GENERAL	311			76	235								
SUMMARY BY ITEM/PRODUCT																	
				MATRIX	31			0	0	0	0	1	5	4	17	4	0
				GENERAL	311			76	235	0	0	0	0	0	0	0	0
				TOTAL ALL 12 MONTHS	342 / 342	2950	95.16	76	235	0	0	1	5	4	17	4	0
ELECTRONIC DIRECTORY	93FAL	413	ADV	MATRIX	42	3615	86.07	0	0	0	0	2	7	33	0	0	0
SUMMARY BY ITEM/PRODUCT																	
				MATRIX	42							2	7	33			
				TOTAL ALL 12 MONTHS	42 / 42	3615	86.07	0	0	0	0	2	7	33	0	0	0
ELECTRONIC LIT NEWS	92NOV	350	PUB	PREMIER	104	1206	33.50									6	98
ELECTRONIC LIT NEWS	93JUN	665	ADV	HI SPEED	36	2537	22.45					4	5	26			
ELECTRONIC LIT NEWS	93AUG	252	ADV	PREMIER	113						33	80					
ELECTRONIC LIT NEWS	93OCT	24	800	PREMIER	741	2537	61.88	90	187	341	123						
ELECTRONIC LIT NEWS	93DEC	24	ADV	HI SPEED	41			41	1								
SUMMARY BY ITEM/PRODUCT																	
				PREMIER	958			90	187	341	156	80	0	0	0	6	98
				HI SPEED	77			41	1	0	0	4	5	26	0	0	0
				TOTAL ALL 12 MONTHS	1035 / 937	6280	33.05	131	188	341	156	84	5	26	0	6	98

Exhibit 14-10
Monthly Advertising Effectiveness Report: Subtotaled by Item/Product

947 - 1

N A T I O N A L   I N D U S T R I E S
MONTHLY ADVERTISING EFFECTIVENESS REPORT
SUB-TOTALED BY ITEM/PRODUCT FOR PERIOD ENDING 31 JAN 1994

SOURCE OF INQUIRY	ISSUE	R/S #	TYP	ITEM/PRODUCT	TOTAL	COST	CPI	JAN	DEC	NOV	OCT	SEP	AUG	JUL	JUN	OTHER 4 MO.	OLDER
ARCHITECTURAL DESIGN	93SEP	28	PUB	MATRIX	73			5	10	12	46						
COMPUTER INTERNATIONAL	93MAY	145	ADV	MATRIX	31							1	5	4	17	4	
ELECTRONIC DIRECTORY	93FAL	413	ADV	MATRIX	42							2	7	33			
OFFICE EQUIPMENT DEALER	93APR	423	ADV	MATRIX	7											7	
OFFICE EQUIPMENT DEALER	93DEC	511	PUB	MATRIX	20										1	19	
PLANT DESIGN & MGMT				MATRIX	127			127									
TYPE OF SOURCE SUMMARY FOR MATRIX																	
ADVERT					80							3	12	37	17	11	0
PUBLCT					220			132	10	12	46				1	19	0
				TOTAL ALL	300			132	10	12	46	3	12	37	18	30	0
				TOTAL 12 MONTHS	300			132	10	12	46	3	12	37	18	30	0
CHEMICAL AGE	93OCT	356	D.M	HI SPEED	45			8	25	12							
ELECTRONIC LIT NEWS	93JUN	665	ADV	HI SPEED	36				1			4	5	26			
ELECTRONIC LIT NEWS	93DEC	24	ADV	HI SPEED	41			41									
PLANT DESIGN & MGMT	93NOV	511	D.M	HI SPEED	269				269								
TELECOMMUNICATIONS TODAY	93NOV30	582	ADV	HI SPEED	51			9	42								
TYPE OF SOURCE SUMMARY FOR HI SPEED																	
ADVERT					128			50	43			4	5	26			
D.MAIL					314			8	294	12							
				TOTAL ALL	442			58	337	12		4	5	26			
				TOTAL 12 MONTHS	442			58	337	12		4	5	26			
COMPUTER INTERNATIONAL	93NOV	132	PUB	GENERAL	311			76	235								
FINANCIAL INDUSTRY	93JUN	666	PUB	GENERAL	45							6	6	33			
MIDSTATE EXPO	93FEB	DALLAS SHO		GENERAL	103											103	
VIDEO NEWS	93JUL	337	M.L	GENERAL	39			2				8	22	7			
TYPE OF SOURCE SUMMARY FOR GENERAL																	
M.LIST					39			2	0			8	22	7		0	
PUBLCT					356			76	235			6	6	33		0	
SHOW					103			0	0			0	0	0		103	
				TOTAL ALL	498			78	235			14	28	40		103	
				TOTAL 12 MONTHS	498			78	235			14	28	40		103	
ELECTRONIC LIT NEWS	92NOV	350	PUB	PREMIER	104											6	98
ELECTRONIC LIT NEWS	93AUG	252	ADV	PREMIER	113						33	80					
ELECTRONIC LIT NEWS	93OCT	24	800	PREMIER	741			90	187	341	123						
ELECTRONIC COMMUNICATIONS TODAY	93JUN20	339	ADV	PREMIER	142							6	20	65	51		
TELECOMMUNICATIONS TODAY	93JUL21	147	PUB	PREMIER	116						11	105					

report particularly helpful when choosing sources and budgeting promotion periods.

Subtotaling by product summarizes the support each product receives, a matter of critical interest to product managers. It shows which sources perform best for the product, in terms of inquiry volume and CPI efficiency. It is especially helpful when building marketing communications budgets in terms of product-by-product support.

Customize Data Breakouts

Of course, your decision-making needs should determine which reports you generate. Do not allow report formats to dictate how you make decisions! Tailor reports to your exact needs. Companies frequently find it useful to sort inquiries by customer classification, or application, in addition to product and source.

Analysis might reveal that certain types of accounts—defined by size, geography, industry, application, purchase volume, etc.—are more active inquirers and therefore more promising prospects. Standard Industrial Classification (SIC) codes provide a ready segmentation method for business marketers backed by extensive government and private databases. Tracking lead volume by SIC code could provide valuable early-warning trends.

Another approach is to compare the relative inquiry and sales volume you derive from different geographic areas to the number and size of your target prospect industries in those same areas—data easily available in the information marketplace. Is your activity in each commensurate with its potential?

It might pay to examine leads by major accounts, particularly those with multiple plant and office locations that require sales attention. Keeping an eye on inquiries per account allows salespeople to review a prospect's inquiry history before making a call, a valuable preparation tool.

Senior Management Reporting

Keeping the boss informed means presenting the big picture, short and sweet. We recommend boiling Advertising Effectiveness Report data down to a narrative format on a single page. Exhibit 14-11 shows an example of a Sales Lead Executive Summary Report.

Qualified Leads vs. Raw Inquiries

The information becomes more instructive when you examine qualified lead generation. Exhibits 14-12, 14-13, and 14-14 show the Sales Lead Qualification Report with data arrayed by source type, individual inquiry source, and product. The format of each is identical to the Sales Lead Qualification Report by Territory discussed above.

Exhibit 14-11
Sales Lead Executive Summary Report

National Industries
Sales Lead Executive Summary Report
May 1994

National Industries processed 329 inquiries for the month just ended, compared with an average monthly volume of 319. May, therefore, exceeded the monthly average by 3 percent.

SUMMARY BY PRODUCT/ITEM:

The National RS232 drew the largest number of inquiries for the month, 228. The number two inquiry generator for the month was Highlite, with 69 inquiries. Lowlite came in third with 22 inquiries.

SUMMARY BY SOURCE TYPE:

Trade shows produced the most inquiries in May, 131. Mailing list came in second with 96 inquiries. The number three source was telephone with 79 inquiries.

SUMMARY BY SOURCE:

PC Magazine produced the most inquiries of any individual source during May: 95 inquiries. Westec was the number two lead generator with 87 inquiries. The number three source for the month was the NCGA Show, with 37 inquiries.

In Exhibit 14-12, inquiries by source type, note the relatively strong quali-fication rates for telephone and trade show leads, as one would expect from media that interactively collect qualification information at the same time they acquire the lead. Your particular qualification criteria will determine which inquiries to count as qualified.

In National's case, for instance, it deemed mailing lists it has used as relatively well prequalified. It judged only half its trade show inquiries as qualified, and many of its 800-number callers were not considered qualified either. Publicity leads through reader service numbers qualified at about average rates.

Exhibit 14-12
Sales Lead Qualification Report by Source Type

NATIONAL INDUSTRIES
SALES LEAD QUALIFICATION REPORT BY SOURCE-TYPE
FOR 12 MO PERIOD ENDING: JAN 94

SOURCE-TYPE SUMMARY	LAST 3 MONTHS TOTAL INQUIRIES	TOTAL CONTACTED	PRE-QUALIFIED INQUIRER	QUALIFIED BY INQUIRER	QUALIFIED LAST 12 MONTHS BY REPRESEN.	BY INQ&REP	TOTAL ALL QUALIFIED	LAST 12 MONTHS ALL NOT QUALIFIED	NO ACTION	TOTAL INQUIRIES *12 MONTHS
ADVERTISEMENT	239 11.4%	23 9.6%	138 9.3%	207 13.9%	172 11.6%	31 2.1%	548 36.9%	55 3.7%	882 59.4%	1,485 30.1%
BONUS INQUIRIES	0 0.0%	0 0.0%	1 12.5%	0 0.0%	0 0.0%	0 0.0%	1 12.5%	0 0.0%	7 87.5%	8 0.2%
DIRECT MAIL	298 14.2%	31 10.4%	20 6.7%	70 23.5%	26 8.7%	1 0.3%	117 39.3%	6 2.0%	175 58.7%	298 6.0%
TELEPHONE CALLS	45 2.1%	10 22.2%	13 9.6%	13 9.6%	34 25.2%	5 3.7%	65 48.1%	6 4.4%	64 47.4%	135 2.7%
POSTCARD DECKS	240 11.4%	23 9.6%	66 12.8%	23 4.5%	54 10.5%	19 3.7%	162 31.5%	2 0.4%	351 68.2%	515 10.4%
MAIL LIST ADDITIONS	2 0.1%	0 0.0%	10 27.0%	2 5.4%	3 8.1%	2 5.4%	17 47.2%	2 5.6%	17 47.2%	36 0.7%
800 LINE CALL	719 34.3%	110 15.3%	70 8.3%	30 3.6%	84 10.0%	6 0.7%	190 22.6%	42 5.0%	610 72.4%	842 17.1%
PUBLICITY	545 26.0%	57 10.5%	135 9.3%	106 7.3%	156 10.7%	32 2.2%	429 29.5%	41 2.8%	984 67.7%	1,454 29.5%
TRADE SHOW	0 0.0%	0 0.0%	51 49.5%	0 0.0%	9 8.7%	1 1.0%	61 59.2%	1 1.0%	41 39.8%	103 2.1%
LETTERS	11 0.5%	0 0.0%	9 16.7%	6 11.1%	10 18.5%	1 1.9%	26 48.1%	2 3.7%	26 48.1%	54 1.1%
TOTALS	2,099 100.0%	254 12.1%	513 10.4%	457 9.3%	548 11.1%	98 2.0%	1,616 32.8%	157 3.2%	3,157 64.0%	4,930 100.0%

Individual Source Accountability

Examining qualified lead information by individual lead source, as in Exhibit 14-13 (the names are fictional), puts media in the hot seat. Qualified lead counts put all media on the same footing, allowing direct comparisons between, say, paid advertising and publicity. Is a page of publicity as valuable as a full-page ad? Let the qualified lead yield decide. Which creative approach will generate more profit? Need the ad be in color? Is each source pulling commensurate with its cost? Again, let the inquiry count reveal the answer.

Plant Design & Management produces the most raw leads over 12 months for this National Industries product, and the most qualified leads. But *Telecommunications Today* produced a much higher ratio of qualified to total inquiries. Assuming, for the purpose of illustration, that both publications reached the same buying influences in the same industries at a comparable cost-per-thousand circulation for the same schedule, *Telecommunications Today* would be the more efficient media purchase. Then again, National's goal is not necessarily generating the cheapest leads, but producing the right number of the best leads to keep sales perking.

Office Equipment Dealer and *Telecommunications Today* are an interesting contrast. They provided roughly the same number of qualified leads over 12 months, but the latter publication produced a much greater ratio of pre-qualified leads. That could be an important media buying consideration for a sales lead management program relying on heavy use of pre-qualifying lead-acquisition tools such as 800-line calls, fax and fax-back inquiries, and sight-qualification criteria such as dual bingo numbers bind-in card returns.

Product Particulars

Brand and product managers will be particularly interested in Exhibit 14-14. It summarizes the quality and quantity of inquiries each product receives, and how well each is followed up—hard evidence of marketing communications and field sales performance.

Media Cost Comparisons

The next step in lead source evaluation takes a closer look at costs and the specific CPI for each of a product's inquiry-producing programs. Exhibit 14-15, for example, reports the CPI of each ad run for a specific product.

The data reveal that Publication C's CPI is more than three times publication A's cost. Of course, that doesn't automatically make it A the superior buy. Although C produces fewer inquiries, it might reach a different audience critical to the selling process, such as senior corporate managers who approve purchases, while A reaches, say, engineers setting purchase specifications.

Exhibit 14-13
Sales Lead Qualification Report by Source

NATIONAL INDUSTRIES
SALES LEAD QUALIFICATION REPORT BY SOURCE
FOR 12 MO PERIOD ENDING: JAN 94

MAGAZINE OR OTHER SOURCE PRODUCT R/S NO ISSUE	LAST 3 MONTHS TOTAL INQUIRIES	CONTACTED	PRE-QUALIFIED INQUIRER CONTACTED	QUALIFIED LAST 12 BY INQUIRER	BY REPRESEN.	QUALIFIED LAST 12 MONTHS BY INQ&REP	TOTAL ALL QUALIFIED	LAST 12 MONTHS NOT QUALIFIED	NO ACTION	TOTAL INQUIRIES 12 MONTHS
ARCHITECTURAL DESIGN	27 1.3%	4 14.8%	14 10.2%	12 8.8%	35 25.5%	5 3.6%	66 48.2%	2 1.5%	69 50.4%	137 2.8%
CHEMICAL AGE	35 1.7%	9 25.7%	6 17.1%	2 5.7%	5 14.3%	1 2.9%	14 40.0%	5 14.3%	16 45.7%	35 0.7%
COMPUTER INTERNATIONAL	305 14.5%	15 4.9%	13 3.9%	2 0.6%	19 5.7%	0 0.0%	34 10.1%	4 1.2%	298 88.7%	336 6.8%
ELECTRONIC DIRECTORY	0 0.0%	0 0.0%	9 21.4%	6 14.3%	4 9.5%	2 4.8%	21 50.0%	5 11.9%	16 38.1%	42 0.9%
ELECTRONIC LIT NEWS	658 31.3%	105 16.0%	84 9.0%	43 4.6%	89 9.5%	6 0.6%	222 23.7%	43 4.6%	713 76.3%	935 19.0%
FINANCIAL INDUSTRY	0 0.0%	0 0.0%	1 2.2%	8 17.8%	4 8.9%	0 0.0%	13 23.9%	4 8.9%	28 62.2%	45 0.9%
HOSPITALITY TIMES	31 1.5%	0 0.0%	1 3.2%	0 0.0%	0 0.0%	0 0.0%	1 3.2%	0 0.0%	30 96.8%	31 0.6%
MATERIAL DESIGN & HNDLG	0 0.0%	0 0.0%	0 0.0%	4 6.1%	4 6.1%	0 0.0%	8 12.1%	1 1.5%	57 86.4%	66 1.3%
MEDICAL LIT REVIEW	0 0.0%	0 0.0%	1 11.1%	0 0.0%	6 66.7%	0 0.0%	7 77.8%	0 0.0%	2 22.2%	9 0.2%
MIDSTATE EXPO	0 0.0%	0 0.0%	51 49.5%	0 0.0%	9 8.7%	1 1.0%	61 59.2%	1 1.0%	41 39.8%	103 2.1%
NEW PRODUCT DIGEST	0 0.0%	0 0.0%	13 5.8%	6 2.7%	34 15.1%	9 4.0%	62 27.6%	0 0.0%	163 72.4%	225 4.6%
OFFICE EQUIPMENT DEALER	119 5.7%	8 6.7%	27 3.1%	107 12.2%	107 12.2%	27 3.1%	268 30.5%	26 3.0%	585 66.6%	879 17.8%
PLANT DESIGN & MGMT	611 29.1%	79 12.9%	137 11.1%	127 10.3%	133 10.8%	32 2.6%	429 34.9%	35 2.8%	765 62.2%	1,229 24.9%
SERVICE MGMT MONTHLY	73 3.5%	14 19.2%	25 14.9%	42 25.0%	15 8.9%	2 1.2%	84 50.0%	11 6.5%	73 43.5%	168 3.4%
TELECOMMUNICATIONS TODAY	60 2.9%	6 10.0%	98 20.6%	73 15.4%	67 14.1%	11 2.3%	249 52.4%	15 3.2%	211 44.4%	475 9.6%
VIDEO NEWS	180 8.6%	14 7.8%	33 15.3%	25 11.6%	17 7.9%	2 0.9%	77 35.8%	15 0.9%	136 63.3%	215 4.4%
TOTALS	2,099 100.0%	254 12.1%	513 10.4%	457 9.3%	548 11.1%	98 2.0%	1,616 32.8%	157 3.2%	3,157 64.0%	4,930 100.0%

Exhibit 14-14
Sales Lead Qualification Report by Product

NATIONAL INDUSTRIES
SALES LEAD QUALIFICATION REPORT BY PRODUCT
FOR 12 MO PERIOD ENDING: JAN 94

PRODUCT SUMMARY	LAST 3 MONTHS TOTAL INQUIRIES	TOTAL CONTACTED	PRE-QUALIFIED INQUIRER	QUALIFIED INQUIRER	QUALIFIED LAST 12 MONTHS BY REPRESEN.	BY INQ&REP	TOTAL ALL QUALIFIED	LAST 12 MONTHS ALL NOT QUALIFIED	NO ACTION	TOTAL INQUIRIES 12 MONTHS
MATRIX	151 7.2%	15 9.9%	23 7.7%	37 12.5%	34 11.4%	8 2.7%	102 34.3%	8 2.7%	187 63.0%	297 6.0%
HI SPEED	389 18.5%	40 10.3%	25 5.9%	103 24.3%	38 9.0%	1 0.2%	167 39.4%	6 1.4%	251 59.2%	424 8.6%
GENERAL	307 14.6%	15 4.9%	69 14.1%	12 2.4%	29 5.9%	3 0.6%	113 23.1%	11 2.2%	366 74.7%	490 9.9%
PREMIER	616 29.3%	102 16.6%	159 14.6%	70 6.4%	111 10.2%	11 1.0%	351 32.3%	58 5.3%	677 62.3%	1,086 22.0%
CLASSIC	282 13.4%	22 7.8%	33 10.3%	27 8.5%	29 9.1%	0 0.0%	89 27.8%	2 0.6%	228 73.5%	319 6.5%
SYSTEM II	121 5.8%	9 7.4%	43 12.1%	10 2.8%	33 9.3%	16 4.5%	102 28.7%	5 1.4%	247 69.8%	354 7.2%
*286 PLUS	0 0.0%	0 0.0%	13 6.0%	7 3.2%	32 14.7%	9 4.1%	61 28.1%	1 0.5%	155 71.4%	217 4.4%
MICRO FAM	65 3.1%	17 26.2%	4 3.5%	1 0.9%	27 23.9%	0 0.0%	32 28.3%	2 1.8%	79 69.9%	113 2.3%
MULTI 8	4 0.2%	2 50.0%	98 8.2%	120 10.0%	158 13.2%	41 3.4%	417 34.9%	31 2.6%	748 62.5%	1,196 24.3%
386 PLUS	164 7.8%	32 19.5%	46 10.6%	70 16.1%	57 13.1%	9 2.1%	182 41.9%	33 7.6%	219 50.5%	434 8.8%
TOTALS	2,099 100.0%	254 12.1%	513 10.4%	457 9.3%	548 11.1%	98 2.0%	1,616 32.8%	157 3.2%	3,157 64.0%	4,930 100.0%

Exhibit 14-15

Advertising History of Costs by Product

Source	Issue Date	Promotional Cost	Number of Inquiries	Cost per Inquiry
Pub A	1/01/94	$ 2,305	153	$ 15.06
Pub B	1/01/94	3,109	251	12.39
Pub C	1/01/94	3,725	72	51.74
Pub B	2/15/94	3,109	127	24.48
Pub C	2/15/94	3,725	75	49.67
Pub D	3/01/94	1,527	46	33.20
Pub A	3/01/94	2,305	139	16.58
Pub C	3/01/94	3,725	103	36.17
Pub D	4/01/94	1,527	30	50.90
Pub A	4/01/94	2,305	163	14.14

Publications A and C advertising produces relatively stable month-to-month inquiry counts, publications B and D relatively less so. Seasonal buying patterns, or supporting special-issue editorial fare might cause the volatility for B and D, particularly if they reach different prospects than A and C.

Eventually, as selling proceeds and some inquiries convert to sales, those conversions can be traced back to the publications—or other source—generating the original lead. Exhibit 14-16 is a table showing representative conversion rates per publication. Publication A appears to be delivering more genuine prospects than the others. Only Publication D can match A's conversion rate.

Publications H, E, and particularly B need a close look before being included on the next advertising schedule. Balanced promotion programs should reach all purchasing influences: specifiers, approvers, and recommenders. Not all those people inquire, sign purchase orders, or respond to Did-You-Buy? surveys. So there might be a good reason to continue using Publication B. It might, for example, be a strong addition to a particular product's schedule, particularly if it delivers new customers not identified by other media.

The closer look at Publication B will include examining each publication's contribution to each product's new customer orders. Exhibit 14-17 shows a basic matrix assigning each converted advertising lead for each product to the publication that generated the inquiry. Publication B, for instance, is not a strong performer overall, and while Product 4 seems to be the one most appropriate to its pages, Product 4 receives plenty of support in Publications D and F. Product

4's product manager has more evidence to drop Publication B, as other product managers are likely to do. Product 2's product manager meanwhile has to examine why her advertising overall is producing few new customers.

Be sure to give credit appropriately. When an inquirer asks for information about the same product from more than one publication or advertisement, and then later purchases the product, log the inquiry to the worksheet in Exhibit 14-17 as many times as necessary. If, for instance, an inquirer responded to ads for product 3 in publications C and H, then purchased product 3, give credit for the conversion to both publications.

You can then calculate the advertising cost for each product's new customers, as shown in Exhibit 14-18. Product 2, which converted the fewest new customers, has the highest ad cost per customer. Perhaps that is justified by the product's price, profit margins, selling complexity, competitive environment, etc. Or maybe the problem is flabby promotion, the product is flawed, or salespeople are not trained properly to sell it. Further investigation will tell.

Exhibit 14-16
Conversion Rate by Publication

Publication	Total Number of Inquiries	Number of New Customers	Percent Conversion
Pub A	1,687	148	9%
Pub B	1,332	22	2%
Pub C	1,240	83	7%
Pub D	1,008	92	9%
Pub E	790	30	4%
Pub F	815	45	6%
Pub G	1,118	63	6%
Pub H	700	25	4%
Average Conversion Rate	8,690	508	6%

Exhibit 14-17
Inquiries Identified As Conversion to New Customer Sales

Product	Pub A	Pub B	Pub C	Pub D	Pub E	Pub F	Pub G	Pub H	Total New Customers
Prod #1	15	0	17	3	9	1	0	0	45
Prod #2	0	4	0	9	1	0	0	1	25
Prod #3	11	0	45	0	4	0	19	5	84
Prod #4	0	12	0	68	3	26	5	0	114
Prod #5	59	4	6	3	9	15	23	12	131
Prod #6	63	2	15	9	4	3	16	7	119
Total New Customers	148	22	83	92	30	45	63	25	508

When an inquirer asks for information from more than one publication or advertisement and the later purchases the product, the inquirer is indicated in the matrix as many times as necessary. As an example, if an inquirer responded to advertisements placed in both publication C and H, and purchased Product 3, both publications would be given credit for the new customer find of product 3.

Exhibit 14-18
Advertising Cost per New Customer by Product

Product	Ad Budget by Product	Total New Customers	Ad Cost per New Customer
Prod #1	$ 523	23	$ 22.74
Prod #2	1,678	12	140.58
Prod #3	2,670	63	37.62
Prod #4	3,917	91	43.04
Prod #5	2,791	117	11.68
Prod #6	2,040	69	29.56
Totals	13,619	375	36.32

This report reflects the actual number of new customers and actual advertising dollars expended by product. The cost per new customer by product is indicated on each individual line.

Did-You-Buy? Survey Insights

The Did-You-Buy? studies we recommended in Chapter 11 fill an information gap between inquiry and order-entry systems that's commonplace within companies. Marketers often gripe about the "black hole where leads disappear" after being sent to the field.

The inquiry handling system reports who has inquired, received literature, and is qualified. The sales and ordering system tracks quotations and eventual orders, as shown in Exhibit 14-19. But, as we've noted, matching those disparate sets of data is an imperfect art.

Did-You-Buy? studies cannot track every lead, unless you contract each inquirer individually, but they do allow you to estimate lead conversion rate, particularly when you telephone a random sample of inquirers and receive a statistically projectable response. (A mail survey cannot easily control who responds and who does not.) Did-You-Buy? studies provide invaluable evidence about the quality of lead follow-up.

To illustrate Did-You-Buy? study findings and what they can mean, Exhibit 14-20 shows the results of a Did-You-Buy? survey conducted by a manufacturer of a $5,000 computer peripheral device, plus the findings from a series of telephone surveys among inquiries to eight computer and electronics advertisers.

The computer peripheral study used the questionnaire shown in Chapter 11 to guide a telephone interviewer. Distributor salespeople handled the field follow-up. The other studies used a similar questionnaire.

Exhibit 14-19
"Information Gap" diagram from workbook

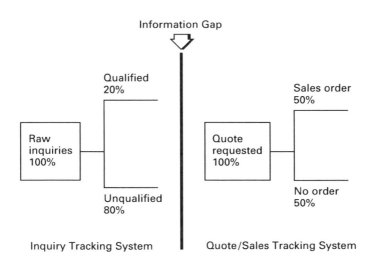

Information Gap

Qualified
20%

Sales order
50%

Raw
inquiries
100%

Quote
requested
100%

Unqualified
80%

No order
50%

Inquiry Tracking System

Quote/Sales Tracking System

Exhibit 14-20
Did-You-Buy? Survey Results: Two Studies

Study 1
Sample: Random sample of inquirers
Product: Computer peripheral equipment
Survey timing: Inquirers called 12 months after they inquired
Survey method: Telephone
Type of lead: 800-number inbound telephone responses to space advertising
Total surveyed: 100 inquirers
Results:

Entire Sample

Percent received information requested:	84%
Percent bought:	31%
Advertiser's share of sales:	58%
Competitors' share of sales:	42%

(No single dominant competitor emerged in the results, among 11 other companies named by respondents)

Percent reporting follow-up by advertiser:	23%
Percent still in the market to buy:	32%

(12 months after original inquiry)
Of those in the market:

Intend to buy within 3 months:	25%
Intend to buy within 4-6 months:	16%
Intend to buy within 7-12 months:	9%
Intend to buy after 12 more months:	16%
Not sure when they will buy:	34%
Would still like a sales call:	50%

Those Followed Up by the Distributor

Percent bought:	52%
Advertiser's share of sales:	83%
Competitors' share of sales:	17%

Those *Not* Followed Up by the Distributor

Percent bought:	27%
Advertiser's share of sales:	40%
Competitors' share of sales:	60%

Inquirers Who Contacted Distributor on Their Own

Percent bought:	66%
Advertiser's share of sales:	82%
Competitors' share of sales:	18%

Study 2
Sample: Random sample of inquirers to eight business advertisers
Product: Computers and electronic equipment
Survey timing: Inquirers called 6 to 12 months after they inquired
Survey method: Telephone
Type of lead: Reader service card and 800-number inbound telephone responses to space advertising
Total surveyed: Minimum 100 per advertiser; 800 total
Results:

Entire Eight-Advertiser Sample

Percent bought:	26%
Advertiser's share of sales:	24%
Competitors' share of sales:	76%
Percent reporting follow-up by advertisers:	42%

Those Followed Up by the Advertisers

Percent bought:	29%
Advertiser's share of sales:	36%
Competitors' share of sales:	64%

Those *Not* Followed Up by the Advertisers

Percent bought:	25%
Advertiser's share of sales:	14%
Competitors' share of sales:	86%

The manufacturers who conducted the studies used the results to advantage in several ways.

- The computer peripheral manufacturer's share of sales was 83 percent among those who purchased the product *and* received a follow-up call from the advertiser's distributor, compared to 58 percent for the entire sample. Among the eight high-tech advertisers, their share of sales was 36 percent among those who purchased the product and received a follow-up call from their sales channels, compared to 24 percent for the entire sample.

- The computer peripheral manufacturer's share of sales was only 40 percent among those who bought but *did not* receive a follow-up call from the manufacturer's distributor. For the eight other advertisers, share among accounts not followed up was only 14 percent, significantly less than half the share achieved among inquirers whom the advertisers did contact.

- The disparity impressed corporate management of the computer peripheral manufacturer with the value of dealer sales training and merchandising programs. And it impressed dealers about the power of pursuing leads, motivating greater cooperation on their part. Similarly, the eight other advertisers used their respective findings to improve their own follow-up rates.

- The computer peripheral advertiser proved to distributors that inquirers who receive "where to buy" information in their inquiry fulfillment and then contact the distributor are especially hot prospects deserving great attention: 66 percent bought, and of those 82 percent bought the advertiser's product.

- Even a year after they inquired, a third of the computer peripheral maker's leads were still saying they planned to buy. Fully half of them said they'd like a sales call. That evidence proved to corporate management that tracking leads over time is well worth the effort. And it impressed salespeople who might otherwise ignore aging leads.

- In all the examples, selling activity probably increased the purchase rate for the entire category as well as for the advertiser's products. Yet the same statistics about percentage of contacted leads who bought also suggest that reps went after the most likely looking prospects first. The lesser purchase rate in the non-contact group suggests both factors influenced sales results.

Did-You-Buy? Trends

Combining the results of Did-You-Buy? studies will paint a broader picture of the health of your lead generation and follow-up programs. Look for consistent weak spots that recur for different products and which reappear at different times. Keep in mind that prospects do not always remember asking for literature, or receiving it, or of being contacted by the company.

Most inquirers do remember, however. Research finds that their recall is fairly stable year-to-year across industries. But some inquiry trends, such as a growing willingness to inquire from multiple vendors, suggest that sales lead management is becoming more competitive and essential to success in the slow-growth 1990s.

Combining the results of more than two dozen Did-You-Buy? mail and telephone studies with more than 2,400 qualified business inquirers over a six-year period, we have found that:

- Around 90 percent of inquirers remember asking for literature and information sent to them. That ratio probably is as good as it gets.

- In recent years, however, the recall ratio has slipped to around 80 percent. Literature memorability affects results; so has the growing volume of business-to-business direct mail during the late-1980s to mid-1990s period of the surveys.

- The percentage recalling sales contact has ranged from 43 to 36 percent. Actual contact is probably somewhat higher. Even so, the statistic reveals flabby sales follow-up.

- Roughly a fifth of inquirers take the initiative to contact a company rather than wait for a sales contact; year-to-year study averages range from 13 to 19 percent. Advertisers cannot afford to wait for prospects to come back to them, when so few do so.

- Inquirers are asking more than one potential supplier to send information more often than they used to. In the mid-1990s, about 70 percent inquired of more than one source for a specific purchase, up from 55 percent in the late-1980s. Even though they are trimming approved-vendor lists and seeking more long-term supplier relationships, buyers seeking new suppliers are casting a wider net. Winning their business increasingly requires a prompt fulfillment response, quality literature, and competitively superior follow-up.

- The proportion of inquirers buying within six months seems to be edging upward, from 26 percent historically to more than 30 percent. While that statistic varies among products and among years, the "Rule of 45" for purchases within 12 months has proven to be a surprisingly stable benchmark (see Appendix A).

- About a fifth of a company's inquirers will buy the product of interest from a competitor within six months. That statistic has remained fairly stable year-to-year.

- Around 50 percent of inquirers in the mid-1990s said they were "still budgeted to buy" the equipment for which they requested information six months after their inquiries. That ratio rose dramatically from 30 percent in the mid- to late-1980s. Evidently, the slow 1990s economy caused more buyers to delay their purchases, making six-month or older leads even more valuable than they've been before.

- Similarly, 66 percent of early-1990s inquirers said they were "still in the market" for the products they inquired about, up from the 48 to 56 percent range in 1985 through 1989. That is additional evidence of delayed purchases, and your best prospects' vulnerability to competitors' selling activity.

Sales Lead Management Is Information Management

This essential fact makes sales lead management part of the core competencies needed to compete in the 1990s and beyond. According to a renowned marketing thinker, Dartmouth University's Prof. Frederick E. Webster Jr., "A company's ability to command natural resources, technology, and capital as sources of competitive advantage is taking a back seat strategically as the ability to control knowledge and information moves to the forefront."[6]

The information contained in sales leads, so woefully underused by most companies today, turns companies into powerful marketing and sales organizations that continuously improve the value they create for customers and the profit they generate for investors. The buyers are out there, waiting for your next move.

Appendix A

Lead Planning Math

The Rule of 45 Lead Conversion Rate

Our ongoing Did-You-Buy? studies find that 26 percent of inquirers from all sources actually purchased the product from the advertiser or from a competitor *six months* after they inquired. And, 56 percent said they still planned to buy while 33 reported they were still budgeted for the purchase.[1] (See Exhibit A-1.)

We've also found that *a year* after responding, about 45 percent of inquirers actually bought the advertised product from either the advertiser itself or a competitor, or intended to purchase soon. That statistic has remained more or less stable over the years.

Exhibit A-1
Lead Conversion Ratios

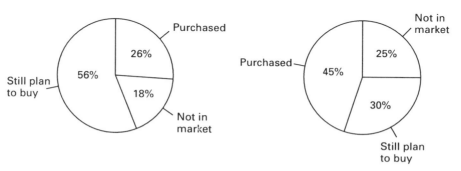

Source: "Did You Buy?" Survey Database Inquiry Handling Service, Inc.

Generally, when the proportion of inquirers who actually bought is much less than 45 percent, those "still in the market" are a correspondingly larger group. That's not unusual during recessions when companies delay purchases, especially for products with year-or-longer purchase-decision cycles. For example, one company selling a $5,000 computer peripheral surveyed 1990 advertising inquirers 12 months later during the recession. It found 31 percent had bought the type of product advertised, while 32 percent said they still planned to make a purchase in the category. Had most of those buying intentions panned out as is likely, close to 45 percent of inquirers would have purchased within 1.5 years.

Individual lead programs often find the proportion of year-later buyers and hot prospects varying around the 45 percent average, depending upon product and market conditions. Yet we've found that it's unlikely to deviate more than 10 percentage points either way.

Additional Lead-Conversion Data

An unusually comprehensive survey by the Advertising Research Foundation of more than 1,000 advertising reader service card inquirers reported behavior patterns related but not identical to our Rule of 45. The classic study, still the most comprehensive investigation in lead management, found an average of 30 percent had purchased the items (or a better substitute) about which they'd inquired during the previous 12-month period. Another 19 percent said they would probably buy those products and services in the future. Only 40 percent of them had asked for information without having a specific purchase in mind.[2]

Other research, covering different periods of time between inquiry and survey, shows roughly similar results.

- When it surveyed industrial magazine readers four months after they'd inquired, *Industrial Equipment News* found 16 percent had purchased and 74 percent intended to buy.[3]

- Within six to seven months, Gordon Publications says, 19 percent have bought the type of product advertised, and 47 percent reported "still a good likelihood" of buying.[4]

- *New Equipment Digest* reported the average survey response of more than 125,000 of its advertising inquirers. More than 35 percent eventually bought the product they inquired about from the advertiser or a competitor. And, another 53 percent said they were still considering the purchase at the time they were surveyed.[5]

- Cahners Publishing Co. surveys of inquirers in 12 of its specialized business publications found 29 percent saying they bought or specified the purchase of the advertised product from the advertiser or a competitor; 59 percent said they filed the information for future purchases, and 12 percent passed the information on to other buying influences for review.[6]

All these figures are broad averages from different databases, however, and none of them are as good for your company's planning as your own lead-performance data. Nonetheless, if you are just starting to collect lead information, these statistics provide ballpark estimates for forecasting and return-on-performance-investment (ROPI) calculations.

The New Business Calculation

Exhibit A-2 shows the New Business Calculation Worksheet. Using it is easy, but plugging in the right numbers might not be.

Exhibit A-2
New Business Calculation Worksheet

1. Target gross annual sales level	$_____
2. Forecast sales from current customer base	$_____
3. Additional sales required (1 minus 2)	$_____
4. Expected lost business from departed customers (lost to competition, out of business, etc.)	$_____
5. Total new customer sales required (3 plus 4)	$_____

Line 1 of the worksheet asks for your sales target for the coming year. You can use either units or dollars. The number should correspond to your sales forecast, including any growth or decline expected from current year levels.

Line 2 asks for an estimate of the volume you will sell to current customers who stick with you. Usually, not every customer will, and sales growth in some customer segments may differ from growth rates in other segments. The estimates are likely to depend heavily on sales department forecasts account by account, tempered by economic conditions and market segment forecasts.

Line 3 indicates how much of your target volume you do *not* expect to get from current customers.

Line 4 can be a particularly difficult estimate because sales departments, which should be optimistic by nature, have a difficult time grappling with the idea of account departures. The larger your customer base, the more you can rely on econometric estimates of attrition. Either way, it takes honesty for companies to recognize how large this number could be.

Line 5 adds the growth you are seeking to the amount of lost business you'll need to make up for to break even with the current year.

Return on Promotional Investment

The ROPI formula reasons that a certain proportion of sales leads will buy, within the following year, the type of product or service promoted by a vendor via advertising, mail, telephone, trade shows, postcards, directories, catalogs, etc. The all-industry average lead conversion rate is 45 percent within a year of inquiring.

Those buyers include companies purchasing competitive brands or superior alternatives to satisfy the applications they had in mind. An individual marketer will reap only part of the sales; the best estimate of which usually is the product's or service's current market share. And, the marketer only has a shot at those sales if the sales force and distributors follow up all qualified leads.

Multiplying share into the formula forecasts the number of your brand's new customer orders, regardless of size. Multiplying in the average dollar volume per new customer order provides the final dollar volume sales forecast.

We simply reverse the process to determine the lead volume required to generate enough new customer business to meet your sales target. Assuming a stable market share, your sales force, distributors, telemarketers, and other channels must pursue a reciprocal number of accounts. For example, if your share is 60 percent and 50 percent of inquirers buy, you must follow up 1,000 new accounts to close 300 of them.

Be sure you use the right market share estimates. It's usually more accurate to apply the ROPI formula to the market segments in which you compete, rather than to a broader market where your share will be smaller. You probably will not draw many leads from segments you do not serve, so it's meaningless to include them in your lead volume target.

The example shown here works within a 12-month period following the generation of inquiries. That's a reasonable time frame for a continuously sold product with a year-long or shorter repurchase cycle. But for more exotic, expensive, higher-risk capital purchases, for instance, an 18-month or longer time frame will be more appropriate for the ROPI calculation.

According to the ROPI formula, to forecast sales in a period, calculate:

Leads × % Buyers × % Market share × $ Average order = $ Sales

Use:

- The number of inquiries obtained from all sources.
- The percentage of those leads that will eventually buy (lead conversion rate). The statistic should come from your own Did-You-Buy? survey results. Absent those data, estimate using the Rule of 45 all-industry average applied to the raw inquiry count. If you estimate against your volume of qualified leads, figure roughly that the conversion rate will be five to eight percentage points greater.
- Unless your ongoing Did-You-Buy? studies indicate your share of inquirers' purchases, use other share statistics you might have from other research, trade associations, etc. to predict how many buyers will buy from you.
- Your order-entry database will indicate the size of the average new customer order.

Rearrange the formula to calculate required lead volume:

$$\text{Leads Required} = \frac{\$ \text{ Sales}}{\% \text{ Buyers} \times \% \text{ Market share} \times \$ \text{ Average order}}$$

Sample Calculations

Manufacturer. A marine radio manufacturer with 27 percent market share needs at least $1.8 million new customer sales to meet its goals for the coming fiscal year. Records indicate that the average new customer order is $2,495. The company estimates the industry's lead conversion rate is 45 percent, and its disciplined sales force will follow up nearly all qualified leads. To achieve its sales goal, it needs 5,938 new customer leads.

Rounding the lead target to 6,000, the company knows its promotional cost per inquiry is $32, not bad for leads producing an average of more than $260 in sales. It budgets $192,000 for lead generation, expecting the same cost-per-lead from a program of 60 insertions in seven industry publications.

Service firm. An industrial heating, ventilation, air conditioning (HVAC) maintenance company's average new client pays $12,000 in fees the first year. It needs about $160,000 in new business to cover client attrition, requiring it to close more than 13 new accounts. Its market share in its three-state region is 15 percent. Estimating a 45 percent lead conversion, the company requires 197 leads. It rounds its target to 200.

Historically, regional leads cost $60 to generate, each producing about $445 in sales. The firm decides to spend its $12,000 budget required to produce the leads in regional Yellow Pages directories and a telemarketing campaign with a free-estimate offer. Because its inquiries come almost totally from inbound and outbound telemarketing, every qualified lead has been followed up.

Consumer durables manufacturer. A maker of expensive consumer electronics gear enjoys an average sale of $1,200 per unit at retail, from which it realizes $700 per unit. Its share of its market niche is 60 percent, and the company needs an extra $1 million in revenue above forecast to meet venture capital investors' requirements. It hopes to stimulate extra sales with a dealer-referral lead program and advertising featuring a prominent 800-number in hobbyist publications.

It hires an inbound telemarketing service adept at asking callers about their existing systems and needs, designating the fulfillment literature to be mailed, and recommending local dealers that can demonstrate the product. The company needs to sell about 1,430 units to make its million, figuring the trade will reorder as consumers buy.

Dealers receive lead information from the telemarketers. Most attempt at least one follow-up call to inquirers in their area. The consensus at the company's annual dealer meeting, held adjacent to its industry's big trade show, is that 30 percent of inquirers eventually buy the types of components in the category, and that qualified inquirer sales seem to be equal to sales to walk-ins. Return-on-promotional-investment (ROPI) calculations therefore indicate that the company needs nearly 4,000 leads. But it recognizes that the ad campaign will draw inquiries from erstwhile walk-in customers, so it bumps its lead estimate up 25 percent, to 5,000 required leads.

Anticipating a $10 cost-per-lead for fulfillment and telemarketing, plus $120,000 in advertising, the company expects a cost-per-lead of $34 and average revenue-per-lead of $100. Competition is squeezing profit margins, however, and the cost-to-revenue mix is tight enough to make the marketing director nervous about whether the ad program will also stimulate an additional 700 walk-in sales as expected. As she runs what-if? scenarios through her computerized planning worksheets, she worries that her already high market share cannot grow much more. Then again, upgrading the equipment with a more powerful chip could expand the entire market rapidly and add price stability, she hopes.

Sales Quota Planning

Similar mathematics can determine the number of leads needed to support sales territory quotas. Say the product manager has to sell 990 units, the brand has a 20 percent share, and to support the product the company needs 11,000 leads spread over the year, or about 920 a month. The company has 25 salespeople, each needing about 37 leads a month, assuming they have the same quotas.

However, the New York rep has twice the quota of the Seattle rep, so the company must apportion leads accordingly. Direct mail, regional print and broadcast advertising, and outbound telemarketing can boost lead-generation in select regions.

Sales Return on Promotion

Return on promotional investment (ROPI) is not the same as a promotion program's return on investment (ROI) as that term is usually defined: ROPI focuses on the cost of generating leads required to meet sales goals; ROI is the incremental profit an investment generates. Decision makers calculate ROI to compare the value of different types of investments.

Yet another return calculation is sales return on promotion, which determines the dollar return on each ad dollar spent. The worksheet in Exhibit A-3 illustrates the math. Note that it credits advertising with two years of the purchases by the leads the advertising produced. For most companies, that is a more reasonable way to assess program return than looking at first-year purchases alone.

Rate Your Media

The best lead-management systems evaluate lead quality carefully, perhaps rating them on a multi-point scale such as A, B, C, and D leads in terms of their potential to be closed. That approach accommodates some of the trickier comparisons, such as rating a trade show's relatively small number of very high potential leads against a publication's large number of inquiries of unknown quality.

Exhibit A-3
Sales Return on Promotion

Period (From April 1, 1988 to March 31, 1989)	12 months
Advertising inquiries received	8,690
New customers converted	375
Percent of new customers converted	4.3%
Average sale per new customer	$720
Total sales for period linked to advertising leads	$269,881
Total sales for next 12 months linked to advertising leads in base period	$299,568
Cost of media in base period	$13,619
Dollar sale per dollar of advertising in base period	$19.82
Two-year sale per dollar of advertising in base period	$41.81

Exhibit A-4 shows a worksheet for adjusting the gross lead yield of each medium according to the mix of high- to low-quality leads it generates. Each inquiry has a weight, and weighted inquiry counts sum to each medium's and the overall program's net leads. That statistic becomes the lead variable in the ROPI equation. Use net lead yield rather than gross yield to calculate the cost-per-lead, making cost comparisons among media more meaningful. Dimensions other than the purchase-timing criterion shown in the example might be more meaningful to your sales and marketing plan.

The A, B, C, etc. percentages will change each time you receive inquiries from a medium. But as your database builds, relationships will stabilize into patterns you can rely on for planning.

Exhibit A-4
Inquiry Scoring Worksheet

MEDIUM	YIELD				*NET LEADS
Tabloid A	_____	A quality	×	1.0 =	_____
	_____	B quality	×	.75 =	_____
	_____	C quality	×	.5 =	_____
	_____	D quality	×	.25 =	_____
	_____	E quality	×	0.0 =	0
SUBTOTAL					_____
Technical Journal B	_____	A quality	×	1.0 =	_____
	_____	B quality	×	.75 =	_____
	_____	C quality	×	.5 =	_____
	_____	D quality	×	.25 =	_____
	_____	E quality	×	0.0 =	0
SUBTOTAL					_____
Big Industry Show	_____	A quality	×	1.0 =	_____
	_____	B quality	×	.75 =	_____
	_____	C quality	×	.5 =	_____
	_____	D quality	×	.25 =	_____
	_____	E quality	×	0.0 =	0
SUBTOTAL					_____
Very Vertical Show	_____	A quality	×	1.0 =	_____
	_____	B quality	×	.75 =	_____
	_____	C quality	×	.5 =	_____
	_____	D quality	×	.25 =	_____
	_____	E quality	×	0.0 =	0
SUBTOTAL					_____
Mail Program K	_____	A quality	×	1.0 =	_____
	_____	B quality	×	.75 =	_____
	_____	C quality	×	.5 =	_____
	_____	D quality	×	.25 =	_____
	_____	E quality	×	0.0 =	0
SUBTOTAL					_____
TOTAL NET LEADS					_____

A leads (immediate need) = 1.0 net lead
B leads (buy within six months) = 0.75 net lead
C leads (buy within a year) = 0.5 net lead
D leads (no buying plans: mailing list only) = 0.25 net lead
E leads (not presently qualified) = 0.0 net lead

*The yield adjustment shown here employs a rating system based on the inquirer's purchase timing. It could just as easily be based on other criteria such as anticipated purchase volume, company size, whether the purchase is budgeted, desire to see a sales rep, etc., or combinations of criteria.

Weighting can be multidimensional as well, requiring a lead adjustment formula such as this for ROPI modeling:

Net Leads = # Raw Leads × Weight Criterion #1
× Weight Criterion #2
× Weight Criterion #3, etc.

Weight criterion #1 could be purchase timing; #2, company size; #3, application, etc. Also you could vary the relationship among the weights assigned to A, B, C, etc. inquiries if, for example, an A lead is not twice as qualified as a C lead.

As a practical matter, that complexity usually is not required for ballpark planning estimates with the ROPI formula. Obtaining the right performance information for a simple analysis is usually daunting enough—unless a company has a lead-management database, programs that ensure adequate follow-up in the field, and periodic Did-You-Buy? studies collecting feedback directly from inquirers.

Appendix B

Inquiry Management Profile: Hewlett-Packard Analytical Products Group

Inquiry and sales lead management is a comprehensive and disciplined process at Hewlett-Packard (HP) Company's Analytical Products Group, where a constant effort to achieve system payback fuels a constant search for system improvements.

The Analytical Products Group generates inquiries primarily from advertising, direct marketing, public relations, and trade show exhibiting to support a sophisticated sales force selling complex instrumentation to highly trained professional buying influences. Group marketing activity focuses on its dominant product lines: equipment for gas and liquid chromatography, mass spectrometry and spectrophotometry equipment, sample preparation and handling systems, and analytical data systems. Individual product units range from $5,000 to $100,000 or more, not including a wide range of accessories, supplies, and consumables.

Relative to other high-technology industries, the analytical chemistry market is fairly mature, with a relatively stable prospect base. But that doesn't reduce HP's ardor for generating inquiries and providing comprehensive customer profile information to the field. The company considers inquiries an essential supplement to its sales force's sophisticated prospecting and market intelligence activities.

Marketing in the analytical instrument field has its challenges. Purchase decision cycles, for example, can run a year or longer, particularly for higher-priced instruments and systems. Multiple levels of purchase influencers within buyer organizations become involved in decisions, depending on equipment complexity, cost, and application. Bread-and-butter business comes from unit upgrades and replacements, and vendors also need to ensure that they don't miss the chance to bid on the occasional yet highly lucrative new laboratory installation. Maintaining support and full communication with the installed base is critical for suppliers. And, not surprisingly, competition consists of dozens of analytical equipment vendors from America, Europe, and Japan at each other's throats.

In other words, the potential stakes running on each sales lead are high. To Allen Owen who runs the inquiry program, the mission is unambiguous. "Our charter is to address sales issues driven by inquiry management and development." As marcom manager running the U.S. Analytical Marketing Center out of the Analytical Products Group's plant in Wilmington, Delaware, Mr. Owen and his department control communications budgets and scheduling as part of the Group's U.S. field sales operation.

A lean and no nonsense professional who joined HP from the rough-and-tumble software world, Mr. Owen demands system accountability: a "payback going in, and going out," as he puts it. "One thing to remember is that when customers contact us they provide a lot of information about themselves. I'm looking for ways to make that information more accessible to the field. Also, the performance reporting information that our inquiry handling service provides helps us to target our promotional investment to the areas that generate the best return for HP."

It's a process with room to grow, he acknowledges. "We're only at about 75 percent of where we'd like to be in this whole inquiry process. We're trying to improve our information handling capabilities," he explains, noting that he'd like to expand his current ability to track inquiries through to sales. He's currently working with his inquiry handling service to expand its database capabilities, for instance.

As his colleague, market research manager K.C. Warawa, puts it philosophically, "There are a million things we can do—in theory." As for actual practice, "We have a vision for our continuous improvement."

The Market Scenario

Analytical chemists are the targets in analytical laboratory equipment marketing. Denizens of giant corporate laboratories or proprietors of modest diagnostic and forensic labs located anywhere, those chemists use chromatography and other analytical techniques to detect the constituent parts of gas, liquid, and solid mixtures. In the arena where HP's Analytical Products Group shines, gas chromatography, or simply "GC" in the industry's parlance, the basic technology goes back to the 1950s. In liquid chromatography, "HPLC," Hewlett-Packard has been a player only since the mid-'70s.

Users' laboratory systems are likely to include a large number of instruments, data systems, and accessories for different kinds of analyses. A sale might well include items as routinely off-the-shelf as personal computers and plotters hooked up to the chromatographs. Technical advances, new software, and instrument and accessory enhancements are frequent in the field, however, making new product activity a vital part of the marketing job.

While use of the instruments is fairly straightforward, applying them to problem-solving can require a great deal of analytical prowess

A chief chemist, sometimes with Ph.D.-level skills, must establish workable methods for the instrument, make critical sensitivity adjustments for the detection task at hand and carefully prepare initial testing samples. Having defined the method, he can oftentimes turn things over to more junior chemists or technicians who apply the method in routine analyses. That's commonplace behavior in several market segments, including environmental testing where HP is a formidable player. "Our instruments can be used by people who aren't as highly trained as those who specify the acquisition," Mr. Owen explains. "That's an important plus in a market where technically skilled people are in short supply."

The sale includes a commitment to ongoing customer service. "In the analytical marketplace, manufacturers are expected to provide on-demand technical and applications assistance. Customers remain very involved with the manufacturer after they have acquired a system. It really is a partnership," Mr. Owen adds. "If you buy a PC from Apple, IBM, or HP, for example, the process of becoming productive is fairly straightforward. You set up your computer, install your software, and you're ready to go. Becoming productive on analytical systems isn't always that easy. Customers may need to have their staffs specially trained on the use of the instrument and on how to perform certain types of analyses.

"They will also want guarantees that their instruments are running without interruption, and that they can get technical advice when they need it. That's where our customer support organization comes in," he continues. Typically, HP prices its services, such as its Atlanta-based training and on-line customer support, on an à la carte basis.

Such customer-manufacturer relationships, when successful, make brand switching infrequent. "Once a system is in place, and a staff person has been trained in its use, there's a propensity to stay with the same manufacturer. You might have to change many of your methods and retrain your staff if you change platforms," says Mr. Owen. "In markets where HP is well represented, that preference works in our favor. But in markets where we are less well represented, it takes more marketing effort to get HP instruments in and our competitors out."

Big sales opportunities occur when a customer opens a new lab or entirely refits an existing facility. At that time, it's easier to switch to a new supplier. "It's not atypical for our competitors to try to break into a predominantly HP lab where they will offer a package deal to switch our instruments out and their instruments in," Mr. Owen continues. Oddly enough, on that rare occasion when a customer considers a competitor's offer, Owen maintains, HP's reputation for reliability and high resale value can hurt a bit. "It's very easy to do because HP instruments have good resale value. The competitor can hand them off to a reseller, who'll take them, refurbish and rent or resell them on the aftermarket."

Selling is largely by direct sales forces. The Analytical Products Group's field deployment, for competitive reasons described only as "fewer than 500 reps," requires highly trained specialists, most of whom are themselves trained analytical chemists. So-called "value-added businesses" service a variety of narrow niche markets, and represent a growing though still small market for HP, Mr. Owen says.

The Analytical Products Group's 1990 order volume of $592 million comprised just 4 percent of total Hewlett-Packard volume, the overall corporation's sales being dominated by measurement, manufacturing, and computing equipment and services. But the Group is a leading player in its field, trailing Perkin–Elmer with an estimated $700 to $750 million revenue. HP's Analytical Products Group achieved an 11 percent volume gain in 1990 vs. 1989, and 12 percent growth the year earlier.

Other competitors include household names like Hitachi, Seiko, Milipore, Philips, Varian, and Beckman Instruments, and a variety of more specialized firms. Across the entire analytical instrument field, more than 400 parent companies and subsidiaries vie for business in what became a comparatively flat market during the 1990–91 recession, compared to boom years in the 1980s. A few sectors glimmered with growth potential during the recession, including environmental testing, an HP long suit, and the biotechnology and pharmaceutical markets. More matured target segments, such as petroleum and chemical companies, have not been keeping pace, Mr. Owen notes.

HP has an industry-leading reputation for reliability and support, which is documented in numerous market surveys. This reliability reduces the chemist's cost of instrument ownership. "Chemists are price sensitive but they are also value conscious. If we can demonstrate the cost-effectiveness of the HP product, we can win every time, even when we are not the low bidder."

Inquiries Ensure Market Coverage

Analytical chemists always search for new capabilities and new products which allow them to conduct analyses they couldn't do before. Typically, they budget in the current year for purchases made in the following fiscal year. "Our customers attend trade shows to evaluate the products of various vendors, especially if they're considering buying hardware of a different class than they've already acquired, or they're interested in evaluating other than their current vendors."

Fortunately for suppliers, the nation's estimated 200,000 to 300,000 analytical chemists aren't frequent job-hoppers and don't share the storied peregrinations of, say, electronic engineers. "There's not nearly as much turnover in the industry. Chemists are very conservative and, unfortunately, theirs is not a growing community," Ms. Warawa explains.

But that doesn't make finding purchase influencers foolproof, because the more expensive and complex the purchase, the more chemists get involved at a company. Purchasing people, as in many technology fields, usually play a support role; chemists, particularly heavyweights such as the 120,000 senior-level members of the American Chemical Society, specify the purchase.

Naturally, it's each salesperson's job to keep track of the players. Indeed, most seem to have pretty good programs. "Like all sales reps they have their own techniques for finding new business," Mr. Owen continues. "They have a steady group of accounts they call on a regular basis. They reference local business publications and keep their ears to the ground for new labs going in, or for new equipment purchases planned. They have tight relationships with other vendors who pass information along to them about new facilities. They also know the accounts where they are not represented but would like to be, so they call on those accounts regularly.

"Inquiries are only one of their information sources, and perhaps not the most important one. But I wish I could say it were. A majority of the prospecting is still a field-based activity. We do supply them with a steady diet of inquiries, a way for them to know a customer has inquired about a technique or technology, but some salespeople claim that nine out of ten inquiries are from people they already know."

Is the "90 percent known" claim of the field force accurate? Mr. Owen can compare inquirers' names with sales reps call lists, but, "We don't routinely compute it," he says. "We have seen the 'unknown prospect' ratio as high as 40 percent for a good trade show, but some of this can be attributed to computerized record-matching routines that do not adequately address actual database matches. The inquiry program probably has greater impact than the sales rep gives it credit for, but we will need better data systems to actually map our performance."

For competitive reasons, HP won't discuss its inquiry volume or costs per inquiry—or its costs per qualified lead, to the extent it calculates that statistic for selected marketing communications projects. Suffice it to say that even with only one in ten inquiries reportedly providing a new prospect name to the field, the Analytical Products Group sees fit to keep its inquiry system humming.

The Group relies on four main inquiry-source types: advertising; direct response, primarily mail; trade show exhibiting; and publicity. "There are discrete information channels to the analytical community," Mr. Owen points out. "Chemists read certain publications and attend certain trade shows. You can use direct mail, and in some cases even the telephone. A discrete, finite community, they are easily targetable, and there are ways to reach most of the people you want to talk to."

Each medium produces a roughly equivalent number of inquiries for the Group, he reveals, but with varying costs per inquiry and varying quality. Publicity, budgeted at much smaller amounts, produces a less expensive inquiry. But publicity—technical articles, new product releases and new literature announcements—on average produces the least qualified leads, he explains.

Trade shows, particularly the analytical instrument industry's annual Pittcon extravaganza, provide the best qualified inquiries to the Group. That's hardly surprising to sales reps; manning the Group's booth and prescreening prospects is recognition for superior selling talent. The Group attends "fewer than 50" shows a year, mostly regional events and national specialized conferences.

The big Pittcon event, for which the Group assembles its formidable 5,000 sq.-ft. island exhibit, is known formally as the Pittsburgh Conference, a privately owned show founded in that city during the 1950s but usually held in other venues. The "value-added businesses," integrators through which the Group sells to specialized market niches, also show up in booths nearby, like satellites to the mother ship. Some 12,000 to 16,000 buying influences attend the show each year, Ms. Warawa estimates.

Notes Mr. Owen, "We only have qualified people representing us in the booth, because of the degree of technical knowledge you need to define a customer's requirements. All of our reps in the booth are highly qualified." Most of them are trained analytical chemists.

And all of them know not to simply give out literature at the show. In fact, HP and most other Pittsburgh Conference exhibitors don't pass out literature at the event, he explains. "We don't even bring it with us. We'd prefer to capture the customer name and profile in exchange for the sending of literature after the event."

Each show produces different information, as reps in the booth complete inquiry questionnaires on promising-looking booth visitors. The Group packs the paperwork off to the inquiry-management service at the end of a show for immediate fulfillment and forwarding to the field, "largely so we can improve the turnaround cycle to the customer," explains Mr. Owen. The service draws the appropriate literature from the shelf, and includes a bounceback card plus information providing customers with the names of their local HP representatives.

For each inquiry, field salespeople receive HP's standard inquiry report, a paper form indicating the prospect's name, company, address, phone number, title, organization type, department, product interest, applications and type of testing conducted, the inquirer's purchasing time frame, whether he or she receives HP's *Peak* magazine, and whether and when a rep should call with what information.

Field feedback generally stays with field management and, at present, does not return to Mr. Owen's department for database updating. Gathering more follow-up and tracking information is part of the Group's long-range plan, however.

Inquiries and the Media Mix

The average analytical chemist reads four to five business publications, so the Analytical Products Group responds accordingly with a year-round ad schedule designed to produce a steady flow of inquiries. Advertising messages, typically single color pages, hardly shy away from the pitch the Group has for the marketplace. "Finally, a real GC/MS for under $50,000!" screams one headline. "Stack up our HPLC modules for a 20 percent saving," says another.

But price appeal isn't the only hand played by the Group. Other headlines cite user benefits, such as, "How to break through the productivity bottleneck," and "When integrating your laboratories, you want the gain, not the pain."

Other approaches claim outright HP superiority, such as "Our new HPLC is built on an excellent foundation," and "You made the HP5890 the industry standard GC. . . . We just made it better."

The Group doesn't use in-ad coupons often; it relies mainly on inbound toll-free response calls and reader service card replies, all of which go directly to the outside service for product literature fulfillment within 72 hours and forwarding to the field.

Inbound 800-numbers, printed in boldface at the close of each ad's copy, feature different extension numbers depending on the ad and product. The inquiry service's inbound telephone reps follow a scripted questionnaire with check boxes to collect information for the field. Operators ask callers for:

- Name, address, and phone numbers;
- The product literature, sales office or other information they would like to receive;
- Testing technology used;
- The types of test conducted;

- The inquirer's type of organization (hospital, industry, etc.);
- Type of material tested;
- Purchase time frame;
- Whether the inquirer currently uses the technology featured in the ad.

If the caller asks a technical question beyond the scope of the questionnaire, the telephone rep refers the caller to his or her local HP sales rep.

Each advertisement, produced by HP's central marketing communications operation on the West Coast, must follow a standard format. The Analytical Products Group has a representative on the communications committee. Once a product is developed and starts shipping to the field, field communications, such as Mr. Owen's department, take over actual ad program scheduling and budgeting specifically to generate inquiries.

Yet response is not HP's sole advertising objective. As Mr. Owen believes, "Advertising provides overall image and awareness benefits, rather than just a quantity of inquiries." Objectives such as market awareness, however, "are not as easy to measure. But it's something we will begin to measure," he acknowledges. "We know that advertising provides a benefit in stimulating awareness in the market, and we need to quantify that."

Media selection is a straightforward process. A variety of horizontal publications serve analytical chemists across industries, and a few verticals specialize in specific market niches. Regional publications such as those published by the American Chemical Society also fit into the plan.

If publishers provide postcard decks, the Group will use them on occasion. It finds they produce a quality and quantity of inquiries similar to display ads, Mr. Owen reports.

Tracking data prepared by the outside service yields total inquiries per publication and insertion, providing planning information. But inquiry totals aren't numbers to be followed slavishly, Mr. Owen cautions. "Using techniques that boost inquiry counts can often reduce inquiry quality as well. A program may call for only a few high-quality inquiries."

Most publications on the schedule provide reader service card (bingo) responses, which they send directly to the Group's inquiry management service. But once fulfilled, bingo inquiries usually go directly to the field without further qualification.

The outside service will qualify reader service card inquiries via outbound telemarketing on special projects, however. And the service may conduct follow-up and Did-You-Buy? studies by phone. Yet the Group is sensitive to the need for trained specialists handling such calls. Although the service's scripts are adequate for inbound, information-gathering-and-fulfillment phone conversations, generalists cannot handle the more interactive outbound contact. "Non-chemists don't have the technical expertise to discuss customer requirements. The words just don't roll off your tongue," explains Ms. Warawa. Technical telemarketing firms, and at times ex-HP employees, are pressed into service for much of the outbound work.

Direct marketing by the Group relies heavily on the mail, a medium that suits Mr. Owen's inquiries-to-the-field objectives well. Each program includes a reply card returned directly to the inquiry management service.

Publicity, run by HP's West Coast departments, generates more casual inquiries for the Analytical Products Group, but at less overall cost than other media used. HP engineers are expected to bolster their careers with some technical writing. And a steady stream of product announcements and new literature releases rounds out the program.

The Analytical Products Group also publishes a customer magazine named *Peak,* a reference to the output of a chromatographic data-handling device. The magazine provides applications and product information of interest to the customer base, and includes a bounceback card should the reader like to request additional information.

Tracking Performance

None of those inquiry-generating activities go unnoticed by the field sales force. Each month reps receive a confidential "AMC Update" report that provides a comprehensive listing of current inquiry-generation projects.

The report booklet includes photocopies of all current advertising and direct mail pieces, a description of all recent publicity releases, and schedules for media placement, industry events, training programs, and technical seminars. It keeps the field posted on the forms used in the inquiry program, and updates the field's phone list should there be product questions needing instant answers. The philosophy behind "AMC Update" is the same as guides the entire inquiry program. "The thing that improves (the field reps') sense of contribution by the program is the amount of information they receive," Mr. Owen maintains.

The Analytical Products Group hired its outside supplier, San Fernando, California–based Inquiry Handling Service Inc., in 1988 to ensure fast literature fulfillment. A specialist can do that work faster and more cost-effectively than the Group can in-house, Mr. Owen reasons. Since he joined HP in 1990, he's seeking additional service from the supplier.

One enhancement is having a strong impact on the quality of data reported to the field: improved database management that allows the Group to spot the names of inquirers who've inquired before. Inbound 800-line operators have on-line access to the HP database. When the operator enters the name of the caller, the system matchs it to the database. If it finds a match, it displays the name, address, company affiliation, etc., for the operator to verify. If the caller has inquired before, the screen displays that information, indicating the number of times the person has inquired, and the source, date, and subject of the most recent inquiry.

More information to the field improves inquiry follow-up. Ms. Warawa and Mr. Owen won't reveal follow-up ratios, although they acknowledge overall performance could be better. The Group doesn't fly blind without information, however. It does receive feedback from field management, and Mr. Owen says the Group runs its own summary analyses off the inquiry service's data tapes. The service provides routine, regular monthly reports: inquiries by project, product, sales territory, and medium. When necessary for special projects, the service reports weekly.

Down the road, conducting more Did-You-Buy? surveys will give him more system diagnostics. Eventually, he hopes to profile individuals, to further refine territory and marketing communication project analyses.

Mr. Owen's conceptual goal is to track inquiries comprehensively through the sale and, more important, get more robust data into salespeople's hands. "Our sales reps get a lot of data, and we have to refine it as much as possible, perhaps making its access user-defined: supplying data on disk, for example, would allow field personnel to conduct their own analyses." HP reps regularly use laptop computers to access corporate databases and manage their territories.

Appendix C

Notes

EDITING NOTE: Endnotes not edited for repeat references (e.g., op.cit., ibid., loc.cit.).

Introduction

1. The lead volume estimate is based on our experience with more than 200 clients of Inquiry Handling Service, Inc., imputed to national business-to-business marketing communications volume. Our data include an independent analysis, by Earl I. Wilson & Associates, of more than 2,000 Did-You-Buy? survey questionnaires completed by those who have directed inquiries to those clients.

2. *Cahners Advertising Research Report No. 210.5C,* (Newton, Ma.: Cahners Publishing Co., 1993).

3. *Reader Action Report: 22 Years of Advertising Effectiveness Research,* (Cleveland: New Equipment Digest, 1990), p. 47.

4. *Cahners Advertising Research Report No. 210.71,* (Newton, Ma.: Cahners Publishing Co., 1990).

Chapter 1

1. *Penton Research Overview Reports No. 101B* (Cleveland: Penton Publishing Co., 1993).

2. Inquiry Handling Service, Inc. estimates adjusting trade press reports for inflation.

3. "Measured U.S. Ad Spending by Category and Media," *Advertising Age* (Jan. 3, 1994): p. 24.

4. Frederick Reichheld, "Loyalty and the Renaissance of Marketing," *Marketing Management* vol. 2, No. 4 (1993): p. 10.

5. Adrian J. Slywotzky and Benson P. Shapiro, "Leveraging to Beat the Odds; The New Marketing Mind-Set," *Harvard Business Review* (Sept.–Oct. 1993): pp. 97–107.

6. Adrian J. Slywotzky and Benson P. Shapiro, "Leveraging to Beat the Odds; The New Marketing Mind-Set," *Harvard Business Review* (Sept.–Oct. 1993): pp. 97–107.

7. Alliances allow companies to integrate critical processes such as just-in-time inventory management and share production information and technologies more intimately than traditional arms-length relationships permit. Partnering has its

downside, however. Even when objective business reasons make alliances look good on paper, "It has been very difficult for managers to adjust to these changes, as partnerships have not been viewed as a natural part of a firm's strategic planning processes," write professors Robert Spekman and David T. Wilson, who observe that most strategic alliances fail. See Robert E. Spekman and David T. Wilson, *Managing Strategic Partnerships: Toward an Understanding of Control Mechanisms and Their Impact On Partnership Formation and Maintenance,* ISBM Report 6–1991, (University Park, Pa.: Institute for the Study of Business Markets, Penn State University, 1991).

8. *Penton Research Overview Reports No. 109,* (Cleveland: Penton Publishing Co., 1993).
9. "What Happened to Advertising?" *Business Week* (Sept. 23, 1991): p. 66.
10. *Profiting from Industrial Advertising Sales Leads,* (Cleveland: Penton Publishing, 1991), p. 13.
11. *Inquiry Cards: Their Sales Potential and How to Exploit It,* Report No. 25 (Princeton, N.J.: Center for Marketing Communications, 1976), p. 19–23. The Center of Marketing Communications is now part of the Advertising Research Foundation, New York.
12. *Cahners Advertising Research Report No. 210.12,* (Newton, Ma.: Cahners Publishing Co., 1989).
13. *Cahners Advertising Research Report Nos. 240.23A and 240.2B,* (Newton, Ma.: Cahners Publishing Co., 1993).
14. *Industrial Equipment News* unpublished subscriber survey PR43C-1089, May 1991, p. 11. The research is part of that publication's ongoing research into inquirer behavior.
15. *Inquiry Cards: Their Sales Potential and How to Exploit It,* Report No. 25 (Princeton, N.J.: Center for Marketing Communications, 1976), p. 19–23. The Center of Marketing Communications is now part of the Advertising Research Foundation, New York.
16. *Industrial Equipment News* unpublished subscriber survey PR43C-1089, May 1991, p. 29.
17. *Cahners Advertising Research Report No. 210.12,* (Newton, Ma.: Cahners Publishing Co., 1989).
18. *Reader Action Report: 22 Years of Advertising Effectiveness Research,* (Cleveland: New Equipment Digest, 1990), p. 47.
19. *Cahners Advertising Research Report No. 210.9A,* (Newton, Ma.: Cahners Publishing Co., 1993).
20. Bob Donath, *Business Marketing 1993–2003: Increasingly Information Intensive,* ISBM Report 14–1993, (University Park, Pa.: Institute for the Study of Business Markets, Penn State University, 1993), p. 20.
21. George R. Frerichs, Inc., *Know the Buyer Better,* (Cleveland: Penton Publishing Co., 1990), p. 14.
22. U.S. Department of Labor statistics quoted in George R. Frerichs, Inc., *Know the Buyer Better,* (Cleveland: Penton Publishing Co., 1990), p. 61.
23. George R. Frerichs, Inc., *Know the Buyer Better,* (Cleveland: Penton Publishing Co., 1990), p. 14, 21, 57, 61.
24. *Industrial Equipment News* unpublished subscriber survey PR43C-1089, May 1991, p. 29.

25. George R. Frerichs, Inc., *Know the Buyer Better,* (Cleveland: Penton Publishing Co., 1990), p. 59.
26. Earl I. Wilson & Associates studies for Inquiry Handling Service, Inc. In the aggregate, the results are based on more than 2,000 did-you-buy survey questionnaires completed by those who inquired of 23 IHS clients.
27. *Cahners Advertising Research Report No. 210.5C,* (Newton, Ma.: Cahners Publishing Co., 1993).
28. *Reader Action Report: 22 Years of Advertising Effectiveness Research,* (Cleveland: New Equipment Digest, 1990), p. 47.
29. Allen Owen, marketing communications manager of Hewlett-Packard Analytical Products Group. Interview, Aug. 28, 1991.

Chapter 2

1. Dartnell Corporation, *26th Survey of Sales Force Compensation,* quoted in "1993 Sales manager's Budget Planner," *Sales & Marketing Management* (June 28, 1993): p. 75.
2. William O'Connell, "A Ten Year Report on Sales Force Productivity," *Sales & Marketing Management* (Dec. 1988): p. 33.
3. *Cahners Advertising Research Report No. 542.1H,* (Newton, Ma.: Cahners Publishing Co., 1992).
4. "1993 Sales Manager's Budget Planner," *Sales & Marketing Management* (June 28, 1993): p. 65.
5. *Cahners Advertising Research Report Nos. 542.2D, 542.21B and 542.9B,* (Newton, Ma.: Cahners Publishing Co., 1992).
6. "1993 Sales Manager's Budget Planner," *Sales & Marketing Management* (June 28, 1993): p. 6.
7. By Cahners' count, the number of calls required to close varies by industry, with manufacturing requiring 4.4 calls on average, and the average service sale needing 2.7. See, *Cahners Advertising Research Report No. 542.5C,* (Newton, Ma.: Cahners Publishing Co., 1992).
8. Richard Brock, comments entitled "Sales Force Automation" to the "Power Selling '91" conference, Chicago, Sept. 10–13, 1991.
9. *Ten Years of Trade Show Bureau Reports in Ten Minutes* vol. 2, (Denver: Trade Show Bureau, 1991), p. 3–4.
10. *Reader Action Report: 22 Years of Advertising Effectiveness Research,* (Cleveland: New Equipment Digest, 1990), p. 47.
11. Cahners polled more than 9,000 inquirers; 94 percent of those responding said they had not seen a salesperson from the advertiser involved. See *Cahners Advertising Research Report No. 220.1,* (Newton, Ma.: Cahners Publishing Co., 1977).
12. *Cahners Advertising Research Report No. 210.9A,* (Newton, Ma.: Cahners Publishing Co., 1993).
13. "Reaching the Unknown Prospect—Trade Show Visitors Not Reached by Regular Sales Calls," *Trade Show Bureau Research Report AC/1120,* (Denver: Trade Show Bureau, 1990).
14. Richard K. Swandby, Jonathan M. Cox, and Ian K. Sequeira, "Trade Shows Poised for 1990s Growth," *Business Marketing* (May 1990): p. 46.

15. *Cahners Advertising Research Report No. 542.6,* (Newton, Ma.: Cahners Publishing Co., 1992).

16. *Penton Research Overview Reports No. 218,* (Cleveland: Penton Publishing Co., 1993).

17. *Profiting from Industrial Advertising Sales Leads,* (Cleveland: Penton Publishing, 1991) p. 16.

18. Bernie McDonald, speech October 7, 1991 to American Marketing Assn. conference, "Implementing Customer Satisfaction in Industrial Product and Service Markets."

19. *Cahners Advertising Research Report No. 210.6B,* (Newton, Ma.: Cahners Publishing Co., 1993).

20. The TF Club of Detroit, an advertising trade association, commissioned Erdos and Morgan, a respected independent research firm, to study the value business-to-business salespeople, distributors, and manufacturer's representatives believe they receive from advertising inquiries. Among the results:
    - 71 percent said inquiries pointed out new prospects in current markets.
    - 60 percent said inquiries provided leads to new prospects in new markets.
    - 66 percent said inquiries led them to new sales opportunities with their current customers.

    See, *Cahners Advertising Research Report No. 210.8,* (Newton, Ma.: Cahners Publishing Co., 1989).

21. For example, a survey for the Purchasing Management Association of Northern California found going around purchasing to be the biggest complaint PAs have with vendor salespeople. See, Milt Grassel, "What Purchasing Managers Like in a Salesperson . . . and What Drives Them Up the Wall," *Business Marketing* (June 1986): p. 72.

22. *Cahners Advertising Research Report No. 551.1A,* (Newton, Ma.: Cahners Publishing Co., 1984).

23. *Profiting from Industrial Advertising Sales Leads,* (Cleveland: Penton Publishing, 1991) p. 4, 45.

24. Unusual research on the subject corroborates attitudes we've seen repeatedly. A survey asked more than 430 business-to-business marketing communications executives about satisfaction with their programs. While 91 percent of those satisfied also had inquiry-management systems, just 83 percent of the dissatisfied managers had an inquiry system. Those satisfied also were much more likely to engage in formal communications planning and research, and use more marketing communications tools than the dissatisfied group. A separate study by the same researchers found 9 out of 10 business and industrial marketers rating inquiry handling as "important," yet 27 percent of respondents acknowledged that they had no structured way of working with their inquiries. See *C.U.R.E. For Business Marketers,* (Chicago: Starmark, Inc., 1988), and *Here's What Really Matters to Today's Business-to-Business Marketer,* (Chicago: Starmark, Inc., 1988).

25. Bob Donath, "Marcom Seeks Its Mission for '90s," *Marketing News* (Aug. 16, 1993): p. 5.

26. A regression analysis of the readership score-to-lead connection, a one-of-a-kind study, found a "weak but statistically significant" relationship between reader-service card inquiries and ad readership "noticed" scores. About 27 percent of

variation in inquiry response could be explained by variations in readership scores. See, Perry Patterson, "Readership & Response: There's a Weak Relationship," *Business Marketing* (Feb. 1987): p. 84.

Chapter 3

1. *Cahners Advertising Research Report No. 210.6B,* (Newton, Ma.: Cahners Publishing Co., 1993).
2. *Reader Action Report: 22 Years of Advertising Effectiveness Research,* (Cleveland: New Equipment Digest, 1990), p. 47.
3. *Cahners Advertising Research Report No. 240.4A,* (Newton, Ma.: Cahners Publishing Co., 1990).
4. *Inquiry Cards: Their Potential and How to Exploit It,* (Princeton, N.J.: Center for Marketing Communications, 1976), p. 1. The successor to the Center for Marketing Communications is the Advertising Research Foundation, New.
5. George R. Frerichs, Inc., *Know the Buyer Better,* (Cleveland: Penton Publishing Co., 1990), p. 77.
6. B.G. Yovovich, "A New Set of Players Drives Technology Purchases, Study Finds," *Business Marketing* (April 1992): p. 12.
7. Jim Holden, "Selling to Buying Committees," *Business Marketing* (December 1983): p. 30.
8. Elizabeth J. Wilson, Gary L. Lilien, and David T. Wilson, "Developing and Testing a Contingency Paradigm of Group Choice in Organizational Buying," *Journal of Marketing Research,* vol. 28 (November 1991): pp. 452–66.
9. *Inquiry Cards: Their Potential and How to Exploit It,* (Princeton, N.J.: Center for Marketing Communications, 1976), p. 3. The successor to the Center for Marketing Communications is the Advertising Research Foundation, New York.
10. *Industrial Equipment News* unpublished subscriber survey PR43C-1089, May 1991, p. 30.
11. *The Blue Chip Advertiser's Research Study,* (Randolph, N.J.: Gordon Publications, Inc., 1985), p. 45.
12. *Penton Research Overview Reports No. 111,* (Cleveland: Penton Publishing Co., 1993).
13. *Penton Research Overview Reports No. 221,* (Cleveland: Penton Publishing Co., 1993).
14. *Penton Research Overview Reports No. 221,* (Cleveland: Penton Publishing Co., 1993).
15. *Cahners Advertising Research Report Nos. 550,1A and 103.1B,* (Newton, Ma.: Cahners Publishing Co., 1990).
16. *Cahners Advertising Research Report No. 120.13,* (Newton, Ma.: Cahners Publishing Co., 1992).
17. *Cahners Advertising Research Report No. 240.23A,* (Newton, Ma.: Cahners Publishing Co., 1993).
18. Roger W. Brucker, "Bingo Card Junkies: Why They Could Be Your Best Prospects," *Business Marketing* (February 1985): p. 102.
19. Richard Brock presentation to joint conference of the MKIS User Forum and the Institute for the Study of Business Markets, March 1, 1994, St. Petersburg, Florida.

20. *Cahners Advertising Research Report No. 140.2B,* (Newton, Ma.: Cahners Publishing Co., 1990).
21. *Industrial Equipment News,* unpublished reader focus group response study, April 27, 1990, p. 7.
22. *Profiting from Industrial Advertising Sales Leads,* (Cleveland: Penton Publishing, 1991) p. 2.
23. Jennifer Cody, "Marketing: More 800 Lines to Dial, More Callers Using Them," *The Wall Street Journal* (Dec. 28, 1993): p. B1.
24. *Industrial Equipment News,* unpublished subscriber survey PR43C-1089, May 1991, p. 29.
25. David Allen, publisher of *Computer Design* magazine. Interview, Sept. 17, 1991.
26. *Industrial Equipment News,* unpublished subscriber survey PR43C-1089, May 1991, p. 15.
27. *Industrial Equipment News,* unpublished reader focus group response study, April 27, 1990, p. 12.
28. *Cahners Advertising Research Report No. 250.22,* (Newton, Ma.: Cahners Publishing Co., 1988).
29. Dale W. Ludlum, "Researching an Inquiry Myth," *Industrial Marketing* (February 1983): p. 61.

Chapter 4

1. *Here's What Really Matters to Today's Business-to-Business Marketer,* (Chicago: Starmark, Inc. and *Business Marketing* magazine, 1988), p. 15.
2. Dartnell Corp. sales research, Chicago.
3. Peter H. Farquhar, Julia Y. Han, and Yuji Ijiri, "Brands on the Balance Sheet," *Marketing Management* (Winter 1992): pp. 16–22.

Chapter 5

1. The American Business Press asked about publication editorial *and* advertising together. The exhibition industry's own survey of how show-attending business "decision makers" rate "extremely useful sources of purchasing information," separates publication editorial and advertising. That puts trade shows ahead of the pack: a 91 percent rating for shows compared to 86 percent for publication articles and 66 for publication advertisements. See *The Power of Trade Shows* (Denver: Trade Show Bureau, 1992).
2. Valerie Kijewski, "Use Marketing Communications to Drive Price," *Journal of Pricing Management* 2 (Winter 1991): pp. 19–22.
   For a complete review of the market performance relationships revealed in the PIMS database, see Robert D. Buzzell and Bradley T. Gale, *The PIMS Principles: Linking Strategy to Performance* (New York: The Free Press, 1987).
3. *Cahners Advertising Research Report No. 210.7A,* (Newton, Ma.: Cahners Publishing Co., 1989).
4. Carl Quintanilla and Richard Gibson, "'Do Call Us': More Companies Install 1-800 Phone Lines," *The Wall Street Journal,* (April 20, 1994): p. B1.
5. *Profiting from Industrial Advertising Sales Leads* (Cleveland: Penton Publishing Co., 1991), p. 39.

6. *Profiting from Industrial Advertising Sales Leads* (Cleveland: Penton Publishing Co., 1991), p. 39.

7. "The Effectiveness of Using Promotional Products at Trade Shows," *Trade Show Bureau Report No. MC23B,* (Denver: Trade Show Bureau, 1992).

8. *Profiting from Industrial Advertising Sales Leads* (Cleveland: Penton Publishing Co., 1991), p. 38.

9. Susan T. Grauff, *Communications Organizations Today and in the Future* (Alexandria, Va.: Business Marketing Association, 1993).

10. *Cahners Advertising Research Report No. 501.2,* (Newton, Ma.: Cahners Publishing Co., 1992).

11. Frederick F. Reichheld, "Loyalty and the Renaissance of Marketing," *Marketing Management,* 2 (Fall 1993): p. 10–21.

Chapter 6

1. *1993 Inquiry Performance Survey,* (San Fernando, CA: Inquiry Handling Service, Inc., 1994)

2. Robert J. Coen, "Ad Gain of 5.2% in '93 Marks Downturn's End," *Advertising Age* (May 2, 1994): p. 4.

3. "What Happened to Advertising?" *Business Week* (Sept. 23, 1991): pp. 66–72.

4. Andrew J. Parsons, "Focus and Squeeze: Consumer Marketing in the '90," *Marketing Management* 1 (Winter 1992): pp. 51–55.

5. Arguably still the most quoted source correlating advertising with perceived quality, market share, sales, and profit, the Profit Impact of Market Strategies (PIMS) database contains extensive performance records from about 3,000 consumer and business product and service business units. See Robert D. Buzzell and Bradley T. Gale, *The PIMS Principles: Linking Strategy to Performance* (New York: The Free Press, 1987).

   Cahners Publishing tracked similar effects working solely with industrial business information in the PIMS database. See *Cahners Advertising Research Report Nos. 2100.01 through 2100.10,* (Newton, Ma.: Cahners Publishing Co., 1989).

   In a classic series of business-to-business studies encompassing 12 major business advertisers, researcher John Morrill found that more advertising teamed with more sales calls on prospects correlated with 40 percent larger market shares on average than did more sales calls alone. Greater share often allows lower-cost production and creates more market clout and consequent profit. See John E. Morrill, "Industrial Advertising Pays Off" *Harvard Business Review* 48 (March–April 1970): pp. 4–14.

   The most ambitious field experiment to test business advertising effects on a real-time basis divided industrial test markets, exposing otherwise identical segments to different levels of specialized business publication advertising. The researchers—the Advertising Research Foundation and the American Business Press, Inc.—surveyed each buyer group and measured inquiry response and buying behavior. A very ambitious undertaking subject to many data collection problems, the study did provide evidence that relatively high levels of advertising produce more inquiries, more sales, and more profit than moderate or low levels of advertising. See the sponsors' own report: *The Impact of Business Publication*

Advertising on Sales and Profits (New York: American Business Press, 1987). For a journalistic analysis of what the study found what it did not, see: Bob Donath, "ARF/ABP Study Confirms It: Advertising Works" and "The Numbers Behind the Research News" *Business Marketing* (November 1986): pp. 74–90.

Also, advertising levels might have to surpass minimum thresholds to have an effect on market perceptions. Research in the semiconductor industry found an S-curve effect for business advertising. Brand preference grew only when advertising weight exceeded a minimum level. See Valerie Kijewski and Eunsang Yoon, *The Brand Awareness to Preference Link in the International Semiconductor Manufacturing Industry,* ISBM Report 12–1990, (University Park, Pa.: Institute for the Study of Business Markets, Penn State University, 1990).

6. Bob Donath, "ARF/ABP Study Confirms It: Advertising Works" and "The Numbers Behind the Research News" *Business Marketing* (November 1986): pp. 74–90.

7. Steven W. Hartley and Charles H. Patti, "Evaluating Business-to-Business Advertising: A Comparison of Objectives and Results" *Journal of Advertising Research* (April–May 1988): pp. 21–27, as cited in Charles H. Patti, Steven W. Hartley and Susan L. Kennedy, *Business to Business Advertising: A Marketing Management Approach* (Lincolnwood, Ill.: NTC Business Books, 1991) pp. 106–113.

8. James G. Kimball, "Mad Dash to Online," *Business Marketing* (March 1994): p. 11.

9. Riccardo A. Davis, "New Advertisers Limit Outdoor Loss," *Advertising Age* (March 15, 1993): p. 40–47.

10. Tom Eisenhart, "What's Right, What's Wrong with Each Medium," *Business Marketing* (April 1990): p. 40–47.

11. "Washington Wire," *The Wall Street Journal* (Jan. 21, 1994): p. 1.

12. Tim Triplett, "Big Names Crowd the Infomercial Airwaves," *Marketing News,* (March 28, 1994): p. 1.

13. "TV Shoppers Are Satisfied," *Marketing News* (Nov. 22, 1993): p. 1.

14. Mark Robichaux, "Highway of Hype," *The Wall Street Journal* (Nov. 29, 1993): p. A1.

15. *Cahners Advertising Research Report No. 442.2B,* (Newton, Ma.: Cahners Publishing Co., 1990).

16. *Industrial Equipment News,* unpublished reader focus group response study, April 27, 1990, p. 11.

17. *Industrial Equipment News,* unpublished subscriber survey PR43C-1089, May 1991, p. 6.

18. *Cahners Advertising Research Report No. 450.4,* (Newton, Ma.: Cahners Publishing Co., 1985).

19. Kate Bertrand, "Catalog Choices," *Business Marketing* (May 1992): p. 43–44.

20. *Cahners Advertising Research Report No. 501.1,* (Newton, Ma.: Cahners Publishing Co., 1984).

21. *Cahners Advertising Research Report No. 501.2,* (Newton, Ma.: Cahners Publishing Co., 1992).

22. *Cahners Advertising Research Report Nos. 211.1A & 412.0,* (Newton, Ma.: Cahners Publishing Co., 1988).

23. *Cahners Advertising Research Report No. 411.1B,* (Newton, Ma.: Cahners Publishing Co., 1992).

24. To examine the method in more detail, see: John M. Klock, "Simple, Efficient Media Selection," *Business Marketing* (March 1982): p. 102.
25. See selected *Cahners Advertising Research Report No. 411.1B,* (Newton, Ma.: Cahners Publishing Co., 1993).
26. *Cahners Advertising Research Report No. 413.3A,* (Newton, Ma.: Cahners Publishing Co., 1992).
27. *Cahners Advertising Research Report Nos. 413.1A & 413.2A,* (Newton, Ma.: Cahners Publishing Co., 1988).
28. *Cahners Advertising Research Report Nos. 4120.1 & 120.12,* (Newton, Ma.: Cahners Publishing Co., 1992).
29. American Business Press, Inc. data reported in "The Case for Frequency," *Metalworking Marketer* (March 1992): p. 2.
30. *Cahners Advertising Research Report No. 3000.6,* (Newton, Ma.: Cahners Publishing Co., 1989).
31. Joan Treistman, "Where the Reader Eye Roams," *Business Marketing* (April 1984): p. 110.
32. *Cahners Advertising Research Report No. 430.1A,* (Newton, Ma.: Cahners Publishing Co., 1993).
33. *Cahners Advertising Research Report No. 440.22,* (Newton, Ma.: Cahners Publishing Co., 1988).
34. Cahners Advertising Research Report No. 116.2B, (Newton, Ma.: Cahners Publishing Co., 1990).
35. Joan Treistman, "Where the Reader Eye Roams," *Business Marketing* (April 1984): p. 110.
36. *Cahners Advertising Research Report No. 430.2A* (Newton, Ma.: Cahners Publishing Co., 1990).
37. *Cahners Advertising Research Report No. 116.2B,* (Newton, Ma.: Cahners Publishing Co., 1990).
38. Joan Treistman, "Where the Reader Eye Roams," *Business Marketing* (April 1984): p. 110.
39. *Cahners Advertising Research Report No. 150.1,* (Newton, Ma.: Cahners Publishing Co., 1979).
40. Perry Patterson, "Readership & Response: There's a Weak Relationship," *Business Marketing* (February 1987): p. 84
41. Sue Kapp, "Media Beat: When Ads Aren't Equal," *Business Marketing* (September 1989): p. 53.
42. Sue Kapp, "Second-Cover Ads Take First," *Business Marketing* (Feb. 1990): p. 28.
43. Joan Treistman, "Where the Reader Eye Roams," *Business Marketing* (April 1984): p. 110.
44. *Cahners Advertising Research Report No. 118.5,* (Newton, Ma.: Cahners Publishing Co., 1991).
45. R.J. Lavidge and G.A. Steiner, "A Model for Predictive Measurement of Advertising Effectiveness," *Journal of Marketing* 25 (1961): pp. 59–62.
46. *Starch Tested Copy* vol. 1, no. 6, Starch INRA Hooper, Inc., Mamaroneck, N.Y., as quoted in *Marketing News Extra* (Winter 1993), newsletter published by the American Marketing Assn.
47. *Cahners Advertising Research Report No. 110.1B,* (Newton, Ma.: Cahners Publishing Co., 1990).

48. *Profiting from Industrial Advertising Sales Leads,* (Cleveland: Penton Publishing Co., 1991), p. 29.
49. *Profiting from Industrial Advertising Sales Leads,* (Cleveland: Penton Publishing Co., 1991), p. 30.
50. *Cahners Advertising Research Report No. 250.2A,* (Newton, Ma.: Cahners Publishing Co., 1989).
51. *Cahners Advertising Research Report No. 110.3A,* (Newton, Ma: Cahners Publishing Co., 1990).
52. Joan Treistman, "Where the Reader Eye Roams," *Business Marketing* (April 1984): p. 110.
53. *Cahners Advertising Research Report No. 540.3C,* (Newton, Ma.: Cahners Publishing Co., 1993).
54. *Profiting from Industrial Advertising Sales Leads* (Cleveland: Penton Publishing Co., 1991), p. 35.
55. *Cahners Advertising Research Report No. 118.5,* (Newton, Ma.: Cahners Publishing Co., 1991).
56. Joan Treistman, "Where the Reader Eye Roams," *Business Marketing* (April 1984): p. 110.
57. *Cahners Advertising Research Report No. 118.5,* (Newton, Ma.: Cahners Publishing Co., 1991).
58. *Cahners Advertising Research Report No. 1310.3,* (Newton, Ma.: Cahners Publishing Co., 1979).
59. *Profiting from Industrial Advertising Sales Leads* (Cleveland: Penton Publishing Co., 1991), p. 33.
60. *Cahners Advertising Research Report No. 1310.4,* (Newton, Ma.: Cahners Publishing Co., 1979).
61. *Cahners Advertising Research Report No. 1310.6,* (Newton, Ma.: Cahners Publishing Co., 1979).
62. *Cahners Advertising Research Report No. 1310.2,* (Newton, Ma.: Cahners Publishing Co., 1979).
63. *Industrial Equipment News,* unpublished reader focus group response study, April 27, 1990, p. 14.
64. *Industrial Equipment News,* unpublished reader focus group response study, April 27, 1990, p. 14.
65. Joan Treistman, "Where the Reader Eye Roams," *Business Marketing* (April 1984): p. 110–114.
66. *Cahners Advertising Research Report No. 114.1B,* (Newton, Ma.: Cahners Publishing Co., 1986).
67. *Cahners Advertising Research Report No. 114.2,* (Newton, Ma.: Cahners Publishing Co., 1986).
68. Bradley Johnson, "Computer Magazines Take Advertising On-line," *Advertising Age* (Aug. 31, 1992): p. 16.
69. *Industrial Equipment News,* unpublished subscriber survey PR43C-1089, May 1991, p. 8.
70. *Industrial Equipment News,* unpublished subscriber survey PR43C-1089, May 1991, p. 10, 15.
71. David Jacobson, "Interactive Fax Speeds Qualification," *Business Marketing* (February 1991): p. 58.

72. Alan Salomon, "Cable System Tests Reach of Broadcast," *Advertising Age* (Nov. 29, 1993): p. 23.
73. *Profiting from Industrial Advertising Sales Leads* (Cleveland: Penton Publishing Co., 1991), p. 58.

Chapter 7

1. Allen Konopacki, "The Different Sell at Trade Shows," *Business Marketing* (July 1982): p. 71.
2. *Tradeshow Week* data cited in *A Guide to the U.S. Exposition Industry* (Denver: Trade Show Bureau, 1994).
3. International Association of Convention and Visitors Bureaus data cited in Robert Dallmeyer, "Bits from Bob," *Ideas* (October 1992): p. 13
4. *Develop Your Prospects and Close Sales for Less with Trade Shows: Report SM20,* (Denver: The Trade Show Bureau, 1994).
5. *1993 IHS Inquiry Performance Survey* (San Fernando, CA: Inquiry Handling Service, Inc., 1994).
6. Trade Show Bureau Research Publications MC14, SM17A, SM17C and SM20, (Denver: The Trade Show Bureau, 1992).
7. *Facts & Figures from Around the Industry,* (Denver: Trade Show Bureau, 1991).
8. "Trade Show Marketing Pays Off," *Business Marketing* (March 1994): p. 42.
9. *A Guide to the U.S. Exposition Industry* (Denver: Trade Show Bureau, 1994).
10. Jeff Tanner, "Attendees and Exhibitors: At Cross-Purposes?" *Ideas* (February 1994): p. 5.
11. *Tradeshow Week* data cited in *A Guide to the U.S. Exposition Industry* (Denver: Trade Show Bureau, 1994), and *Advertising Age* data cited in *Facts & Figures from Around the Industry* vol. 4; (Denver: Trade Show Bureau, 1993).
12. James Head, *Positioning, Objectives, and Selection Factors for Trade Shows: Report MC24,* (Denver: Trade Show Bureau, 1992).
13. William W. Mee, "Trade Shows: This Medium Means Business," *Association Management* (June 1988).
14. Bill Kelley, "Trade Show Tips and Travails," *Sales & Marketing Management* (July 1991): p. 47.
15. Srinath Gopalakrishna and Jerome D. Williams, "Planning and Performance Assessment of Industrial Trade Shows: An Exploratory Study," *International Journal of Research in Marketing* 9 (1992): 207–224.
16. Richard K. Swandby, Jonathan M. Cox, and Ian K. Sequeira, "Trade Shows Poised for 1990s Growth," *Business Marketing* (May 1990): p. 46.
17. *A Guide to the U.S. Exposition Industry* (Denver: Trade Show Bureau, 1994).
18. "Reaching the Unknown Prospect—Trade Show Visitors Not Reached by Regular Sales Calls," *Trade Show Bureau Research Report AC/1120,* (Denver: Trade Show Bureau, 1990).
19. *Trade Show Bureau 10-10,* (Denver: The Trade Show Bureau, 1991), p. 16.
20. "The High Technology Trade Show Audience," *Trade Show Bureau Research Publication AC-24* (Denver: The Trade Show Bureau, 1991).
21. Joan Hough, "Corporate Executives' Perceptions of Trade Expositions—Factors Which Influence Attendance Decisions," *Trade Show Bureau Research Report No. 1030* (Denver: Trade Show Bureau, 1986).

22. Joan Hough, "Corporate Executives' Perceptions of Trade Expositions—Factors Which Influence Attendance Decisions," *Trade Show Bureau Research Report No. 1030* (Denver: Trade Show Bureau, 1986).
23. "An Analysis of First-Time and Previous Trade Show Attendees," *Trade Show Bureau Report AC23* (Denver: Trade Show Bureau, 1991).
24. "What Trade Show Attendees Want from Direct Mail," *Ideas* (Dec. 1993): p. 7.
25. "The High Technology Trade Show Audience," *Trade Show Bureau Research Publication AC-24* (Denver: The Trade Show Bureau, 1991).
26. "The High Technology Trade Show Audience," *Trade Show Bureau Research Publication AC-24* (Denver: The Trade Show Bureau, 1991).
27. "The High Technology Trade Show Audience," *Trade Show Bureau Research Publication AC-24* (Denver: The Trade Show Bureau, 1991).
28. Richard K. Swandby, Jonathan M. Cox and Ian K. Sequeira, "Trade Show Audience Trends," *Exhibitor,* August 1991, p. 32.
29. Jonathan M. Cox, *Measuring Trade Show Results: Report SM11,* (Denver: Trade Show Bureau, 1983).
30. For example, under the specific and limited conditions studied, lead efficiency (the exhibitor's share of all potential leads) correlated positively and significantly with:
    • Show verticality;
    • Exhibit expenditure per show attendee;
    • The ability of booth personnel to contact interested visitors and screen out casual ones, and
    • Booth personnel performance compared to the average booth's staff, as rated by attendees.
    See Srinath Gopalakrishna and Jerome D. Williams, "Planning and Performance Assessment of Industrial Trade Shows: An Exploratory Study," *International Journal of Research in Marketing* 9 (1992): 207–224.
31. *Six Tips for Measuring Exhibit Effectiveness: Report SM16,* (Denver: Trade Show Bureau, 1989).
32. Industry survey data cited in: John D. Jack, Jr., "Chairman's Column," *Ideas* (November 1991): p. 3.
33. Valerie Kijewski, Eunsang Yoon and Gary Young, "How Exhibitors Select Trade Shows," *Industrial Marketing Management* vol. 22, no. 4 (November 1993): pp. 287–298.
34. Valerie Kijewski, Eunsang Yoon and Gary Young, "How Exhibitors Select Trade Shows," *Industrial Marketing Management* vol. 22, no. 4 (November 1993): pp. 287–298.
35. Srinath Gopalakrishna and Jerome D. Williams, "Planning and Performance Assessment of Industrial Trade Shows: An Exploratory Study," *International Journal of Research in Marketing* 9 (1992): 207–224.
36. To calculate required booth space, consider that the average booth person can engage 12–15 visitors an hour. (That estimate differs from the Trade Sow Bureau's estimated 10 minutes per average visit.) At that rate, two booth people per 100 square-feet can handle 700–900 visitors during the average 30-hour show.
    See, Robert Firks, "In Search of the Cost-Effective Exhibit," *Industrial Marketing* (March 1980): p. 40.
37. *Trade Show Bureau 10-10,* (Denver: The Trade Show Bureau, 1991), p. 20.

38. Srinath Gopalakrishna and Jerome D. Williams, "Planning and Performance Assessment of Industrial Trade Shows: An Exploratory Study," *International Journal of Research in Marketing* 9 (1992): 207–224.

39. Robert J. Francisco, "Face Up to Winning Exhibit Design," *Business Marketing* (March 1988): p. 80

40. *Trade Show Bureau 10-10,* (Denver: The Trade Show Bureau, 1991), p. 18.

41. Everett L. Butler, "Separating the Expo Expert from the Amateur," *Industrial Marketing* (October 1981): p. 72.

42. Srinath Gopalakrishna and Gary L. Lilien, *A Three-Stage Model of Industrial Trade Show Performance,* ISBM Report 20–1992, (University Park, Pa.: Institute for the Study of Business Markets, Penn State University, 1992), p. 14. The same statistic is summarized in *Cahners Advertising Research Report No. 533.2,* (Newton, Ma.: Cahners Publishing Co., 1993).

43. "The Effectiveness of Using Promotional Products at Trade Shows," *Trade Show Bureau Report No. MC23B,* (Denver: Trade Show Bureau, 1992).

44. *Facts & Figures from Around the Industry* vol. 4, (Denver: Trade Show Bureau, 1993).

45. Richard Manville, "Sales Lead Management That Works: Qualification Is the Key Step," *Business Marketing* (February 1987): p. 77.

46. Research suggests that technical personnel should always be on hand, senior executives should be available for existing customers stopping by the booth, and that the special skills of sales personnel are required when booth visitors know what they need and are shopping for vendors. See, Lawrence B. Chonko, John F. Tanner, and Joyce McKee, "Behind the Booth," *Marketing Management* vol. 3, no. 1 (1994).

47. *Research Shows Exhibit Manager Involvement an Important Element of Trade Show Success,* (Denver: Trade Show Bureau, 1990).

48. Interview: Allen Owen, August 28, 1991.

49. Srinath Gopalakrishna and Gary L. Lilien, *A Three-Stage Model of Industrial Trade Show Performance,* ISBM Report 20–1992, (University Park, Pa.: Institute for the Study of Business Markets, Penn State University, 1992).

50. Dick Miranda, "Who Says Advertising Specialties Improve ROI?" *Ideas* (July 1992): p. 14.

51. Jerome D. Williams, Srinath Gopalakrishna and Jonathan Cox, "Trade Show Guidelines for Smaller Firms," *Industrial Marketing Management* (November 1993): pp. 265–275.

Chapter 8

1. Robert J. Coen, "Ad Gain of 5.2% in '93 Marks Downturn's End," *Advertising Age* (May 2, 1994): p. 4.

2. Cable News Network "Factoid," Dec. 28, 1993.

3. *Cahners Advertising Research Report No. 560.0,* (Newton, Ma.: Cahners Publishing Co., 1991).

4. Gary Levin, "Package-Goods Giants Embrace Databases," *Advertising Age* (Nov. 2, 1992): p. 1.

5. According to Chuck Kettler, of DID Associates, Inc., Somerville, N.J., the USPS services available include the following:
   - *National change of address* (NCOA) indicates that an addressee has moved. Frequently it provides the new address for lists that are accurate and complete.
   - *Delivery file sequence* (DSF) validates street number and unit number addresses and sorts a list by the route the carrier actually walks.
   - *Name and address list correction service* (NALCS) has the route carrier correcting your list, in effect catching the inaccuracies NCOA and DSF cannot identify.
   - *National deliverability index* (NDI) measures the completeness and accuracy of your list.

   Source: Chuck Kettler presentation July 20, 1993, to the MKIS User Forum meeting in Newport R.I.
6. Bob Stone, *Successful Direct Marketing Methods,* fifth edition (Lincolnwood, Ill: NTC Business Books, 1994), pp. 3–5.
7. *Cahners Advertising Research Report Nos. 250.4, 250.6, and 250.7A,* (Newton, Ma.: Cahners Publishing Co., 1991).
8. Linda C. Andrews, senior vice president, Wunderman Cato Johnson; presentation to American Marketing Association Business-to-Business Marketing Conference; March 28, 1993, San Francisco.
9. In testing lists, be sure test samples fairly represent the full lists. That's not always easy, particularly if an unscrupulous list broker seeds the list samples you order with particularly responsive names. That is, you may ask for a random (*n*th name) selection from a broad list, but the broker really provides a sample from a portion of the list known to have high potential.

   Direct mail expert Shell Alpert has suggested ways of coping with that problem. One is to order a sample consisting of all the candidates list's names from one state or similarly unbiased portion of the list and compare its test performance to that of the *n*th-name sample. A wide variation may be revealing a seeded *n*th-name draw.

   Or, you can ask that the *n*th-name sample be drawn from only certain zip endings, say every zip code ending in a 2, 4, and 6. That makes seeding the sample with hot names much more difficult. Alpert adds that simply asking a broker for such out-of-the-ordinary draws may preclude any funny business; your request has put the broker on notice that you're aware that seeding does happen.

   For a strong tutorial on testing tips and traps, see the three-part series by Shell Alpert, "In Testing, Details Can Be Everything," *Business Marketing* (Feb., March, and April 1984).

Chapter 9

1. Udayan Gupta, "BMC Software Develops a Program for Rapid Growth," *The Wall Street Journal* (July 3, 1991): p. B2.
2. Steve Idleman, "The Future of Telemarketing," *DM News* (June 15, 1992): p. 43.
3. Jennifer Cody, "Marketing: More 800-Lines to Dial, More Callers Using Them," *The Wall Street Journal* (Dec. 28, 1993): p. B1.
4. Tom Eisenhart, "Telemarketing Takes a Quantum Leap," *Business Marketing* (Sept. 1993): p. 76.

5. Carl Quintanilla and Richard Gibson, "'Do Call Us': More Companies Install 1-800 Phone Lines," *The Wall Street Journal,* (April 20, 1994): p. B1.
6. Tim W. Ferguson, "Better Aimed to Please," *The Wall Street Journal,* (March 22, 1994): p. A15.
7. *Cahners Advertising Research Report No. 413.6,* (Newton, Ma.: Cahners Publishing Co., 1990).
8. In a study of recognition scores for more than 1,800 advertisements, ads with 800-numbers averaged 20 percent more readership than those without. See *Cahners Advertising Research Report No. 119.1,* (Newton, Ma.: Cahners Publishing Co., 1986).
9. Carl Quintanilla and Richard Gibson, "'Do Call Us': More Companies Install 1-800 Phone Lines," *The Wall Street Journal,* (April 20, 1994): p. B1.
10. Tim W. Ferguson, "Better Aimed to Please," *The Wall Street Journal,* (March 22, 1994): p. A15.
11. Richard L. Bencin, "First, A Solid Foundation," *Sales & Marketing Management* (June 1991): p. 97.
12. Philip E. Varca, "Power, Policy, and the New Service Worker," *Marketing Management* (Spring 1992): p. 16–23.

Chapter 10

1. *Cahners Advertising Research Report No. 210.71,* (Newton, Ma.: Cahners Publishing Co., 1990).
2. See, for example, Bob Donath, *Harnessing MKIS for "Marketing Engineering"* ISBM Report 9–1994, (University Park, Pa.: Institute for the Study of Business Markets, Penn State University, 1994), p. 3–9.

    Also note the regression-based modeling discussed in, Robert D. Kestnbaum and Lester Hsieh, "A Yardstick to Measure Inquiry Quality," *Business Marketing,* August 1983, p. 70.
3. *Profiting from Industrial Advertising Sales Leads,* rev. ed. (Cleveland: Penton Publishing Co., 1991), p. 77.

Chapter 11

1. *Penton Research Overview Report No. 224,* (Cleveland: Penton Publishing Co., 1993).
2. *Cahners Advertising Research Report Nos. 240.23A and 240.2B,* (Newton, Ma.: Cahners Publishing Co., 1993).
3. *Industrial Equipment News* unpublished subscriber survey PR43C-1089, May 1991, p. 11.
4. *Cahners Advertising Research Report No. 550.2,* (Newton, Ma.: Cahners Publishing Co., 1990).
5. *Profiting from Industrial Advertising Sales Leads,* (Cleveland: Penton Publishing, 1991) p. 14.
6. Huntington D. Lambert, executive director, market strategy development, US West, Inc. "Strategic Marketing," presentation June 16, 1993 to the Institute for the Study of Business Markets, Pennsylvania State University.

7. Betty Ann Tinnelly, "Interactive Fax: A Hot Tool for Marketers," *High-Tech Marketing News* (September 1992): p. 1.
8. *Cahners Advertising Research Report No. 210.12,* (Newton, Ma.: Cahners Publishing Co., 1989).
9. Vic Cherubini, "PC Presentation Dazzles Audience," *Marketing News* (Oct. 28, 1991): p. 13.
10. *Cahners Advertising Research Report No. 210.12,* (Newton, Ma.: Cahners Publishing Co., 1989).
11. *Cahners Advertising Research Report No. 210.12A,* (Newton, Ma.: Cahners Publishing Co., 1993).
12. *Profiting from Industrial Advertising Sales Leads,* (Cleveland: Penton Publishing, 1991), p. 80.

Chapter 12

1. *Cahners Advertising Research Report No. 210.8,* (Newton, Ma.: Cahners Publishing Co., 1989).
2. Howard L. Gordon, partner Chicago research firm George R. Frerichs, Inc., interviewed July 29, 1991.
3. *Cahners Advertising Research Report No. 542.4B,* (Newton, Ma.: Cahners Publishing Co., 1992).
4. Howard L. Gordon, partner Chicago research firm George R. Frerichs, Inc., interviewed July 29, 1991.

Chapter 13

1. Professor Philip Kotler of Northwestern University, quoted in: Bob Donath, *Business Marketing 1993–2003: Increasingly Information Intensive,* ISBM Report 14–1993, (University Park, Pa: Institute for the Study of Business Markets, Penn State University, 1993), p. 19.
2. *Profiting from Industrial Advertising Sales Leads* (Cleveland: Penton Publishing, 1991), p. 109.
3. H. G. Bissinger, "Is Your PC All That It Can Be?" *Lotus* (July 1991): p. 84.
4. Albert R. Karr, "Labor Letter," *The Wall Street Journal* (June 23, 1992): p. 1.
5. Marc Ferranti, "Sales Force Automation Goes Client/Server," *PC Week* (September 27, 1993): p. 41.
6. Rowland T. Moriarty and Gordon S. Swartz, "Automation to Boost Sales and Marketing," *Harvard Business Review* (Jan.–Feb. 1989): pp. 100–108.
7. Todd C. Schofield and Donald R. Shaw, *Sales Automation* (New York: Amacom, 1992), p. 4. The book is a useful primer on field sales force automation strategy, tactics, and information sources.
8. Van Mayros, presentation to the MKIS User Forum, Parsippany, N.J.: Nov. 1992. Mayros heads InfoMarketing Systems, a consultancy in New Port Richey, Florida.
9. Todd C. Schofield and Donald R. Shaw, *Sales Automation* (New York: Amacom, 1992), p. 4.
10. Louis A. Wallis, *Computer-based Sales Force Support* (New York: The Conference Board, 1990) p. 26.

11. Charles W. Stryker, "The Revolutionary on Your Desktop," *Business Marketing* (June 1990): p. 96.
12. Tom Eisenhart, "Automating the Last Frontier," *Business Marketing* (May 1989): p. 41.
13. Richard Brock, presentation to *Sales & Marketing Management* magazine's "Power Selling '91" conference, Sept. 10–13, 1991, Chicago.
14. *Computerized Lead Processing for Business-to-Business Communication,* White Paper Series No. 2 (Alexandria, Va.: Business Marketing Association, undated), p. 1.
15. Donald R. Shaw, "Glitch-Free System Start-Ups," *Business Marketing* (June 1990): p. 58.
16. Richard Brock presentation, "Critical Success Factors in Sales Automation," quoted in: Bob Donath, *Harnessing MKIS for "Marketing Engineering,"* ISBM Report 9–1994, (University Park, Pa.: Institute for the Study of Business Markets, Penn State University, 1994), p. 25.
17. Thayer C. Taylor, "Choosing the Right Software Vendor: A Case Study of Natural Selection," *Sales & Marketing Management* (October 1991): p. 46.
18. Donald R. Shaw, "Glitch-Free System Start-Ups," *Business Marketing* (June 1990): p. 58.
19. Donald R. Shaw, "Glitch-Free System Start-Ups," *Business Marketing* (June 1990): p. 58.
20. Donald R. Shaw, "Glitch-Free System Start-Ups," *Business Marketing* (June 1990): p. 58.
21. *Desktop Marketing Alert* 1, no. 1 (Sept. 1991): p. 1. The newsletter is published by Cruxpoint Publishing Co., Los Altos, Ca.
22. *Profiting from Industrial Advertising Sales Leads* (Cleveland: Penton Publishing Co., 1991), p. 111.
23. Louis A. Wallis, *Computer-based Sales Force Support* (New York: The Conference Board, 1990), p. 21.
24. Professor Philip Kotler of Northwestern University, quoted in: Bob Donath, *Business Marketing 1993–2003: Increasingly Information Intensive,* ISBM Report 14–1993, (University Park, Pa: Institute for the Study of Business Markets, Penn State University, 1993), p. 19. Also see Arvind Rangaswamy and Yoram Wind, "Information Technology and Marketing," *Encyclopedia of Microcomputers* 9 (New York: Marcel Dekker, 1992), p. 67–83.
25. Donald R. Shaw, "Glitch-Free System Start-Ups," *Business Marketing* (June 1990): p. 58.
26. Thayer C. Taylor, "Choosing the Right Software Vendor: A Case Study of Natural Selection," *Sales & Marketing Management* (October 1991): p. 46.
27. Russell Thomas, editor and publisher of *Desktop Marketing Alert* newsletter, Cruxpoint Publishing Co., Los Altos, Cal., interviewed November 21, 1991.

Chapter 14

1. Gary L. Lilien presentation: "The Market-Driven Customer Information System," quoted in: Bob Donath, *Harnessing MKIS for "Marketing Engineering,"* ISBM Report 9–1994, (University Park, Pa.: Institute for the Study of Business Markets, Penn State University, 1994), p. 3.

2. *C.U.R.E. for Business Marketers* (Chicago: Starmark, Inc. and *Business Marketing* magazine, 1988), p. 5.

3. Gordon S. Swartz and Rowland T. Moriarty, "Marketing Automation Meets the Capital Budgeting Wall," *Marketing Management* vol. 1, no. 3 (1992), p. 9.

4. Charles W. Stryker presentation. "Marketing Information Systems," quoted in: Bob Donath, *Business Marketing 1993–2003: Increasingly Information Intensive* ISBM Report 14–1993, (University Park, Pa.: Institute for the Study of Business Markets, Penn State University, 1993), p. 24.

5. William M. Bulkeley, "Databases Are Plagued by Reign of Error," *Wall Street Journal* (May 26, 1992): p. B6.

6. Frederick E. Webster Jr., "Defining the New Marketing Concept," *Marketing Management* vol. 2, no. 4 (1994): p. 22.

Appendix A

1. Earl I. Wilson & Associates studies for Inquiry Handling Service, Inc. In the aggregate, the results are based on more than 2,000 Did You Buy? survey questionnaires completed by those who inquired of 23 IHS clients.

2. *Inquiry Cards: Their Potential and How to Exploit It,* (Princeton, N.J.: Center for Marketing Communications, 1976), p. 9. The Advertising Research Foundation, New York, is the successor to the Center for Marketing Communications.

3. *Industrial Equipment News* unpublished subscriber survey PR43C-1089, May 1991, p. 14.

4. *The Blue Chip Advertiser's Research Study,* (Randolph, N.J.: Gordon Publications, Inc., 1985), p. 45.

5. *Reader Action Report: 22 Years of Advertising Effectiveness Research,* (Cleveland: New Equipment Digest, 1990), p. 47.

6. *Cahners Advertising Research Report No. 210.0A,* (Newton, Ma.: Cahners Publishing Co., 1993).

Index

Inquiry Handling Service, Inc.

Inquiry Handling Service, Inc., San Fernando, California, sponsored the writing of this book as a contribution to the science of marketing and sales. Its executives contributed their time and effort to present a fair and logical guide useful to all companies in all industries.

As the pioneering company that in 1966 identified the need for professional inquiry management, Inquiry Handling Service serves more than 200 companies from all sectors of business including electronics, computer hardware and software, medical and laboratory equipment, food services, building materials, financial and insurance services, and industrial manufacturers and distributors. Inquiry Handling Service processes more than two million inquiries a year.

Terms coined by Inquiry Handling Service that are gaining universal acceptance include Power Profiling, Promotional Portals of Entry, Return on Promotional Investment (ROPI), and others. Inquiry Handling Service hopes those terms, and all the information in this book, contribute to stronger sales and marketing programs throughout business worldwide. The core message is unambiguous: "If you can't control sales leads, you can't control sales."

American Marketing Association

As a marketing professional or student you'll never get enough information about marketing.

One way to stay up-to-date with the latest academic theories, the war stories, the global techniques, and the leading technologies is to become a member of the American Marketing Association.

For a free membership information kit

Phone: 312-648-0536,
FAX 312-993-7542

or write to

American Marketing Association
250 S. Wacker Drive
Chicago Illinois 60606.